Rambo and the Dalai Lama

The Compulsion to Win and
Its Threat to Human Survival

Gordon Fellman

STATE UNIVERSITY OF NEW YORK PRESS

Published by
State University of New York Press, Albany

© 1998 State University of New York

For information, address State University of New York
Press, State University Plaza, Albany, N.Y. 12246

Production by E. Moore
Marketing by Patrick Durocher

Library of Congress Cataloging-in-Publication Data

Fellman, Gordon.
    Rambo and the Dalai Lama : the compulsion to win and its threat to
human survival / Gordon Fellman.
        p.   cm. — (SUNY series, global conflict and peace education)
    Includes bibliographical references and index.
    ISBN 0-7914-3783-3 (hardcover : alk. paper). — ISBN 0-7914-3784-1
(pbk. : alk. paper)
    1. Social conflict. 2. Aggressiveness (Psychology) 3. Mutualism.
4. Conflict management. I. Title. II. Series.
HM136.F425 1998
303.6—dc21   97-30351
                                                                              CIP

10 9 8 7 6 5 4 3

To the struggles and joys
of my mother
Rose Mae Shyken Fellman (1908-1992)
and my father
Charles Fellman (1902–1997)

Contents

Foreword

It may often seem that violence around us is growing, but we should be aware that violence reveals only one aspect of the human personality. We must remember that we all have a most remarkable potential, the ability to develop infinite altruism and compassion and a brain capable of unlimited knowledge and understanding. This intelligence needs to be used in the right way, for it is also capable of unlimited destruction.

Human happiness does not come about in isolation, but is dependent on the kindness of others. Our own success and happiness are closely related to that of others. Therefore, being of help to others and being considerate of their rights and needs is not just a question of duty, but also has a bearing on our own happiness. We human beings are social animals. No matter how powerful or how intelligent we are, it is virtually impossible for us to survive without other human beings. We need others for our very existence. Therefore, the practice of compassion and nonviolence is in our own self interest.

The events and developments of our century have encouraged human beings to become wiser and more mature. In many countries, there is a growing sense that active nonviolence is very relevant to our own times. Nonviolence does not mean just being passive, but active in helping others. Nonviolence means that if you can help and serve others you should do so. If you cannot do that, recognizing their rights and needs, you should at least restrain yourself from harming others.

We must cultivate the motivation that develops from compassion and make a commitment to nonviolence. We must attempt to stop producing weapons and close the great complexes that manufacture them. If there is the will, we can change and start making tools for construction rather than destruction. The scientists who are involved in the making of military equipment can turn their talents to other more useful fields. The human brain should be used for constructive purposes.

Today's world requires us to accept the oneness of humanity. In the past, isolated communities could afford to think of one another as fundamentally separate. Some could even exist in total isolation. But today, whatever happens in one region eventually affects many other areas. Within the context of our new interdependence, our self-interest clearly lies in considering the interest of others.

Each of us has a moral responsibility towards humanity. I say this as a fellow human being and a simple Buddhist monk. Every one of us has a responsibility for the future of humanity. I hope the readers of this book will think over the issues it raises and ask yourselves how you can contribute to the peace and happiness of all sentient beings.

THE DALAI LAMA

Acknowledgments

During my 1987–88 sabbatical year in Israel, when I began the first of what became five drafts of this book, I became so caught up by the *intifada*— the Palestinian uprising—and Israeli reactions to it that I decided to remain in Israel one more semester. Thanks to two Hebrew University research centers that were kind enough to provide funds—the Truman Institute and the Leonard Davis Institute—I was able to stay on. I am especially grateful to Prof. Edy Kaufman, then head of the Truman Institute, for enthusiastically supporting my request for funds, and to Prof. Gabi Sheffer, who was director of the Davis Institute, for financial support and for encouraging me to write the first formulation of my ideas as a paper in a Davis Institute series.[1]

It was my good fortune in the summer of 1993, with the generosity of a grant from the Faculty Office at Brandeis University where I work, to hire Josh Neuman, a former student of mine who seemed exceptionally drawn to my idea and unusually competent with it. Indeed, it was he who observed with great emotion and clarity, in a class where I first presented some of this material, that my paradigm analysis was the most adversarial thing he had ever encountered. This remark led me to some fundamental rethinking.

Josh was an excellent reader and editor of the second draft of this book, and he did most of the research for the three chapters on seeds of mutuality and wrote the first draft of them. Analyses of the slam-dunk, the play element in sport, and the music group Arrested Development are his ideas and almost entirely his formulation. For the rest, he worked with great capability and imagination from fairly vague instructions from me. The summer we worked together was a continuing thrill of a full-time, stimulating seminar; Josh, once my student and then my research assistant, became colleague and friend as well.

Draft number three of the book was the last reading for my graduate seminar on Psychoanalytic Sociology in spring term 1994. I thank my six graduate students—Scott Blake, Marion Hecht, Dan Miller, Heather Pillar, Victoria Pitts, and Dave Shafer—for their perceptive, useful discussion of it in class and for their additional comments. Marion and Victoria, together with Colquitt Meacham, pointed to places where I could be more aware of and sensitive to gender issues. Thanks to them and other friends and colleagues, my feminist awareness continues to grow.

Again thanks to the Faculty Office at Brandeis, in the summer of 1994 I was able to hire sociology graduate student Mathew Johnson to check footnotes and quotations for accuracy. Over the next two years, Mathew also offered countless excellent observations and suggestions for changes. During the same summer, Mathew and I completely rethought and redesigned two courses, War and Possibilities of Peace and Sociology of Empowerment, in which he assisted me the following three years. Ideas from this book were crucial to the conceptual frameworks and organization of both courses. Mathew helped me rethink some of these issues in the context of the classroom, helped me work on my own issues with the issues I raise in the book, and worked with me in preparing the courses we taught together. With Mathew I again had that delightful experience of colleagueship and friendship and of a blurring of lines between student and teacher.

In the spring of 1996, I taught my graduate seminar on Psychoanalytic Sociology again, this time assigning draft number four, which I completed in the summer of 1994. My students Anne-Marie Asner, C. J. Churchill, Mathew Johnson, Kees Kleywegt, and Andy Simmons provided thoughtful, clear, helpful, and shrewd criticisms of the manuscript.

In another piece of incredible good fortune, in the summer of 1996 I was able with the partial assistance of the Faculty Office to hire Marin Goldstein as my research assistant. Marin, who had spent his senior year as a work-study student helping me organize and run the interdisciplinary undergraduate Peace and Conflict Studies Program, had just graduated from Brandeis in sociology, with an independent concentration in East Asian studies, and in the Peace and Conflict Studies Program. Marin, who had studied with me in several courses, offered countless suggestions, small and large, on the manuscript, did further research for the chapters on seeds of mutuality, drafted the bibliography and pieces of other chapters, and helped with numerous niggling problems of finding sources, checking out references, and the like. Throughout, we maintained stimulating discussions of this and numerous other topics, including the Buddhism he knows so much better than I.

In addition to those of Neuman, Goldstein, and Johnson, exceptionally close readings and numerous excellent suggestions for changes were helpfully offered on one draft or another by a number of colleagues and friends: Steve Berger, Michal Conford, Phyllis Greenwood, Lee Halprin, Karen Klein, Larry Miller, Richard Onorato, Shula Reinharz, Eli Sagan, Ted Sasson, Morrie Schwartz, and Philip Slater. Phyllis Greenwood read the manuscript remarkably closely and carefully, with great patience, and offered extraordinarily useful advice. It was in my reactions to her observations and recommendations that I learned ever more about my own struggles with the major themes of the book, and in my political behavior and my sociological thinking, writing, and teaching. Phyllis also compiled the excellent index.

Many others read parts or all of the manuscript and offered invaluable counsel. They are Ariela Bairey, Graham Cassano, Naomi Cotter, Fred Dobb, Phyllis Fisher, Mindy Fried, Bill Gamson, Karen Hansen, Roger Hurwitz, Cecil Lubell, Michael Macy, Jonathan Martin, P. J. McGann, Debi Osnowitz, Lisa Peattie, Maurice Stein, Steve Wangh, Jonathan White, Kurt Wolff, and Elie Yarden. Tom Doherty, who heads the Brandeis Film Studies Program, located some film references for me; Rabbi Albert Axelrad helped me track down some religious textual references; and Tom Rawson's computer expertise got me through a puzzling moment or two, as in how to convert footnotes to endnotes. In her drawings for the cover, artist and scholar Karen Klein used her great talent to capture the spirit of the book. The superbly skilled designer Chuck Dunham brought the drawings, the title, and the idea of the book together into a nuanced, exquisite design for the cover. I thank my neighbor, the skilled photographer, Margaret Lampert, for the photo on the back cover. My profound gratitude also to Judy Hanley, Academic Administrator of the Brandeis Sociology Department, who was efficient, helpful, and patient throughout; and to Gnomon Copy's Mike and Connie Welch, who Xeroxed numerous copies of my manuscript at numerous stages of development. I am deeply grateful for the interest, friendship, and support of them all.

Part I

❦

Background, Method, Problem

⊱∿⊰

ONE

On Cruelty and Social Change

My Context, Briefly

Why, I wondered as a child, are people so cruel to each other? On the playground, in the classroom, in families, in the media (the Second World War was under way) and elsewhere, the question asserted itself almost daily.

Although never an activist, my mother often exclaimed as she read an account of brutality in the newspaper, "Why do people *act* that way!" or "That's *terrible!*" or "It isn't *right* that people do things like that!" Those out cries seared themselves into how I viewed the world and felt about it.

Neither Mother nor Dad presented their values didactically to my older brother Gerry and me; we simply witnessed them in their behavior and talk. The decency of both my parents, my mother's exasperation with cruelty, and my father's steadfastness and sense of humor have been among the strongest influences of my life.

By the time I entered Antioch College, I had vague desires to change society. I thought I should run for office but decided that a lower-middle-class Jew from Omaha would not get very far in politics. To raise money, I'd have to compromise myself too much. Maybe, I thought, it would be possible to learn through sociological inquiry how society works and how to take part in transforming it. Prof. Everett K. Wilson helped me learn that society can be studied systematically. When my adviser, Prof. Nolan Miller, suggested I might make a good college teacher, I was flabbergasted and flattered. Five minutes later I made up my mind: I would get a Ph.D. in sociology, teach, write, and be an activist. By searching for underlying principles and dynamics, I would try to understand how power and suffering are organized, how they proceed, and how they might be changed.

I went to graduate school at Harvard University, where I was introduced to the work of Karl Marx by Prof. Barrington Moore Jr. and that of Sigmund Freud and Erik Erikson by Prof. Erikson himself. I discovered rather early that these would be the thinkers who would preoccupy me for a very long time, but I did not know then exactly what I was looking for.

It took two more decades after graduate school to reformulate my boyhood question about cruelty into more elaborate ones: Why do people dominate each other? What are sources of unnecessary human suffering and how can it be reduced? How can satisfaction—human happiness—be increased?

In the courses I teach, I have spent years trying to explore what I see Marx and Freud as having in common—the project of identifying sources of unnecessary human suffering and figuring out how to reduce it. I have spent years trying to understand why social class, gender, race, religion, and other divisions and antagonisms persist in societies, and how complex early experiences in families shape people's senses of who they are, what they can try, what to fear, what to love, how to fulfill or not fulfill themselves in human relationships, nature, work, art, society. I have kept teaching about these matters, probing, and exploring, but only about a decade ago did I begin to figure out the insight I sought, and what to do with it.

My Insight, Briefly

In the 1980s, I turned to the nuclear threat as a primary area of concern in teaching, activism, and writing,[1] and I involved myself in Middle East political work, about which I also wrote and taught. In the Israeli-Palestinian struggle, I saw something similar to the U.S.-Soviet confrontation: each nation appeared fearful of the other and determined to defend itself.

As I pondered these two conflicts for years, and countless others like them, I found an idea gradually taking form: people not only have issues with each other; they *find* ways to oppose each other in virtually all contexts. In 1987–88, a sabbatical year in Israel brought me face-to-face with the first year of the *intifada*, the Palestinian uprising against the Israeli occupation of the West Bank and Gaza. The drama of daily confrontations and Israeli reactions to them, from strong opposition to Palestinian nationalism to a proliferation of movements against the occupation, sharpened the issues for me and provoked a more systematic formulation of my insight. I came to articulate what

I see as tension between tendencies to oppose, or adversarialism, and tendencies to connect, or mutuality.

I decided to call these two forms of behavior *paradigms*. A paradigm is a model, an explanation of complex phenomena that allows people to grasp hold of them in a full way. There are, for example, two competing paradigms in U.S. society about origins of human beings. The biblical one assumes a God who created Adam and Eve on the sixth day after setting the universe in motion. Although biblical explanations can be taken as extraordinary literature and exquisite metaphors, those who hold to the paradigm of creationism believe the bible narrative is literally true. In the alternative paradigm, scientific techniques are used to calculate the age of the universe and deduce the ways in which species, including humans, evolved from simpler forms of life. In Western medicine, the leading paradigm focuses on diseased parts of the body or psyche as objects to be treated by way of medicines, operations, and other objective procedures. It contrasts with an alternative paradigm of holism, where attention is on the full human, whose mind, soul, and body interact in complex ways.

In this book I suggest that the assumption that human life is based on conflicts of interest, wars, and the opposition of people to each other and to nature exists as a model, a framework, a paradigm that supplies meaning and orientation to the world. An alternative paradigm sees cooperation, caring, nurturing, and loving as equally viable ways of organizing relationships of humans to each other and to nature.

This is not to pose mutuality as good and adversarialism as bad. Both must be honored as expressing real parts of the self and configured differently in different historical moments. So far in history, adversarialism appears unavoidable in many situations and is often experienced as positive in contexts where it appears not especially harmful. The case for appropriate adversarialism can perhaps be made, although with conscious effort it is possible to reduce its deleterious effects. Correspondingly, mutuality can be fulfilling and liberating; it can also be inauthentic and thus lose its capability for bringing about desirable consequences.

The idea of mutuality can be raised now as attractive and attainable because mutuality is becoming more familiar, more routine, in the world. Human rights, one of its political manifestations, has in the last two decades become a world issue. Considerateness and empathy in child rearing have been forcefully promoted by many people concerned with raising healthy, unafraid, forthright children. If humans are to survive the environmental devastation common in our current stage of industrialization, nature will have to—and it already is in some quarters—be reconceived from nuisance or enemy to an integral part of us with which to live in the greatest harmony possible. The lethality of war and the waste of resources spent on waging and preparing for it, as well as lives taken and environment despoiled, all express adversarialism at its most devastating and call to mind an alternative vision that fits into what I am calling mutuality.

I see the shifting of relative emphasis from adversarialism to mutuality as essential to the survival of our species, of other species, of nature itself. I am not predicting that in the face of possible human-engineered extinction, we will opt for life; I am only suggesting that with the proper analysis and appropriate behaviors that follow from it, we can find our way to renouncing the predominance of adversarial ways and creating a fully elaborated mutuality as an essential piece of a survival strategy.

Individuals cannot help but reflect currents in their society. Once I named adversarialism and mutuality in my understanding of the world and myself, I began working on this book and also on my own struggles with both these modes of relating. As I worked on this idea of two contrasting paradigms, I realized that at one level I was examining society and history and at another, I was working on some troublesome issues in myself. With much trepidation and backsliding, I looked into my personal inclinations toward adversarialism and mutuality as well as what they are historically and sociologically.

My Methods

Films

I illustrate many of my points, particularly on the nature of rituals by which people maintain adversary distance or connect with others, by way of movie metaphors. In our culture, film is more than entertainment; it is also shared ritual and collective dreaming. It is a form of mythologizing appropriate to a dispersed, heterogeneous, officially secular, high-tech society. Film metaphors arise in conversation. Their ritual implications are dramatically illustrated, for example, by the highly stylized ways in which many young filmgoers have made a cult of the film and their behavior in repeated viewings of *The Rocky Horror Picture Show*.

Films show paradigmatic heroes, villains, role models, and alter egos. Just as Shakespeare and the Bible advance powerful images of Hamlet and indecision, Lady Macbeth and ambition, Solomonic decisions, prophetic wrath, and messianic hopes, so do movies like *High Noon*, *Rambo*, and *Thelma and Louise* present compelling metaphors for deep tensions, conflicts, and confusions. Like religion and art, and partaking perhaps of both, cinema offers cultural materials that illuminate and clarify our condition.

Rituals

Brief discussions of *adversary rituals* are woven throughout my book. I use this term to refer to practices like blaming, hurting, and avenging—mundane, familiar behaviors by which people oppose each other. I had thought of calling these actions routines but decided on rituals to underscore what I see as the stereotyped, unreflective, familiar, comfortable ways in which adversarialism is reinforced in everyday life. My listing could also include stereotyping, ridiculing, using sarcasm, judging, interrupting, ordering, threatening, preaching, interpreting, advising, and many, many more. There are probably countless ways by which tendencies to oppose become repeated in highly stylized patterns.

Scholarship, Observation, the Classroom, and Myself

I have proceeded in this study by way of introspection and scholarly investigation as well as observation, some of it as participant, some of it not. I see my social observations as metaphors for certain inner observations, and vice versa. Many of my concerns and insights grow from years of social activism and also years of struggle to come to terms with personal conflicts and their ramifications. I have worked in social movements for change of parts of society that have puzzled and troubled me, and I have worked with dreams and other parts of myself that have troubled and puzzled me. The latter method is unorthodox for sociology, as it has involved systematic conversations with people whose profession is to help guide and understand the fruits of introspection.

As part of my ongoing grappling with my own compulsive adversary tendencies, and in my effort to free up more of those parts I call mutualistic, I have asked a few colleagues, friends, and students to read drafts of this book critically. With many of these people I have over the years explored inner issues, outer ones, and the relationship between the two.

Some of my deepest illuminations come from what is for me a major area of praxis, the classroom. I have found the joys of teaching to include the chance to try out insights and ideas with enthusiastic people new to examining them. As with those of other readers, my students' hesitations, qualms, and recommendations have been as important as their interest and support of the project. Partly through and with them, I have more and more felt the writing process taking on mutuality characteristics, as I thrilled to finding people excited about my ideas contributing their insights and understanding for extending, rethinking, and rewriting.

This book grows out of continuing struggles to rein in and move beyond my adversary tendencies when they are destructive of others and myself and to be freer in enjoying mutuality. The book is itself a major piece of the struggle. And it goes on.

Naming the Paradigms

It was difficult to find adequate names for the two modes of behavior that I describe throughout the book. For one, I initially played with the term "opposition paradigm" until my friend and colleague Richard Onorato suggested "adversary paradigm," which I think is a more felicitous and accurate choice.

I thought I would call the complement to the adversary paradigm the "cooperation paradigm," but that lacks a sense of interaction and relationship I was seeking. After two years, I realized I already knew the term I needed: *mutuality*, central in the work of Erik Erikson.

Struggling with the Paradigms

I had trouble getting to the ideas in this book, and I struggled for years with trying to make them clear, accepting the possibility of their accuracy, and understanding their complex places in my life. I can imagine other people engaging in similar struggles. If readers find some of the ideas threatening, if they feel uncomfortable questioning some of their assumptions about the world and their place in it, I sympathize with their discomfort. I continue to grapple with my own version of this.

People can respond to new ideas the way they often react to new buildings: with some combination of apprehension, alarm, and scorn for disturbance of the familiar landscape. I have rarely met a building new to me in places I know, that was not unwelcome at first. I hope that readers will be in touch with their misgivings about what I claim in these pages and will approach the ideas playfully. I hope they will try the ideas on, roll them around in their minds and mouths, touch them and taste them for a while and see what they feel like if they let them become increasingly familiar. I hope they will grant that these ideas may have something useful in them and that they will think of Coleridge's advice about poetry: approach it with a "willing suspension of disbelief."

It might be illuminating to imagine these ideas not as opponents to be overcome but as partners in figuring out the great challenges of the coming turn of the century and millennium. I hope that readers will consider these ideas and reconsider them, amend them, supplement them, criticize them constructively while keeping in mind the question, How can we do more than we have done to reduce human suffering and enhance human fulfillment?

꧁꧂

TWO

To Overcome or Not to Overcome: That is the Question

> The price of fruitfulness is to be rich in internal opposition; one remains young only so long as the soul does not stretch itself and desire peace. . . . One has renounced the *great* life when one renounces war.
>
> —Nietzsche,
> *Twilight of the Idols*

> The object, in Washington, is not to improve America. The object is just to win the game. Republicans just want to beat the Democrats, and the Democrats just want to beat the Republicans.
>
> —Letter to the *Boston Globe*,
> July 5, 1996

The Practice of Overcoming

This book builds from a proposition: *An essential piece of most encounters as they so far appear in history in most societies is that each party tries to overcome the other.* Thus in numerous circumstances men to women, whites to nonwhites, rich to poor, straight to gay, tall to short, verbal to less verbal, well-armed to less well-armed, and so on.

The problem is not just the practice of overcoming. It is what I see as the compulsive exercise of that tendency in some people that accentuates and prolongs the ill effects of adversarialism. We cannot come to terms with adversarialism, in its more destructive forms, even if we want to, until we deconstruct the compulsion. We can then take back into ourselves the parts that have fragmented off in the service of maintaining the compulsion. We can also recognize that nonadversarial ways of behaving are, though often in minor forms, all around us, there for the plucking and participating.

Part of our turmoil at the turn of the century and millennium is that old patterns of domination—historically the most striking form of adversarialism—are not only resented by the dominated; demands are made that they be ended. Those on top, so to speak, combine bewilderment, frustration, hurt, and anger when their privileges and worldview are questioned. And they seem reluctant to join in efforts to reconstruct the social order so that respect and compassion replace strength, indifference, and triumph over others, as ways in which people recognize and relate to each other.

The idea that encounters are ordinarily organized as "zero-sum" games, where one either wins or loses, is not new. Columnist William Raspberry refers to Search for Common Ground, a Washington-based organization that seeks to reduce the adversary nature of politics in the United States:

> So much of our public debate—from elective politics to welfare to educational reform to race relations—is unnecessarily bitter because we insist on treating those who disagree with us as enemies. We deliberately ignore points of agreement for fear that acknowledging that the other side has a point will weaken our own position. Then we complain about the mean-spiritedness and intolerance that are sweeping the land.[1]

What Is the Status Now of the Determination to Overcome?

The second half of the century almost completed is filled with movements like civil rights, anti-imperialism, feminism, and nationalisms meant to end the power of any group to limit the freedoms of members of any other group. Such movements proceed in fits and starts, often exercising power and cruelty over enemies and dissidents even while resenting and hating power and cruelty exerted upon them. All politics moves unevenly, and political movements whose understanding precludes awareness of their and their members' internal contradictions tend to repeat the outrages they so resented as victims. This in a nutshell is, for example, a piece of the history of virtually all nationalist movements, whether among Irish people, Jews, Palestinians, Serbs, Croats, Bosnians, Tamils, Sinhalese, or anyone else. I attribute the agonies thus continued less to malice or hypocrisy than to genuine inner confusion. Even while the mind suggests moving in one direction, habits and feelings often dictate another.

The reappearance of militant fundamentalism in Judaism, Christianity, and Islam seems similar to the reappearance of militant nationalism in the world. The pitting of good against bad, the hallmark of what might be called nationalist fundamentalism, becomes in religious fundamentalism the pitting of right against wrong. As each side "knows" it fathoms divine truth, it can only oppose people it sees as either intending evil or promoting mistaken messages from true divinities or ignorant ones from false divinities.

Militant nationalism and fundamentalist religion are not new to this way of thinking. What is new lately is growing numbers of fervent adherents. Perhaps because of fears of nuclear holocaust, the passions of militant nationalism and religious fundamentalism have turned more inward, within nation-states, than outward. With the end of the Cold War, the passion to overcome appears to have shifted to structures within nations more than those between them.

The Reformation and the Renaissance brought the world a gleaming promise: the individual, freed from coerced bonds to the medieval Church and the stagnation of feudalism, could explore and express talents, desires, impulses to create on a level never before possible in human history. Capitalism and the beginnings of democracy emerged as the institutional contexts in which freed individuals would come into their own.

Capitalism, and the politics that allowed and promoted it, did indeed produce. People in numbers greater than ever imagined before have become physically comfortable, enjoying automobiles, television and computers, air travel and appliances almost beyond counting. Good housing is no longer limited to a tiny elite; it is the privilege of majorities in many societies. And thus with education and adequate health care as well.

Capitalism, along with the political institutions that promote it, has indeed thrived. And it has encouraged people with great creative gifts to invent, produce, buy, trade, consume, and live in physical comfort and, sometimes, great display.

That the same system that brings enormous benefits to so many people could also generate new difficulties was perhaps inevitable. As this remarkably energetic, expanding economy proceeded, hundreds of millions of people would be forced off the countryside into urban misery and would have to do body- and mind-deadening work at low wages. The hunger of capitalism for resources, markets, and labor would drive empire and the despoliation of peoples and cultures. The integrity and health of the environment itself would be endangered by the eagerness to make products and profits.

All these downsides of the brave new productive system revealed themselves gradually as capitalism proceeded. By the mid-nineteenth century, one thinker fully appreciated the dynamism and productivity of capitalism and thought he foresaw something happier and more equitable beyond it. He wrote that capitalism had to appear in history; it was, he said, the only system that could provide the material basis for real comfort for all people. We will become fully human, he claimed, when we produce so much, and distribute it so fairly, that scrambling for survival and dignity will be things of the past for everyone. Only then, he concluded, will real human potential—for everyone— flower. This will come, Marx insisted, only after capitalism is fully developed and binds all peoples in the world together into a single market system.

Enter Lenin, who thought that Russia, then in early capitalism, could bypass its dislocating, cruel stages. Russia would, he believed, proceed rapidly to the fair and universal distribution of goods, services, and dignity. Stalin decided that the way to do this was through massive industrialization and coercion. For whatever complex of reasons, in 1989 the system, only seventy-two years after it started, collapsed.

This unexpected turn of events supposedly left the alternative system, capitalism-plus-rudimentary-democracy, as the "victor." Victor? In the capitalist countries, particularly the United States, which emerged after the Second World War as the capital of capitalism, the gap between rich and poor widens. More people, rather than fewer, are denied the fruits of the remarkably productive economic system. In the richest country in the world, several million people have no homes. Many have no work either. Public services deteriorate, education worsens, the literacy rate lowers, drug use increases, hope diminishes, despair rises, and wealth disparities grow.

The logic of a system is playing itself out in complicated ways. If chemicals increasingly poison land, water, and air, it is not entirely the fault of the rich or the managers of industry. If rain forests, essential to the planet for the production of oxygen, are thinning out in favor of lumber profits, it is not entirely the fault of the lumber merchants or the bankers behind them. Not to say they are not all responsible for their actions but to acknowledge that their views of the world are shaped by institutions that do not direct their attention to human and planetary well-being.

To the extent there is a problem, it lies with institutions and the assumptions behind them as well as with individuals in them. Once the people in charge understand the frameworks that govern their practices, they can emerge, if they so choose, as creative changers of what they do and the context in which they do it. Transition to a world that respects all people and the planet would do well to draw on the talents of the very people who have pushed it in the opposite direction, if they are willing and visionary enough to take up the challenge.

Dissatisfaction with health care, unemployment, environmental devastation, and the like can lead in four possible directions. One is to continue things as they are as closely as possible: this is the "conservative" approach to the world. It is thoughtfully fearful that experimenting with institutions could make matters worse. Another approach is to make some minor adjustments within the system so as to soften its cruelties to people and nature; building

[margin handwritten note: globalization... what does this mean its coming in a world so petrified of communism?]

from human decency and compassion, welfare politics, environmental controls, and federal regulation of industry are parts of what defines the "liberal" approach to the world. A third direction, the "radical" one, would overthrow institutions that appear to be at the heart of the inequalities and miseries of the world and replace them with new ones. Experiments in creating new institutions have, though, so far not been altogether happy, even if the matter has often been complicated by outside interference and often by new systems of internal control that become coercive. The fourth and last possibility is the "reactionary" effort, however earnest, to return to some earlier time in history when, in retrospect, things seemed to function more effectively.

All these approaches to coping with real problems have the integrity of belief and, each in its own way, logic compelling enough to persuade large numbers of people of its correctness. The reactionary option, currently in sway in many parts of the world, is anchored in fundamentalist religion and militant nationalism, which are meaning systems that dominated human consciousness (and never fully left it) before capitalism and democracy emerged. It is quite possible that capitalism and democracy as evolved so far fail, to the extent they do, partly because they recognize neither the blood ties so essential among peoples until then, nor the spiritual involvements that brought people intimation of the divine, the holy, the transcendent. If secularization was part of a process of freeing people from the constrictions of tribe and parochial religion, it also was a way of leaving people unmoored loosened from the familiar, adrift into material comfort and rudimentary democratic processes offered as successors to blood and divinity. Among many people, the substitution did not fully take.

As this book proceeds, I will argue that capitalism and what is so far called democracy have been steps, however partial and hesitant, beyond naked adversarialism, even as they have embodied it. Similarly, militant nationalism and fundamentalist religion promote love and human connection even as they militate against people of different blood and religious beliefs.

All of these systems embody the cruelties and opposition I call *adversarialism*, as well as the hopes and visions of decency and peace I call *mutuality*. I will define these terms more fully and carefully very soon.

If the world has for millennia been steeped in war, hatred, and environmental ruin, is this not an unstoppable steamroller? Is there any chance of reducing the destructive powers?

Enter Feminism

I am not alone in having experienced feminism as the most revealing, insightful new system of analysis available to people who worry about human suffering and planetary survival.

As history has evolved in the past ten to fifteen thousand years, men have come to dominate women, nature, and other men. It appears this was not always the case.[2] Qualities that are part of all humans came to be allocated according to gender: men became external, strong, hard, determined, aggressive, public, competitive, warlike, dominative. Women became internal, weak, soft, hesitant, passive, private, cooperative, peaceful, submissive. This division of character and personality was never complete. History reveals strong, dominative women and weak, passive men as well as the opposites, but the opposites have for a very long time defined what is proper for each gender in all but a handful of indigenous, premodern cultures. True, there are pockets of resistance here and there in the technologically more complex societies—like utopian experiments, communes, kibbutzim, and consciousness-raising groups—but even these efforts rarely transcend gender stereotyping and have not yet inspired successful mainstream social change movements anywhere.

For whatever reasons, for the most part women have wound up, more than men, caring about caring, nurturing, and emotional honesty; respecting vulnerability, hurt, and emotional complexity; loving new life and seeing it through from fragile infancy to competent adulthood.[3] It is my claim that these qualities, allocated to women historically yet available to all people and the proper birthright of everyone, will either make it fully into mainstream consciousness and behavior, or we will die of our shortsightedness and confusion. The Burmese democracy movement leader Aung San Suu Kyi put it this way in a videotaped address to the U.N. Fourth World Conference on Women, held in Beijing in 1995:

> For millennia women have dedicated themselves almost exclusively to the task of nurturing, protecting and caring for the young and the old, striving for the conditions of peace that favor life as a whole.
>
> It is time to apply in the arena of the world the wisdom and experience [that women have gained].[4]

Something is playing itself out now. Limiting compassion and caring to nursery and household is no longer tenable. These qualities will become public virtues, or we will die before our time.

My argument is thus ultimately biological: what I will soon define more fully as compulsive adversary behavior has brought us to the brink of destruction. At the same time, a greater expression of mutuality, also to be explicated shortly, can not only save us but can bring us to far more gratified states than most people have known in the last several millennia.

On Paradigm Shift

In *High Noon* and just about everywhere else I look, I identify what seems to me an underlying tendency, wherever it comes from, *to oppose for the sake of opposing.* This bent appears not only in nearly all organized human endeavor but also in the foundation of ecological crises. Nature itself has been implicitly defined in the industrial world as an enemy to be overcome.

I also identify a complementary inclination to connect, to respect, to feel with and for the other and for nature. These two urges coexist in everyone and are weighed and expressed by societies in different ways at different times. For example, in our society today, in business, politics, and sport, opposition is given free rein in relations with the other side, while affection and caring, if expressed, except when inauthentically offered for instrumental purposes, tend to be limited to one's own side. In many families, love and care are allowed open play, even though partners, siblings, and members of different generations often also experience themselves as adversaries.

That there is tension between adversarialism and mutuality is a very old idea. I suggest that now is the time to entertain the possibility that a historical attachment to the adversary model as primary can give way to an emphasis on mutuality as primary. This would realize the ideals of both individual fulfillment and community in bringing self and others, and individual and society, together in reciprocally strengthening, gratifying ways.

I am convinced that although this shift is desirable, it is not inevitable. Yet it is essential if humans are to survive the dangers posed by the nuclear threat, environmental crises, rapid population growth, massive renewals of militant nationalism and fundamentalist religion, and a host of other perils that are logical outgrowths of the adversary paradigm. Having lived for millennia in a paradigm that mandates brutality and war, we can choose to move to one that renounces them.

The possibility of paradigm shift is highly controversial and as such is more likely to appear in the works of people marginal to mainstream social analysis than of those in the center. It is, all the same, in numerous works of this century, especially those of the last two decades or so. Veritable compendia of such names have been compiled by Marilyn Ferguson and Fritjof Capra.[5] Ferguson's message is that something is abrewing. Capra goes a step further in arguing that systems thinking, or overcoming Cartesian dualism, is what is under way. Other thinkers offer different emphases.[6] Sociology developed from efforts to understand the brutalities and dislocations of industrialization. It has identified changes it judges destructive of human dignity and potential and has opened the way for imaginative projections into the future, from those of Karl Marx to numerous others also critical of the peculiarities of society as it has developed industrially. Many thinkers agree that massive transformations are under way that could lead to something better. Although that is usually identified in terms of freedom, fulfillment, community, and the like, most of these thinkers focus on structural conditions like social class and social psychological mechanisms like self-deception that appear to interfere with movements in what they see as desirable directions.

My goal in this book is double. I conceptualize a mechanism that drives adversarialism, a paradigm whose power seems to be undoing us. By examining that mechanism in great detail, I work toward a way to move past its debilitating effects.

The second part of my goal is to offer a vision of the expansion of another paradigm that could serve as an essential agent of our liberation from the destruction that awaits us if unbridled adversarialism persists. Toward that end, I develop vocabulary I hope will be useful and claim that following suggestions available to us now, the self can be more capable in determining its destinies than it has been so far in modern history. I assert further that the seeds of a freer human situation are already planted in institutions where they are ready to develop, and can be harvested into a coherent, mutualistic society.

Part II

ჽↄↄↄ

Paradigm Shift

This part begins with a discussion of the paradigm issue as I see it in the film *High Noon*. Then the adversary paradigm is defined and its dynamics are explored. I make a distinction between adversarialism proceeding in a way that need not be highly destructive and its taking a compulsive form where it is responsible for great damage to people and nature.

In its compulsive mode, adversarialism is described as being very much like an addiction. Its destructiveness appears most often in images of external threat, typified, for example, by Franco Fornari's concept of the Terrifier, a constellation of fear and terror, anger and rage. Following one social psychological tradition, I offer the proposition that destructiveness is a natural response to wounds to self-esteem. Unfaced and unresolved hurt, to put it another way, appear to form a major root of the compulsion to oppose. I claim in my analysis that adversarialism diverts anger and rage from their real sources and binds them to culturally approved substitutes, commonly in systems of competition and domination. Finally, the compulsion to oppose is tied to being taught to achieve as much as possible, at the cost of passing up opportunities to connect amicably, cooperatively, and pleasurably with other people and with nature.

we need to change our culturally approved substitutes

THREE

ৎ৴৴৹

"Oh to be Torn 'twixt
Love and Duty"

> [I]t is best to do to another what will
> strengthen you even as it will strengthen him
> [sic]—that is, what will develop his best
> potentials even as it develops your own.
>
> —Erik H. Erikson,
> *Insight and Responsibility*

High Noon is a classic good guy-bad guy film. Newly married to
Quaker schoolteacher Amy Fowler (Grace Kelly), town marshall Will Kane
(Gary Cooper) postpones his retirement in order to rid Hadleyville of Frank
Miller (Ian MacDonald), who is coming to seek vengeance on Kane, who sent
him to prison. Recently released in some political deal, Miller, with his min-
ions, vows to kill Kane.

The movie's theme song presents Kane's conflict:

Do not forsake me oh my darlin'
On this our weddin' day. . . .
The noon-day train will bring Frank Miller;
If I'm a man I must be brave,
And I must face that deadly killer . . .
Or lie a coward in my grave.
Oh to be torn 'twixt love and duty,
S'posin' I lose my fair-haired beauty. . . .

Love and duty define the contest, which is not between two gunslingers
but between two genders and the paradigms that broadly define them. Amy,
who became a Quaker after her father and brother died in gunfights, embodies compassion, restraint, nonviolence, love. Will's "duty" is a traditional

masculine commitment to the imperatives of the power-and-danger view of the world.

Amy represents the caring, nurturing, supportive possibilities in Will. These vie with his loyalty as a law enforcement officer to normative male virtues of toughness, confrontation, and victory. If the film's showdown is between two paradigms, the middle lines of the song explain why there is no real choice for Will: "And I must face that deadly killer, or lie a coward, a craven coward, or lie a coward in my grave." Murder is the only possibility the story offers for resolving hatred and desires for revenge. Bad guy Miller apparently has had nothing on his mind during his jail years but getting even. He surrounds himself with paradigm partners who share with him (and Will as well), the assumption that the world is this way, must be this way, and will be this way forever. Will is in a sort of prison too. Made in 1951, the film reasserts the worldview that underlay the World War recently ended and the Cold War that followed.

For Will to abandon male imperatives would be to deny his very masculinity. Will has "never run away from any man before," he explains to Amy as they leave town following their marriage. After a few miles, Will turns around because "I've got to, that's the whole thing." The *whole* thing. Not I choose to, I want to, I ought to, I feel obligated to, but "I've *got* to." I am, in other words, compelled to. And that is all-encompassing.

Frank and Will (his male commitment suggests the power of will itself; and is the proper spelling of his last name Kane or Cain? Is not Cain the first killer, and does not the Bible imply that killing was in his nature? Miller is perhaps completely "frank" about this?) share allegiance to imperatives of encounter and bloodshed, and if Will does not acquiesce to them, he will be a coward, a failed male.

Amy does not offer Will a nonviolent alternative. She simply objects to killing and pleads with him to flee from it. In a crucial scene, Helen Ramirez (Katy Jurado), who has been lover to both Miller and Kane, scorns Amy's nonviolence, declaring that if she were in Amy's place, she would stand by her man. Amy protests that she opposes killing, but without a credible plan to accompany that stand, she cannot convince Will to rethink his decision. Will responds to the demands of a destructive man rather than the values of a good woman. And so, finally, does Amy. Transformed by the threat to Will's life, she seizes the chance to shoot one of the antagonists in the back and then helps Kane kill Miller. Amy's nonviolence is revealed as undeveloped, a simplistic, weak alternative with no program, no imagination, and no real integrity. By the film's end, she has abandoned her nonviolent ideals, and the killed gunman triumphs: he, Amy, and Will have reaffirmed the validity of the worldview underlying vengeance.

The story offers Will no way to play out his assertive, competitive self but mortal confrontation; he is presented no context in which to enact his life-affirming inclinations but the conventional one of protecting innocents by fighting.

The male adversary ethic is not simply of good men against bad men, but also of men unable or unwilling to rise to the paradigm's imperatives, deferring to the hero who can. Will's deputies back off from Miller's challenge. They live in Hadleyville, a name that echoes Mark Twain's "The Man That Corrupted Hadleyville," a story of supposedly honest, virtuous people who sell out their ideals when tempted by gold they think they can—dishonestly but with impunity—claim. Twain's town is one where folks widely admired do not really have the courage of their convictions. In *High Noon*, the townsmen who present bravado and cool mastery of weapons find reasons not to join Kane in freeing the town of the Miller menace. Will recognizes that everything depends on his strength of character and his capacity to lead.

One film critic, not alone in this criticism of *High Noon*, complains that such towns did not shrink from the challenge of defeating threats like Miller.[1] What is probably thus a historical inaccuracy makes sense in metaphoric terms; the refusal to take up the issue mirrors the fragmentation, confusion, and fears of communities in the 1950s, provoked by Senator McCarthy's accusations and character assassinations.[2] This theme dovetails with the larger one of the film that mirrors Cold War polarization.

The central conflict in *High Noon* is not between Will Kane and Frank Miller but between Will Kane and the men of the town, and between Will Kane and Amy Fowler. The townsmen are, in the Miller crisis, failed adversaries. Amy in French means "friend," the opposite of adversary, and her last name suggests she would befoul the world of might and combat, of masculine "will." (In perhaps an ironic reference, a "fowling piece" is a light shotgun, while a chicken, a common word for coward, is a fowl.) Yet having renounced violence after the brutal deaths of two men dear to her, Amy, through love, comes full circle in accepting the film's teaching that there is no other way to order relationships in the world than by the good men—sometimes assisted by good women—shooting it out with the bad. Amy comes to accept the proposition that loving a man includes embracing his worldview.

Arriving in the wake of the end of the Second World War, *High Noon* can be read as a reaffirmation of adversarialism and violence, a warning not to let down our guard and imagine, let alone work toward, a peaceful world. As economic and political decision-makers were deciding to maintain a war economy and to gear up for the Cold War, this classic Western helped lay the ideological groundwork for the direction they chose for the country.

The best one can hope for, according to this film, is not justice, restraint, or the adversary mode transcended, let alone questioned, but rather a quick draw, a good aim, and luck. But there is more to *High Noon* than that. Not a straight formula Western, it suggests two significant steps beyond pure male adversarialism:

1. The blonde middle-class woman leaves the pedestal common to the genre by actively helping her man in the classically male endeavor of protecting the vulnerable townsfolk, albeit by killing. Although she fails to realize her nonviolent ideals, Amy rises above the usual dichotomy of passive female/active male by joining Will in his fight.
2. Just by raising the issue of nonviolence, *High Noon* offers a fragile bud, a tantalizing hint of the mutuality alternative. Even if the story finally reaffirms violence as inevitable, nonviolence is at least glimpsed for a moment, as if to imply, by raising the issue in the first place, We'll hear more about this as time goes on.

FOUR

⌒⌣⌒

Two Paradigms

Out of civil states, there is always war of every one against every one. Hereby it is manifest, that during the time men live without a common power to keep them all in awe, they are in that condition which is called war.

—Thomas Hobbes,
Leviathan

War is . . . an act of force to compel our enemy to do our will.

—Carl von Clausewitz,
On War

Victory creates hatred, defeat creates suffering. Those who are wise strive for neither victory nor defeat.

—Buddha

The Adversary Paradigm

The perils of nuclear combat need not mean the end of war. They could induce the use of weaponry that risks less than complete annihilation, or of a few, limited nuclear devices. But the enormity of our danger could move our species in another direction altogether.

The nuclear threat enables humans, albeit not consciously so far, to begin to come to terms with a crucial postulate I call the *adversary assumption*, that underlies the nuclear moment and other major perils we face. This is the belief that winning an encounter is the point of engaging in it. If that is not possible, according to the assumption, one is supposed to submit.

Philip Slater observes that the ancient Greeks staged contests over just about anything: "beauty (male, of course), singing, riddle-solving, drinking, staying awake. Nothing seemed to have meaning to the Greek unless it included the defeat of another."[1] "To achieve revenge and arouse envy were the twin delicacies of everyday life."[2]

In the adversary assumption, that parties oppose each other's interests more than sharing anything *is taken for granted.* Like the string attached to the center of a puppet's back that guides its movements, that conviction led the superpower relationship until the dissolution of the Soviet Union in 1989 and, until the Rabin-Arafat handshake in September 1993, that between Israel and the Palestinians. So fragile are these tentative moves that the victor of the 1996 Israeli election, which cast from power the party pursuing the peace process begun by Rabin, appears, as of this writing, to be moving back to the prior norm of a fuller adversarialism.

The adversary assumption forecloses all options but antagonism and one form or another of battle. It means that self and relationship are defined in terms of winning and losing, conquering and submitting. It is as if conflicts are the essence of life, and living means enduring them, winning as many as possible and learning how, when it comes to that, to live with failure. An especially familiar context that promotes this view is that of "sportsmanship," which, when not cynical or manipulative, expresses this essence.[3]

Many readers at this point will say, "What else is new? The pervasiveness of adversarialism is obvious. It is neither good nor bad. It is life. It is reality." And what can I say in return? If competition is life, then bemoaning its ill effects is nothing more than blowing in the wind.

In *No Contest,* subtitled "The Case against Competition," Alfie Kohn explains that the supposed virtues of competition are not supported by the data.[4] He analyzes what he calls the four myths that justify competition as ideology and practice: (1) competition is fundamental to human nature, (2) it is more productive than cooperation, (3) it is more enjoyable, and (4) it builds character.[5] Kohn demonstrates that each of these beliefs collapses when closely examined. What remains is that *competition is a gigantic cultural defense system that promotes circumvention of the work needed to face and surmount unnecessary and destructive tensions in the larger society and in the self. Full immersion in competition also forecloses most people's chances for fulfillment of broad ranges of their possibilities in life.*

By revealing its rationalizations and destructiveness, Kohn undoes the pretense that competition is healthy and productive of anything worthwhile. But he does not ask what motives underlie it or whether they are, without systematic self-consciousness, beyond individuals' voluntary control.

The adversary assumption and behavior following from it combine into the *adversary paradigm,* an interpretation of the world in adversary terms. Whereas I intend to be critical of adversarialism for its own sake—which means engaging in adversary behavior in order to overcome the other—this is

failure of imagination

not an objection to conflict in general. There are conflicts whose goal is liberation of the self and others (as in arguments and political activities that challenge domination), and there are conflicts wherein by presenting contrasting views, people at odds with each other are able to enrich and develop their understanding and gratification in learning and in action.

There is a deep level of adversarialism that is essential to the human condition altogether.[6] To eat is to pit oneself against what is eaten. With consciousness, humans can evaluate whether and where to draw lines—for example to include animal flesh or not in their diets—but certain basic ambivalences and contradictions of living cannot be erased.

Morality, or the sacred, works toward ever greater human inclusiveness. Charles Nathanson sees a creative process in history toward including more and more diversity into a single sacred, or moral, system, and he discusses how and why cooperation evolves among humans.[7] Food sharing, necessarily a cooperative endeavor, is basic to human evolution.[8]

In a fundamental way, life is about the tension between adversarialism and mutuality. Both sets of forces are inevitable; the question is how they are expressed and in what degree of saliency. In this book I try to identify the tensions, the paradigms that correspond to them, and possibilities for renegotiating their various expressions at what I see as this critical moment in history. I am not claiming that all adversarialism is bad and all mutuality is good. I am, rather, talking about relative emphases and their consequences.

The Mutuality Alternative

The alternative to adversarialism assumes deep fulfillment in social connections and a more or less peaceful relationship with oneself. Even within the adversary paradigm, competitors, whether in business, sport, or politics, coordinate with teammates, enjoy the thrills of game and victory, and share chagrin in loss.

Pleasures of cooperation that depend on opposing other groups peak in war and other forms of intense competition. This need not be organized. Group hatred like racism and sexism is a stylized way of opposing on the one hand, while enjoying solidarity with similarly inclined people on the other.

Adversarialism culminates, individually, in feelings of rage that can escalate into total hatred and violence. Mutuality culminates in love: love for self, love for lover, love for parents, love for children, love for friends, love for group, love for humanity, love for nature, love for planet, love for life— love for a work of art, a sunset, a seascape, a walk in the woods. Whereas hatred wants to destroy, love wants to celebrate, to embrace, and finally, to merge. Adversarialism expresses Thanatos, the death force, the determination to separate, to distance, to define the self in terms of what one is not. Mutuality is Eros; it flowers in the subtle, caring, loving recognition of parent and child delighting in each other. Mutuality, like love that is its essence, expresses the yearning to merge with something higher. Some people call this spirituality, the sense that there is a higher, inclusive force in the universe. This force may be named God, Jesus, Allah, Buddha, Brahman, spirit, love, transcendence, enlightenment, nirvana. The names are numerous and reflect the striving, the yearning for union.

For reasons yet to be understood, in the ongoing tension between adversarialism and mutuality, the former is so far in history more powerful than the latter. It is as if the buried issues underlying adversarialism must first be discovered and taken care of, to pave the way for mutuality in its rich and cosmic implications. It is perhaps telling that until very recently, historians concentrated on wars and dynasties, to the exclusion of the daily lives of ordinary people.

Alternatives to adversarialism so far play a secondary role in most of public life. I remember a golden moment in the 60s when I, a nonathlete, joined a game of noncompetitive volley ball. The idea was to keep the ball in motion for as many hits as possible. To that end, we could change sides whenever we wanted. It was in everyone's interest to help us all; we wanted to see how many hits we could achieve by working together. On both sides of the net we were all driving at the same thing; there was a sublime feeling of doing it together, and of pure fun.

Historically, women as well as men operate in both adversary and mutuality modes, but friendship, nurturance, and compassion are more central to most females' training in most societies than to that of most males. Mutuality qualities are especially in evidence in family life, friendship, and love—the so-called private sphere. It follows that until women enter the adversarialism of public life, they may be more familiar with mutuality than are men ordinarily. It is not to be ignored, though, that women can also be adversarial inside the family and beyond. The advances of the women's movement in the last quarter century make it very clear that in public life, as they enter politics, business, law, and other traditionally male occupations, women can be as adversarial as men.

Consider nonadversarial values such as savoring good health, feeling comfortable in the environment, exploring sensuality, caring for others, finding pleasure in a great range of people. Why is it that in public life, battle and tough-mindedness are considered more real or fundamental than friendship and serenity?

In many ways complementing "object relations" theory,[9] the work of Erik Erikson emphasizes the reciprocal relation between infant and mother, self and others, and self and society. Erikson uses the word *mutuality* to describe the process by which two people support and nourish each other, to

[margin note, handwritten: humans are especially susceptible to self-fulfilling prophecies]

the enhancement of both.[10] By *mutuality assumption*, I mean an inclination to believe that trusting, satisfying relationships with others are desirable *and possible*. The view of behavior and corresponding practices that follow from this assumption constitute the *mutuality paradigm*. So far mutuality has played a role less prominent than adversarialism in the ways societies and their institutions are structured and in ways people behave toward each other in most settings other than friendship, family, and love.

These adversary and mutuality paradigms are two ways of defining the world. According to the adversary paradigm, people are dangerous, potential competitors, inevitable combatants. In the mutuality paradigm, people are potential friends who can be trusted to respect feelings and vulnerabilities and who can be known partly through knowing oneself.

Suppose that the chance of realizing mutuality hinges on assuming it is possible. Conversely, suppose that failure to realize the appeal of mutuality is a function of an incorrect conviction that it cannot be. Humans construct meanings, including the sense of what is possible and what is not. The predominance of conflict could be part of the human condition; it is more likely a self-fulfilling prophecy, something that becomes true because one is convinced it is true and makes it happen that way.

To live more harmoniously with others would mean developing potentials of the self to enjoy emotional interdependence. These pleasures depend on adjusting needs and desires to those of others. That adjustment is possible by virtue of the capacity to "take the role of the other,"[11] a central form of which is empathy.

Empathy is the opposite of competition. It means feeling with the other for the pleasures of connecting. It requires recognizing and respecting the integrity and feelings of the other. It means appreciating the other in the self and vice versa. Schemes and hatreds can be identified through empathy; shared fears, needs, aspirations, and desires that exist outside the adversary framework can also be identified through empathy. All of this is anathema to the adversary paradigm.

Consider the rhetoric of war, business, politics, sport. "The other" is dehumanized, ridiculed, vilified. During the Cold War, President Richard Nixon said, "It may seem melodramatic to say that the United States and Russia represent Good and Evil. But . . . it helps to clarify our perspective on the world struggle."[12] When demonization is used to characterize an adversary, the adversary's skills, sincerity, intelligence, and capacity are mocked in favor of one's own supposed superiority.

Even if projection is central to adversarialism, it ought not to be understood that projection is all that adversarialism is about. My focus on it is to emphasize something commonly ignored in much of social inquiry: the social psychology of opposition, and two of its central constituents—anger and rage.

The Range of Possibilities within the Two Paradigms

Both modes of relating, adversarialism and mutuality, can be expressed in different degrees. Most people, most of the time, are probably not aware of the many ways in which they might express either tendency.

Energies of conflict, as distinct from the goals of adversarialism, can mark play for its own sake (see chapter 16 on the relationship of play to competition in games) and can be used to help improve a skill. They can also help oppose forms of domination like racism, sexism, and classism. These kinds of conflict can be seen as socially useful and, again, differ from the domination and submission that usually follow adversary encounters.

Adversarialism appears in institutions like business and politics, where in order to win profits and office, it is necessary to undermine respect for and trust in someone or something else. Desires for justice, safety, and non-exploitation are sacrificed for "victory." In its most virulent forms, adversarialism is murder, war, and environmental destruction.

Most people go along with all these forms of adversarialism because they are socialized into doing so. The key players in such behavior are a minority of people, the compulsive adversaries, whose personalities are so constituted as to drive them, as if addicted, to fight and win or lose. Their insistence, and their leadership, solidify and reproduce the norms of adversarialism that most people are taught not to question and with which they learn to play along.

There are corresponding degrees of intensity—and, consequently, effect—in mutuality. In its most limited expression, people cooperate for self-interest, simply to gain something for themselves that they consider desirable. A further stage of mutuality is cooperation for mutual interest, where goals and feelings of others with whom one identifies, as well as one's own, are taken into account. The next step is love of family and friends. Then collaboration with and feelings of love for others for the common good, the good of the community, small or large. Mutuality at its fullest involves feelings of unity and love, and actions to realize those feelings for the human species, others species, nature, the entire planet.

It is the compulsively mutualistic people who through their insistence, often rigid and dogmatic, on their version of morality, seem unable to bend, to appreciate humans' shadowier inclinations and allow for them too. But mutuality compulsives rarely have the influence of adversary compulsives. Even though most people would go along—probably with enthusiasm—with people who would lead them to greater mutuality, they are easily swayed by people who believe that adversarialism is the only way.

On Capitalism and Adversarialism

Since the integration into it of the former Soviet and East European "communist" countries and China, world capitalism includes nearly all nation-states. So complex and contradictory, capitalism embodies adversarialism among its many characteristics.

In this era, transnational corporations, backed by various governments' foreign policies, perceive workers, competitors, and other governments as adversaries. Developed countries buy resources and labor from the Southern Hemisphere cheaply and use populations there as markets for goods thus produced. Except for small elites at high levels in the transnational international system, the majority of people in countries in the Southern Hemisphere have become adversaries of the corporations, their own governments, and consumers in the more developed societies.

Rather than seeing workers as skilled others with whom wealth can be produced and enjoyed and fellow humans with needs, fears, and hopes—most investors, owners, and managers tend to experience workers as adversaries who want to extract wealth from their employers. Rather than seeing owners and managers as sometimes frightened, even confused people who may act compulsively on what are called their "economic interests" in ways that do not gratify them fully, workers see them either as adversaries or as remote figures who cannot be affected or maybe as admired role models, exemplars of "success." While ordinarily corporations' power is vastly greater than that of workers because of the role they play in the economic system, owners may be surprisingly limited in their ability to reconceptualize their situation and that of workers and may not be able to imagine breaking free of outer and inner constraints that prevent them from enjoying empathy and other emotions prohibited by the adversary mandate. Owners' roles may constrain them from initiating change just as much as, in far different ways, constraints on workers prevent them for acting for change. Like owners and managers, workers often have difficulty finding the means and, sometimes, the concepts, that would allow them to break through the internal and external constraints that prevent them from acting effectively toward their own greater gratification and that of everyone else in the economic system as well.

Like nearly everyone else, the rich are usually convinced that adversarialism is not only necessary but also productive. Conventional criticism of the rich tends itself to be fully adversarial. It ignores complex motives among the wealthy. Many people of great means see themselves as stewards of public well-being. Foundations may mean tax breaks, but they also express genuine desires on the part of some of the very rich to do good with wealth, the complex sources of which may be less important to them than some of the good they wish to do with it.

Capitalism is about profit and comfort. It is an economic system that organizes resources, labor, talent, and markets so as to produce goods and services efficiently and in abundance, and this is its virtue. It stimulates great entrepreneurial creativity and the pleasures thereof, and it frees up some of the stifled aspects of traditional societies. But it is an economic system that appears incapable of distributing goods and services equitably, respecting nature, and liberating human potential for social creativity. Capitalism assumes scarcity of what is desirable, and seems to demand the separation of people into the categories of haves and have-nots. These are limits of capitalism and also a major piece of its tragedy.

Although welfare capitalism as practiced in countries like those in Scandinavia softens the rough and cruel edges of the system, it cannot dissolve feelings of emptiness and aimlessness in life, for capitalism replaces human connectedness and fulfillment with comfort and appearances. Eating well, using electronic appliances, and surrendering to distractions that pull attention away from compelling issues—for example, most of the content of television and consumerism itself—are integral to the system.

Capitalism is about making money. It is also about philanthropy, which benefits its recipients, helps alleviate guilt in the wealthy, and distracts the attention of both from what might be fundamental injustices in a system that allows some people more than they need at the expense of the deprived majority. Philanthropy, whatever its motives and consequences, is secondary to the power that comes from making money and esteem for consuming in whatever is the going style in one's social class at a given moment in history. Money and living well are about security and hope for the future, but not about nuanced motives, connectedness, vulnerability, tenderness and love, growth and exploration, spirit and soul. Capitalism is about conquest of markets rather than of deep inner fears. It is about the satisfaction of organized productivity, not the pleasures of cooperation and interdependence. In capitalist society, children are potential power-wielders and displayers of wealth, or potential quiescent workers, or even disposable surplus population. They are not vulnerable beings who need to be supported in strengths and aided to overcome fears and confusions. They are not people with numerous and wondrous talents eager for discovery and development, development that has nothing to do with the excessive comfort, obsessive appearances, and deadening work discipline that capitalism demands from all but a minority of people fortunate enough to enjoy fulfilling work or to enjoy not working at all.

At a broad level, my critique applies to capitalism as an economic-political-social-cultural system. The adversary paradigm is the underlying dynamic that not only keeps capitalism going in its more destructive phases, but that also that sustains much of what goes on in just about all institutions. I see capitalism not as the source of adversarialism but rather a historical form of it. It was preceded by other adversary forms (patriarchy, slavery, feudalism, tribalism, nationalism, racism, anti-Semitism, combative religions) and, unless its social psychology is fully understood and used as the basis for a politics of genuine liberation, will give way to still others.

On Patriarchy and Adversarialism

Although it is tempting to identify adversarialism with men and mutuality with women, it is more accurate to recognize that both enact both paradigms. Some men are more mutualistic than many women and some women are more adversarial than many men. All the same, men have, in most societies and certainly in industrialized ones, been more fully involved with, and accepting of, the adversary paradigm, and women, far more with mutuality.

We don't know how and when adversarialism arose in human history.[13] Riane Eisler speculates, from anthropological and archaeological evidence, that peaceful agricultural societies in the Mediterranean region, where no one dominated anyone—she calls these "partnership" societies—gave way, after invasions by animal herders from the north, to what she calls "dominative" societies.[14] Daniel Quinn, by contrast, sees the settling down of people into agricultural communities as laying the groundwork for food surplus, which allows for population increase and the growth of hierarchy and domination.[15] The differences between these two theories need not concern us here. What they share is the awareness that somewhere around ten to fifteen thousand years ago, domination and hierarchy, male-controlled, began.

Marx speculates that domination starts with the onset of economic surplus: whenever there was more than enough of something that people found desirable, someone grabbed it. Whoever got it presumably had to protect his gains by force. The male musculature worked to men's advantage in this respect, while childbearing and nursing worked to women's disadvantage; stronger men were positioned to subdue women and weaker men.

Pace Marx, it is not difficult to make the case that much international and domestic violence has to do with who gets how much of resources defined as scarce. But while Marx taught us to keep our eye on the big political-economic picture, he had little to say about the social psychology that sustains it.

The relationship between the social psychology and the political economy of adversarialism can be argued endlessly, in chicken-and-egg fashion. The relatively neglected social psychological component intersects with the political economy of the matter. People are trained in the small-scale setting of the family, with all the complex dynamics implied, in the minutiae of competition as well as all other forms of normative behavior.

In most cultures, sons are socialized into traditional masculine traits by fathers as well as mothers. Ordinarily, both parents encourage independence and aggression. Fathers may be in charge of techniques like circumcision, scarring, war training, and isolation from women, which help effect the transition from a boy's dependence on his mother and identification with her to dependence on and identification with the authority and power of men.[16]

In addition to mixed feelings about their dependence on women, boys may suffer from feelings of inferiority that come from comparing themselves to fathers who have sexual ties to their mothers and greater size, abilities, and strengths. If boys feel competitive with their fathers, they may compulsively try to outdo other men as a metaphor for wanting to have outdone their fathers. Since in both cases, the underlying motive is not conscious, the only trace of it that is apparent is adversary behavior, which may be expressed toward women as well as men. The adversary tendency can be expressed toward women then as a displacement from the male object, but as boys also have to distance themselves from dependence on their mothers in order to become acceptable men, the desire to remain dependent on mother can be turned, by way of "protesting too much," into its opposite, scorn and contempt.

By now in advanced industrial societies, there is no clear process for inducting boys into manhood. Even war, which had for millennia served that purpose, is fading from favor in societies of affluence, at least among the classes that benefit most from it. But warrior qualities do not thereby wither. They are sustained in other forms of adversarialism in virtually all institutions.

The growing elucidation of the nature of patriarchy by feminist scholars contributes as much to understanding domination, as has a century of Marxian analysis. There is as yet no general theory of domination that makes sense of all its forms, but at this point in our understanding, I believe it is accurate to say that patriarchy and capitalism define two of the major dimensions of domination as it has appeared in history. My claim is that both these forms can be located in the still larger adversary paradigm. Powerful feminist critiques of domination ordinarily stop short of acknowledging and criticizing the adversary paradigm. Even some feminists take part in domination structures such as racism, nationalism, and bureaucracy, although others resist and rebel, turning to forms of art, religion, politics, and relationships that express care, love, and human support.

Although gay-lesbian-bisexual literature has revealed much about heterosexism, that too is analyzed inside the terms of the adversary paradigm. Heterosexuals (like homosexuals in this respect) are seldom offered, except in combative ways, the pleasures and apprehensions involved in reexamining the assumptions behind their sexuality. And debates within the homosexual community, especially on sadomasochism, do not locate it in its larger paradigm context.

There are by now many offices where secretaries, mainly women, are treated as rudely by women who outrank them as by men. Although of course many are not, women lawyers, college presidents, physicians, and other professionals can be as cold, ruthless, careerist, and narrow-minded as men in corresponding positions.

It is not that such women—and others less accomplished—are stupid, inconsiderate, or consciously contradicting egalitarian feminist values; it is that the overarching adversary paradigm is so powerful, so compelling, so successful in its seductive ways, that even people who on other grounds appear critical of what it is about, succumb to the tantalizing call of the adversary sirens.

The deprivation that lies at the heart of adversarialism—the teaching that there is not enough for everyone of what one needs, particularly of love— is anchored in the family. Like most men, most women raise children to be adversarial. Even though girls and boys may learn this in different ways, adversarialism is thus reproduced between mothers and their children as well as in their relationships with men.

Men can be "successfully" masculine in all-male groups as long as they can define themselves as "better than" other groups that have failed in masculine rivalry. Even successful men, though, suffer from the nervous apprehension of not being masculine enough. It is unclear whether women's adversary determination derives from that of men who define the dominant norms or whether it has independent origins in female experience.

David Bakan speculates that once men discovered their role in procreation, they wanted to know who their children were.[17] He sees this as a step toward feminizing men who wanted to take parental responsibility for their children and could identify them only by controlling the sexuality of women. It is likely that knowing who their children are also has something to do with men passing on property, but analysts who observe this fact do not, as far as I can detect, ask why men would invent the ideas of property and inheritance in the first place. Neither is obvious in nature.

Oddly, although Freud made much of "penis envy" in explaining vast reaches of female behavior, he ignored the all but transparent parallel of vagina or womb envy, male jealousy of female capacity to bear life.[18] Suppose that men, fascinated, frightened by, and covetous of what are to them the mysteries of menstruation, pregnancy, childbirth, lactation, nursing, and the mother-child bond, react in ways ranging from exclusive male bonding (to "get even" for feeling excluded from the mother-child tie and for having to give up the child's part in it) to creating their own forms of "life," such as property and the state.

In Western law, corporations, a form of property, are treated as persons. Money invested accumulates "interest," an abstract form of growth that is mainly under male control. Men "create" products, trading systems, employment, monuments—all, perhaps, unconscious metaphors for creating life itself. Believing that women enjoy biological secrets men cannot fathom, men construct secret societies and state secrets to which women are ordinarily denied access.[19] Men also make war. I imagine that part of the agony on the part of some men in admitting women to military training is based in the historically secret rituals it entails, which will be hidden from women no more.

It is observable that, as women gain entry to the public world, they also struggle for the right to decide when and whether to have children. While this recent historical development is a gain in freedom for women, it could at some levels be confused with men's disparagement of women as part of men's complex sour-grapes reaction to exclusion from the bearing and nursing of children.[20] It could also be that women's desire to succeed in adversary institutions reflects their internalization of men's assumption that the male role in having children is somehow more crucial or significant than the role of mothers.[21]

The complexity of socialization suggests that both genders recognize both paradigms as their legacy. The "gentleman," for example, is a man who in particular historical circumstances values consideration, honor, decency, and gentleness in addition to knightly virtues of combat.[22] Cervantes's Don Quixote is a delightful caricature of this conflict. Females such as Kali, a Hindu goddess representing both destructiveness and life, and Lady Macbeth embody both love and adversarialism.

When the dominated object to domination, they violate the implicit rule of the adversary paradigm that if one cannot overcome, one is supposed to submit. The dominators do everything they can to reassert themselves or find new people or groups to dominate. Countermovements to liberation movements are not only directed at perpetuating the structure of domination for whatever financial and power benefits may ensue; they are also meant to reaffirm the normative adversarial *process* of domination.

Paradigm Shift

This book does not predict a shift from adversarialism to mutuality as the primary emphasis in human encounters. Rather, it argues that *such a shift can be made if people identify what drives them to oppose each other and ways to release the complementary tendencies of mutuality.* I claim that *unless such a choice is made, we are as a species probably doomed to early extinction.*

By using the concept of paradigm shift, I am on somewhat dangerous ground. Thomas Kuhn advanced the term in 1970 in his celebrated, controversial book *The Structure of Scientific Revolutions.*[23] Kuhn writes about "hard science," not about how people understand the social world to work. He questions the heretofore popular assumption that scientists accumulate knowledge and that its objective weight leads inevitably to changes in how they, and often the public itself, understand the world to work.

Kuhn portrays the difficulties in science of retiring a paradigm that no longer works and the struggles to maintain it in the face of evidence that cries for casting it aside. Whether or not Kuhn has it exactly right in science, and although social science is much more slippery than natural science, I believe paradigm shifts work in Kuhnian fashion in social science and also in ordinary public understanding of the world.

Although they may differ in detail, models by which the world is understood have tended to take adversarialism for granted. Nonmainstream models, like those advocating cooperative ownership of industry and nonviolence at all levels of organization, have been marginal both to social science and to the public's understanding of how the world could work.

Indeed, paradigms in social science do not ordinarily stray very far from the "common sense" of the multitudes. Thus, for example, Marx and Freud, while continuing to influence some people, are widely rejected in the academy and on the street. Both these thinkers attempt to unsettle dominant paradigms, one about the organization of power, the other about inner workings of the self. Both have fallen from favor for many reasons, such as understandable efforts to hold on to pre-Marxian and pre-Freudian "commonsense" paradigms. Marx and Freud insist that people are governed by principles and processes that are not obvious—social class, ideology, and the dialectic for Marx, and the unconscious, ambivalence, and metaphoric associations for Freud.

The idea of forces not readily identifiable in everyday lives appears to remain anathema to most people, and for good reason. It is chilling and initially insulting to face the possibility that control, so precious and fundamental in the pictures most people entertain of themselves, is not subject simply to the whims of unjust others and one's personal decisions but resonates to entire societal structures and inner processes that people are trained to overlook or simply to ignore. The concepts I present here are of the same order; they are my effort to synthesize what I have found most powerful and useful in Marx and Freud.

Political economist Herman E. Daly is concerned with human survival. Toward that end, he sees the possibility of moving from the paradigm of a growth economy, which he calls "growthmania,"[24] to one of nongrowth, or steady-state. He recognizes that

> Even under the stress of facts that don't seem to fit, paradigms are not easily abandoned. . . . Indeed, even logical debate between adherents to different paradigms is often very limited, for proponents of two paradigms may not agree on what is a problem and what is a solution.[25]

Daly writes that the paradigms by which we (usually unknowingly) operate determine the kind of society we have. "Even if we wish to be neutral or 'value-free' we cannot, because the paradigm by which people try to understand their society is itself one of the key determining features of the social system."[26]

Structures and processes are maintained partly according to what we think they inevitably have to be; that concept of inevitability is a product of the governing paradigms. These assumptions guide our investigations. This way of thinking is Daly's way of stating the concept of the self-fulfilling prophecy. In his discussion of what he sees as the necessity of a nongrowth or "stationary state" or "steady-state" economy, Daly quotes John Stuart Mill, who touches strikingly on my topic:

> I confess that I am not charmed with the ideal of life held out by those who think that the normal state of human beings is that of struggling to get on; that the trampling, crushing, elbowing, and treading on each other's heels which form the existing type of social life, are the most desirable lot of human kind, or anything but the disagreeable symptoms of one of the phases of industrial progress. The northern and middle states of America are a specimen of this stage of civilization in very favorable circumstances; . . . and all that these advantages seem to have done for them (notwithstanding some incipient signs of a better tendency) is that the life of the whole of one sex is devoted to dollar-hunting, and of the other to breeding dollar-hunters.[27]

I believe it is time to identify the adversary and mutuality paradigms, to understand the motive behind fixation on the former, and to work to bring mutuality to the central place in our lives so far held by adversarialism. My hope is to provide a useful vocabulary and an analysis of adversarialism that suggests ways to move beyond it. I also hope to offer at least a glimmer of what a mutuality society might be and to call attention to essential elements of it that I believe are already in place.

FIVE

Two Compulsions

Winning isn't everything, it's the only thing.
—Red Sanders[1]

All you need is love.

—The Beatles

The Urge to Kill

In the summer of 1988, sociologist James William Gibson enrolled in the American Pistol Institute of Pauldin, Arizona, nicknamed "Gunsite Ranch." Half the forty-some students in the class were from military and federal agencies and police forces; the others were civilians like him.[2]

Gibson writes that instructor Cooper, in the manner of a military drill sergeant or athletic coach, urges the students to summon the psychological energy necessary to fight to the death. "Anger and fear are similar," Cooper emphasized. "You need to flip a switch to transform your fear into rage. You should be angry at your adversary. By attacking you he deserves no consideration."[3]

A Texan who learned hunting as a boy, Gibson rejected it later. Taking the gun course was returning with new insight to something familiar. He recounts his rigorous training in Pauldin:

As I sucked that desert air deep into my lungs, the conditioned reflexes Gunsite had programmed into me during the week finally took over, flipping switches I didn't even know existed. Cooper's philosophy of violence had become part of me. Political ideas, shooting techniques, and flesh united to form a cold killing machine. It felt like massive whirls of energy came up from the ground, ran up my legs, raced through my torso, and grabbed my shoulders. It felt like the energy roared down my arms until it formed a tunnel that extended out to wherever I aimed my weapon.[4]

Gibson took part in contrived encounters and shot at lifelike targets. He was amazed at how easily he entered what he calls a paranoid world of attack, fear, rage, and counterattack.

I was hungry for the unseen adversaries. I knew they were out there. I wanted to kill them. I wanted revenge for all the fear they'd caused me the day before. I wanted the thrill of a gunfight I knew I would win. I wanted Boom! Boom! and to see my hits go dead through the heart.[5]

When it was time for Gibson to leave this particular session, he refused.

I was furious the hunt was over. Then it hit me—the week of intense training had created conditioned reflexes and an adrenaline rush strong enough to break through all the inhibitions that normally keep aggression under control. As a result, I'd loved the power of destruction. I'd loved the sensory distortions of time. I'd loved the adrenaline rush and that feeling of being so close to death, the "you're dead and I'm not" unspoken dialogue between shooter and target. I'd loved the way my mind and body worked together, remembering moves without consciously trying, dancing in one seamless flow. I had become the *armed man*—a reborn warrior.[6]

Reflecting on his training at the American Gun Institute, Gibson saw the skilled use of a weapon, in a world where few people feel control over their lives, as "a kind of grand compensation prize," which even if never used is comforting to have in reserve, should the occasion arise when one wanted and had to use it.[7]

Gibson brings the reader into the meaning of guns in a society whose promises of upward mobility are pretty much frozen and mocked by the economic policies and realities of the 80s and 90s. He also suggests in vivid ethnographic detail the emotional power and worldview behind the gun version of adversarialism.

I finished reading Gibson's account with a gripping fantasy that I would take the Gunsite course. I wanted to feel the thrill and power Gibson did. I know murderous rage, but for the first time, I felt something in me that would like to soldier, to shoot and slay. I imagined killing Nazis in muddy battles in World War II and hunting down rapists and child-molesters in big cities and beating, strangling, and shooting them. I imagined myself, Rambolike, living on the edge, honing survival skills and cleverly fashioning weapons to destroy my enemies with perfect mastery and no aftermath of guilt.

I remembered a scene in seventh or eighth grade when a tough boy I ached to emulate slapped around a timid boy who could have been me. I loathed the brutality but as I turned back to the scene in high school years and later, I imagined myself the roughneck, not the victim, not the teacher, not the victim's rescuer. In more recent times, when I am angry at people I sometimes envisage the violent ways I might harm them. I continue to choose not to act on those Gunsite parts of me, but I was startled, indeed shaken, to admit them more fully to my consciousness than I ever had before.

In thinking how I deal with rage, I realize that sometimes my violent fantasies go on and on. Other times—and I like this resolution better—I pour my angry energies into some project. It may be as simple as tearing through a closet and throwing out clothes no longer worn, or engaging in a workout with special vigor, or it may be as complex as spending nine years writing this book about rage and love. It may be working in a political movement to challenge racism or anti-Semitism, or it may be a single political action on campus or in my community. Occasionally I feel consciously that the anger driving my determination to work for a cause comes from many sources, some of them deeply personal. And that is all right, for serious efforts to bring civil rights to people or to end a war or to do anything else that enhances human well-being have got to draw on personal subjective history as well as objective history and compassion. One identifies with the hurts of others by recognizing one's own hurts and the energies of resentment and rage bound up with them.

It is possible that Gibson's feelings and mine, on violence, are typically masculine rather than universal in U.S. culture, but I am not sure. While I observe that women tend to turn aggression inward more than men do, this generality may apply to fantasies as well as behavior; I expect that it does. Yet I know that women can be brutal, even if oftener verbally than physically, and many men turn anger inward more than outward. Even though there seem to be general tendencies like these, the range within each gender between expressing destructiveness outward and inward is enormous.

Social science has for the most part sidestepped issues of such fundamental power as fear and terror, anger and rage. It may be that much social inquiry includes as an unstated, unrecognized project, the avoidance of issues so seemingly powerful and threatening as to be hidden from consciousness.

The Adversary Inclination

Arthur Koestler writes about an experiment by Henri Tajfel:

Parties of schoolboys aged 14 to 15 were subjected to a quick—and bogus—psychological test; then each boy was told that he was either a

"Julius person" or an "Augustus person." No explanation was given of the characteristics of the Julius or Augustus people, nor did the boys know who the other members of their group were. Nevertheless, they promptly identified with their fictitious group, proud to be a Julius person or an Augustus person to such an extent that they were willing to make financial sacrifices to benefit their anonymous group brothers, and to cause discomfort in the other camp.[8]

In 1968, Jane Elliott, an Iowa third-grade schoolteacher, responding to the assassination the day before of Martin Luther King Jr., divided her class into blue-eyed children and brown-eyed ones. She called the latter cleaner, more civilized, and smarter than the former. They were given special privileges and encouraged to discriminate against blue-eyed children. The next day she reversed the roles. On both days, the children in the "inferior" group quickly learned to act like losers, while the "superior" ones did better work. Members of each group bonded together through their common circumstances. The experience was striking, and later it was repeated in a number of settings with adults.[9]

In his *Conflict*, Georg Simmel speaks of an "abstract impulse to opposition," which "emerges with the inevitability of a reflex movement."[10] Referring to "the incredibly picayunish, even silly, occasions of the most serious conflicts,"[11] he observes that

> In human hostility, cause and effect are often so heterogeneous and disproportionate that it is hard to determine whether the alleged issue really is the cause of the conflict or merely the consequence of long-existing opposition. . . .[12] The observation of certain antipathies, factions, intrigues, and open fights might indeed lead one to consider hostility among those primary human energies which are not provoked by the external reality of their objects but which *create their own objects out of themselves* [my emphasis].[13]

Although adversarialism can reflect differences in interests and opinions, more often it *concocts* them. Angry people can latch onto anything—nothing is too trivial, too insignificant—as a way to release anger. Just as the content may be all but arbitrary, so may the person attacked be just about anyone.

The adversary impulse seeks contexts, even invents them, for expression. Winners, in their implicit commitment to the adversary paradigm, believe and feel they have no equally powerful or attractive choice than competing to win; they reject, ridicule, or deny alternatives. It is not only *believed* to be necessary, it is *felt* to be right, natural, even moral, to seek advantage over others, to "win" what one's culture defines as worth having.

Normative Adversarialism

If people are reluctant to identify adversary behavior as problematic, it is not only because they find it satisfying but also because of the comfort of living according to majority norms. Normative adversaries go along with what their society prescribes as battles and rewards. They compete on the playground, in business, conversation, sex, love; they cheer their nation in war and are loyal to athletic teams representing school, city, nation. They do this in company with family, friends, fellow citizens. Because the practice is so widespread, it feels right and true. There may be an edge of discomfort, as in disliking political rhetoric more focused on vilifying the opponent than on dealing with real problems, and in wondering if all the advertisements and the seemingly eternal indebted buying are really worth the bother.

Norms that define one group as automatically better than another, at a particular task, abound. Even in the 1990s, the normative assumption that males do better at math than females continues to influence education. When challenged, some girls reject the normative definition of themselves as losers in the mathematics game and find to their pleasure that they are skilled in math. They transcend the adversary assumption that pits males against females in the math classroom as in so many places.

Despite common expectations that they are not as good as the dominant group, some women, people of color, and others seeking greater freedom succeed in bucking traditions of discrimination. They find ways to move beyond them internally as well as externally. One of the powerful meanings of women's consciousness-raising groups has been their support of women who can, with encouragement, put aside assumptions that had held them back.

Most people who go along with adversary expectations could, if they choose to, recognize them, assess them, and renounce them in favor of the more appealing pleasures of working with others and caring about them. When such choices are within conscious control, we can recognize such people as having been normative adversaries. They engage in adversarialism not as a complete commitment but rather part of a familiar, understood way of life.

The Adversary Compulsion

Unnecessarily destructive consequences of the adversary paradigm follow from what I believe has not previously been identified by people who study competition: its compulsive nature among its most fervent performers.

Compulsive behavior is beyond conscious control. In this respect, compulsions are like addictions. We recognize alcoholics as unable to control their intake of alcohol. Their bodies become accustomed to a level of chemical stimulation and demand it even if their minds recognize that alcohol is not good for them.

Many people suffer no harmful consequences from alcohol, nicotine, and other drugs. What distinguishes the addict from them? While this is an area of great unclarity, one interpretation that may help is the suggestion that the substance is not the issue but what it stands for. The bodies of drug addicts do not genetically crave drugs even though in some there may be an in-built low capacity to handle them. Rather, addicts seem unable to cope with many of their life stresses, past as well as present, and they may take drugs to numb themselves from feeling pain and anger. (Addiction to drugs in such ways is different from the recreational, creative, "mind-expanding" use of drugs. I am talking here only of compulsions carried to the point of destructiveness toward others and toward parts of the self.)

What about overeaters? Twelve-step programs for alcohol and drug abusers have as their goal cessation of the activity. Food addicts must have a different agenda: to reduce intake of the problematic substance, not to end its use. I accompanied a friend to two meetings of Overeaters Anonymous, which reminded me of an Alcoholics Anonymous meeting I had earlier attended with another friend. At AA, I was struck with the friendliness, warmth, democracy, and inclusiveness of the addicts, and with their oral fixation. The AA members I saw smoked a lot and ate huge amounts of cookies during their meetings.

At Overeaters Anonymous, something more subtle was in play. No one claimed victory over eating, although many, like alcoholics, said they were recovering addicts. For some members of OA, as in AA, group support and concern appear crucial in coming to terms with the problem. Others pursued such questions as, What pains and fears underlie compulsive eating? Discovering the *meaning* of the troubled behavior and the *feelings* that accompany it help the person seeking change to gain the energy and insight to make it.There is a Gamblers Anonymous. Unlike alcohol, drug, and food addictions, gambling does not concern something taken into the body. Rather, it engages some part of the self other than mouth and skin.

Gambling is a taunting of fate, a playing with odds, a passion to make money without doing anything serious to earn it. If a substance is the taboo for the other addicts, gambling is a clever avoidance, through the magic called luck, of the mundane reality of what it takes to make money. It is also an appealing determination to mock the existential nature of chance. Unlike substance addicts, zealous gamblers seem to yield with unusual fervor to fantasies of *winning*, of honoring the adversary imperative in a unique way calling less on work than on gaming skills and luck.

Is the gambler much different from the investor in the stock market?

Indeed, is not the recent proliferation of legal gambling in the United States an extension and caricature of the dominant market behavior upon which our society is based? There too, playing with chance and avoiding work are at stake and appear to involve peculiarly intense, even frantic, passions. Charles Derber analyzes "wilding," at both gang and corporate levels, as a passion for illegal activity, fed by risk-taking and thrills that are legal and socially legitimate in one case and illegal and scorned in the other.[14] Domestic and international banking scandals of the past several years seem to underscore the point.

The adversary compulsion is addiction to victory, a drivenness to win. Prevailing is not, for such a person, a rational decision. It is not, in some utilitarian way, self-interest. Rather, it is if anything a bit mysterious. One has to compete to win because one has to compete to win. For the compulsive adversary, there is no other reason for the encounter, for if one does not win, one loses, and losing is unacceptable.

There is, in the logic of games, a set of terms that can be useful here. If two people are in an encounter, both can win ("win-win" solution). Or—the assumption behind most adversary behavior—one can win while the other loses ("win-lose" solution). No one seems drawn to the remaining logical possibility, of "lose-lose." The compulsive adversary does not have emotional access to win-win logic, let alone the pleasures of mutuality. The idea of caring, understanding relationships with others is a puzzlement, or a treasure to be limited to family and close friends. It may even be a prize so appealing and tantalizing as to be experienced as taboo. It may be of a piece with a peculiar human tendency, under some circumstances, to avoid having what one most wants, for fear of guilt, sin, or what is experienced somehow as too much pleasure.

Why does one feel one *has to* win? What is so important about winning that dictates that people die in wars so that a country can retain access to cheap oil supplies, or that permits athletes to damage their bodies on steroids so they can take home medals from major competitions, or that permits some businessmen to lie, bribe, cheat, steal, and even kill in order to win contracts and profits?

The compulsive adversary—the competition addict—assumes scarcity of money, medals, promotions, honor, acceptance, love, whatever. Note that it is not only material rewards that are assumed to be scarce, but nonmaterial ones as well.

Compulsive adversaries, restless with success, may act partly from desperation. They are driven by what feels like an unidentifiable force to accomplish ever more and then still more. As with any addiction or compulsion, there is no satiation, no moment or achievement that allows relaxation, no grasping the brass ring and saying happily, gratefully, Now I can take it easy.

As with any addict, the person acting under the adversary compulsion hints at something repressed, something avoided. Just as the alcoholic is not really looking for yet another chemical high, but rather for peace, so compulsive adversaries do not know what inner issues are driving them to win-lose strategies in politics, business, sport, or anything else. Is the recognition that comes with fame, for example, a substitute in some ways for the recognition needed in childhood and thereafter, in simple daily encounters? Might admiration by others shore up a complicated, uncertain inner sense of esteem and self-acceptance?

Compulsive adversary behavior has numerous origins. In Freud's sense, more streams feed into its explanation than are logically necessary: it is "overdetermined."

What Does It Mean to Lose?

For the compulsive adversary, public recognition is, peculiarly, defined as scarce. *The winner can feel accomplished only at the expense of the loser.*

The adversary and the entire supporting culture assume a particular rule in competition: the loser must accept loss as part of the "game." The "sore loser" or "spoilsport" is the one who demands the rematch or the recount or who, in the political sphere, may even protest the rules of the game. Those who challenge the outcome of conflict are not welcomed by the winners. The increase in social disorganization in the United States, expressed in illiteracy, homelessness, drugs, and murder at a time of reduced chances for upward mobility, is such a challenge. The alarm and outrage of "winners" reveal genuine concern with social problems. At the same time, that alarm and outrage also suggest, implicitly, that the "winners" prefer not to recognize the implicit criticism of assumptions that losers are supposed to accept losing and do nothing about their displeasure and pain. By ignoring the unsatisfactory circumstances of life for "losers," "winners" allow themselves to ignore the consequences of adversary triumph for free choices, self-respect, and even life itself, among "losers."

Ordinarily, "losers" do not object to the system that has defeated them, they just want to be let in on a share of the goods, services, and honor. There is an alternative: to redefine goods, services, and honor as abundant rather than scarce. But adequate respect and resources for all, although realizable, would undermine the governing rule of adversarialism. It is not that paradigm adherents disavow pleasure in cooperation, but rather that they *favor* adversary contest. With the *partial* exception of friendships and family, non-adversary relations may even seem wrong, as if they are sour-grapes alternatives for losers or as if they are life choices made by people who could be winners in the conventional sense but who commit themselves to a non-adversary life in ways that puzzle and threaten committed adversaries.

Indeed, as at Gunsite Ranch, everyone can be feared *and expected* to be an enemy. Think of joking metaphors even within marriage, that site of especially intimate relations, like the "battle of the sexes," "battleax" as a name for a wife, a spouse as a "ball and chain."

For committed adversaries, even to suggest virtue in a collaborative mode of relating is to set up a contest. Kindness, empathy, and sharing resources, sometimes identified by "winners" as characteristics of "losers," defy the adversary commitment and must be staved off by argument, attack, even murder.

People skeptical of visions of humane reorganization often view them not only as jeopardizing their privileges, but also, implicitly, as subverting the adversary paradigm itself. One of the central failings of societies calling themselves socialist and communist has been, following Marx, their blindness to this issue. Although in areas such as education and medical care, something more nearly universal evolved, elsewhere, particularly in government and economy, the adversary mandate has prevailed.

Left and right alike, celebrating liberation, all but choke on their unacknowledged commitments to winning for its own sake. In all political systems, whether new nations, new companies, or new voluntary organizations, it can be predicted with near perfect accuracy that oppositional fights will emerge, often destroying unity and resulting in organizing new units, themselves subject to the same centrifugal struggles, *ad infinitum.*

The Dynamics of Adversarialism

Anger and Rage

Anger is problematic for just about everyone. Rather than dealing with anger on its own terms as it is aroused in families, at work, and in public life, it can be redirected at opponents—team, gender, sexual orientation, ethnic group, nation, or any structure one's society or some part of it defines as a legitimate enemy. And one can take on ideas as well as groups.

This can be done vicariously rather than directly. People watch organized sport. They follow election contests, often centered more on sensational personal charges than on political issues. They watch war as if it were entertainment.

Sigmund Freud suggests that one way to handle fear and anger is to "displace" it from real sources onto substitutes. This capacity allows enemies to be designated toward whom anger and rage are to be directed, whatever their original sources. A classic example is the harried parent who, chastised by the boss, comes home and abuses the spouse, who then takes it out on the child, who in turn kicks a younger sibling or the dog. Racism and other forms of domination proceed in about the same way. The dynamic is simple: striking out at the cause of one's ire is often more troubling and frightening than holding it in. But the ire festers and demands release. So it comes out in "safe" ways that will not get the releasers in trouble with the powers over them. Unexpressed, the rage is like money in a bank, deposited into a resentment account with seething interest compounded every minute. There seems to be a point beyond which the vault can no longer contain that amount of currency, and it explodes.

Projection of anger onto others allows one to preserve an image of oneself as not angry, but reasonable and right. It is a way of denying part of the complex reality of the self. By this device, one not only avoids facing one's own anger, one may even create it in others and self-righteously take umbrage at its being directed against oneself.

Cultures socialize some groups passively to receive anger from dominators and not to return it. Recent revelations about the startling extent of partner and child abuse demonstrate how effectively victims have for generations been taught to accept it. Roman law permitted men to kill their wives and children. One social psychological function of slaves is to serve as meek recipients of their master's anger, to be yelled at, beaten, raped, abused at the owner's whim. The slave is a sanctioned substitute for the real objects of the abuser's wrath. Racism, sexism, anti-Semitism, homophobia, national hatreds, ridicule of the disabled—all these, in a social psychological manner, expand slavery, allowing perpetrators to remain unharmed by the people they hurt. Civil rights movements and other challenges to these practices are in effect challenges to the entire set of adversary assumptions behind them. The social psychology of adversarialism intersects with its political economy. Elites encourage deflection of anger onto objectively irrelevant substitutes to avoid the wrath they would otherwise receive for maintaining inequality and domination. However one evaluates such behavior, it is understandable. The adversary compulsion is the point of convergence of objective advantage and subjective gain.

Socially sanctioned displacement is often effective because victims of anger, even if unable to confront their abusers, gain seeming control over their humiliation and anger by dumping them onto someone else. Their passive victimization becomes seemingly bearable as they become active victimizers.

The gleeful hatred radiated by white racists, the macho brutality of mercenary soldiers, the sickening obsession of serial rapists—all suggest not only warped consciences but overflowing reservoirs of bitterness. Unbound, they brutalize traditional scapegoats, national enemy groups, and random passers-by.

Societies are fascinated by these dramatic figures because they caricature "normal" behavior. Burning a cross on a lawn, raping a woman, shooting
a stranger are but exaggerations of everyday acts of cruelty and thoughtlessness so normative as to be unacknowledged by their perpetrators.

Competence and Self-Esteem

A core human need is the need for self-esteem.[15] One learns to feel good
about oneself by having good feelings mirrored back by others who feel good
about the same self and their own selves. Children need lots of such mirroring. They need not only praise and love but recognition of the full range of
human feelings. They need to have all their selves recognized—their loving
selves and their hating selves, their cuddly selves and disgusting selves, their
generous selves and stingy selves, their cheerful selves and morose selves,
indeed *all* parts of themselves.

Parents who are not very good at affirming the child's full self might
reward accomplishments more than feelings, and normative feelings more
than counternormative ones. The child is celebrated for good grades but is told
to "snap out of" a bad mood or to "straighten up" and renounce annoying
behavior.

If the self is rewarded primarily for accomplishments, then they can be
noncompetitive or competitive. It is one thing to tell a child that its drawing
uses colors in very vivid ways and another to give it a gold star to distinguish
it as better than other children's drawings.

Adversary training may begin with gold stars and go on to grades,
prizes, trophies, salaries and promotions, elections and wars. Feelings of self-
worth are tied to *winning* something at the price of another's loss. This cannot be stressed strongly enough. In *No Contest*, Alfie Kohn distinguishes
between pleasure in developing and refining one's skills and talents and doing
so *at someone else's expense*. Only the latter is competition. Thus one does not
compete against oneself.[16]

Underlying all compulsive behavior is fear. Overdetermined in its
meaning, the fear from which the adversary compulsion builds is seldom
acknowledged. Its principle component is the apprehension that something
more vital than the contest can and will be lost in "defeat": feelings of competence, respect, esteem, love. Loss in all its forms—punishment, ridicule,
isolation—means feelings that are the negative of these. There is growing evidence that the Kennedy-Khrushchev face-off over the Cuban missile crisis
had more to do with each man's sense of masculinity than with military and
political issues.[17] Loss of self-esteem in extreme form means loss of a sense
of one's own viability and reality.[18]

All people need and enjoy competence and its accompanying *emo-

tions.[19] One common way to symbolize the feeling of competence is by feelings of body strength, because differences in intellectual, emotional, and other capacities are less visible than the physical. Men frequently establish dominance over women, children, and other men through physical force.

In metaphoric form, hierarchies in organizations are something like physical domination; "strength" in the form of political coercion takes the place of physical power and resembles it; both involve imposing one's will on others, against their will. There are hierarchies of competence, as in playing music or games, that may refer purely to talents. This is different from hierarchies based on physical or political power. By forcing oneself as if competent on others, one can still one's doubts about one's own competence. Such doubts, universal, are often shunned, it seeming easier to make others acknowledge one's competence in physical and/or political skills and thus avoid the realities of struggles with competence in other areas, like friendship, sex, and love. It is tempting thus to avoid facing real problems with incompetence and instead to designate entire individuals or entire other groups as incompetent in areas where one is denying such issues in oneself.

Common male obsession with physical strength is one basis of sport and, until the advent of high technology, of war as well. Fearing weakness and unable to face inner weaknesses, many men strive to be physically superior. This is necessary in a system where other men, operating according to the same unfortunate premises, could cause them harm. If this sounds very crude, it is. Detached from context and consequence, yearning for superiority is one of the reasons for body-building.[20] It is the social psychological basis for foreign policy and the final justification for the state as a political and social form. Institutions as diverse as business and the academy also rely heavily on metaphors of strength, whether of the dollar, markets, or the faculty.

Domination appears in other forms, particularly ideology. The ill-effects of force on victims of projection do not lie only in the pain of the force itself. They also lie in the consequences of *conceptions* of inferiority. Attitudes of condescension and disgust and all institutionalized domination are *ideas* as powerful as and arguably more insidious than the exercise of brute strength.

Women's "consciousness-raising groups" of the 1970s and 1980s helped many women, in a socially supportive setting, to confront and overcome internalized ideas of weakness forced onto women for millennia. Black power and Black nationalist movements have encouraged African Americans similarly to face hurtful stereotypes maintained by White majorities and forcefully to reject them. Zionism, seen by many as a project to liberate Jews from the vicissitudes of host peoples who have often turned against them, has played a corresponding role for countless Jews.

Taboos and Ideals

People carry around two sets of ideals with them: what they strive to be, and what they strive not to be. The one can be called aspirations or ideals, the other, taboos. Both are learned.

Adversaries project onto others characteristics and feelings like timidity, rage, weakness, and meanness that they split off from themselves. Having been taught that these are undesirable qualities, they have learned to prefer not to recognize them as their own. Just as likely, they may attribute to others feelings of heroism, altruism, and compassion they deny in themselves. Although they are taught these are desirable qualities, they are also taught that few people can achieve them. The other as adversary thus can be considered superior *or* inferior or, even, both. (Jews are unusual as a scapegoat group in that anti-Semites tend to consider Jews both superior, in numerous fantasies of Jewish money and power schemes, and inferior, in numerous demonic images, to themselves.)

Shared opposition often enhances group cohesiveness. In an adversary system, "Each needs its opposite number to complete itself." Howard Stein calls this "adversary symbiosis."[21] Through "projective identification," one feels "identified with the other because one attributes his [sic] own qualities to the other."[22] *Projective identification, central to the adversary system, means at the level of the unconscious not that the other is an enemy or inferior but rather that the other and I are one; fighting the other is a metaphor for unfaced internal struggle.*[23] Once an enemy is defeated, it must be replaced by another, for fear ultimately is of the pain and bewilderment that would accompany recognizing certain complexities, understandably but incorrectly experienced as too hurtful to handle, within the self.

Refusal to acknowledge the injustice of discrimination against others implies not just callousness or ill will but the sad victory of pressures to feel contempt for innocent others rather than deal with personal hurt, fear, anger, competence, and ideals in their own real contexts. The refusal adds up to what Erikson calls pseudo speciation, the tendency to define other groups as behaving

> as if they were separate species created at the beginning of time by supernatural intent. Thus each develops not only a *distinct sense of identity*, but also a conviction of harboring *the* human identity, fortified against other pseudo species by prejudices which mark them as extra-specific and inimical to "genuine" human behavior.[24]

The pseudospecies becomes defined as a gigantic winner or a gigantic loser. As the latter, it represents split off parts of winners' selves, violations of the self by the self, the self's lies to itself. All this helps maintain the precarious integrity of the self and its society and the precarious rule of elites.

Such processes as these can themselves be engaged actively or passively. Joel Kovel distinguishes between "dominative" and "aversive" racism.[25] Feelings and behavior explicitly contemptuous toward people of another race constitute dominative racism. There are other feelings and behaviors by which people take part in racism without even knowing it. For example, as African Americans suffer disproportionately from unemployment, policies that permit it are part of the gigantic puzzle of racism. Ignoring the societal problem of unemployment is an aversive way of perpetuating racism and classism as well and thus subtly taking part in both.

And thus with people who turn their backs on underfunded inner city schools, discriminatory hiring, and homelessness. Aversive racists, like aversive anti-Semites (the "good Germans" of World War II who feigned ignorance of Nazi extermination policies or actually kept themselves from knowing), aversive sexists (who insist that rape victims "ask for it"), aversive anyone—through inaction play a crucial role in perpetuating the adversary structure known as domination.

Adversarialism and Leadership

It is likely that those who feel adversarialism most deeply (the compulsives) drive themselves into elite positions and define their experience as universal. The majority, whose adversary needs are milder (the normatives), either act as "believers" in adversarialism or simply go along, through ambivalence or feelings of helplessness or both. It cannot be too strongly emphasized that the strength of adversarialism varies enormously from one person to the next. It is the pressure to accede to it, whether dominatively or aversively, which involves nearly all players in it.

Societies and institutions appear to be run, for the most part, by compulsive adversaries whose satisfactions must be primarily external, not internal. They use winning as a way to avoid dealing directly and in liberating ways with the whole inner cauldron of feelings like doubt, anger, rage, fear, weakness, failure, and guilt. "Winning" also allows them to bypass other inner issues like affection, vulnerability, tenderness, and love as they apply beyond immediate relationships.

Most leaders by choice and/or acquiescence wind up as adversary specialists. Through them, competition offers itself as a gigantic theater of denial and displacement, where "winning is the only thing" not in contrast to losing but in contrast to the option of genuine inner exploration and the painful, complicated, and also euphoric and liberating work of honestly facing the full range of what is the inner self and coming to terms with it. Compulsive adversarialism is an implicit admission of bewilderment before mutuality, empathy, and love and a determination to belittle and ridicule what one feels unable to grasp.

Ambivalence

One can pit oneself against an opponent—consider the friendly tennis game—as a compromise between conflicting desires to merge with others and to separate. Unconsciously, this ambivalence may underlie all adversarialism, and mutuality as well. On a well-functioning team as in a good tennis game, mutuality relations, valued as they may be, are premised on combating others.

If Freud is right that we are inevitably ambivalent toward parents, others, self, even life, then people either face and enact both positive and negative valences or they act on some and deny others. One may love conscience, for example, for exalting culture's highest aspirations; one may also resent it for inhibiting yearned-for pleasures in spontaneity, sensuality, and destructiveness. The usual resolution of such ambivalence is to decry or admire others who express what one dares not allow oneself, whether that is noble behavior or base. When the other behaves especially virtuously, admiration is public and decrying is private. And vice versa when the other behaves despicably.

Conscience develops slowly. Part of the charm of young children is their comparative lack of it. As conscience sets in, children need to do something with their longing to return to the simpler pleasures of preconscience days. Their cultures offer entire groups as supposedly lacking conscience: Blacks, Jews, women, homosexuals, Communists, infidels, Westerners, animals, and even slightly younger children. In struggle with ambivalence toward their own consciences, many children learn to mock and hate scapegoated others as insufficiently moral and ethical.

Loving a flag, political party, or religion and hating another is less challenging and less honest than acknowledging mixed feelings toward any nation, political program, or religion. The convenience of this splitting of emotions reflects a child's common difficulties in relating to parents as both loved and hated. Charles Pinderhughes reasons that "differential bonding is easier to handle than ambivalence. It is as if there were a drive to avoid the acceptance of ambivalent feelings."[26]

The hypothesis that people are ambivalent about any person or phenomenon about which they have strong feelings allows sense to be made of seemingly contradictory behavior. Among highly competitive people, affection for its own sake may typically be experienced as too threatening to bear. Thus it is common among men in U.S. culture to feel more comfortable competing with other men—and women—than caring for them and feeling affection toward them. Even though sometimes oppositional and unfeeling, homosexuality often implies tender and warm responses that puzzle many men when they feel them toward women, let alone men. For such people, it feels safer to oppose than to connect. Yet the deep yearning for connection and love cannot go away. It is the deepest yearning of all.[27] It can be grudgingly if privately respected in others and, in classic ambivalent behavior, also ridiculed there. A common meaning of opposition is the warding off of attraction to the other's virtues, accomplishments, wickedness, elan, body. Often in relationships inside and outside of families, a stylized "picking on" the other can be seen as both a form of intimacy and as disguised adversarialism suggesting unfaced ambivalence.[28]

The most treasured resource in the nuclear family is love. Around ages 3–5, many children imagine exclusive enjoyment of the love of one parent. Especially in a context where competition is prized, a child who finds love scarce, contingent, or unavailable is more likely to compete for love than one who feels more or less adequately loved. The reality that parents have other needs in addition to desires to satisfy children's needs and also have other people to love is accepted reluctantly, if at all, by any child, but especially one trained in adversarialism.

Competition probably begins, then, with children learning from parents who themselves must have experienced love as scarce. But love is not really scarce. It is an abundant good of a peculiarly startling sort: the more there is, the more there is.

Love by its nature can be boundless. This is the furthest implication of Erikson's critique of "pseudo speciation." Love is a major component of the fundamental drive Freud names Eros, and of what Marx calls species-being, the capacity of humans to recognize themselves and others as members, much alike, of the same species. (Although their makers may not have intended this, both concepts can be extended logically to concepts like Gaia and to feelings of connection with all of nature, the cosmos, and life itself.)

The economics of love, so to speak, in the nuclear family, might determine far more of human behavior than is ordinarily imagined. How much easier to contemplate and fight over wages, productivity, and ownership than to face painful memories, often not consciously remembered, that stem from life in the family.

As love is problematic, so is violence. That some cultures know little of it could mean that some peoples have more of it than others but more likely suggests that some cultures have managed to strike bargains whereby inner restraints on violence substitute for outer confrontations.[29] Basic images of the uninhibited self are few: children, criminals, and the satyr-devil metaphors. Because of their vulnerability, children are the easiest prey of projections, and because of what has until very recently ordinarily been constructed as their comparative physical weakness, women have also long been subject to such projections. In degrading women, men make them into children metaphorically (from time to time, the depiction of women in magazine ads does this literally), and work out upon them their own repressed desires for exactly what they ridicule and condemn: passivity, gentleness, sensuality, vulnerability, spontaneity, openness with feelings, love. Women struggling with these issues project them onto children or people of other ethnicities and social classes, options obviously available to men as well.

The negative side of ambivalence can be expressed viciously in domination or less harmfully in fantasy. The culture of driven achievement surreptitiously allows for resentment at being driven and for longings for quiet and desert islands; such yearnings are enacted in personal reveries and collective escape fantasies promoted by certain religions, literature, and mass entertainment, including advertisements. They are not acted on in healthy, socially fulfilling ways.

Recognizing ambivalence can allow integration of the full range of one's humanity. One has options for which valence to enact when in the throes of ambivalence about anything. Normative adversaries who can face their ambivalences see beyond adversarialism to mutuality. They are best positioned to challenge compulsive adversaries and even to invite them into a more satisfying, life-enhancing mode of relating.

The Mutuality Compulsion

It took me several years of working on this project to realize that just as there is an adversary compulsion, so is there a mutuality compulsion. Like adversarialism, mutuality also comes in normative and compulsive forms. If compulsive adversaries displace their mutuality needs onto other people as if they did not exist in themselves, something similar is true in people who are compulsively mutualistic.

People who enjoy affection, empathy, and caring in everyday life *and also* accept seamier parts of themselves might be said to enjoy the fruits of mutuality. These are people at ease with their subterranean, more destructive impulses as well as their sunny ones and who are capable of finding helpful outlets for them all.

There are, though, others who are compulsively mutualistic in ways that give many people the chills. The mutuality of such people is driven, frantic, strained. They mistake others' cautious and even disapproving attitudes toward them for rejections of mutuality. Such may be the case, but it need not be. Skepticism about compulsive mutuality or goodness (think of "goody two shoes" and the "boy scout" as examples) is often a realistic response to what is felt to be inauthentic about the compulsively mutualistic person. In place of traces of competitiveness, cruelty, or anger, they show self-conscious qualities of being upbeat all the time, of self-righteousness, humility, and martyrdom. I think of people who appear completely even in temperament, forever cheery, to the point where it seems quite forced. While they may be expressing true character inclinations, they must also be hiding from others and themselves a more petulant, angry side of themselves.

Journalists discover, with tedious regularity, that the mass murderer was often a nice person who played the organ in church and taught Sunday School. How, the neighbors inquire incredulously, in story after story after story, could such a quiet, sweet man take a machine gun to a school or a mall and mow people down? The answer in part is that no one is really as virtuous as they seem. That particular stereotype of the good citizen is a classic example of repressed rage that cannot even be expressed in normative adversarialism and that gives false comfort to onlookers who are taken in by it.

Some people are so giving and caring that they are referred to colloquially as "saints," but not with unmixed regard. While our consciences may lead us to admire and celebrate such people, we usually find ourselves coming up short in comparison with them. It is not that we want to emulate them but that we feel somehow judged by their goodness and moral rectitude. But more than that, we also may have an edgy feeling that the price paid for such sainthood is a deep, complex inner inauthenticity. Something in U.S. culture in particular seems to want saintly perfection in leaders. When they turn out to have feet of clay, rather than therefore identifying comfortably with them, which would be a reasonable response, the public seems to be disenchanted, feeling somehow betrayed. It would help the public and the "saints" themselves were all to acknowledge the possibility of inner struggles with what Jungians call shadow parts of themselves. That repression of the shadow, the dirty, mean, destructive, unsavory parts of the self, underlies compulsive mutuality. It is not exactly parallel to compulsive adversarialism, for the compulsively mutualistic person is usually trying to create something of value, while the compulsively adversarial person is usually destroying something of value. The point of similarity is that just as the latter is ungenuine in repressing mutuality inclinations, so is the other ungenuine in repressing adversary inclinations. Neither are authentic, at ease with the entire range of what they really are.

If compulsively mutualistic people are met with guarded admiration and suspicion, as they often are, it is because they seem unable to recognize their contradictions. Denial of anger and rage probably costs them much in symptoms and feelings of unworthiness. Genuine mutuality finds ways usefully to express "bad" parts of self as well as "good" ones and recognizes both as integral to being human. The dialectical counterpart and counterpoint to adversarialism, it leads beyond it.[30] But we are not ready to turn to it before examining further facets of adversarialism.

SIX

ᗝᔕᨥᑐᔕᗞ

The Terrifier

> Man does not live by bread alone, but also by the nourishment of animosities, and the objects of our animosities are crumbling across the communist world.
>
> —George Will,
> "The Morose Liberals"

> Idealistic reformers are dangerous because their idealism has no roots in love, but is simply a hysterical and unbalanced rage for order amid their own chaos.
>
> —William Irwin Thompson,
> *Evil and World Order*

Franco Fornari suggests that the specter of nuclear holocaust makes its execution so unlikely that states may gradually move away from war altogether.[1] If this happens, the state's many functions will have to be renegotiated and expressed in unaccustomed ways.

War offers justification—political, economic, military, or all three—for release of inner destructiveness. Defining sovereignty as the right to intimidate others,[2] one can see how citizens, unable to handle intense anger in its real contexts, turn it over to the state. The state then binds its people's anger in policies toward other nations (and also, although Fornari does not take this up, policies that perpetuate internal population divisions, as in racism and battles over reproductive rights and taxation). The populace, to put it simply, allows the state to manage what might be called the public's surplus destructiveness.[3]

All people are ambivalent about people close to them, but it is not yet commonplace to permit direct expression of ambivalence. The emotion of each valence is fulfilled to some extent through displacing it onto structures

this makes sense but he does not attempt to prove it

beyond the context that evoked it. Love for country and flag has meaning in and of itself, but it is also mislocation of the fierce love children ordinarily feel for parents, love often not returned with equal passion, love muddied by competing feelings of rage which, to continue the example, can be redirected onto the flags and countries of others. This is in large part how enemies are constructed.

At one level, an emotion seeks complete expression, but it is not clear if that is ever possible; culture usually limits it and anyway, most people accept good-enough satisfaction[4] and probably let the rest of the demand go. But some people, inadequately satisfied by partial expression, may yield to the seduction of culture's abundant metaphors for the emotion. God becomes the wished-for idealized parent: caring, knowing, forgiving, and loving in ways more complete than those of any real parent. Demanding and protecting his authoritarian, patriarchal interests, God can also be the punitive, unforgiving, condemning parent. God can be the best of what one wishes for in one's parents and also the worst of what one fears. The latter is so much harder to take than the former that followers of a religion different from one's own and those who stray from the fundamental position in one's own are often made to substitute for the feared, hated aspects of one's god. To them is attributed evil far beyond that feared and felt from and toward one's parents.

And thus with the nation. To love ideology, leader, flag, is for many, among other meanings, to mislocate early love from its seemingly too threatening contexts onto substitutes approved by one's society. And so, correspondingly, with hatred and enemies.

Although Fornari works in the tradition of Freud, and Freud sees love and destructiveness as inseparable, Fornari does not examine love in his psychoanalysis of war but rather aggression, destructiveness, anger, rage, and hate. In his famous letter to Albert Einstein in 1932, published as the essay "Why War?"[5] and in the prior (1915) "Thoughts for the Times on War and Death,"[6] Freud explains destructive impulses as very flexible in the choice of suitable objects and explores ambivalence as a fundamental human trait. It is on this basis that Fornari builds his argument.

Fornari names a universal Terrifier: an "internal, absolute enemy similar to a nightmare."[7] The Terrifier is the self's destructive parts that *feel* alien to it. It is a component of what Freud called "es" in German, transformed and dulled a bit by translators into the Latin "id," or what in English is "it," that part of the self whose power is so overwhelmingly disquieting, indifferent to morality, and insistent on full release as to be experienced as a strange, adverse force, "it" rather than "I." The Terrifier is awesome destructive urges, that, whatever their sources, frighten and intimidate so powerfully and unconsciously as to lead one to distort them, deny them, displace them onto others rather than face them in their seemingly implacable fury.

Nightmare terrors in child and adult are insistent visits by the Terrifier.[8] Common pleas that "An impulse came over me," "I don't know what got ahold of me," or "Something made me do it"; cultural themes of devil, demon, and dybbuk-possession; Jekyll-and-Hyde and Frankenstein fictions[9]—all suggest coping with the Terrifier by unconsciously estranging it from the self. Either "it" invaded the self, or the horrors of "it" are experienced as if beyond the self. The human psyche has the remarkable talent of projecting the Terrifier onto cultural motifs in movies, "evil" people, and war itself, providing endless fascination-horror.

Referring to an "internal and unknown" "instinctual enemy," Edward Glover writes that "Projection implies a psychic displacement; *an attempt to convert an inner (psychic) stimulus into an outer (reality) stimulus, an inner enemy into an outer enemy. . . . [I]t operates with especial vigour in most group relations.*"[10]

Surely the deepest reason for continuing preoccupation with Hitler and the Nazis is that *in extreme form they represent the Terrifier that lurks in everyone.* People tend to be confused about fantasies of violence and their possible expression. It is that confusion that accounts for denial of ordinary destructive wishes, which in many people stop far short of consciously imagining murder, or really permitting the free play of the Terrifier.

The final secret of the fascination with and revulsion toward Hitler is the universality of the repressed longings, fears, and fantasies that Hitler surfaced and enacted. Hitler is not unique in the *content* of his depredations, which is the stuff of fiction, pornography (of violence as well as sex), and ordinary human desires and nightmares. Hitler was unique in fully *acting out* in extreme forms the routine horrors of conventional fantasy life.

Hitler can be mastered not by isolating him as sui generis, as evil incarnate, but, upsetting and difficult though it may seem, by finding points of connection that make the Nazi phenomenon *personally understandable.* Many people assume that if we do that, what the Nazis did will somehow become acceptable. They fear that to react in anything but total horror is to compromise with Hitler, to give in to him, so awesome and final is his embodiment of the most degrading, sickening potentialities of our species. But people retain choice, and the more fully the effort is made to understand, and to understand one's understanding of Hitler, then, and only then, will freedom be increased to reject all temptations to rationalize echoes of him. *Otherwise Hitler will have won after all.* To deny inner familiarity with Hitler is to sanction the license to destroy that Hitler claimed as the essence of the viable Nazi, the superior human being.

It is no shame to admit to feelings of anger and rage, and even to fantasies of killing, to grant rage the privilege of an honest and unfettered imagination, as Freud himself does so vividly in quoting Heine:

Mine is a most peaceable disposition. My wishes are: a humble cottage with a thatched roof, but a good bed, good food, the freshest milk and butter, flowers before my window, and a few fine trees before my door; and if God wants to make my happiness complete, he will grant me the joy of seeing some six or seven of my enemies hanging from those trees. Before their death I shall, moved in my heart, forgive them all the wrong they did me in their lifetime. One must, it is true, forgive one's enemies—but not before they have been hanged.[11]

Hitler's continuing victory lies in people's inability to admit to the entire range of reactions to him, running all the way from familiar revulsion to shamed attraction to secret adoration. His triumph also persists in one consequence of that seeming inability, unwitting tolerance for forms of destructiveness that governments claim is necessary and present to their populations as routine.

Liberal good conscience and radical determination to end injustice both suffer from refusals to acknowledge the full scope of inner human complexity. In its own way that refusal is as toxic to the project of liberation as are conservative and reactionary insistence that domination is inevitable and to be accepted rather than fought. One group underestimates the destructiveness of humans and refuses to deal with it realistically, and the other underestimates the decent social inclinations of humans and declines to deal with that realistically. *By the ego defense of splitting, both groups act out tendencies shared by everyone.* Both groups are thus in a crucial way—one that would surely bother both endlessly—remarkably similar to each other.

If liberals and radicals hate conservatives and reactionaries, it is not only because of the intransigence, cynicism, and destructiveness they believe they represent, it is also because of at least a trace of envy, a sigh as it were, for the repressed longing for unambivalent clarity and a firm certainty that the existing order is just. And if conservatives and reactionaries hate liberals and radicals, it is not only because of the disruption of the order of privilege that liberals and radicals advocate and their seeming naivete, it is also because of at least a hint of jealousy of people who are forthright in their visions of a just society and sympathetic human connection and who are comfortable with warm human feelings rather than contemptuous of them.

At various times in my life I have seen the conservative, liberal, or radical position as "right." I entered college an Eisenhower Republican. Even though I had little idea what that meant, there was something in Eisenhower's calming voice, his military record, and Republican assurances that their way was the true way that appealed to me. I had no idea of what Adlai Stevenson, Eisenhower's opponent, stood for. I admitted to a friend half way through college that I still had not figured out the differences between the two parties.

Then I sort of did. I became a liberal, expecting that beneficent government programs and well-intentioned leaders could make good changes in our society. (Twenty years later I refigured what the parties meant; this time the differences seemed rather slender even if significant.)

In the sixties, I became passionately antiwar and more or less radical. During that wondrously alive, tragic time, I deepened my analysis of society and my understanding of power. I worked for the end of the war and hoped for but did not expect radical changes in U.S. politics and society. My teaching turned to analyzing the roots of domination and oppression, and I found publications that informed me and political activities that engaged me. *By now I see all those visions, including the ones I find most attractive, as limited by violating and denying what is true about the others. Political struggle in our society is framed almost entirely in the adversary paradigm, and that is what is most fully the matter with it.*

While claiming to make the world free for investment capital, open elections, socialist democracy, workers' rule, or whatever, political factions are engaged *also* in trying to overcome each other. Ideologists are usually sincere, but ideology rationalizes fighting. If Hitler could have killed all his intended victims—always for compelling reasons—he would have moved on to others. Had he killed all the non-Germans on the planet he would have had to turn on Germans and differentiated them even further than he already had in terms of ideology or body characteristics, or something else he could define as threatening to him and his supporters. Hitler, as pure a total adversary as has existed, needed an enemy; he could not define himself otherwise. In this as in many other respects, Hitler was not unique.

Hitler's Germany illustrates obsessive opposition *for its own sake* with barely any restraint. One reason Hitler bothers and bewitches (there are people, including some scholars, who are fixated on Hitler in what look to me like unselfconsciously unhealthy ways) is that he represents, in extreme form, the order most people accept as normal. What people find intolerable is that he reveals its ultimate implications, which if taken seriously lead inevitably to a critique of the order itself.

Ah but, the friendly critic is likely to reply, one cannot compare genocide with the contempt and indifference shown by well-off people toward the poor or the viciousness of racism. Well, one cannot and one also can. One cannot, in that hating a group of people and denying them some of their rights is not the same as physical annihilation. But the degradation and killing remind one of lesser versions of those final acts. A child beaten to death is different from a child hit, but the killer shares with the hitter a rage that could be faced and dealt with nonviolently or expressed in socially useful behavior that would not harm a child.

When Kurt Vonnegut Jr. says, "We are what we pretend to be," I think he means that what we are in fantasies is as truly what we are as what we present to the world in our neat or messy ways. Hitler reminds people not of what they have done or intend to do but of what they imagine and repress. The closet sadist is enraged by the out sadist. Prudes aching to be free loathe hippies; hippies shove aside secret yearnings for discipline and recognition by people overtly scorned. Thus did Jerry Rubin and numerous other hippies become straight arrows with a vengeance. And thus did countless people who scorned and even attacked hippies eventually adopt aspects of their life styles.

Hitler is the adversary compulsion incarnate. However partially repressed, everyone knows desires to cause pain, get even, violate norms, destroy, avenge insults, the appetite for power that Nietzsche saw more clearly than any recent thinker. Yet one must not focus exclusively on Hitler in this respect. The Israeli-Palestinian conflict was, until the September 1993 rapprochement between Arafat and Rabin, also the adversary paradigm incarnate and may be now, under a right-wing government in Israel and tortured politics among Palestinians, become so again. Both Palestinians and Israelis continue to harbor rejectionists of the social-political-existential reality of the other community. The peace forces on each side are those who recognize the other's claims to dignity and place in the compromise form of mutuality rather than holding on to the pure win-lose insistence of adversarialism.

Attachment to a leader, destructive or not, duplicates attachment to any powerful other; it recalls the rapport and dependency of child and parent, and the fear and confusion as well. Yielding responsibility for action to a leader gives the Terrifier free reign, at little or no moral cost. War leaders/Terrifiers—military, civilian, and religious—permit forbidden games like murder, rape, and looting. That is part of their appeal.

Demonizing the other is a way of externalizing the Terrifier. It happens in war as well as in less violent forms of political confrontation. Until their recent beginnings of rapprochement, Palestinians and Israelis can be interpreted as recognizing but not acknowledging in each other denied parts of themselves. In each people, there is a tendency to generalize from extremists on the other side to the whole of the other side. Former Israeli Prime Minister Shamir declared that Palestinians hate Israelis, covet their land, and want to push them into the sea. Thus were Israelis encouraged to hate Palestinians, covet their land, and push them into the desert. Palestinian imagery of demonic Israelis wanting to take land from them mirrors the hatred and land-aspirations many Palestinians feel toward Israelis and that have been nurtured by many of their leaders.[12]

In Fornari's analysis, war is not only defense against external enemies but also defense against external representations of *internal enemies.* Culture allows *"a maneuver which transforms this terrifying but ultimately unaffrontable and invulnerable entity into an external, flesh-and-blood adversary who can be faced and killed.*"[13] The people who conduct wars locate enemies who can be made, unconsciously, into the Terrifier, or even invent enemies to serve this purpose. The same process is as common within societies as between them, as, for example, in attitudes and behavior of the majority toward ethnic and race minorities on one hand, and lawbreakers on the other.

Internal destructiveness (the Terrifier) is directed toward what is loved as well as what is not loved. An infant's rage at beloved parents can terrify it (and, sometimes, them). As the child develops a conscience in the household of parents who may not be secure and aware enough to permit all the child's feelings full expression, hating parents and even momentarily wanting them to die can be so troublesome to the child as to be forced out of consciousness. The anxiety that something bad may befall loved ones is a twisting of the unfaced desire that they be harmed, however momentary that desire and however counteracted by love.

Destructive energies can be turned outward into sadism, and also turned inward into masochism. People who seem to be morally neutral harbor sadistic and masochistic feelings they dare not admit to themselves.[14] Lying to itself about wishes it finds morally repugnant, the self represses consciousness of the wishes, but it does not and cannot cancel them. If a wish is made conscious, a person can choose how to control it in nondestructive ways; but shoved into unconsciousness, the wish demands release and may find it directly or metaphorically in either socially sanctioned destructiveness or in an idiosyncratic, personal form.

Denied rage toward parents, for example, can be turned into self-loathing or, in a subtler version of that, into physical illness or depression. But that is an unhappy condition too, and it is more tempting and conducive to untroubled feelings to project hatred outward. If a culture offers enemies as parts of mundane reality—and it often does—then one can not only avoid coping with ambivalence toward people one loves, one can unite with others doing the same thing. Embracing one's culture's Terrifier by hating proscribed enemies helps create good feelings with neighbors, solidarity, "us" against "them." Almost all these manipulations of destructiveness are *socially learned*; people are trained into them as surely as they are trained into language, patriotism, and sport.

The enemy metaphor fulfills one more crucial function. The fury of the Terrifier seems boundless, and one fears that it might, as it can, cause endless suffering, as in overwhelming guilt. It is always in potential a merciless inner tyrant.

> [M]ore profound than the anxieties caused by the external world, there exist . . . deep anxieties created by the purely illusory, fantasy dangers of the internal world. . . . [I]f we succeed in finding something bad (an

study the psychology of fear of the other & self

THIS IS WHAT I WANT TO DO

enemy) to destroy in the external world, we are able to reassure ourselves both against the fear that this bad something may hurt us (reassurance against persecutory anxieties) and against the danger of our destructive attacks being directed toward what we love (reassurance against depressive anxieties).[15]

War can be seen then as a form of therapy, "a costly and tragic system of security, involving an intricate interplay between the inner and the outer world, between illusion and reality."[16]

If war is a form of therapy, an attempted cure of seemingly unbearable inner anxieties, it seems to the self, albeit incredibly, *less terrifying than facing the repressed inner emotional reality.* But given the certainty of massive, total destruction that all-out nuclear confrontation would mean, war has lost its primary psychological, therapeutic advantage. "The war institution, which until now could be fantasied as the powerful sorcerer who protects us, is now on the verge of becoming the sorcerer who kills us."[17]

Thus it is urgent in this era to renounce war and to relocate the energies that feed war into alternative behaviors. The same tendencies that lead to planning, fighting, and supporting wars can be redirected willfully and ethically into behavior such as working with compassion toward others, toward ending war, racism, and other forms of domination. All the same, even the prospect of ending war can arouse inner anxieties that had been "taken care of" through externalization into war. Social norms so far make it difficult for most people, regardless of political orientation, to imagine handling those anxieties by changing destructive institutions rather than taking part in them.

The state is that political unit which can direct force toward other nations or its own people.[18] At the extreme, the state organizes violence into the prospect of nuclear annihilation. Citizens can take back the violence from the state and figure out more constructive things to do with it.

> The reappropriation by each individual of the aggressiveness saved by him [sic] and deposited into the state, as if into a bank, thus appears to be the path that must be taken if the state is to be liberated from the accumulation of private violence which it has monopolized, capitalized, and finally increased to nuclear proportions. . . . [T]he growing destructive intensity of war, having reached its apex in the nuclear era, has thrown war into a state of crisis; herein lies our hope.[19]

Not only war but the state is in an unprecedented predicament; this could mean that the abolition of the sovereignty of the state is inevitable.[20] Thus not only is war possibly approaching its logical end, but so may be its guarantor and sponsor, the state.

we are adversarial even subconsciously, when we don't know it or mean to. When we do not understand our own feelings (more taboo for males) we project onto others, this being okay means we never have to honestly examine ourselves

64 ∽∽∽ *Paradigm Shift*

War is not about events per se but about the interpretations of those events by leaders and followers.[21] War allows the projection of violent intentions onto the other side and of guilt as well. It is enemies, then, who not only are vicious but who, one often seems convinced, should feel guilty for their aggression. Consider how furious we often feel when opponents do not admit their guilt. The Israeli-Palestinian conflict was for half a century replete with demands from both sides for confessions of guilt, and outrage when, as is all but inevitable so far with the nation-state, admission and repentance are not forthcoming.

War is the ultimate extreme in yielding to the temptation to project outside what one wants to avoid inside. Whether or not some wars are inevitable, adversary tendencies could lead to honest inquiry and mutuality rather than erupting in war. It is perhaps paradoxical yet necessary to suggest that adversary energies be used to overcome adversarialism. Other liberating alternatives include cultivating inner honesty—facing destructive impulses and the depression that comes from *wanting to* express them (as distinct from actually doing so). This approach to dealing with destructiveness is addressed in disciplines as diverse as psychoanalysis and Buddhism.[22]

The state presents itself as the protecting parent. Clients transfer needs for security and understanding onto therapists, and populations transfer the same needs onto the state. But now the state can no longer provide even the fantasy of such security and is thus an unsatisfactory parent. If citizens feel anger toward that parent-surrogate, they are likely to feel guilty. The bind that arises is this: citizens seem willing to meet the state's demand to be loyal, but the state frustrates and angers citizens as well as providing for them. Ordinarily, the state can then divert that anger outward, but it is increasingly risky to do so, so the state is caught between angering its citizens and leaving them few choices but to express their anger either against the state or against groups within their society. The rise of militias in the United States and the general turning against government and so many of the services it provides is a less volatile form of the intrastate hells created in former Yugoslavia and in places like Somalia, Sri Lanka, Myanmar/Burma, and parts of the former Soviet Union.

If anger against demands of the state is not to be expressed destructively, it can be expressed constructively. To understand how this can be so, it is necessary to speculate what lies behind politically expressed anger in the first place.

Part III

❦

Adversary Rituals of Coercion

Committed adversaries take for granted that competing to "win" is so natural that, like the unquestioning belief in divinity that characterizes pious people, the proposition is taken as axiomatically true. This is so not by revelation or reasoned conviction but rather, in pure form, by unacknowledged presumption.

When challenged, or faced with even an approximate definition of it, defenders of the adversary assumption justify it. One way is to invoke philosophies of competition, such as Nietzsche's image of the superman and Hobbes's claim that opposition of interests is in our nature. Another approach cites cliches about human nature, the human condition, and other collective deflections of debate over the issue: it's a dog-eat-dog world; it's a jungle out there; to the victor go the spoils; winner take all. Undergirding an epistemology that justifies competition and the ranking that follows from it, these forms of explanation are supposedly objective, eternal truths. They are also excellent examples of adversary rituals, in what might be called the justification mode.

Cultures sustain rituals, stylized ways of behaving, for many reasons: to bind anxiety, to enjoy the familiar, to celebrate unity, to avoid having to figure out each new situation. Friendly greetings are ritualized, as is much of conversation. Squabbles and arguments are often ritualized too.

In ritual behavior there are no surprises; participants fulfill expectations of what will be said and done. They are used to this proceeding even when boredom, exasperation, and anger are associated with it, and sometimes find great satisfaction in renewing acquaintance with what is routine and known.

Erikson writes of ritual as mutually affirming, a basis of the human need for recognition.[1] Parties to rituals may affirm each other's strengths, as Erikson observes, but they can also affirm distance and deprecation. "That was a great performance" is a ritual expression of recognition and appreciation. "You're full of baloney" is a ritual expression of disparagement.

Some rituals allay fears. The fear of being hurt is aroused when spontaneous behaviors could result in pain or where something happens that reminds one of pains suffered in the past.

Religion is ritual par excellence, but all institutions, from sport to politics to education to business proceed with ritual as well. The singing of the national anthem at a baseball game, the wearing of suits by basketball coaches during game time, post-game reactions by players are almost perfectly ritualized; true spontaneity is usually bizarre and suspect in such contexts. Election campaigns, from conventions to "debates" and advertisements to acceptance and concession speeches are as heavily ritualized as the liturgy in a mass. From the use of texts, exams, and grades through commencement proceedings, education is highly ritualized too. Standard rhetoric about merchandise, sales, and pleasing the customer as well as about the ruthlessness of the competition defines common rituals of business.

In adversary rituals, cultures bind anger and accusation, defamation and humiliation, subjugation and victory, in order to sustain hostility in structured, predictable ways. Adversary rituals serve one further and crucial function: they are collective clichés, ways of avoiding possibilities of real dialogue and real changes in understanding and behavior. It is in this context that I examine a number of adversary rituals.

I distinguish between *rituals of coercion*, whose goal is to force, harass, distance, humiliate, subdue, and *rituals of resistance* that are meant to overcome rituals of coercion.

I present four sets of rituals of coercion. One is rituals of killing; in maximum and collective form, this is war. In more limited form it is mafia murders, gang killings, and whatever goes into individual homicide; I focus on war and avenging.

The second set are rituals of undermining, in which insulting, frightening, abusing, and unnerving are examined. In the third set, a party presents its supposed superiority to another by comparing or contradicting, or by constricting feelings. In the fourth set, mistrusting, blaming, and displacing define the other as at fault, with the self as innocent and fair in its behavior. All these rituals are proactive in the sense that they initiate a fight of one kind or another. Once the fight is going, each step of response is reactive to the fight under way.

By contrast, two forms of *rituals of resistance* oppose forces that inhibit freedom and life itself. One is *adversary rituals of resistance*. These include revolutions, strikes, and humiliation of the opponent. When they take this form, resistance helps perpetuate coercion by seeking to win encounters.

Rituals of resistance can take another form as well, *mutuality rituals of resistance*. They build from respect for the other and the desire to relate to the other mutualistically. They assume nonviolence as a framework for action and may include civil disobedience, demonstrations, and other challenges that maintain the humanity and dignity of the other, speak to maximizing integrity of all parties involved, and seek solutions that are least harmful to everyone. The goals of such rituals include efforts to change all parties rather than over-coming anyone.

In this part, I focus on rituals of coercion. Mutuality rituals of resistance appear in part IV of the book.

My discussion of adversary rituals is a sampling, not an exhaustive inventory. Here are others that come to mind: ridicule, sarcasm, cursing, posturing, hostile looks, contradicting, negating, debasing, ignoring, caricaturing, attacking, scolding, reproaching, humiliating, trivializing, mocking. The reader can undoubtedly think of more.

unless you
are psychotic,
who would not
prefer
this?

꙰

SEVEN

Rituals of
Killing and Revenge

War is the father of all things.

—Heraclitus

Our future is Oklahoma City. I have a deep
and abiding faith in the ultimate depravity of
mankind. There will be no love or brother-
hood . . . only racial hatred and contempt and
fear and loathing and rage until one side or the
other in this titanic struggle has perished.
Count on it my friend. There is a cruel wind
blowing and a cold, cruel time coming.

—From an antigovernment,
pro-"Patriot" journal

Violence is the quintessence of the adversary paradigm; war is its ultimate display.

Enemies

Theorists of power and conflict often assume the rationality of differences of interests. From "self-interest," enemies are assumed rational in vying
for money, power, or anything else defined as valuable and scarce. It is taken
for granted that the item struggled for is worth the struggle and must be
claimed by one party at the expense of the other.

If, contrary to conflict of interest theory, the adversary compulsion creates conflicts in which to act itself out, it does not always, or perhaps even
often, matter what the content is. It can be war over possession of a piece of
land or a hair of the prophet or the bone of a saint. It can be a quarrel over who

this is true because one could negotiate control of these things so that everyone benefits and this could happen if we didn't have some sick want of being the ONLY controller → to dominate

is the best pitcher in baseball or the best way to organize an economy or whether women have the right to control their bodies. It can involve *anything*. This principle is keenly caricatured by Dr. Seuss in *The Butter Battle Book*, a nuclear arms race parody that starts with an argument between two neighboring peoples over how to butter bread.[1] The story ends in total war.

The enemy relation culminates in war; combatants and civilians on the other side are killed, and members of one's own side are "sacrificed" for the "common good." The overt goal is control of markets, raw materials, land, honor, or some such resource, but the covert goal is to *overcome* the other.

Two armies face each other. They share a tacit issue with the publics that support them: not knowing how to release anger in a gratifying way toward whoever instigated it. The anger, felt to be bad and hence unacceptable, is rejected.[2] Deprived of access to this compelling, real part of themselves, people yield easily to the temptation to experience it outside themselves, as if directed *toward* them instead of *by* them. The consequence: normative paranoia, constructed and experienced in terms of group and persecution.

> The members of each community . . . rid themselves of their hostile, destructive impulses by projecting them into their armies for deflection against the enemy. Paranoid anxiety in the total community, Army and civilian alike, may be alleviated, or at least transmuted into fear of known and identifiable enemies, since the bad impulses and objects projected onto the enemy return, not in the form of introjected phantastic persecutors, but of actual physical attack, which can be experienced in reality. . . . The bad sadistic enemy is fought against, not in the solitary isolation of the unconscious inner world, but in co-operation with comrades-in-arms in real life. . . . [M]embers of the community also avoid guilt by introjecting the socially sanctioned hatred of the enemy. Such introjected sanction reinforces the denial of unconscious hatred and destructive impulses.[3]

Diverting thwarted feelings toward "enemies" is a collective alternative to emotional illness. People who claim instructions from another planet to oppose anyone are considered disturbed, but accepting what is said to be God's or the government's directions to attack enemies is called religious or patriotic or loyalty to one's group.[4] Thus can people become collectively ill.[5]

Underlying these processes is a crucial problem of esteem. When a society ties self-esteem to something that seems in finite supply, like wealth, battles over economic "worth" *are* battles over self-worth as well as over who gets to drive what and live where.

Domination, a core form of adversarialism, is coercive. The dominated are designated as the enemy by the dominator who inevitably becomes the adversary of the dominated.

Domination may, though, involve more than suffering at the hands of the dominator. Free-floating guilt, of whose sources one may be unaware, can lead people to feel they somehow have punishment coming. Thus the dominated, like a partner in an abusive relationship or the law-breaker who deep inside wants and unwittingly arranges to be caught, may unconsciously accept domination as expiation for shared feelings of guilt or for unconscious decisions to direct aggression inward.[6]

Winning, Losing, and Rituals

The adversary compulsion culminates in murder. But the hatred and rage implied in adversary encounters are usually modulated by society through internal and external restraints—conscience, law, and morality—that prevent people from killing. National leaders encourage displacing daily brewings of anger onto enemies in stylized antagonism. For men, this often means taking part in killing; for women, preparing sons and husbands for war. It can also, for women, mean turning destructiveness inward into obsessions with body-hate and dismay with the self.

Like most adversarialism, war proceeds through rituals, the first being the *casus belli*, the formal reason for combat. Leaders cannot say, "We want war" or "We recommit ourselves to conventional masculinity." Instead, they invoke stylized words about defending national interests, opposing evil, and promoting divine intentions.

Basic training (increasingly, for women as well as men) is a ritual in which conscripts lose civilian identity, assimilate technologies of fighting, and learn to follow orders quickly and unthinkingly. Soldiers hear commanders and politicians glorify the nation (often with assurance that God does likewise) and vilify the enemy (also with God's alleged support). Other rituals mobilize civilians by urging them to donate gold, food, and offspring for the war. Military music and flag-waving; accounts of evil, heroism, and sacrifice; and exaltation of the bereft contribute to the drama. War rituals train people to dehumanize and loathe the other; enemies are not born, they are made.[7]

The binding and projecting of anger has to be cultivated. Anti-Asian racism already normative in the United States was easily engaged when Japan bombed Pearl Harbor in 1941. The internment of Japanese-Americans in camps was a ritualized way of containing fear and anxiety about the war. It made no more sense than would have interning German-Americans, but even given the history of the First World War, there was no inclination to do that in 1941.

Germans had, all the same, to be made into enemies. Without the prior racism against nonwhites, prejudice against Germans could not cut quite so deeply as against Japanese. Paul Fussell claims that for many U.S. troops, the war was fought because of Pearl Harbor and that Germany was considered our enemy because it was allied with Japan.[8] There was, he adds, little understanding of fascism or the reasons for fighting it, among Allied forces.[9]

War propaganda portrays enemies bent on evil deeds menacing "our" women.[10] Sam Keen illustrates *Faces of the Enemy* with war posters that demonize the enemy.[11]

War rituals enhance the zero-sum (all or nothing) definition of war. They stifle critical examination of political discourse and alternatives and still doubts about justice, violence, and victory. Because enemies do the same thing, the absolutism and denial in both sides' patriotism dovetail perfectly.

War ritual plays on generations in conflict. It is like initiation rites in some cultures[12] where boys, said to be made into men,[13] are introduced to metaphors for acting out murderous rivalry between fathers and sons. Thus in war as in peace, rituals bind young men's aggression that threatens the authority of older men; by threat, fear, and punishment, the elders socialize the youngers into accepting their authority.[14]

If war serves to divert sons' rage from fathers, there are other ways to do this. The U.S. tradition of college education for over half the population allows at least a minority of courageous, thoughtful late adolescents to confront elders with challenges to their ideas and values. (Most college students learn the adversary rituals taught in the academy and challenge very little. They are not dumb or thoughtless so much as scared of authority and of their own critical powers, with few ways of admitting and dealing with their fears.) The anti-Vietnam War movement and the counterculture that accompanied it developed into the kind of threat—that of widespread social criticism and demands for change—from which war is meant to distract the young. Both weakened within a few years of the war's end; thus the war paradigm, questioned not quite to its very roots, was restored, albeit shakily.

For all its ritualization, the accounting at combat's end of losses does not touch pride, grief, tragedy, and other feelings pricked by war. Although rituals of victory abound, like parades and selecting great warriors for high office, there is no vocabulary or ceremony for coming to terms with the *emotional* meanings of losing in ways that avoid desires for retaliation, feelings of self-deprecation, and realities of self-destruction. (Consider suicides, crime rate, and massive drug use among U.S. veterans of the wars in Southeast Asia.) In the United States, Southern reactions to losing the Civil War have led to endless efforts to come to terms with it, in ways ranging from defiant uses of the Confederate flag to the rich and complex body of literature by Southern writers who explore meanings of the defeat.[15]

In war as in most opposition, the loser is expected to accept misfortune and go on. If the defeated, the poison of whose losses festers, explode into protest or violence, "victors" cry foul and vilify the vanquished and their refusal to accept defeat.

Recognizing despair, hatred, and vengeance is either factored out of the winner's consciousness or assumed, with grim resignation, to be unavoidable. This rationalization reveals the flaw in the paradigm expectation that losers resign themselves to failure. It is by now common to observe that Hitler's temporary success in Germany was due at least in part to the yearning by Germans to negate the degradation of defeat in the First World War and of the subjugation crafted in the Versailles Treaty afterward.[16] The common euphoria in the United States over "victories" in Grenada, Panama, and the Persian Gulf likely reflects a widespread wish to compensate for the "defeat" in Vietnam. George Bush treated the Gulf War in these terms.

A peculiar defect in the adversary paradigm then is the incapacity of victors to understand defeat and the burning determination to overcome it. Sadly, the vanquished rarely confront the paradigm but rather strive to win within it. Tragedies of domination will continue until participants understand the constraints imposed upon them by the adversary paradigm and the liberating potential in shifting attention to mutuality instead.

While entire peoples can be inspired to support war, it is small elites— economic, political, military, and sometimes religious—that make war decisions and stimulate the passions of their followers to join them (or threaten to punish for refusing). Emotions that could lead to criticism and opposition to domination are redirected onto foreign "enemies," with slogans like "national interest," "security," and "God's will." Unscrupulous elites, touching the yearnings and confusions of masses of people, can persuade them to "act out" leaders' personal pathologies. A peacetime mass murderer of twenty people is considered deranged whereas a president who orders the killing of thousands of foreigners for a flimsy reason is hailed as a leader. Society could construct definitions of pathology to include any people—including elites—who sanction killing for any reason at all.

War Technology and the Future of War

War is the most mechanized sector of human existence, which adds another clue to its significance. War technologizes murder, and it does something strange thereby. Killings within societies are usually performed by weapons that bring killer and victim together through poison, hands, rocks, knives, clubs, ropes, guns. Although some victims are "chosen" at random, murderers typically know their victims face-to-face. They encounter them directly, act on personal motives, and are held responsible for the killing.

The primary difference between tools for individual murder and those for war is the distance of the killer from the killed. The more sophisticated the war technology, the more depersonalized the killing. Yet even though war permits killing, not everyone signs up. Many American soldiers during both world wars—perhaps as many as 80 percent in the Second—would not shoot at the enemy even in the thick of battle. It is not unheard of for entire units to agree not to shoot, in collaboration with the enemy at whom they are supposed to be shooting. Thus it appears that conscience often rejects even depersonalized and sanctioned commands to kill.[17]

All the same, disengaging murderer from quarry makes it easier to kill. Helicopter pilots in the film *Apocalypse Now* bomb Vietnamese while listening to Wagner on tape. Not only do they not see their victims, the bombast distracts them from feeling or thinking about them. No problem here of the infantry soldier hesitating to kill a real human being standing before him.

Like the politics of which it is a part, war has become rationalized, that is, made bureaucratic and impersonal.[18] The glamour and inspiration of the charismatic military leader have given way to the routine of rules and machines. By the time of the Vietnam War, no one was kindling the enthusiasm of U.S. troops in a cause that meant anything to them. Indeed, Vietnam failed as a patriotic crusade partly because the passion of world anticommunism had begun to wane and bureaucrats had decided to try to "win" the war with fancy technology run by anonymous men who became its acquiescent appendages.[19] Further, the passionate guerrillas who believed in a cause had an advantage over massed parts of an impersonal machine. The Persian Gulf War marked a return to faith in high-tech warfare, but again U.S. soldiers appeared not to believe in what they were doing.

Impersonality in war did not begin with Vietnam, nor did the massive brutalities of high-tech killing. In World War I, poison gas killed in a way other than by impact of explosives. (This was not new; disease was used as a weapon in killing Native Americans in the settling of the United States,[20] but the use of toxins on a vast scale is very recent.) World War II brought developments in the use of nonimpact killing technologies. Although more people died in the U.S. fire-bombings of Dresden, Cologne, and Tokyo than in the nuclear destruction of Hiroshima and Nagasaki, it is the latter cases that excite the world's awe and dread. Like Zyklon B, nuclear devices are nonimpact killers and break a taboo. Poison gas, outlawed internationally after World War I, was supposedly not employed in World War II. Yet if Zyklon B is understood to be a poison gas and radioactivity a still more efficient form of nonsolid, nonimpact killer (and a vastly more destructive one as well), then both Nazi Germany and the United States violated the injunction by moving poison gas use from the trenches, its locus in World War I, to warfare against civilians, with consequences far more monstrous than those that led to the original ban.

The death camps replicated and extended familiar technologies of killing. The release of atomic energy in war signaled something new. A vivid if limited metaphor for the atomic invention is a distortion of the double-barreled shotgun. Imagine that one barrel points outward, destroying the enemy society. This feat is possible only at the price of triggering the second barrel pointing inward, annihilating the aggressor society. Nuclear technology makes it highly probable that large-scale homicide is now inextricable from suicide.

If nuclear omnicide—the destruction of everything—is the ultimate expression of the adversary compulsion, the final implication of the adversary paradigm, and if it is understood that war is too costly to pursue at maximum level, then something new in history happens to war: it has the potential to become obsolete. "Nuclear war" is an oxymoron. Until now, war has meant an armed contest that can be won or lost. With no victor, the word *war* loses its meaning. And so with "nuclear weapon." A weapon is a device to overcome another. An apparatus that kills aggressor and victim alike can no longer be called weapon.

After two generations of the nuclear threat, humankind appears to have begun to integrate its awesome knowledge; sophisticated measures minimize accidental or unauthorized ("madman") nuclear holocaust. Thanks to Gorbachev's decision to opt out of the arms race, the main nuclear stockpiles are being reduced.

While such moves could be seen as nothing more than mollifying nervous publics and responding to economic imperatives, they could also be interpreted as realistic measures to wind down the lunacy of the threat to destroy the planet. But, the skeptic reasonably continues, even if nuclear confrontation is avoided, conventional wars can continue ad infinitum (as of course can the incremental destructiveness of reckless treatment of the environment). So it would seem, even though the most likely scenario for a major nuclear catastrophe is escalation from conventional war.[21]

Although the United States started several wars in recent years, none of them threatened to escalate into larger ones. It is too early to know whether Russia will be tempted to engage its considerable war arsenal at some later time.[22] War for the moment seems to be almost entirely intrastate and to be limited to violence fueled by ethnic hatreds that surface in the processes of state-disintegration and economic development.

What, then, of the possibility of small regional wars getting out of hand? If they escalate and one of them draws in a nuclear power, it might be tempted to unleash a nuclear device; or if a smaller state with nuclear technology enters the fray, nuclear madness could ensue. Prevention of conventional wars is the best safeguard against that qualitative jump to the once unthinkable.[23] Thus the nuclear threat *implies* the end of war. It does not guarantee it; there are wars all over the globe. But those wars suggest possible changes in the nature of the outcome of war. The Iran-Iraq conflict, for example, was a conventional war that escalated with the addition of chemical and biological toxins. The war persisted for eight years; at its end, neither side "won" in any sense in which we are familiar with that word.

It was important to major states that neither Iran's Islamic fundamentalism nor Iraq's aggressive nationalism would triumph. External actors arranged arms supplies so as to allow a near-even match. The war's duration as the longest war of the century, its viciousness, and its casualties could imprint on late-twentieth-century human consciousness the message that a major war of that sort cannot, for whatever reasons, be won.

More recently, the European community, the United States, and the United Nations are gingerly entering various frays with peacekeeping politics and forces, hesitantly employed. They are not very good yet at bringing about peace, but they are refraining from escalating war. The Soviet Union's pullout from Afghanistan, like the U.S. withdrawal from southeast Asia, reveals the limits of the most powerful nations attempting to impose their wills on dissident movements in client states. In a rare move, the Soviet Union admitted the illegality and immorality of its Afghanistan involvement. The suggestion that morality ought to play a central role in world affairs was made by Gorbachev in his remark that

> A way of thinking and a way of acting, based on the use of force in world politics, have formed over centuries, even millennia. It seems they have taken root as something unshakable. Today, they have lost all reasonable grounds. Clausewitz's dictum that war is the continuation of politics only by different means, which was classical in his time, has grown hopelessly out of date. . . . For the first time in history, basing international politics on moral and ethical norms that are common to all humankind, as well as humanizing interstate relations, has become a vital requirement.[24]

The United States has limited itself since Vietnam mainly to small wars it can win directly (Grenada, Panama), or by proxy (Nicaragua, El Salvador). Yet what of the seeming anomaly, the Persian Gulf War? The reasons it was fought are confusing and unclear, but the one the U.S. public seems to have responded to most fully was the perceived threat of Iraq's using nuclear devices.

Whatever else it was, the Gulf War might have been an effort to stave off transition to peace, a desperate affirmation by both George Bush and Saddam Hussein of the conventional appropriateness, inevitability, and masculinity of war. The excitement about redeeming American honor can be read as just that, but it can also be read as a lamentable attempt to breathe life into a collapsing war paradigm. It is too early to tell if this was a war to deny the ending of war or just another in a continuing series of nonnuclear confrontations.

Within the Eastern bloc, objections to Soviet domination had, until December 1989, traditionally been contained with little or no armed resistance. Dissident movements in Poland, East Germany, Czechoslovakia, Hungary, and elsewhere used the spoken word, the written word, and the streets for their protests. Intimidations and arrests were common, but torture and killing were nearly passé by the time Gorbachev made his startling decision that self-determination for East European nations was more important than Soviet domination. Much must have changed among Soviet elites that they could select him as their head and that they could accept, however grudgingly, the extraordinary decisions he made in their name. The stunning events in Eastern Europe since 1989 reflect a unique combination of grassroots and top-down actions, most of which have avoided large-scale violent confrontation. Even within the former Soviet republics, though wars abound they are so far of very small scale.

In 1989, China presented the curious spectacle of several weeks during which little force was used against vehement antigovernment protest. When other "socialist" governments began to honor dissidence and respond positively to it, China wavered. Whatever conflicts among Chinese elites were played out in that waiting period, the Chinese government ended the Tianenmen Square demonstrations by reverting to the classic state adversary response of brute force. If the time is ripe to work at weakening the adversary paradigm, then some societies get the point while others fearfully shore up old ways.

Despite dozens of wars, there is evidence of growing war-weariness in the world. States not at war struggle to figure out how to be useful in ending wars. The United States and Russia play this role occasionally, and Norway showed it in dramatic fashion in bringing Israel and the Palestinians together in 1993. If war could wind down, three recent examples of lightning-swift victories further demonstrate the point rather than, as might seem at first glance, contradicting it. In a burst of jingoism in 1982, the British defeated Argentina in the matter of who owns the Falklands/Malvinas Islands, which are of little objective value to anyone but their handful of residents. It appears that few Britons had ever heard of the islands or knew their location until then Prime Minister Thatcher aroused her countrymen's and women's passions for faded empire by offering a tiny taste of what it was like to do battle and win. The minuscule scale of the conflict, the paucity of stakes, and the uneven match between the warring parties made the confrontation more farce than war in the usual sense.

The unevenness of the match was exceeded in the subsequent encounter between the United States and the island nation of Grenada in 1983. Whatever the point of the exercise—to shore up a flagging anticommunism in the United States, divert attention from the immediately prior massacre of several hundred marines in an ill-considered U.S. adventure in Lebanon, or forestall a possible chain of revolutions among tiny Caribbean nations, all these reasons or others still—a face-off between nations of 240 million and 120,000 was not war in the grand style. Nor was its successor war, that of the United States government against the president and people of Panama.

The very brevity and limited scale of those conflicts make them seem more like caricatures than the massively destructive wars of this century. It is too early to know if this period is only an interim between the Second World War and the Third, or if efforts to move away from war are gaining acceptance and adherence.

More problematic are the massacres in the 1990s in several parts of what used to be Yugoslavia, in Somalia, Rwanda, Burundi, East Timor, Tibet, Angola, and elsewhere. These are mostly wars among peoples once part of empires and then of fragile multinational states held together by tyranny. None of these wars threaten to escalate into nuclear confrontations, and without the Cold War, the involvement of superpowers is unlikely.

Several ethnic wars reflect an unpredicted tendency in the post-modern world: the disintegration of the multinational state. Even as the European community moves to weaken the autonomy of the individual state by political and economic integration, components of what were the Soviet Union and Yugoslavia move in the opposite direction, fashioning one non-multinational state after another. Outcomes implied are less clear in current wars in Asia and Africa, except for the prominence of ethnic-national identification.

A Note on Revolution and Possibilities of Ending War

History can be read, among its multitude of ways, as a dialectic between adversarialism and mutuality. Marx identifies the dialectic as in effect adversarial, primarily in the form of class conflict, with cooperation and decency (mutuality) mysteriously emerging from the final confrontation of workers and owners in the late stages of capitalism, thus ending the major effects of adversary relations.

But it is not only that the objective interests of slaves and masters, serfs and lords, workers and owners contradict each other. All those people also have glimmerings of a mutuality society in their daily lives. In families, religions, guilds, neighborhoods, taverns, sports teams, and other places, the mutuality principle holds in significant ways, albeit secondarily.

Rebels seek to overcome their degradation, and seek freedom from domination itself. But then, almost without exception, they recreate it. They unwittingly find ways that can be seen as compulsive, to renew the domination they dedicated themselves to terminating once and for all. It could be that revolutionaries perpetuate what they sought to overthrow because that process is inevitable until material prosperity makes possible its final overcoming, the conviction of the Marxist tradition. But I am convinced that the process itself lives to some major extent independent of its material base.

Marx expected an ending of the pernicious effects of capitalism to emerge from class struggle in and of itself. I suggest, to the contrary, that the adversary paradigm continues to define the nature of relationships in parties endeavoring to overcome domination just as it does in those making no such claim. Even if material scarcity were originally the basis of adversarialism, and even though adversarialism is an adaptive response to scarcity as defined in society, by now adversarialism has developed a life of its own. (In the United States, abundance could be distributed fairly to all, but compulsive adversary pressures, led by the very wealthy and their friends in power, prevent humane distribution of goods and services. Indeed, one of the most enduring accomplishments of the Reagan administration was a dramatic redistribution of income *upward* rather than democratically to all.)

Paradigms of proper behavior in prerevolutionary societies do not bend easily to ideological or material change. They persist both in revolutionaries' minds and in objective reality; they also exist in revolutionaries' emotions, in their subjective reality. Assumptions of what is proper are not put into mothballs when developing political forces define as outmoded what has become experienced in some conscious way by *some* people as archaic.

Erikson imagines global mutuality:

> Insofar as a nation thinks of itself as a collective individual . . . it may well learn to visualize its task as that of maintaining mutuality in international relations. For the only alternative to armed competition seems to be the effort to *activate in the historical partner what will strengthen him [sic] in his historical development even as it strengthens the actor in his own development—toward a common future identity.* Only thus can we find a common denominator in the rapid change of technology and history and transcend the dangerous imagery of victory and defeat, of subjugation and exploitation which is the heritage of a fragmented past.[25]

Ethical strength as well as destructive rage build upon unconscious components as well as conscious ones.[26] Erikson's radical insight here, following from Freud, is that not only have modern people repressed more of their rage than is healthy for them and their society, they have repressed crucial aspects of their nobler, mutuality yearnings. What psychoanalysis identifies as the superego includes both the taboos of a society and that to which people aspire. Many components of superego, as well as of id, do not come easily, if they come at all, to consciousness.

Where there is domination, substantial numbers of people may challenge it. However genuine their intentions, though, however strong and authentic their determination to change their society in good ways, rebels are ordinarily socialized into the orders they attempt to replace. Once the old structure is ended, its norms seep into the new structures, for their inventors feel compelled unconsciously to recreate that which in their deep inner recesses they feel or even "know" to be real and proper. When they thus revive and revise the secret police, or develop new forms of oppression (neighborhood surveillance committees, public confession of errors and guilt, ideological reeducation), they act out of an inner compulsion they do not recognize.

One possible exception to this generalization is parts of the feminist movement that work consciously on resocialization away from domination altogether. Yet since such efforts come out of adversary experiences, it is likely that in one way or another they continue them. That is almost always the result of efforts to end adversarialism. Only deep inner awareness of adversary tendencies and a methodology to come to terms with them, together with mutuality structures that invite participation, can be adequate to the task of really getting past adversary destructiveness. The last part of this book is devoted to this topic.

Revolutionaries are attached to authoritarianism learned in the patriarchal family.[27] "They secretly loved the authority they subverted and reestablished domination when they were able."[28] Revolution cannot succeed

> so long as it only changes the institutions and ignores the men [sic] who live by them. If humanity is a function of institutions, so are institutions a function of humanity. For a transformation of the world to be radical it must grasp things by the root. The root is man. Education changes man. This is the path that is given to us.[29]

Sad though it may be, it appears that buried rage is easier to exhume than buried wishes for mutuality. This is not because human nature makes it so; it is because the adversary paradigm, still pre-eminent in most cultures, dictates that adversary behavior is more acceptable, "natural," permissible than mutuality and thus encourages attention on adversarialism and away from mutuality.

we have inherent destructive tendencies within ourselves but it is taboo to express them so at this age it becomes scandalous to do so, but also admit, Need to admit to them before we can understand them,

Revolutionaries are puzzled by their inability to reach as deeply inside for ethical energy and inspiration as they do for revenge and triumph. They miss altogether the saliency of the paradigm, and for many of them *the compulsion* that governs this norm. Given that reality, and the accompanying tendency to avoid facing feelings of hurt, it is no wonder that love, respect, and mutuality seem so elusive, even "utopian," despite the fact that people yearn for them, not for hatred and killing.

In their confusion, revolutionaries commonly locate people supposedly antagonistic to the revolution and persecute them rather than accurately identifying their own inner processes that contradict their conscious intentions. (Hitler and Stalin are conspicuous and grotesque examples of this. So are Mao in the cultural revolution and Deng in the destruction of the pro-democracy movement in China.)

Emotional reality unacknowledged is stronger and more influential on behavior than perceptions, ideology, conscious intentions, and determined political organizing. Among the frequently ignored inner issues that would-be change agents are reluctant to address is ambivalence about victory itself. The prospect of winning

> may . . . stir unconscious fears of disloyalty to our parents, whose lives were firmly enmeshed in powerlessness. . . .
> Here we have the primary inner contradiction of progressive politics. People both do and don't want to succeed. . . . [A]nybody who has been part of a movement for social change cannot fail to be impressed by the sincerity, dedication and willingness to sacrifice that are characteristic of many movement activists. . . . With rare exceptions, most of the core activists in movements for progressive social change tend to be intelligent, caring and giving people. . . . Very often they are people whose talents, if applied in a more self-centered way, would have brought them many more rewards at the level of money, power and recognition from the marketplace. . . . Yet, at the same time, *they are also deeply committed to losing* [emphasis added]. Over and over they will choose paths of action that are guaranteed at seizing defeat out of the jaws of victory. The double message of progressive politics is to be strong and visionary, but act in ways that prove you are going to lose.[30]

Thus may war and the fighting of it be more complex than simple desires to win. Just as in sporting events it sometimes appears that a party lacks the will to win, so in war. In both cases, the issue is less likely having or not having the will to win, but ambivalence about the endeavor.

One can oppose domination and war by loving peace. This practice includes comfort with one's loving and hating tendencies. Effective peace work proceeds best from people who know themselves well and accept the full range of their feelings and ambivalences.

Hurting, Avenging, and Killing: Boyz N the Hood

Hurt and rage are twinned—two aspects of one experience. People insulted, negated, humiliated, respond in rage. Attacked, one either replies in kind, imagines doing so, joins in cultural metaphors for assault, or turns the anger inward. Or one leaves the adversary system and finds constructive ways to deal with hurt.

One could write the history of a child's day in terms of its happy moments. Another way to record it, complementing the first, would be in terms of fear and pain. The exuberant two-year-old, helmeted and strapped in, sits on the child seat on the bicycle. Hitting a bump in the road, his father flies over the handlebars. Bike and boy fall, and the boy's face is scraped. His father comforts him; later his mother holds him lovingly as a nurse scrubs his scuffed skin very hard. He cries a lot. Over several days, with his helmet on his head, he acts out the scene over and over. After a while, when he sees his father about to ride the bike, he tells him to be careful not to fall.

A child is supported in his efforts to come to terms with a major hurt, and he comes to terms with it. But what of children not so lucky to have parents who recognize and sponsor such events? And what of numerous lesser daily hurts? Fear and anger may be acted out by turning on another child or a toy. Or in fantasies, dreams of vengeance, culture's metaphors. In games, the child fears and hates and hurts criminals or cops, Indians or cowboys, Blacks or Whites. The child can, if exposed to someone modeling it, victimize another child.

Revenge is reactive hurting, an effort to negate the hurt self, or compensate for it, as if by displacing the hurt to someone else—either the person who caused it or a substitute—one could get rid of it or at least alleviate it. Satisfaction in revenge is dimmed by the possibility of more revenge still (as in *Boyz N the Hood*). But revenge appears to be not so fulfilling as anticipated anyway. Rambo breaks down, Don Corleone is empty and alone, Hamlet perishes in a frenzy of violence after ruining his chance for love. To examine revenge as a ritual, begin with hurt, with being narcissistically damaged, as Gregory Rochlin puts it.[31] Then comes the desire to "get even." "The need for revenge, for righting a wrong, for undoing a hurt by whatever means, and a deeply anchored, unrelenting compulsion in the pursuit of all these aims gives no rest to those who have suffered a narcissistic injury."[32]

I remember a particular insult, in the form of an action I interpreted as personal criticism of a very severe and unfair sort. I think the action was not meant consciously as cruel, but I became enraged. A conversation with the wounder led to no satisfaction. His explanation did not make sense to me, he did not apologize or make any effort at restitution, and he rejected my suggestion that we talk the matter out. This left me angrier than before. I would have been willing to settle for a long conversation to explore what perhaps had been mutual hurts, insults, whatever, but I could discover no point of entry into such a talk.

I then turned to fantasies of revenge, and I was fascinated to watch them unfold. The insulter became an enemy in my mind and gut. I imagined ways of humiliating him in print, of disgracing him in public, of making him squirm with remorse that he had hurt me so. But that would not suffice. I wanted him dead, preferably after a slow, horrible torture during which he would be forced to face his cruelties, especially what I felt was the gross injustice done me. But that was not enough. I wanted him pulverized, turned not into ashes but powder, and the powder blown by the winds. But that was not adequate either. I wanted all memory of him blotted out, forever. And even that would not do.

At this point I recalled the biblical portrayal of a God of vengeance. Through the prophet Samuel, God reminds Saul, first king of the Jews, that their enemies the Amalekites had "laid wait" for the Israelites when they came up from Egypt.[33] God commands Saul to annihilate the Amalekites (or Amaleq), "utterly destroy all that they have, and spare them not; but slay both man and woman, infant and suckling, ox and sheep, camel and ass."[34] God goes considerably further in declaring (to Moses, earlier, but that seems not to matter) "that I will utterly blot out the remembrance of Amaleq from under the heaven."[35] This sentiment, I was embarrassed to admit to myself, is familiar; whatever the metaphor is, I think I finally get it.

Revenge is a desire to hurt in return for hurt; at its maximum, though, it is a desire to annihilate, *an unbounded urge to return hurt in far greater measure than it was given*, as if such action would somehow cancel or undo the hurt. (Thus it is widely understood that the injunction to take "eye for eye, tooth for tooth."[36] was in its time a moderating principle, a mandate for restraint.) Revenge can become obsessive, and wars have been based at least in part upon it, as have countless daily brutal acts. Several women colleagues and students have told me that their revenge fantasies are not violent but involve humiliating the other. I expect that some women imagine violence while others do not and that the same is true among men, although men may learn to imagine violence more frequently than do women. It is likely that the desire for revenge is universal, but that forms in which it works itself out vary with gender socialization and culture.

The event in question happened many years ago. I did not let go of the anger until I discussed it with a number of people and then poured it into an article that related to the content of the issue between me and the other person. I find that anger can sometimes be dissipated by talking to people other than the original source of the anger, by writing, and in physical activity. Indeed, I expect that releasing anger safely is one of the principal reasons for using gyms; it is certainly one of my principal reasons for using gyms.[37] When the energy of anger and rage pour into physical exercise, one's body and soul benefit thereby. This is a form of sublimation where the payoff for the self is in self-development, and for society in channeling anger and rage away from harming people.

Among the options for dealing with rage—which crossed my mind in the incident above but which I rejected—is revenge. As a ritual, revenge begins with offending pride and undermining respect. This is the major theme of the 1991 movie *Boyz N the Hood*, which portrays hurt, threat, and revenge in a larger structure of oppression. The police daily buzz an African American ghetto in Los Angeles. We never see the helicopter, and the feeling we get is of military occupation. The oppressor is so remote and vague that whatever resentment and anger build toward it have no logical outlets against it. Hence, the film suggests, the anger is turned to relations within the ghetto.

Revenge is the middle term between hope and hopelessness. In *Boyz*, Ricky (Morris Chestnut), handsome football hero and potential college student, accidentally brushes against another young man, who is incensed. Quietly vexed but not combative, Ricky walks away. Some days later, accompanied by friends, the man whom Ricky had inadvertently annoyed kills him on the street. Ricky's brother Doughboy (Ice Cube) finds Ricky's killers, kills them, and later is killed in turn by their friends.

The impulse to avenge destroys Ricky, his killers, Doughboy, and countless other ghetto men. Ricky's friend Tre (Cuba Gooding Jr.), the film's protagonist who epitomizes lower-middle-class struggles to leave the ghetto, is tempted to join the killing party but backs off. His father Furious Styles (Larry Fishburne) teaches Tre to emulate him in sublimating his fury; avoiding street violence is crucial to leaving the ghetto.

Counterpoint to Tre, Doughboy is a youth with a short fuse. His contempt for law and aspiration combine with a full commitment to the macho *trompe-l'oeil* that makes a thin skin appear to self and others as a thick, coarse hide. Only through stylized posturings do such "tough guys" hide their hurt from self and others and let it rot them away. Not focusing on the larger structure of oppression or finding political ways to act against it, ghetto men often transmute frustration into fratricide and other forms of self-defeat. (Once again, women do not so often seem to choose this way to act upon frustrations but tend to limit themselves to verbal criticisms, gaining support from other women, and self-castigation.) Thus does the majority culture contain and deflect the rage it instigates, away from itself.

Among the angry, low-status young men of *Boyz N the Hood*, revenge is reduced to its simplest, purest form. Someone brushes up against someone else, and the tragedy proceeds. There is a comic taste of this in *Midnight Cowboy* when down-and-out Ratso Rizzo (Dustin Hoffman) screams at a taxi driver who invades what Rizzo perceives as "his" space on a busy New York intersection: "I'M WALKIN' HERE!!!"

This is about as full as "touchiness" can get. A brittle self, when grazed, responds with hurt and anger meant to protect the self's integrity. In polite society, an accidental collision is accompanied by, "Oh, I'm sorry," which is met by "That's okay," "No problem," or simply "Mmmm." If, at worst, the offending action seems motivated and there is no apology, one might be miffed and mumble an obscenity. These are gestures of grudging acceptance or politely expressed annoyance, as alternatives to battle.

Full-blown revenge is a decision not to let an offense, however slight and unintended, go by gracefully. It is a judgment, rarely conscious, that misdeed and vengeance should preoccupy one, a decision not to let go but be consumed by the circuit, followed compulsively: hurt/anger/vow-to-vengeance/retaliation. In a single name and image, it is Ahab.

Revenge seems to touch on something at the deepest level of hurt, a sense of unbearable violation that feels as if it can be assuaged only by retaliation. Steve Wangh suggests that "all anger is simply a physical container for and denial of pain."[38] If the pain is expressed and the hurter apologizes for causing it, then the anger might be either assuaged or finessed. It is in this context that Palestinians' request that Israelis admit the pain they have caused them makes perfect sense. It also makes perfect sense that the request is difficult for many Jews who experience their history as one of frequent and brutal violation by tormentors who do not apologize for the suffering they have inflicted.

The explosion of interethnic conflicts in Eastern Europe and Central Asia brings hurts and anger massively to the surface. People who have injured and loathed one another for centuries had a temporary cease-and-desist order forced on them by the Communist governments they despised. With that imposed control gone, loathing erupts anew, thus demonstrating that every generation has been socialized into its parents' pains and hatreds. Each side in each conflict accuses the other, rehearses the history of wrongs, and self-righteously proclaims or assumes its innocence of wrong-doing and its purity of intentions. It is difficult to envision national rituals of admitting culpability, asking forgiveness, and accepting it, but such rituals would help reduce the festering sores that nationalism appears inevitably to breed. In 1993, a new government of Japan began a series of gestures moving toward apologizing for Japan's role in World War II.[39]

The famous Rabin-Arafat handshake in September 1993 is a striking example of a mutuality ritual that contrasts with a history of extreme adversarialism. The power and simultaneous fragility of such gestures is revealed by Rabin's fate two years later. In November 1995, Rabin was celebrating and celebrated at an outdoor rally in Tel Aviv, in support of the then ongoing peace process between Israel and the Palestinians. The rally featured two more mutuality gestures. In one, Rabin, known as a dour fellow who rarely if ever sang, stood with 100,000 supporters singing a peace anthem known by heart to nearly everyone there but him. Someone passed him the words on a piece of paper, and he sang along. In the same evening, Rabin publicly embraced his long-time political nemesis and partner Shimon Peres.

The rally signified Rabin's transformation from successful warrior to nascent peacemaker. It was exactly at that moment of consolidation of his new identity that a representative of the old paradigm literally came out from the shadows of the event and engaged the quintessential adversary implement, a gun, to kill Rabin. The bullet was aimed not just at a particular human being and his historic role, it was aimed at the entire paradigm embodied by the shift toward nonviolent resolution of a continuing conflict.

Revenge can localize in time and space what is otherwise diffuse. The Simi Valley jury's acquittal of police officers in the videotaped beating of Rodney King was widely experienced among African Americans in Los Angeles as yet another manifestation of racism. The subsequent riot released years, even centuries, of accumulated humiliation, frustration, and pain. And it is that accumulation that is suggested by the revenge killings in *Boyz N the Hood*.

Revenge then, whatever its other meanings, especially when it is chronic, can be understood to be defensive "against the awareness of anxiety-laden, repressed emotions . . . particularly . . . repressed grief and separation-anxiety."[40] It is not the norm of insult and forced respect (so common in Mafia movies) that is the issue so much as accumulated rage.

Not so angry as Doughboy and the killers, Ricky and Tre each enjoy a parent who supports them, mirrors back strengths and weaknesses, and helps them withstand the mundane hurts of racism. Ricky and Tre were surely hurt less by their parents than were Doughboy and many other children; that their anger was no doubt honored by those parents helped them plan to leave the ghetto. Not vengeful, Ricky is his mother's favored child, a handsome and successful athlete, popular with his peers, a contented mate and father. It appears that his mother also favored his father over Doughboy's father, vengeance toward whom she takes out on Doughboy.

The redemptive message in Ricky's character is that people not victimized by those immediately around them need not capitulate to temptations to avenge; they are not even drawn to them. Ricky's friend Tre is the transitional case. Tempted to join the action but not really needing to, Tre recedes from the abyss; he frees himself from loyalty to revenge and thus saves his life.

Vengeance occurs when apology, forgiveness, and restitution are forsworn or thought to be impossible. My fantasy of annihilating my antagonist followed not the insult but rejection of my proposal to talk about it. The rage in revenge reveals failure to connect in other ways with the objects of one's wrath.

Hurting another is a way of turning a passive experience into an active one. It is a primitive attempt to gain control over pain. Much human hurt is caused by perverting the Golden Rule into: Do unto others what has been done unto you. Anna Freud calls this "identification with the aggressor."

In the humiliation in military training, the trainee is made to feel hurt, angry, and afraid. It is actually the trainer who is the enemy, but a complex of clever strategies moves the trainee's rage onto a substitute, usually women, who are mocked in chants when trainees are all male, and the vague, shadowy "enemy."

Ghettos and military units, like most such groups, hold seeds of their own liberation. Affection for peers, delight in adventure, pleasure in joining something beyond the self can flow into mutuality as easily as into adversarialism. The point is not to sacrifice feelings of camaraderie and accomplishment but to find more constructive ways to enjoy them than avenging a slight or satisfying the complex needs and longings of forces that for whatever reasons promote displacing attention from individual and collective hurts onto scapegoat pseudo-enemies.

EIGHT

୧᠊ᢏᢏᢏ

Rituals of Undermining

That which is hateful to you, do not do to your
neighbor. That's the whole Torah. The rest is
commentary. Go study.
            —Rabbi Hillel, *The Talmud*

If you do not care for each other, who will care
for you?
                        —Buddha

Rituals of undermining are without number. Although I limit myself in
this discussion to *insulting, abusing, and hurting,* a full treatment would
include sarcasm and ridicule, humiliation, and all other forms of belittling.

Insulting

From the prosaic (nerd, jerk) to the vulgar (motherfucker, bitch), the
insult carries a striking emotional charge. Its object is accused of lacking adequate checks over sexual or violent impulses ("Can't you control yourself?"
"What are you, some kind of rapist?"), or of enacting inclinations that many
people are reluctant to fancy in art, let alone their own imaginations (murder,
perverse sex), or of not having the inhibitions of a satisfactory superego
("He's a moral cretin," "She eats her young"), or of failing to meet the challenges of ordinary life demands ("You're a congenital loser," "Everything you
touch turns to dirt").

The most intense insults pass beyond simple abuse; they caricature the
object by reducing it to one unflattering dimension. Not, "What you did is stupid," but rather, "You are stupid." Not, "What you did makes me angry," but,
"You are a destructive person." By generalizing a response to an act (verbal
or otherwise) into a characterization of the actor, the entire person is made

into an inferior and an adversary. The humane alternative is to replace typifying the whole person by a response to specific behavior. This kind of de-demonizing and de-dehumanizing is one of the genuine mutuality buddings of our era.

Commendable as this development is, people careful enough to make such efforts among family and friends often revert to conventional insulting of another political party, religious persuasion, social class, or nation. This is not to suggest hypocrisy. It is, rather, to suggest that the ambivalence anyone feels toward differences needs to be recognized. Once fully apparent, the options for what to do about it increase. For example, upper-middle-class people scornful of lower-middle- and working-class lives might reflect on their own struggles to consolidate entry into one class by exaggerated separation from another, or their efforts to justify privilege and not feel compassion for those of less privilege. Disparagement of upper-middle-class life by people of other classes could mark frustration with blocked mobility and fear of changes in familiar life ways.

Fascination with "lower classes" accompanies conflict about class itself. If working-class clothing is now all but universal in the upper-middle and upper classes for casual wear (tee shirts, leather, blue chambray and denim, work boots and cowboy boots), is this not in emulation of the body confidence of less well-off people who until recently were the principal wearers of such clothing? Does not the massive turn to gyms, renamed athletic clubs, health resorts, and spas among the privileged, reveal for men a yearning for the body competence and rugged look long associated with blue-collar workers and athletes? and for women, cultural pressure to look like models and movie stars and, increasingly, like athletes?

People in higher classes mocking and emulating people from working and lower-middle-classes suggests not confusion or duplicity but ambivalence, and it is mirrored in the other direction. The counterculture introduced long hair and earrings for men and short hair and tattoos for women. It was upper-middle-class men and women, mostly high school and college students in the beginning, who delighted in the new body freedoms. They were vilified for this by working-class and lower-middle-class agemates. After some years, the hair and adornment styles of the counterculture caught on there too, suggesting that what had been derided as pretentiousness and arrogance was covertly envied. Whether the epithet is "Joe Sixpack" or "faggot," insulters broadcast their fascination with what they mock.

Philip Slater observes that sensory experience tends to dim with upward class mobility: colors are muted, sounds are softened, emotions are more controlled.[1] He implies that upward mobility includes greater control over others' lives as well as overcontrol of one's own, and an attempt to put down one's origins that in confusion and ambivalence may still be felt attractive.

Secret desires are common to everyone: for example, struggles with impulse control. Imagining inventive sexual acts and forbidden partners is probably common to members of both genders. Contempt for antisocial fantasies and behavior is a way of distancing oneself from unacknowledged desires to do the same thing. Hence collective fascination with crimes and sexual "deviance."

Consider a game played by some African Americans (oftener men than women): "doing the dozens." A male insults another's mother or sister. The second's reply, insulting the mother or sister of the first, is more offensive. The first tries to top that. And so on. The game is a way for men to disparage women and thus either avoid physical expressions of their own anger toward each other or evade feelings of affection and closeness that are felt to be taboo to express. They also, by attribution to the other, sidestep their own negative feelings about their mothers and sisters and by extension, women in general.

The sexual insult reveals profound involvement in what Freud calls erotogenic zones of the body. Exceptionally emphatic insults in U.S. culture refer to mouths, anuses, and genitals. Intensity of feeling, repressed memory, and body desires are detached from the speaker's consciousness and attributed to another. The very reading, let alone hearing or speaking, of such words commonly evokes very strong emotions.

To the adversary then is attributed *absorptions denied in the self*. Humor can serve the same purpose. The other is mocked for a misunderstanding, foolishness, or slip of the tongue that might just as well have happened to oneself and probably has.

Insults, curses, and humor are rituals in group adversary relations as well as individual ones. Alleged laziness of Blacks, immorality of Jews, inadequacies of women, sex obsessions of homosexuals—all represent fears of those qualities in the insulter. In insulting, the self strives to cope, however sadly and unjustly, with its less agreeable and often seemingly scandalous parts. It does this by employing the technique of "splitting," of separating off one part of the self from another and denying contact and integration between them.

Frightening

Hurting others is a common adversary ritual. Slaves, prisoners, children, and women commonly learn to fear their dominators and follow their orders rather than submit to pain, even though compliance does not always prevent punishment.

Fear is the negative of trust. To mistrust means to anticipate harm. Like children who try to cope with fears by pretending to be monsters, those who induce fear do so from denial of their own fears. In *First Blood*, Sheriff Teasle tries to make Rambo fear him by threatening punishment. Rambo's breaking point is a moment reminding him of capture and pain in Vietnam. He responds by giving Teasle reason to fear him. In *The Godfather*, the Mafia makes sure that everyone fears everyone; afraid even of himself, master fear-inducer Michael Corleone becomes his own ultimate victim.

The Boyz N the Hood who kill Ricky are unnamed. They represent the pathos of brutal ghetto realities and also the unnamed parts of men who, by ignoring their true inner lives, act out inner confusions through violence toward other men and toward women. All of these men could act compassionately, but they are estranged from that part of themselves; they are socialized to lie to themselves about themselves.

Social structure parcels out parts of the self to different individuals and entire groups. It is in this respect that "all the world is a stage." As in many families, Ricky and Doughboy's mother assigns each son different parts of who she is. Doughboy's capricious, self-defeating actions are not simply self-willed; they are implicitly encouraged by his mother who thus avoids facing those issues in herself. She fulfills her strengths in doting on her other son. Like *Rambo* and *Godfather*, *Boyz* dwells on fathers and sons. The male (as usual in U.S. films, females are background) who will escape the stultifying life of the ghetto is the only one raised by his father. It is never explained why Tre could not continue to live with his mother. We know only that he was a discipline problem in school, and we are led to believe that only fathers can handle such matters.

A child begins life with a self that can be loving and lovable. Those forces grow when nurtured in patient encouragement, sensitive touching, and loving help from caring others. When needed responses are not forthcoming, the child learns to doubt its viability. Ridiculing, disparaging, and ignoring are some ways a child's confidence is violated. (They are also routine adversary rituals in military training.) Once in place, such patterns cement the child's fear of being undermined.

Not being responded to, as if one did not fully exist, is, like negative response, experienced as punishment. This violation of self-esteem, like others, leads naturally to feelings of rejection and then to rage. Rage is not only a sign of hurt and frustration, it frightens its bearers to the extent they do not know where it and the fantasies it generates might lead. To imagine annihilating an offending other can be as terrifyingly real as imagined punishment from others for expressing rage.

Abusing

Thanks to the women's movement, spouse and child abuse became a major public issue in the 1980s and 1990s. It was underlined dramatically in the U.S. obsession in 1994 with the O. J. Simpson case. As a society, we seem to be moving, however hesitantly, toward discouraging the infliction of pain by people in close relationships.[2] Abusing extends of course beyond the household, in rituals like rape, street attacks, and police brutality.

Even though psychological abuse is at least as painful and devastating as the physical form, the former is not yet taken so seriously in our society as the latter. In both forms, the other is dehumanized. Rituals for this include words of humiliation like those in sarcasm and deprecating humor, which help instill self-doubt, shame, and guilt and undermine efforts and achievements.

Psychological abuse is the opposite of "mirroring," that process by which good parents reflect back to their child its strivings for recognition of its goodness and its feelings, and also recognition of the limits it needs to have affirmed. This is an essential part of parenting and is crucial in relationships that encourage good feelings and growth.

Just as family physical violations until recently (and not yet universally) were considered private matters, so is the continuing attitude toward psychological abuse. It is beginning to be addressed in the United States in the form of workplace and campus attention to verbal as well as physical harm.

In general, all abuse is abuse of the spirit, but one can be abused spiritually in a more technical sense. Spiritual leaders, however well-meaning, can hurt followers, by disempowering by threats of eternal damnation and by forbidding criticisms of religious dogma and prescriptions. It is understandable that people who were themselves abused spiritually would, like victims of physical and psychological abuse, find it "natural" and necessary to do the same to others; they might have no experience or concept of any other way of encouraging "civilized" behavior. Like physical and psychological abuse, spiritual abuse tends to deprive victims of confidence in powers of observation, critical analysis, action, and self-esteem.

There is a fourth form of abuse: intellectual. It is the use of ideas to maintain power over other people. Promoting inaccuracies—lies—infuses appeals in activities such as campaigning, advertising, and nationalism, all of which promulgate distorted versions of others' realities in order to firm up loyalty to idea, candidate, leader, product, or state.

Presidential campaigns commonly offer intellectual abuse in the form of lies about economic prospects if one or another tax plan or deficit reduction plan is enacted or is not, lies about international dangers, lies about the heroism of party allies, and lies about opponents. Perhaps in reaction to understanding that one is being thus abused by candidates, about a majority of U.S. voters decline to participate in presidential elections.

Students risk learning enough to want to change something. A classic way to forestall that is to break the connection between learning and action. The political system promotes clichés that encourage passivity: "You can't fight City Hall," "The system is too big and complex to change," "It doesn't matter who is in power; they are all corrupt." Classrooms employ other rituals with similar consequences: memorizing and repeating, grading (a major form of intimidation and control), ridicule by teacher and by other students, the bizarre insistence that action lies outside the scope of education. Intellectual abuse includes advertising that mocks understanding of products and their limits, the unscrupulous use of symbols, and such classic devices of intellectual confusion as scapegoating and distraction through entertainment.

Unnerving

Whereas in mutuality, one supports others' strengths and helps them cope with weaknesses and uncertainties, in unnerving, one does the opposite. The unnerver finds points of vulnerability and exploits them, reducing the other to an obsessively doubting, frightened, pathetic lump.

Part of the fascination of the film *The Silence of the Lambs*[3] is the mastery by Hannibal Lecter (Anthony Hopkins) of the adversary ritual of unnerving. The role is archetypal. Lecter carries adversary behavior to a point rarely seen in film or life. It appears that nearly everyone is his enemy, and he overcomes them, when possible, by verbal or physical assault, murder, and ingestion.[4] Whether Lecter is expressing himself in a particularly hideous macho aggressive way, revealing unusually deep sadism, or combining rage and affection as a child might at its mother's breast, his cannibalism is the striking extreme point of the adversary attitude he embodies in his unique way.

In a maximum security prison for several murders, Lecter is a psychiatrist with an exceptional talent for locating raw nerves and exploiting them. Sophisticated, charming, and highly intelligent, he cannot relate in ordinary ways, even in ordinary seductive ways. Bound to an apparatus that allows him only to speak, Lecter meets the mother of a woman kidnapped but likely not yet murdered. Lecter is to be moved to more comfortable quarters in exchange for helping the FBI locate Buffalo Bill, a serial killer who is making a garment of his female victims' skins. Instead of soberly bargaining for advantage by cooperating, Lecter asks the mother how she nursed her daughter and how she might feel in her body seeing her daughter on a mortician's slab. The mother is shocked and disgusted. Rather than deal with the woman civilly for his own purposes, Lecter undoes her through unnerving, thus demonstrating according to some criterion dear to him, his superiority over her. It can be deduced that his killings are done in the unnerving mode, his victims reduced to quivering jelly before he destroys them.

Unnerving is not limited to cannibals, psychopathic or otherwise. Boxers, swimmers, and track stars try to unnerve their opponents. Politicians try to unnerve rivals by accusations and scandals. Courtroom lawyers unnerve witnesses and defendants in cross-examination. Some men and women unnerve each other in intimacy power plays, and parents often unnerve children to control them. The rebellious child also may employ unnerving to disturb parents and separate from them.

Vulnerability is also a central point of contact in mutuality. A friend respects and acknowledges the other's sensitivities and relates them to her own. Lecter does the opposite. But he does more than simply unnerve his victims. He kills and eats them. It is as if he wanted the other to be part of him all along. Or as if he was trying to contact the vulnerable parts of himself by physically incorporating their analogs in others.

Adversaries may mean something far more complex than zero-sum encounter. To bother to oppose another is to admit to serious relationship. Lecter fixates on the earliest way an infant relates to a mother, by taking her into its mouth. It is one thing to nurse, another to eat a victim. In both cases, that which one does not want to go away is ingested. Cannibalism is a very peculiar and literal way of relating to that which one admires or fears, or more fundamentally still, that which one feels to be a part of oneself but elusive. Because the cannibal warrior wants to be as powerful as he sees his victim to be, even as he violates his victim through murder he also honors him by idealizing and eating him. Strengths he seems unable to embrace and enjoy in himself are projected onto another and vicariously appropriated. If that applies to strength not fully mastered in oneself, it can apply equally to weakness.

By killing the Jew, the Nazi attempted to kill real parts of himself that were not permitted in what it meant to be a Nazi. This principle applies to all forms of domination, including that of people of color, women, and homosexuals. In killing the Jew, the Nazi created the ghastly bond of killer and killed wherein the Nazi implicitly acknowledged his similarity to his victim.

The Schwarzenegger, Stallone, and van Damme film figures of cyborgs, soldiers, and brutes all give vent to desires to be hard, strong, cruel. Such quasi-barbarians share with Nazis and the physically unremarkable Lecter, denial of their own vulnerability. Brawn and swagger conceal confusion so powerful as to be felt as overwhelming. These tendencies may be, among other things, ways of denying inner weaknesses, longings, and hurts.

Lambs explains why Claryce Starling (Jody Foster), an agent-in-training whose task it is to enlist Lecter's aid in finding Buffalo Bill, becomes a federal agent: her law enforcement father was killed in the line of duty. Lecter, by contrast, is presented as unmotivated. If Starling has a life story and real human characteristics (a starling is a fragile creature of the air), Lecter caricatures his profession in his secrecy about his own story. We learn nothing of his fears, confusions, hurts, nothing of parents, childhood, traumas.

Unable to face and come to terms with his life, Lecter employs three strategies in the terrible effort to destroy others:

1. He turns his own doubts and fears into fearlessness and aggression; this is "reaction formation," the twisting of feelings into their opposites and acting as if one is feeling only those opposites. The more troubling, confusing, frightening parts of the self are thus massively denied.
2. He "identifies with the aggressor," taking on the other's characteristics that have so troubled him in a desperate attempt to master them. Lecter must have been scared of someone in his life, most likely one or both parents. He apes and exaggerates parental power in a way that hints of tragic misconceptions of it.
3. He "turns passive into active." Abused children often later abuse partners and children. They attempt to master the humiliation and pain of victimization by taking the active role in the encounter as they experienced it, rather than continuing the passive one. Following what must have been his own experience early in life, Lecter humiliates, terrifies, unnerves, and then—the last step foregone by whoever traumatized him—kills.

Lecter, prime abuser, listens and talks. But he does not talk about himself (a "lector" reads scripture in church; he lectures). Instead, he uses words to bring the other under his control. In an especially hideous way, Lecter comes to terms with Fornari's "terrifier" by *becoming* it. Thus do those who kill in the name of freedom often become what they intended to destroy. Thus do people who undermine others perpetuate what must have hurt them so much they could never face and come to terms with it.

NINE

Rituals of
Supposed Superiority

Hierarchy is a form of adversarialism in which someone or some group claims to be superior to someone or a group of others. Among the rituals by which hierarchy is maintained are *comparing*—claiming privilege over another; *contradicting* the claims, reality, and observations of the other; and, more subtly, gaining advantage through physical force at the cost of *constricting feelings*.

The Ritual of Comparing

One way adversarialism proceeds is by comparing measurable outcomes. More esteem is granted to people who have more of something conventionally valued—like property, power, status, or honor. Although human encounters can also permit support and love, in many contexts these experiences are secondary to the comparison ritual. Supportive outcomes may even be suspect or forbidden.

In comparing, victors are judged superior in either (1) an achievement, as in athletics, business, or war, or (2) an inborn trait, like gender, race, or build. Comparing makes it *essential* to strive to outrank the other. *Ranking itself* is the issue. Thus, whatever the intrinsic value of material and social rewards, they also indicate adversarial victory or defeat.

The phenomenon of comparing appears in the controversy in the United

States in the 1990s over multiculturalism. Opponents argue for the superiority of Western history, texts, values, and culture. Advocates support pluralism, diverse traditions celebrated without ranking in terms of worth.

Those opposing multiculturalism fear that if what is Western is not superior, it is inferior. That the strengths and weaknesses of cultures might be appreciated without invidious contrasts is outside the boundaries of the adversary paradigm, which is assumed.

When Black Power asserted itself in the 1960s and 1970s, there was a variant that saw it as superiority (Malcolm X in his middle period, the Nation of Islam more generally) and that continues today in the rhetoric of Louis Farrakhan and Leonard Jeffries. But the later Malcolm X, Martin Luther King Jr., Maya Angelou, bell hooks, Thurgood Marshall, Jesse Jackson, and other African American spokespeople have seen the issue of human rights and pluralism not as zero-sum but in terms of universal respect and rights.

The slogan "Black is beautiful" exemplifies the pluralist approach. It implies turning around the contempt in the eye of the white beholder of Blacks and of the Black self-maligner as well. The motto is not "Black is better," which would assert Black pride in adversary terms, it is "Black is beautiful," suggesting the recognition that accompanies mutuality. "Black is beautiful" opens the way for white, yellow, brown, and red to be beautiful too.

Rejecting mutuality is not simply a way of looking at the world, or a value held with conviction. It is much deeper; it is anchored in fear. In this respect, right and left are not far from each other. The right wants to overcome the left, and does so through violence or visions of superiority or ruthless economic and military competition. Left adversaries lean toward liberation fantasies that include victories over right and center; for many on the left, universalism, generosity, and love are to *overcome* parochialism, tribalism, and hate. Few leftists or rightists imagine social change created together by people from varied political backgrounds who learn a new form of politics—creating structures and processes that work in everyone's behalf—rather than reaffirming old goals of "right" triumphing over "wrong."[1]

Univalent thinking is shared by right and left more than either side would care to admit. There is little notion on either side of facing ambivalence or of coming to mutuality with the "other." Thus, both pro-choice people and pro-life people assume the adversary must be defeated in court or on the streets or in legislatures. Each side compares itself with the other, which it finds morally inferior. Each stance is a point in a two-point space, and like opposing magnets, it can only repel the other.

Genuine conversation and openness to change are ordinarily forbidden by the imperatives of the adversary paradigm. Whether the issue is foreign policy, marijuana, or nuclear power, one side will be for certain measures and the other side against. Beneath and often interlocking with objective differences is the adversary compulsion: *the need to oppose for the sake of opposing.*

Comparison can be along any lines whatsoever: Which gender's body parts are better? Which musical form is best? Who are the greatest athletes? The size of anything—car, house, audience, penis, breasts, hard disc, grade point average, foundation grant, bank balance, GNP—is taken up with enthusiasm by the comparer as if it mattered very much and as if that were not a way to avoid more pressing issues of greater significance to all concerned.

Differences in skin color and physiognomy are objectively trivial, yet often become bases for adversary comparison. Although I tread here on very sensitive ground, I want to raise the question of how it is that certain features are considered more attractive than others. I struggle with this. A product of my culture, I find some faces and shapes (as well as landscapes, buildings, and paintings) more "beautiful" than others. Can we demarcate the differences between aesthetic response and insidious evaluation?

As aesthetics is one of many bases of interclass hostility and feelings of superiority by educated "higher" classes, what is to be made of it? First, why evaluate others' taste? I wore a light blue suit with what I consider a spectacular necktie that perfectly matched a new striped shirt of several colors, to a summer wedding where nearly all the other men wore tuxedos or dark suits and white shirts. I pay almost no attention to fashion and sometimes don't know if what I am wearing is appropriate till I get where I am going. Before attending the wedding, it could have occurred to me to ask what I should wear, but it did not. At this social event, where most men were suburban lawyers, doctors, and businesspeople, all of them more prosperous than I and accustomed to a social life and subculture foreign to me, I found an alien aesthetic. It struck me as drab, uniform, boring. I imagine some people found the way I was dressed to be gaudy, tasteless, gauche. Still, even as I try to see what people wear as an expression of their social context and commitments, it is difficult for me not to evaluate those differences, and herein lies a paradox with which I must contend, or I negate my entire argument. For what lifestyle details are to me, with whatever inner struggle, race is to another. Granted the consequences of one form of judgment are vastly different from those of the other, we all do tend to construct hierarchies of worth. What makes jade plants preferable to poinsettias, orchids superior to daisies? Or vice versa?

Processes of judgment and scorn work in two directions. Wealthier people do not want to be thought vulgar by imbibing cheap wines or domestic beers. Working-class people do not want to be considered haughty by drinking expensive wines or imported beers. One group may have more power than the other, but the processes of distancing and judging are similar in both. If the imbalance has a sting, it lies in comparisons that mock and patronize.

Colleges and universities, facing a shrinking applicant pool in the 1980s and 1990s, have become increasingly aggressive in "marketing" themselves.

The better known ones strive for high rankings in such apparently influential guides as the *U.S. News and World Report* annual listing, "America's Best Colleges." To be ranked favorably, a school must score high on "objective" criteria—reputation, selectivity, faculty salaries, financial resources, student satisfaction. Not only are such data reported by the institutions themselves and hence not necessarily accurate, the very indicators of worth are stacked toward the usual "winners" like Harvard, which obviously do well on those terms.[2] What an education actually means or does for a given student cannot be quantified and compared. Yet colleges and universities are driven, in a society with a free market ideology, to be as competitive as fast-food chains and athletic shoe companies.

Overtly, competition reaches its peak in U.S. society in spectator sport. Why is so much invested in athletic contests where success is more ephemeral than in any other setting? Sport is one of the primary training grounds for adversarialism. Indeed, General and President Eisenhower suggested that "the true mission of American sport is to prepare young people for war."[3]

For participants and audiences alike, success in sport is the triumph of skilled over less competent players; it is also a metaphor for the attempted triumph of competent parts of the self over less competent parts. We prize competence, and sport is a repeated demand that we display it. Some days athletes win, some days they lose. The ritual enactment of success-failure and all it stands for goes on through the entire season, day after day, year after year, life after life. Contenders' worst fears of failure alternate with fulfillment of yearnings for success. And thus with vicarious involvement of onlookers as well; the audience enjoys the ritual thrills of confrontation, victory, and defeat. In athletic leagues, teams can take on dramatic roles, like that of perennial stars (Chicago Bulls in basketball as of this writing) or perennial losers (staying with Chicago for the example, the Cubs of baseball).

In boxing, adversary rituals of hate (insulting, swaggering, glaring) help motivate good performance. In his clever posturing, Mohammad Ali was brilliant at burlesquing enemyness. His famous line (from his trainer Bundini) "Float like a butterfly, sting like a bee" is a description of good fighting and poetic self-promotion at the same time. Ali's knack was in presenting adversary and audience with essence of contrived conflict, a significant part of what sport is about. Because real opposition can be experienced by most people as too hot to handle, athletes and audiences welcome escape into stylized, pleasure-giving metaphors.

Creating and maintaining enemy relations in sport reaches its most blatant, caricatured form in professional wrestling. In this contest, highly skilled athletes mimic confrontation, attack, and malice in the ring and in intermission rituals in which they loudly, pseudo-viciously badmouth each other. Some people appear to believe that wrestling is serious and real. This self-deception is not far-fetched; it is like blindness to the game aspect of politicians vilifying each other. There, too, attack often has little meaning beyond the battle itself. The point in politics is oftenest to win. As in wrestling, the contest is in the drama of adversarialism, not in actual performance. The public is not naive about this. A letter-writer to a newspaper observes, "The object, in Washington, is not to improve America. The object is just to win the game. Republicans just want to beat the Democrats, and the Democrats just want to beat the Republicans."[4]

By reducing competition to its barest form, opposition and hatred, and by doing it tongue-in-cheek, "wrestlers" enable their audience to enjoy the entire drama without concerning itself with integrity, pain, or real earnestness of combat. Well-disciplined bodies give and take "punishment" that they are trained to sustain. Distinct from most other forms of opposition, sport engages the bodies of observers as well as participants. Physical skills, as well as clashes between opponents, excite the audience: grace, strength, coordination, expertise in intricate moves. Viewers are encouraged to project their own unfulfilled body aspirations onto players. Desires for the pure joy of lithe body motion, erotic pleasure in movement, and contact with other bodies are present for both player and audience in the ritual of sport.

This is not to suggest that confrontation is all there is to athletic contest. Given that they are frequently poorer members of minority groups, many athletes become socially mobile through sport; the opponent merges with all the obstacles that social class and racism set before each person. Without feelings of contempt, superiority, and determination to overcome, there is no battle and hence no chance to advance in conventional adversary ways.

Sport is an economic issue for owners as well as players. Marx predicted that everything in capitalist society would become a commodity. Sport brings handsome incomes to athletes because it is very big business for team owners, media broadcasters, and companies whose products are endorsed by athletes.

The Ritual of Contradicting

One person says "You're looking great"; the other replies "I look terrible." The initial comment is an offer to connect, to affirm the other's dignity and worth. It can be accepted by a simple "Thank you." If this sounds Ann Landers-ish or Miss Manners-ish, that is because such columnists often steer readers away from adversary behavior and toward mutuality.

By its nature, mutuality is not so dramatic or troublesome as adversarialism. It is, rather, graceful, polite, responsive. Mutuality invites completion of a loop. An invitation to relate is tendered; one accepts as if catching a ball tossed in a friendly, hopeful manner, with good feeling lofted back to the sender. The contradictor rejects the simple advance, distancing the hopeful one who wants to touch. The ball is thrown instead at the head of the inviter, or simply thrown away. "You're looking great" does not mean, "Do you think you look great?," which is the unasked question the second person answered. The original comment is simply a request to share in gladness about the pleasure the first person feels in the presence of the second.

When the person to whom a compliment is extended feels unwilling or unable to join the complimenter, it is as if to say:

> I reject your advance. It is more important to me to control you by negating the feeling of your choice which you present to me and instead forcing another feeling, of my choice, on you. It may be that I do not feel worthy of your compliments and take refuge in deprecating myself. Even though the feeling I return to you is less pleasant than the one you bring, this is another way I control the situation. Otherwise I would be yielding control to you, and I cannot bear that. To me, control is every-thing. Either you dominate me by my submitting to your invitation to share the good feeling you are having, or I dominate you by forcing a feeling on you. I see no alternative to adversary relations, and I am determined to win them.[5]

Thus a piece of the adversary compulsion. The principle of contradicting means changing the question or comment offered by the other, negating it as well as the feeling and intention behind it. In pushing the other away, the negator appears to preserve some fragile autonomy, a tenuous individualism. The commonly experienced fear of engulfment, fear that accepting the initiative of the other is somehow to become controlled by the other, thus dictates the terms of relationship.

The principle of contradicting, easily identified in one-on-one conversations, expands to institutions. At its best, politics is a system of allocating power and resources justly. Like religion, politics articulates ideals of mutuality; inauguration addresses and Independence Day speeches celebrate ideals of mutuality and universal fulfillment.

Even if postelection and post–July 4th reality is otherwise, intentions of the rhetoricians are usually honest and real. But politics as we have known it, from routine elections to war, *is* adversarialism. The format in election campaigns is heavily based on the adversary ritual of contradicting; indeed, campaigns are often little more than adversary entertainment. The content of nearly any issue is less important than the style (sarcasm, ridicule, innuendo, character assassination) with which the candidate responds to any position taken by the opponent.

Although campaigns offer means for aspirants to persuade voters of their good intentions and their worthiness for office, they also permit them to lie, raise money from people to whose adversary agendas they are then obligated, malign opponents, make promises they do not intend to keep, and in general seduce, cajole, and scare voters as best they can. This proceeds in part by contradicting whatever the other candidate says and stands for.

Journalists rush to determine who "won" a debate on stylistic points, not on policy recommendations or understanding or compassion. Polls usually ask which candidate one favors, not which policy one prefers and why, or even reasons for supporting one candidate over another.

Voters not too put off by all this to decline to vote, participate in elections emotionally as well as "objectively." Candidates are discussed, even unto details of their private lives, and are voted for or against sometimes on the basis of issues, sometimes on party loyalty, sometimes on promises, sometimes on what appears to be glamour or decency.

Politicians dance the adversary whirl because electoral victory is an end apart from actual or expected performance in office. Professional consultants coach candidates in forcefulness and feigned sincerity, remodel their "images," market-test substance and approaches, and divert voters' attention to melodramatic and trivial issues. If "all is fair in love and war" (an aphorism curiously joining mutuality and adversarialism in their extremes), conquering the other candidate, not offering real options and change to the voter, is the nub of elections as process. Just as the consumer relates more to the promise of a product than to the product itself, so it is the candidate's emotions and image that are meant to move the voter more than the performance that follows.[6]

Candidates' rivalries continue after the election in barely disguised form as politicians protect their self-esteem while attacking that of others. Elected representatives, for example, are charged with malfeasance. Party colleagues of the accused stand by them, mock the charges, and cast aspersions on those who bring them. The most wondrous accusation, usually uttered in tones of disbelieving scorn, is "That's just political," as if the essence of politics were somehow something other than politics.

This claim is not only self-serving; it implicitly recognizes that destroyed or defamed careers are one of the costs of the adversary system and that compassion and justice are undermined by it. Because of the unrecognized compulsive nature of the adversary encounter between public and accused, those bothered by the destructive nature of the system reveal exasperation rather than glimpsing other ways of organizing public business. Such critics' commitment to the system, even as they defame it, is too deep to recognize and overcome; they remain loyal to the compulsion itself.

The deepest level of adversarialism in politics is not politicians against each other; it is all of them *against the public*. The public wants various issues addressed, as do business interests. As the business agenda often runs counter to public desires, politicians join their sponsors—"special interests" in the most powerful sense—in working against the majority.

The adversary principle in politics means that public needs for adversary dramas are met while needs for safety, due process, free expression, and community services are shortchanged. And the public does need adversary dramas, which is probably why even in cynical detachment it is ordinarily willing to put up with the travesties that electoral politics so commonly present.

The limits of adversarialism in politics reached a most appalling moment when military planners in the 1970s and 1980s sought levels of "acceptable" human loss in nuclear showdown. Herman Kahn asserted that twenty million U.S. lives lost would be acceptable;[7] others suggested that if two Americans survived a nuclear holocaust and only one Soviet citizen did, the U.S. would have won. The terrifying doctrine of "massive retaliation," to discourage nuclear initiatives from the other side, was appropriately known as MAD (Mutually Assured Destruction).

It is a truism that the U.S.-Soviet antagonism was a stabilizing force in the world for several decades. The shared policy of nuclear "deterrence" was its fulcrum of organization. If the USSR supported the struggles of Nicaraguans, Chinese, Cubans, and others for self-determination, the United States opposed it. If the United States complained about human rights abuses in such societies, the Soviet Union opposed that. Whatever their strains, though, except for the Cuban missile crisis, neither side would protect its clients or oppose those of the other to the point of risking nuclear confrontation.

The two superpowers proceeded, now hobbling, now marching. Neither risked the final fire, but until Gorbachev, neither moved very far toward overcoming what was clearly an enervating, resource-draining arms race and political stalemate. A prime reason both could not accept the reasonableness of the other is that *the adversary relationship itself was far more fundamental and powerful in the world system as the two superpowers organized it, than the justice, accuracy, or human worth of any of their claims.*

In his remarkable move, Gorbachev withdrew the Soviet Union from the adversary encounter,[8] unilaterally renouncing the contradiction rituals that had been normative since the end of World War II. He wrote of the relation between survival and allocation of resources:

> The necessity of effective, fair, international procedures and mechanisms which would ensure rational utilization of our planet's resources as the property of all mankind becomes ever more pressing.

And here we see our interdependence, the integrity of the world, the imperative need for pooling the efforts of humanity for the sake of its self-preservation, for its benefit today, tomorrow and for all time.[9]

The objective realities of economic drain and nuclear terror, together with his universalistic views and values, seem to have convinced Gorbachev to take the daring step in world politics of renouncing the adversary "game" itself. The nuclear arms race helped force the issue; Gorbachev emerged as a superpower leader with the courage and imagination to open up the adversary frame and move beyond it.

> The new political outlook calls for the recognition of one more simple axiom. . . . The only solid foundation for security is the recognition of the interests of all peoples and countries and of their equality in international affairs.[10]

The United States, its economy and infrastructure deteriorating, its population beset with troublesome malaise, its public scorning homelessness and feeling helpless before problems like joblessness and white collar crime, nonetheless claims to have "won" some sort of contest with the Soviet Union. By summer 1990, U.S. citizens apparently were not fully convinced of this "truth," though, and the White House found a way to have a war whose outcome would be so clearly a "victory" that doubts about what had been won in the Cold War could be subordinated to conventional notions of war "success." The Gulf War shored up a weakening adversary paradigm. One reason the war "worked" to the extent it did was each leader's compulsive commitment to the adversary paradigm and to contradicting in particular. The Iraqi president's attachment to adversarialism seemed so firm and foolish that he apparently deluded himself into thinking he could by force of will alone defeat his formidable antagonist. Bush's faithfulness to the paradigm and the contradiction ritual was strong enough that he evidently preferred war to more inventive, daring diplomatic and economic alternatives that, had they been pursued and effective, would have been of great historic significance.

A current example of contradicting is the abortion issue, where each side contradicts the other side's claims. If war is a collective decision by elites of when life for many people will end, the reproductive rights issue presents the inverse concern. "Pro-life" people present their case as a concern with when life begins, while "pro-choice" people focus on the mother's autonomy and on quality of life for would-be mother and would-be child.

All this takes place as it becomes increasingly unclear medically when life *ends* and when and how the decision can be made, and by whom, about when to terminate it.[11] If at the margins, it has become unclear when life stops and when it starts, it is also increasingly difficult theologically, morally, and sociologically to define the relationship between father and fetus, mother and fetus, and mother and father during the time when the mother is bearing a fetus, and, if the biological parents do not keep the child, to define their relationship to adoptive parents and the child's relationship to both sets. If there is a hired surrogate mother, problems are compounded still further.

It is unclear what is violence and what is not in the "war" over reproductive rights. From the side of the "pro-life" people, abortion is violence as is demonstrating in its favor. From the "pro-choice" point of view, "pro-lifers" are violent in harassing women seeking abortions and the people who support their decision, murdering doctors who perform abortions, attacking property, and implicitly advocating return to self-induced and back-alley abortions which cause unnecessary deaths. "Pro-choicers" see coerced childbearing as violating women's rights and conducive to violence against unwanted children and the potential antisocial violence of people who have been neither desired nor loved.

The abortion issue contrasts the rights of the mother and the rights of the fetus. Each side claims its concern as the true or more humane one and insists that the other side is wrong. Each accuses the other of obduracy, callousness, and disregard for life.

A second comparable issue is drugs. Except among the wealthy, drug use sometimes means theft. Violence among dealers, struggle between the drug business and the federal government, and tensions between the United States and countries of drug origin are among the conflicts that may be replacing war on the grand scale.

If conflict supports dominant elites, it is in their interests to sustain it. This is, in part, why media present conflict powerfully and pay little attention to efforts to alleviate it. It also is why commitments to end drug use ring hollow. Drugs distract users from problems that propel them into drug dependency in the first place. Such problems run from the fear of being defined as a loser without a job or housing or dignity and self-respect, to the fears of "successful" people who suffer from spiritual and psychological emptiness and confusion.

Boredom, fashion (including what it means to some people to be sophisticated or "cool"), and healthy experimentation are sufficient to explain recreational drug use. But the compulsive use of drugs suggests despondency without them. To transform feelings chemically is to give up on living real feelings in real contexts in a satisfactory way. It suggests that work, relationships, and citizenship are so meaningless that only the drug-crutch can make life bearable. It indicates helplessness with respect to the outcomes in one's life and to possibilities for change. Official drug policy ignores motives for drug use and focuses entirely on behavior. It is a simple-

[handwritten marginalia:] changing the law not the people or their motives   this is why laws against drugs fail so miserably   Must take away the motivations for drug use, which would require inventiveness

minded approach to compulsive behavior to command people to stop it or to punish them for it. Imagine advising Lady Macbeth to "just say no" to her ambition or her hand-washing.

It may be that people attack drug behavior rather than seek underlying motives because they intuitively grasp that whatever the individual pathology, the compulsive drug user is a social critic as well as a breaker of laws. It is the implicit criticism more than the drug behavior itself that "must" be stopped by the law enforcer and moralist. As the critique obviously holds as long as the conditions objected to obtain, there is no logical end to drug use or its persecution except fundamental social change.

The "war" on drugs is a clever if absurd replacement for what is conventionally meant by war. It provides enemies (drug pushers and users for one side, federal agents and moralists for the other), ideologies ("clean" living vs. individual "freedom"), and self-righteousness for everyone. Intelligence services, informers, guns, raids, courts, prisons, and rhetoric itself suggest war in a way the "War on Poverty" never did. The war includes fighting within one side over profits and turf and within the other over program funds, prison construction, and law enforcement budgets.

One side can deny its own despondent tendencies, its boredom, its yearning to be daring, break the law, violate communal norms. The other can dodge desires for conscientious commitment to society and for ways to reduce boredom, alienation, and despair without recourse to drugs.

And so with racism, tax rebellion, homelessness, and other leading sociopolitical issues of our time.

The Ritual of Applying Physical Strength While Constricting Feelings

Whatever rage is and wherever it originates, when fully mobilized it can temporarily obliterate feelings such as hurt, sorrow, and longing. Constricting feelings, or limiting their range in the face of vulnerabilities one assumes one cannot handle, is a standard adversary ritual, brilliantly exemplified in *First Blood*, a movie about a Vietnam veteran named John Rambo.

Capturing the imagination of millions of viewers not only in the United States but throughout the world, the Rambo films offer an exceptionally vivid glimpse of an adversarial form of masculinity and its exaggerated expression in the warrior. In *First Blood*, John Rambo (Sylvester Stallone) illuminates crucial aspects of the soldier's social psychology.

Contrast the Rambo films with *All Quiet on the Western Front* and *Grand Illusion*, war movies that portray authentic human conflict in all its complexity and tragedy. The genre in its classic form reveals confusions and contradictions of decent people whipped about by historical forces they can neither fathom nor control.

And what is Rambo? On the surface of the most intricate and revealing of the three Rambo films, *First Blood* is about the individual against society. Rambo is the loner determined not to be pushed around. He employs ferocity to redress insult and glorifies violence in the name of one man's freedom. Beneath these elements lie others that suggest the self-strangling effects of the adversary ritual of constricting feelings.

Whatever anger is, it mobilizes the body for "fight or flight." Since men have defined flight as cowardice and fight as heroism, it is the body's fighting potential as much as the actor that draws the viewer's attention in the Rambo films. They miss no opportunity to present well-sculpted, gleaming muscles, straining under the inner tautness of hatred, self-righteousness, and revenge and the external pressure of assault by unrelenting enemies. Sylvester Stallone has established himself, in both the Rambo and Rocky series, as the not very articulate, quietly wounded hero who through brawn avenges being underestimated and pushed around.

In real human beings, the power of muscle is limited. Weapons are prostheses, wish-fulfillments for more powerful biceps, triceps, power, reach, and throw. In Rambo, as in the even greater caricatures of "bionic" people, muscle literally takes center stage. The brilliance of Stallone's achievement in the gym is that he uses it, in Rambo, to return war to the human body. Although Rambo employs a variety of weapons against his enemies, they are presented more as adjuncts to his muscles than extensions or substitutes. The film implicitly accepts the demise of high-technology war that was one of the consequences of Vietnam, and returns the actor and the viewer to the original condition of war: pitting a man's body, a few simple weapons, and his cunning, against adversaries. (*First Blood* was made in 1982, nearly a decade before the Persian Gulf War revived faith in high-tech killing.)

In an age when the nuclear threat parodies male strength—it is the ultimate but disembodied muscle, male fantasies of brawn gone completely mad—Rambo is a wondrous return to human muscles themselves, every last bulging, shining, sweating one of them. Son of the Vietnam War, Green Beret, and holder of the Congressional Medal of Honor, Rambo is trained in survival and killing under the most trying circumstances. In that jungle war, he mastered small-scale weaponry, one-on-one encounter, and living off the land.

A Vietnam veteran passing through a small town in Washington state, John Rambo is jailed by Sheriff Teasle, who seems to see him as a potential troublemaker. Sullen and quiet when arrested for no misdeed at all, Rambo will not answer any questions, will not even give his name. The police decide to clean him up for court. After hosing him down, his captors try to shave him. Approaching from behind, officer Galt whips his police stick around Rambo's neck and holds him taut. As the straight razor approaches Rambo's face, the audience sees in a flashback that he was tortured by the Vietcong. Pressed tight, his mighty torso stripped bare, Rambo endured the blade of a sword repeatedly slashing his chest. The terror and fury of that prior moment explode now, and the prisoner, in classic comic book fashion, breaks free of his tormentors, bang-sock-pows them senseless, tears the place apart, and flees.

He heads for the mountains. Rambo, who must have been a marvelous soldier, uses everything he knows to overcome his pursuers. He recreates Vietnam in Washington state (which may well stand for the national capital). And he does it all defensively. Master of survival and fighting skills, Rambo becomes a perfect one-man army. Like the cowboy in American folklore, he is self-sufficient and self-contained. And whereas Washington, D.C. could not organize itself to allow heroes like Rambo to win the war in Vietnam, this veteran hero vanquishes Washington. Reversing the U.S. disgrace in defeat, Rambo avenges his personal degradation by the law enforcement men dogging him.

First Blood offers a twist in the adversary paradigm in that the stalker of one encounter becomes the pursued of another. As if the United States could not face its own participation in Vietnam, its exemplary military hunter is transformed into prey; at the same time, government becomes villain.

The movie not only tries to redress the supposed shame of "losing" Vietnam; it also caricatures power, war, and the individual soldier. The skills Rambo learned against Asians are his arsenal against fellow Americans. The training is transferable to *any* adversary situation. What matters is not logic, justice, or emotional acuity, what matters is brute conflict.

Rambo is the personalization of war, the reduction of it to its pure elements of men facing each other in all their anger, toughness, power, confusion, and fear. Rambo rids conflict of technology—airplanes, missiles, and napalm. He reduces it to its quintessence: a man on an adrenalin high, inspired by hurt, determination, and rage to take on other human beings who have nothing to do with what originally provoked him. Sheriff Teasle's eagerness to engage Rambo suggests the same kind of process in him. All complexities of ideology, history, political economy, feelings, and strategy are finally boiled down to one man pitted against enemies. The entire range of human issues is eliminated from consideration, in favor of pure brute strength.

Gone are abstractions of "communism" versus "democracy," of helicopter bombing with stereoed Wagner distracting the pilot, of innocent women, children, and men subjected to the whims of self-seeking machismo-obsessed political and military leaders. Gone too, for Rambo, is the shame of the returning soldier mocked and scorned by his sponsoring society. Vanished is the degradation of the fighter unable to win the war, failing to bring that massive muscle to its proper conclusion in victory. Rambo is getting even, for himself, for his comrades killed in Vietnam, and for feelings of betrayal by the entire U.S. army, government, and public.

Rambo's hurt triggers his war with the locals in Washington state, and that hurt is clue to his wrath. The subtext of the film is that some men do not know how to deal with pain and fear except by lashing out. Rambo could have told the sheriff that he was a Vietnam veteran who had just learned that his buddy died of Agent Orange–induced cancer. He could have revealed how troubled he was over his war experience. He could have explained that his jacket, with its American flag at the same spot as on the jackets of Teasle and his men, was not hippie chic but a garment provided by the U.S. Army. He could have defended his unkempt appearance by celebrating an American man's right to shave or not to shave as he wishes.

But Rambo *says nothing in his own defense*. Acting as if he owes words to no one or as if he does not know how to use words or as if they are not effective in tight situations anyway, he rejects the possibility of words for the certainty of sinew. Gone is the chance of mutual understanding; replacing it is violent showdown. Rambo's hurt is based partly on his perplexity about being harassed, that his intentions and condition were not apparent to that hapless sheriff. He reminds us of the child who expects the parent, or the lover who expects the beloved, to understand without conversation, to anticipate without prompting, to respond as desired with no cues as to wishes and needs. The simple, innocent terms of Rambo's brief visit to that small town in Washington are drowned in misunderstanding, injury, and revenge on the one hand, and scorn, stranger fear, and boredom on the other—all this the consequence of forgone conversation.

If the hurt begins with Rambo's pain at being misunderstood, it escalates to memory of physical pain melded to emotional anguish, sword against chest and soul, blade taunting the hard fullness of his muscled manhood and integrity, threat to his power as an American, by smaller, weaker, slighter foreign men with simple weapons and a winning war strategy. Rambo is the soldier charged to fight an enemy he knows nothing about, disciplined to follow orders even when his life is endangered, trained to blind himself to historical, political, economic, emotional complexities in favor of those of immediate threat, survival, and command.

As a helicopter passenger, Galt, his earlier tormentor, pursues Rambo. To save himself, Rambo hurls a rock at the chopper; it swerves, and Galt falls from his unsteady perch to his death. Rambo, within shouting distance of Teasle, roars, pleadingly, referring to Galt's death but also the entire set of circumstances that led to this moment: "It's not my fault; I didn't do anything."

This must be the inner plea of any Sgt. Calley, any killer in a nation's uniform. Rambo means simply to say, as he later tries with his mentor and inspiration Troutman, that he just wanted to have lunch in that town, that he was harassed and reacted only in self-defense. War is always justified as self-defense, and Rambo believes in his innocence in Washington state as much as he surely believes in his innocence in Vietnam. Back in his home country, dishonored and unemployed, Rambo becomes the low-tech Vietcong guerrilla pursued by helicopters. And like the Vietcong, he outwits his pursuers. Rambo is thus able to identify both with those who made him a warrior and with the guerrillas who defeated him. The pathos of the tough soldier knuckling under to stronger authority and modeling himself after it, could not be clearer.

The Rambo who obeyed directives in Vietnam, even ones that put his life in mortal danger, now gets even with authority that cares nothing for him by striking out against it. Practiced in deferring to uniformed command, Rambo attacks brash, cold-hearted civilian police, a barely disguised metaphor for the depravity and arbitrariness of the entire structure that led him to, and deceived him in, southeast Asia. But the attack is not a challenge to irrational authority. It is only rage at a disappointing one.

The Vietnam War was a historical turning-point. An aggressor society was faced with protest against the blind obedience of war education. It echoed Nuremburg by ignoring Nuremburg. Rambo returns to the United States vanquished, as if on trial for his defeat. Whether the small-town sheriff thinks of Rambo as veteran or hippie, he sees him as nothing more than a drifter and in effect pronounces him a failure. And now Rambo's inability to defend himself in the few words it would have taken, becomes clear.

A soldier is schooled in *not* explaining himself. A soldier is forbidden to think, let alone ask, why he is commanded to use deadly devices to destroy strangers. He is disciplined to define the enemy as ruthless and armed. He is forbidden to learn anything about his opponent from the opponent and often does not have even a common language with him. To explain himself would be to acknowledge the possibility of *misunderstanding*, the chance that force is not the only way to manage human encounter.

Rambo is a comic-book emblem of a war that taught him one thing only: to be effectively, innovatively ruthless in any circumstance of threat. He is a pre-cyborg killer, a human killing machine who was not programmed to develop parts of himself that might be useful in peacetime. That his emotions might lead him in other directions is irrelevant since he has been educated to deny feelings except in the rage-violence range, that, at its maximum, is war. Professional in muscle and survival and amateur in heart, Rambo is sucked into Teasle's trap because he is waiting for it, *he is looking for it.* Deny it though he may, Rambo needs the war with Teasle as much as Teasle needs the war with him; neither has any other justification for his adult existence.

Each blames the other as victimizer, and although the audience is primed to identify Teasle in that role more readily than Rambo, each can be seen as responsible for the havoc. Both are victims *and* victimizers. Neither can recognize the larger institutional forces that define him in such constrained, limited ways. Each is blind to the pitfalls in his society's instructions on how to respond to frustration, how to handle feelings, how to be a man.

Teasle, essence of macho adversarialism, risks lives, property, and sanity itself to pursue his quarry. Had Rambo told Teasle his story, had he asked Rambo for his story, Teasle would likely have sympathized, particularly with Rambo's rage at the heartless and moronic government handling of the war. Rambo might have created friends and sympathizers in law enforcers who probably share his worldview. But Rambo, perhaps closer to a real male than a cartoon after all, does not know how to do this. And he fears to make that kind of connection anyway, for it would break ranks with masculinity as Rambo knows it; it would be to betray feelings and ask for empathy, to recognize force not as the essence of male purpose but as a failed alternative to conversation.

Victim of attacks on his body, Rambo chooses not to denounce and renounce that mode of relating but rather to return it in kind. Blindly, as if driven by an inner force fused to his military expertise, Rambo does unto others what he most feared and hated having done unto him. He aggresses against the aggressor with whom he has identified completely. The soldier, humiliated and made dumb in learning how to kill, does not strike back at trainers who drained away his humanity in making him a "man." The successful warrior learns to look away from officers, government, society, and culture that replaced personhood with an outmoded form of manhood, defined only in terms of submission, force, and fear denied.

Rambo challenges obedience, which he had learned so well, by disobeying Teasle. This from a fighter who had never challenged orders and never questioned the justification of brawn. Rambo becomes the essence of the fighter dishonored, veteran of an incomprehensible conflict. No longer a soldier, he cannot even hold a job, he confesses to Troutman. He is nothing in experience or potential but the hero-soldier. He holds onto that in the only way he knows, by "defending" himself.

The American soldier in Vietnam played sheriff to the Vietnamese Rambo. Mistaking people fighting for their freedom for threats to American security, the U.S. government and military treated the Vietnamese, already devastatingly hurt in their war with the French, exactly as Rambo was treated in that small town: with suspicion, violence, and contempt.

The least of *First Blood*'s significance is its caricature of the individual against society, the wronged soldier getting even in cartoon sock-bam fashion. Rambo is the confused American; Nixon's pitiful, helpless giant; the beer ads' tough, mesomorphic, fleshy male with nothing substantial opposing his muscle and no logical partner for his very being; a man caught up in narcissistic self-absorption at its classic price of isolation and self-pity.

The Vietnam War might eventually be seen as the beginning of the end of war, for a substantial portion of the citizenry of the mightiest power on earth brought morality and political analysis to what cannot succeed as an institution unless accepted on blind deference to authority: war. They brought empathy and compassion to the forbidden territory of war; they rejected the annihilation of that very broad range of human feelings essential to making war. *First Blood* hints at the necessary transition from war. Troutman and Rambo finally meet in a police headquarters Rambo devastated one night along with a filling station, dozens of vehicles, a munitions store, and the lighting system for much of the town. And now Rambo's emotions, beyond anger and determination, become clear for the first time.

When he returned to the United States, Rambo tried to contact Troutman, only to get a runaround. He was hurt that he could not see the man who tells Teasle that he is the only family Rambo has. Here then is an archetype of the disappointing authority, the father who coaxes his son out of humanity and sends him off to war. With Troutman beside him, his life in shambles, Rambo's emotions explode: he cries, he yells, he explains that he did not start the war with Teasle, that the sheriff and his men drew first blood.

In his heart-rending tantrum, Rambo accuses Troutman and everyone else of not understanding what it was like to see his buddies killed in Vietnam, to have one burst apart all over him by an exploding shoe shine kit. He shrieks that "nobody would help," "somebody wouldn't let us win." In agony he tells Troutman he is haunted by his Vietnam years: "I don't talk to anybody," and "I can't do it any more." In Vietnam, people covered for each other, but not in civilian life. His whole meaning was in fighting, and now he cannot, Rambo confesses, even hold a job parking cars.

This is a plea for mutuality, for understanding and compassion. Rambo demands from Troutman what Troutman taught him to suppress. After a career of dumbly following orders that destroy the very vitality, the exuberant life-force, in the soldier, Rambo's repressed humanity screams for release. Rambo is the perfect soldier, and the film explains to us the dreadful cost of his perfection.

Vietnam was for what? Troutman has no answers for Rambo. He tells him he is the last of a special group (apparently the only survivor of his elite unit). Troutman is the helpless pitiful giant himself, and he has no words of consolation for his star pupil. He sees Rambo as not only the final member of a unique fighting group in Vietnam, but perhaps the last warrior altogether. We even see a flicker on the otherwise impassive Troutman's face that intimates he wonders if it was worth it after all. As Rambo cries out his story, Troutman stands apart, squelching, except for a quiver of the lower lip, whatever human feelings must be aching to surface for this fighter he made and whose life is in ruins.

Sobbing, Rambo falls into Troutman's arms. Slowly, reluctantly, hesitantly, as if he must but wished he didn't have to, Troutman touches Rambo's back. He betrays no feeling and does not hold his creation close. Troutman, severe representative of the adversary male order, tells Rambo that Vietnam is over; he can do little more than inform him that he is surrounded by 200 troops with M16 rifles, outside the wrecked police department.

And now Rambo realizes he must give up. The film ends with lyrics of a man's confusion about struggle, betrayal, and pain. It is the plaintive song of the soldier, the cowboy, the lonesome macho male who feels he has to be better than those who oppose him, even if that means dealing from a very limited deck of emotions. Only men can be his companions, but they are killed in the same war that could kill him. He is drilled into confusing this isolated, hurt-filled, angry, fearful condition with life.

☙✦❧

TEN

Rituals of Faulting

We are not independent but interdependent.
—Buddha

Mistrusting, accusing, blaming, shaming, and inducing guilt are ways, often ritualized, of creating and maintaining separation in an adversary fashion. They shift responsibility for behavior and feelings from oneself to someone else. The other is considered at fault for behavior or character defects that, it is implied, make positive regard and connection impossible; these flaws, according to the claims of those making them, justify distancing, domination, and other forms of adversary behavior.

Mistrusting

The Godfather is a Mafia variation of the classic gangster tale. Beneath its surface of illegal business and gang warfare is the ethnography of mistrust, whose numerous rituals run all the way from piercing glances to murder. The complex emotional ties and struggles in *The Godfather* are between men; male-female relations are unemotional, exploitative, and distant. Connie Corleone (Talia Shire), sister of Michael (Al Pacino), is a battered wife whose husband-abuser is killed by her family; she is not an active agent but victim and onlooker. Michael's wife Kay (Diane Keaton) also plays a minor role. Unlike Amy Fowler in *High Noon*, none of the women in *The Godfather* even suggest a mutuality alternative to the adversarialism of the Mafia life that defines the entire drama.

The role of women in *The Godfather* is painfully clear from the opening scene, a mechanically joyous celebration with a side moment in which the bride's brother Sonny (James Caan) screws a guest in a bedroom while his sister is being married in the garden below. Behind the religious and ethnic formalities sanctifying conjugal union, we are informed, lies unfeeling, macho sex.

The movie never leaves that tone in its portrayal of gender. There is softness, though, and what appears to be reciprocated love, in Michael's attraction to a Apollonia, a young peasant in Sicily, whom he meets while waiting for tempers to cool after murdering some East Coast Mafia competitors in New York. Apollonia is suspicious of Michael at first, but after he lets her father know there is no choice but to let the couple marry, they do, and they seem quite taken with each other.

Mafia rivals kill his bride, as if to remind Michael that real men are concerned only with power and vengeance. Even the hint of a caring, gentle love has no place in the world these men inhabit.

The film proposes that life is about men and power and insists that mistrust is inevitable. In gaze, speech, and actions, the men engage in adversary rituals by which they brutalize each other at least as terribly as they do the women.

Whereas mistrust is personified in *High Noon* in the two male antagonists and their supporters, *The Godfather* is more of a Hobbes war of all against all. What becomes clear is that trust, the beginning of mutuality, is impossible for adversary acolytes. The mistrustful Don Corleone (Marlon Brando), in trying to pass his life and fortune on to his boys, sees his hotheaded son killed. Only the level-headed brother is left to absorb the don's adversary principles as he takes over ruling the family.

Just as the story begins with the exclusion of women from commanding roles in sex and business, it ends with the insight that one other group threatens the hegemony of the adversary male commitment: children. The aged Don Corleone plays in a backyard vineyard with his little grandson. Delighted with the boy, the sick old man pretends he is a monster chasing him. Scared at first, the toddler soon finds fun in the pursuit. The scene suggests that opposing others is in some essential way a game, and that Don Corleone knows no other way of relating, even to a child, than as adversary. It is fitting that when a heart attack fells his grandfather, the boy does not realize he needs help. Corleone gets back what he gave: the boy responds to him as nothing more than a player in an adversary game.

Michael announces early in the film that he will not join the Mafia family, which, he says, is nothing but a business. Michael does not elaborate; what I make of this remark is that in legitimate business, literally killing the competition is extremely rare; but murder in the form of ruined careers, destroyed competition, abused employees, betrayal of the public trust, exploited workers and customers, abandoned communities, and devastated environment is, in some lines of commerce, routine. Despite the great prosperity and means of comfort that business brings, and despite the monumental historical accomplishment of contract, which implies at least limited mutual trust, business, like organized crime, also often abjures trust.

Fondness of men for each other appears throughout the film, but it is undone by the stronger enactments of mistrust that define almost every scene. The young Michael hints at an alternative way in his initial rejection of the human bankruptcy of the world in which he has to select his role. Later, when he accepts his legacy and grows into his Don's job, his dark and troubled eyes radiate mistrust. He winds up isolated, totally alone, a caricature of what it means to trust no one and be trusted by no one. Like Midas, he carries the macho paradigm to its ultimate implication: total competition and complete success mean emptiness, solitude, sadness. The adversary prize cannot be enjoyed in partnership with anyone, because it is defined as being against everyone.

An associate of another Michael—Milken—the junk bond expert who went down on racketeering charges after prospering for a decade, said, "In addition to being a talented, creative genius, Michael is among the most avaricious, ruthless, venal people on the face of the earth." According to another, "Michael is interested in power, dominance, one hundred percent market share. . . . He is the most unhappy person I know. He never has enough."[1]

Eventually Michael Corleone mistrusts not only his comrades in business but also his parents and siblings, his wife, his children (toward whom we never see him act as father), and himself. The younger, vulnerable Michael, a spark of whose compassion appears at moments with Kay and his Sicilian wife, is mistrusted and ultimately rejected by the adult, role-bound Michael.

Erik Erikson[2] reasons that trust and mistrust are the earliest human qualities that make relationship possible. Children must learn when and how to trust parents and also when and how to mistrust them. No parent can be perfectly reliable, meeting a child's numerous needs and wishes all the time; thus a cautious, careful mistrust is essential in a family as well as beyond it. Mistrust of the parent, though, at least in U.S. society, is, according to Erikson, too difficult for most children to integrate with trust. It appears, as he sees it, that most parents are unable to present trustworthiness effectively enough to provide a foundation upon which inevitable mistrust can successfully be joined with it. Mistrust is either factored out and displaced onto "enemies," or it becomes the entire relationship.

Erikson claims that the longing for total trust never ends. Even the reality that any loved person disappoints some of the time can, as I interpret Erikson's reasoning, be assuaged by attachment to divinities or idealized leaders, who provide balm to the wounds of mistrust experienced early and later. As Freud also suggests, God in formal religion can be trusted completely. For many worshippers, God, in both Freud's and Erikson's understanding, has something in common with children's wishes for parents who are omnipotent, all-knowing, all-caring, and all-forgiving. This is not to reduce religion to early developmental issues but to suggest some involvement of the latter in the former.

Erikson illuminates the possibility of religion as, among its many meanings, a place where needs for perfect trust can be met. He does not, though, extend his analysis to the secular equivalent, with all its problematics, the state. Absolutist systems, in both right and left variants, claim perfection and full trustworthiness of leader, party, and government. Like dogmatic religion, this absolutism draws on residues of infantile yearnings for perfect trust. And like dogmatic religion, it allows the disappointed seeker to mistrust another whole people—the enemy—completely.

Just as some institutions may serve to embody perfect positive qualities that are imperfect in individual relationships, so do others serve as metaphors for the negative counterparts of these qualities. Society is upset about crime; then it identifies people in its midst upon whom others can project mistrusting tendencies that they avoid facing in some day-to-day encounters. Although enemies may be reviled, they may also serve as groups toward whom people can in socially approved ways feel scorn and mistrust.

Films like *The Godfather* ritually satisfy needs to anthropomorphize mistrust. Even while viewers may find the story appalling, they may also find it, like the violence in the film, gratifying. It is tempting to represent less pleasant parts of the self externally, since disapproving of what is seen there is easier—for good reason—than facing such issues inside oneself. It seems that people strike a bargain: so much pain and doubt would attend introspection into terrifying parts of the self that people who act out such behavior publically, in reality and in fiction, will somehow be tolerated, even if disapproved, by society.

Accusing, Blaming, Shaming, and Inducing Guilt

Those who blame the poor for their poverty avoid facing the complexities of a social order where gender, class, and race load opportunities in favor of some people and against others. It is not their callousness or ill intentions that motivate them to blame the poor, but a reluctance to examine the institutions themselves. The social psychology of class relations lets us discover embarrassment on the part of the higher-class person when confronting the class left behind, fear of falling into a lower social class, and an unconscious struggle against recognizing "failed" parts of oneself. It is easier to define others as failed and to despise or patronize them accordingly.

The same blaming tendency operates at petty levels. Someone who hates whiners and blames them for their annoying, disrupting ways acknowledges herself as mightily tempted to whine. Blaming someone else for thoughtlessness is a way of evading one's own tendencies in the same direction.

Ordinarily, one who is blamed feels hurt and insulted at what seem to be unjust accusations and gets angry in return. Although this makes the blamer feel uneasy, it becomes justification for the original act of blaming. Now the blamer can claim and believe that the anger really comes from the other, *toward himself*, not vice versa.

There is no reason people should accept their role as objects of projection and misdirection of emotion, so devices are engaged to keep them in their place. Through demonization, entire groups, even nations, are blamed as weak, subversive, degenerate, dirty, sex-ridden, evil. When the blamed responds, "No, I am not," the blamer uses the protest as an example of the other's perfidy. A woman, for example, who objects to the label "aggressive" applied to her for behavior found admirable in men, is dismissed as having just demonstrated how aggressive she is.

When the blamed responds in kind to the blamer, an "adversary symbiosis"[3] is formed. It is constructed of reciprocal accusations and recriminations, each party tacitly helping the other avoid the inner honesty that could free both from blaming and being blamed. In the films *Boyz N the Hood* and *Menace II Society*, angry young African American men whom the viewer has every reason to see as vulnerable and frightened, act violently against each other to express collective and individual hurts and the rage ensuing from them. Their hatreds form a symbiotic system whereby all are involved with vengeance and countervengeance and exclude inner considerations or possibilities of changing the larger social order that creates and sustains their festering problems.

Blame proceeds from either-or thinking, which assumes that any act with deleterious consequences is the responsibility of one and only one agent, animal or human, demonic or divine. The logic of shared accountability or institutional accountability or some piece of responsibility inhering in the blamer is ignored. People can recognize and probably even remember from their own childhoods the aching fear and anger that grip the child who insists that a sibling, cousin, neighbor, or monster started it, whatever it may be: a fight, a plot to steal the cookies, tormenting a pet, a day of hooky. Children, like anyone else, may be tempted to try to avoid punishment by vilifying another rather than facing themselves.

Optimally, elders will respond compassionately and justly to the child's real thoughts, feelings, and actions. But many parents, caught by memories of their own early abuses, may not know how or even whether to accept unpleasant parts of their children as inevitable or whether to see these unpleasant qualities as identical to corresponding parts of themselves. Our culture is not alone in failing to teach people how to be aware of themselves in this way.

Rituals of shame and guilt often accompany blaming. Shame is a strong form of disapproval of self. The child who breaks wind at the dinner table or breaks a vase is made to feel ashamed and unworthy for disrupting the civil order of the household rather than simple discomfort for the act committed. Shame reflects a transgressing of norms; one has not lived up to society's expectations of behavior. Guilt, by contrast, is a feeling of evil, wrong; one has done something not simply clumsy or thoughtless but *bad*. Cosmic laws of morality have been violated.

Blame is *accusation*, a shortcut past inner struggle that rejects seemingly problematic parts of oneself. Shame and guilt imply not only judgment but the appropriateness of punishment. How tempting to find someone else— or indeed whole groups—who ought to be feeling shame and guilt *instead of* oneself and members of one's group.

Children can sometimes mistake thought for deed and not be certain whether they are to be punished for *attacking* another, for merely *wanting* to do so, or for simply *imagining* it. It is also unclear to children whether adults are aware of their children's fantasies and, in subtle ways that do not reveal their awareness, punish them accordingly. This confusion about wish and action and about how much adults know about a child's inner life may continue in adulthood in a mistaken equation of thought/desire and deed.

In 1971, William Ryan brought the world the book and phrase *Blaming the Victim*.[4] Social science welcomed insight into a process by which the poor are blamed for being poor, the raped for being raped, the exploited for being exploited. Unfortunately, a frequent choice of some politicians and many other people for dealing with homelessness, inadequate medical care, AIDS, and poverty, is to blame the victim. Ryan's suggestion enables readers to see blaming as a mechanism by which people with wealth can keep the poor poor, rapists can violate the raped, and exploitation can be rationalized. In every case, though, rather than blaming the blamer, it is more useful and accurate to see the blamer as needing a way to make sense of behavior that may appear too bewildering and painful to face in any other way.

Thanks partly to Ryan's analysis and partly to the women's movement, blaming the victimizer has replaced blaming the victim as the method of choice of large numbers of activists and social scientists concerned with victimization. It is as if to say that if you are holding me down, I demand that you remove the barriers you have erected to my success. Legislation, law suits, and public humiliation are likely to be the lot of people who blatantly victimize African

Americans and Jews in public. This model is followed too by organizations promoting the rights and dignity of women, gays and lesbians, people with AIDS, disabled people, the aged—indeed, virtually all the put-upon of our society.

Blaming the victimizer is usually joined to the demand that victimizers change their objectionable behavior. Indeed, like all people, victimizers are morally responsible for what they do, but stopping overt discrimination does not address the motivation, dynamics, and institutions that keep it going. It seems assumed by those who blame the victimizers, that what motivates them is of no concern to the dominated, whose task is to shake off the tormentors by confronting them in united, forceful ways. I remember a student in the early 70s screaming that she did not care if men have trouble expressing their feelings, she was only insisting that they stop mistreating women. She would not entertain the possibility, any more than do most other dominated peoples, that the dominator was acting less from malevolent commitments than from confused, compulsive behavior not under conscious control.

Liberation is usually understood to be one-way, the dominated freeing themselves from the dominators. For it to move beyond recrimination and adversary somersaults, though, liberation can be seen as *a mutual process whereby dominator and dominated free themselves and each other from dynamics that account for both parts of the transaction. Blaming dominators presumes either that they act rationally but against the interests of the dominated, or that they are unfathomably evil and can be undone only by overpowering them. The adversary paradigm is assumed.* This is seemingly the reverse but actually the complement of the conservative/reactionary assumption that the world is composed of contending, antagonistic interests that must be fended off as well as possible. The only difference, in this respect, between conservatives and reactionaries on one hand and liberals and radicals on the other, is that the former group urges that the order of domination remain intact, while the latter claims it can be overcome. But the changes accomplished by the latter, if any, are a *restructuring of the order of domination. This is the consequence of not identifying the adversary paradigm and its underlying dynamics and facing them on their own terms.*

All of this makes sense if one realizes that victims are ordinarily limited to the adversary framework in analyzing their pain. If they are not to blame for their condition, then it must be the blamers who are at fault. Exiting the paradigm that makes this analysis plausible requires awareness of alternatives. It is very hard to locate them, and most contexts lack them altogether.

If no possibility of moving beyond adversary binds is recognized, then choices are limited indeed. Consider pornography. Without attempting a rigorous definition here, let it stand that pornography is a popular culture form in which women and children (and sometimes men) are objectified and violated physically and verbally by men. In complicated ways, many people fail to experience the simple, natural pleasures of their bodies and of human connectedness and are drawn instead to the dehumanizing, dissociated sensationalism of pornography that is profitable for its purveyors and that arouses lustful and destructive feelings in its consumers. It is one thing to deplore this, it is another to ignore the forces that make it attractive to people.

Freedom from pornography might imply freedom from unnecessary constrictions on eroticism, love, and the playfulness of sensuous, lustful impulses. To end pornography or at least to reduce its appeal means serious social reconstruction. And the same is true of all other adversary behavior that is coercive and destructive.

Like the antipornography effort, the War on Drugs limits attention to *behavior*. It confuses recreational and expansive drug experiences with troubling motives and consequences that, when destructive, call for understanding rather than simple censure. Just as Prohibition did not address the reasons that people drink, the so-called War on Drugs seems to ignore the pervasiveness of feelings of dislocation and despair that underlie those people who use drugs to numb feelings, mind, and soul and the role of the drug business as yet another business in a "free market" society. The "War" neglects to seek the motives underlying the behavior and the social structural realities that shape and sustain them.

Correspondingly, both sides in the abortion controversy tend to ignore underlying structural issues. Each blames the other for sanctioning violence as each side defines it. "Pro-lifers" deny what can be seen as the violence of rapists, poverty, inner turmoil, and social institutions in helping determine whether a given woman feels inclined to grow and bear a baby. "Pro-choice" people rarely take as their central focus underlying social and economic conditions that lead to unwanted pregnancies.

Each side in the conflict is caught up in a frenzy of blaming the other. Virtually no "pro-life" activist admits to feeling any kind of attraction to the democratic principle of freedom to control one's own body and life, and "pro-choicers" rarely grant any interest in the intense refusal of their opponents to end, for any reason, that which has been conceived, for any reason. Each side to the controversy distances itself from what is probably somewhat appealing and understandable in the other.

Part of the way out of confrontations like the Cold War is to shift from nations in adversary contention to seeking ways to end war as an institution. Then nations can work together to safeguard themselves not against each other or simplistically against war but against conditions that perpetuate war. That is the principle of "common security,"[5] and it is a model for moving toward mutuality. A sane survival politics of mutuality would build from such questions about how best to use resources for the benefit of everyone, so as to eliminate most of the reasons for war.

And so with racism, sexism, and all forms of domination. Yet working at systemic change rather than blaming can be frightening, for several reasons:

1. It is threatening and potentially overwhelming to confront the problematic nature of entire social-economic-political-historic processes. Who can fathom their intricacies? Who has the audacity to imagine, let alone recommend, fundamental change in them?
2. What will happen if others see one as an active seeker of change? In many circles, that is a sure recipe for ostracism; under ordinary circumstances, few people seem willing to risk it.
3. If one does pursue change, there can be trouble with the law as well as public opinion. Thoreau, Gandhi, and King come to mind, as well as numerous people engaging in civil disobedience in recent decades. Fear of legal and social censure dissuades most people from working for serious change.
4. A stable milieu, however hated, is familiar. Fear of the unknown may explain, in part, ties to unsatisfactory institutions.

Law and law enforcement are especially involved in rituals of blame in our society. Among professionals, lawyers represent far more clearly than physicians, professors, engineers, and other professionals, the essence of the adversary complex. Even lawyers whose work is environmental protection, family law, labor law, and other social issues ordinarily work in adversary contexts. Divorce attorneys work against other divorce attorneys. Environmental lawyers pit what they consider the public interest against what polluters consider their economic interests. Even legal work on wills and taxes often proceeds in an adversary framework.

If law is there to regulate conduct, regulation usually is framed in adversary terms; the point of nearly any legal proceeding is to win whatever is being contested. At its most dramatic, this process is enacted in courtroom law. Toward the end of victory, the subtlety of the legal mind in sifting through precedent and principle can give way to the cleverness and suppleness of that mind in figuring how to plant doubt and prejudice in judge and jury, how to aggrandize the client, and how to ridicule the other side. The O. J. Simpson case is an extreme example of spending vast sums of money on lawyers and consultants to manipulate public opinion and selection and behavior of a jury.

Advocate and client engage in a series of adversary relations: client against client, lawyer against lawyer, and each lawyer and the other's client against each other. Judge and jury are adversaries to be bested by lawyers, rather than, as in classroom legal theory, neutral instruments plucked to play the sweet sounds of justice. Lawyers often pit themselves against laws, trying to defy or distort those that weaken their clients' interests and to manipulate those that work in their favor. Lawyers can also implicitly oppose the claims of society for justice. Although some have this in mind, lawyers are not enjoined to work for outcomes that would minimize harm to each client, reestablish peace between them, and serve the community's needs for harmony.

Lawyers collectively represent *both commitment to law and defiance of it*. The goals of decency and justice, pursued in the legal system, are undermined by actual practice. (As Abbie Hoffman put it, in the halls of justice, the only justice takes place in the halls.) It is easy to dismiss the discrepancy cynically, even despondently, but it can usefully be seen as expressing fundamental contradictions of a society with democratic and egalitarian claims. The practice of law symbolizes both ambivalence about submitting to social order and also what underlies that ambivalence: the disparity between ideals and the emotional capacity to realize them under conditions where emotions that oppose the ideals are not brought to light, examined, and integrated with them.

Law also presents the drama of individual against society. Lawyers enact the common desire to be clever and persuasive enough to get away with breaking the law. Law fascinates partly because the citizen accepts *and resents* the superego that law represents and thus, even if grudgingly, admires professional circumventers of it. If judges represent superego, lawyers stand for the ego clever enough to get what it wants in spite of superego.

Law enforcement complements law in its adversary nature. If judges stand for superego, police are like lawyers in symbolizing the collective ego, negotiating between rational norms of conduct encoded as law and either impulsive or deliberately planned violations of them. But unlike lawyers, police are trained in violence. If officers are admired, feared, and hated, even by the same person, this befits their mandate to stand for conflicting aspects of the person: conscience (enforcing ethical and legal codes), competence (maintaining order, negotiating between desire and conscience), and unsocialized desire (violence in self-defense, real or contrived). Doubts about police and resentment toward them surface in dramas about corrupt cops. Speaking to the audience's ambivalence, television police sagas (somewhat like westerns in an earlier era) most likely represent continuing public fascination with conflicts among impulses, conscience, and self.

Criminals act out what the public reins in. Feelings of horror and disgust toward lawbreakers, like demands for the death penalty, are genuine responses based on honoring the superego *and* secret expressions of envy; they are veiled, sometimes desperate attempts to keep one's own antisocial inclinations in check.

Conscience guides and also torments. Corruption scandals reveal the ordinariness of law-breaking and also the recognition that as terrible as this is, it is also fathomable. "Everybody does it" is not only a statement of cynicism or despair, it is also tacit rebellion against conscience.

Those who violate laws remind us of our own antisocial urges though we belong to the "law-abiding" majority. Guilt about our own impulses may explain, at least in part, why many people are less concerned with rehabilitation and prevention than with vengeance and punishment. But scapegoating criminals also victimizes the law-abiding majority because the scapegoaters thereby deny themselves the potential liberation of recognizing denied parts of themselves and learning how best to manage them.

Rationality, Bureaucracy, and Displacing

In addition to profit, efficiency and rationality are high aspirations in capitalist society. As productive as these matters can be, they also tend to subordinate love and fulfillment in favor of comparisons, power, and material comforts.

At the heart of putative rationality and efficiency in the capitalist economic system is what appears to be a peculiar irrationality. It is hard to see a rationale for the contrasts between opulence and poverty so common throughout the world. The turmoil that ensues works against the economic interests of the people who sustain the conditions that bring forth the turmoil. What is rational about the stock market fluctuating wildly after the death of a world leader? Or the insistence on inventing technology that, if used for its intended purposes, even and especially by accident, would destroy it. Capitalism is productive and appealing *and* includes practices that deny emotional realities that are not irrational but that follow a rationality that is different from that of productivity and profit.

It is easy to knock bureaucracy, which is no stranger to adversarialism, but its virtues can be acknowledged as well as its limits. Large-scale societies need organizations to perform complex tasks. If we do not yet know how to organize these institutions in humane, compassionate ways, our challenge is to learn how to do so. Toward that end it is useful to discover systemic limits and problems of bureaucracies. Some bureaucracies welcome clients and serve their needs admirably. Along with and often in place of brutes who are commonly identified with bureaucracies are people who care about each other, help colleagues in crises, and treat clients humanely. That life is bearable at all in institutions is due to decent people acting honorably.

Many people, though, experience bureaucrats as frustrating, withholding, even sadistic. Although the bureaucratic mode of organization is meant to be efficient and fair, it is more often experienced as hostile, sloppy, and permeated with injustice and petty corruption. The problem is not theories of bureaucracy or character flaws of bureaucrats, it is the unfaced adversary assumption underlying so much bureaucratic activity. It is that assumption that guides the structure itself and that determines the normatively objectionable practices of its officials and employees.

Consider the insurance industry. The customer, without whom the insurance firm cannot exist, is the firm's source of income and also, in some ways, its adversary. When a customer makes a claim to get some money back, maybe even more than was put in—the possibility of which is part of the endeavor—the insurer sometimes finds ways to escape paying the insured. The latter sees the company that acts this way as the enemy and sometimes has to hire a lawyer (an adversary technician) to help with the claim.

I have noticed at universities that if I ask a question of a secretary on the telephone and do not give my title, I often get suspicious, hesitant, or even hostile replies. When I identify myself as a professor, the person is almost always cordial and forthcoming. Suppose I were a student or a parent or someone else on the outside. I know how I would be treated since I am an outsider at other bureaucracies.

Bureaucracy has many meanings. In some ways, it appears that its formal organization and procedures substitute for the weak inner selves of many bureaucrats. Bureaucracy thus serves as a prosthetic ego for some people and also as a formal excuse for avoiding spontaneous, compassionate interactions. Those who hide behind bureaucratic procedures may find those human qualities bewildering, problematic, or a threat.

Bureaucracy sanctifies adversary behavior. It tends to split the world into acceptable intimates, or friends, and unacceptable others, or enemies. The former group comprise a kind of community, the latter, its opposite.

Approach a certain common kind of bureaucrat. The first feeling you may get is that you are seen as determined to get something you don't deserve—money, privilege, time, human consideration, anything. It is as if they are afraid that you will cheat them out of something, and will, if unchecked, damage their self-image or waste their time.

For some people in bureaucracies, intra-office intrigues, from malicious gossip to schemes for advancement at others' expense, define office reality as much as work. As in other institutions, the adversary principle reproduces at all levels of relationship, internal and external. Bureaucracies have gradually become associated with issues of mistrust, contentiousness, jealousy, competitiveness, backbiting, and hostility. Max Weber's fatalism about the nature and future of bureaucracy[6] reflects his inability to imagine alternatives. He reifies bureaucracies, making them immutable things unto themselves rather than structures that reflect unfaced issues that people assume to be inevitable in human behavior. It is Weber's lack of a sophisticated social psychology that prevents him from imagining ways to move beyond the problems with bureaucracy that he so cogently examines.

The cruel treatment of people and the removal of hearts and faces from petitioners in many bureaucracies are models for the deeper depersonalization, brutalization, and efficiency of war. In all cases, the commitment to produce in the smoothest manner is a way of ignoring, even denying, the human costs involved.

The "rationalization" of activity includes neglecting emotions. In bureaucratic society, this intersects with the "rationalization" of individual motives. "Rationalization" in the former sense means organizing an activity as logically and productively as possible, but in the second sense, "rationalization" means covering up, with socially acceptable explanations, motives hidden from one's audience, one's self, or both.

One of the classic justifications for bureaucracy and its rationality is its efficiency. Complex tasks do have to be done, somehow. But the vaunted efficiency of bureaucracy is often oriented toward a goal that ignores human needs and feelings. In addition to whatever else it is, I suggest that bureaucracy is commonly a system of *organized, systematic aggression.* Hiding behind rules and maintaining distance from clients and workers on which bureaucracy depends, a functionary who is susceptible to these opportunities is enabled to administer punishments that masquerade as procedures, budgets, and bureaucratic imperatives. Vagueness of accountability in bureaucracies, expressed in dryly written, incomprehensible regulations, often forecloses confrontation with client-victims. Who was the aggressor against Vietnamese peasants? the U.S. president? Congress? capitalism? the U.S. public who supported presidents waging war? confused young men trained to kill? anticommunist ideology? journalists on a battle high? a military hierarchy receiving confused and contradictory messages from those to whom it is responsible?

In efficiency, the very concept of separating humanity and productivity is commonly carried to its extreme implication: dehumanization in each step of the productive process. Attention is on product—whether car, baby formula, or pesticide—not on the consequences for people involved in the product's manufacture, sale, and use. With rare exceptions of visionary entrepreneurs, feelings and conscience play lesser roles in entrepreneurial activity than productivity, consumption, and profit.

The efficiency principle bifurcates in its application to war in modern history. Nazi death camps industrialized killing but in horrible ways that were not entirely depersonalized. Guards and executioners saw their victims, mocked them, reviled them, tortured them, beat them, killed them at close range. Demonization, degradation, and hatred in their most virulent forms defined the relationship of Nazi and victim.[7]

Nazi killings show the driven quality of the adversary compulsion.

Nazis did not invent a mode of murder, though, so much as they carried a familiar one to one of its two possible ends.

The United States chose the other extreme. Nazis, inventive in ways that caricatured science and technology, conceived of both death camps and atomic bombs. The use of Zyklon B made it possible for Nazi soldiers and prison guards to see real victims, but the use of the nuclear device depersonalized even more than the V-2s that devastated London. Rocket victims were identifiable, and the memories of the London blitz yielded endless stories of steadfastness and heroism. The nuclear explosion, which the Nazis were unable to perfect but which the United States created and twice used, meant by contrast obliteration of entire cities. Dying, like the release of the bomb itself, would be anonymous.

Nazi death camps embodied industrial dehumanization, productivity, efficiency, and aggression gone totally mad. Fighting a war to regain lost honor and rebuild a ravaged economy fused with Hitler's personal needs to demonize and dispose of a number of populations and an obsession with obliterating one of them completely. Most of the German people went along with him. The mass camp killings became a caricature of what is perhaps the ultimate implication of the "rational" economy: death. Nazi Germany harnessed the deadness of bureaucratic functionaries to the impersonality of technology, led by the contagious passion of a crazed charismatic leader with monstrous *idées fixes* about Jews, gypsies, communists, homosexuals, disabled people, the retarded, and Slavs. In some metaphysical way, the death camps were a consummation of the West's commitment to heartless efficiency.

Are we to feel doomed by the impersonality and frequent depredations of bureaucracy? I think not. Understanding their social psychological underpinnings is a piece of a strategy for inventing ways to rectify their shortcomings. It cannot be impossible to construct humane behavior as a norm in institutions, no matter how complex they are. It is one of the greatest challenges to ingenuity to shift inventiveness from products, manufacture, and sales to mutualistic social forms. If there are few decent bureaucracies but only many decent people scattered throughout them,[8] then the task is to create ways to work together that welcome clients and co-workers as colleagues, not antagonists. The place to begin is those institutions, however flawed, that build upon mutuality in their work and procedures. Chapters 14 through 16 present such options as already exist.

Part IV

❧⌘❧

Mutuality under Way

In mutuality, people cultivate feelings of pleasure and joy in their relationships in every context: family, lovers, friends, groups, species, cosmos. No one is debased, no one is made to feel inferior or superior. If each relationship can be felt as enhancing and if the goal is bolstering others rather than embarrassing, humiliating, or otherwise overcoming them, the relation strengthens all parties involved.

Think of athletes and craftspeople, lovers, friends, parents and children, artists and entrepreneurs urging each other on to growth in skills expanded and developed, deepened emotional experiences, and ever deeper fulfillment, in contrast with people bent on winning. Imagine selves so well integrated that they need not attribute unwanted and unmet parts of themselves to others and either admire or persecute qualities and deeds they thus project outward from their proper location, their own selves.

There is tension in mutuality, but it is not the tension of confrontation and defeat, it is the tension of efforts to grow and to connect. The tension in mutuality is that of expectation, of potential hurt, of risk, of anticipation, of disappointment, of challenges and fantasies unmet or inadequately met, of delight and of sorrow. The goal of mutuality is not to end tension but to cultivate those tensions that produce growth and pleasure.

If, as humans, we can find alternatives to the unnecessary destructiveness fostered by adversary assumptions, we can also figure out how to relate to nature as friend rather than foe. While this does not mean welcoming hurricanes, it would mean an end to overfishing the seas and misusing topsoil and water.

Human fear of nature is complex. Because it can destroy humans and their endeavors, experiencing nature as adversary makes some sense. But we can treat the force of nature with respect, and people can select settlement sites, grow food, and fish seas in ways that honor the intricate realities of nature and our relationship with it.

As drama is built on tension, mutuality does not easily lend itself to dramatic representation, but the tension between adversarialism and mutuality does. In the major paradigm shift that may be under way, that tension could replace conventional adversary tension. Artistic ways of representing the skills and growth of mutuality are likely to evolve.

In this part, I define and explore mutuality. I suggest that it could be achieved by reappropriating childhood, feelings, body, and altruism lost or wounded in historical processes of fragmentation. The movies *Thelma and Louise*, *Close Encounters of the Third Kind*, *E.T.*, *Strangers in Good Company*, and others are examined as metaphors for aspects of such reappropriation. Seeds of mutuality are identified in familiar institutions, and I describe some newer institutions organized around cooperation as the main mode of relating. Although they do not yet appear to be as dramatic or clearly definable as their adversary counterparts, mutuality rituals are stylized ways of enjoying the humanness of others, empathy, support, and caring. Handshakes originated as a way of showing one had no weapons at hand; they now represent, as in the handshake between Yassir Arafat and Yitzhak Rabin on the White House lawn in September 1993, a step toward mutuality. So do embraces, smiles, and collaborating on common goals, whether in sport, work, art, conversation, or politics.

Most humans have learned adversary skills or failed in that endeavor. Fewer have learned mutuality skills with equal success. All institutions can figure out how to proceed to take part in this teaching and this learning.

ELEVEN

The Other As Complement Rather Than Threat

The infant needs . . . parents and their affection, needs a world of varied impressions, yet one with regularity, needs objects to manipulate and master, needs a chance to develop . . . modes of controlling . . . excitements and hungers and of turning off to sleep or to disengagement. There is some deep biological principle that abhors the imposition of one person's will on another—even when one is mother and the other infant, or vice versa. The deepest principle is mutuality, and it begins early.

—Jerome Bruner,
foreword to Barry Brazelton,
Infants and Mothers

Transitions to Mutuality

In *Thelma and Louise*, two women respond forcefully to hurts they have felt from men. The film is about adversarial encounters between men and women and about rape, one of its quintessential forms. And it is a film that points toward mutuality.

Friends Thelma (Geena Davis) and Louise (Susan Sarandon) leave their partners for a weekend trip. A stop-off at a roadside bar turns into Thelma's near-rape by drunken mauler Harlan and his unintended murder by Louise.

For reasons not clear for a long time to Thelma, Louise will not call the police to report the near-rape and accidental killing. Louise insists on running. When they are broke, they are brought money by Louise's lover, but it is stolen by a hitchhiker on a one-night stand with Thelma.

Inspired by the thief's tales of derring-do, Thelma robs a convenience store. Now the police have two reasons to find her and Louise. Racing through several states in their attempt to escape, they are caught and, surrounded by law officials at the brink of a canyon, deliberately drive over the edge to their deaths.

This is a film in which two women take charge of their lives. It is also a film in which one will not talk about her rape, even with the friend she has saved from rape. Nor will she discuss the powerful effect her rape has had on her with the officer who is trying to save her life. Tough, clear-headed, and cynical, Louise has adopted many male ways of seeing the world. She radiates an attitude of strained self-sufficiency, but her humanity endures.

When she explains with great passion—first to Thelma's would-be rapist and later to the truck driver whose sexual overtures repel her and Thelma—that women do not like to be violated, Louise is hoping for understanding and the possibility of change. When her attempts fail, she turns on each of these men who neither get it nor back away. She could have told Harlan off rather than shooting him, and she could have targeted the tires of the oil rig rather than the tank. Only gradually does the viewer realize that when Louise insists, after the killing, that there is no point in going to the police, she must have tried that after her rape and gotten nowhere. For a moment, Harlan was her rapist, and he paid for that and all his rapes committed in the tavern's parking lot.

The humiliation and pain of rape do not go away. The story is powerful in portraying the pervasiveness of those feelings in Louise's life and her inability to transcend them in her everyday surroundings. Victims of men's adversary predations, she and Thelma become reactive victimizers and outlaws.

With the important exception of Clyde's companion in *Bonnie and Clyde*, outlaws in American film iconography are usually male, adventurers, and remarkably vital. The negative of the bored citizen who leads a life of "quiet desperation," outlaws reject conventional adversary relations—like business and politics—and take pleasure in illegal ones instead. Although early experiences may contribute to their choices, their escapades are at their own initiative, in contrast to the reactive ones of Thelma and Louise. The film makes clear that violating women is normative not only in the larger culture but even among male guardians of the law. Asking Thelma's husband Daryl to sound considerate when Thelma calls from the road, the police chief adds, "Women like that shit." The cop reading a girlie magazine, *Boudoir*, unwittingly enjoys the sexist culture he presumably monitors for brutality.

Slocum (Harvey Keitel), the detective trying to coax the women to stop running and face charges, seems an exception. He could be feigning compassion and understanding as part of his strategy, but his concern feels deeper than that. In an encounter with the newly apprehended hitchhiker (Brad Pitt), Slocum is enraged that his theft of Louise's money is what led Thelma to rob the store. His fury would be out of place were he not genuinely moved by the women's story. But his empathy is not enough for Louise. Slocum cannot make up for her history of hurts and disappointments, reinforced daily by what she sees in her job as a waitress.

Thelma, by contrast, is inexperienced and hence less guarded with her feelings. Her misery is more forthright than Louise's, and her delight is stronger. She gives in to Harlan on the dance floor and to the hitchhiker in the motel. The message is that indiscriminate openness to opportunistic men is not good for women. Some reviewers have taken this as man-hating. It is not.

The women in the film develop a relationship; the men do not. Rapist Harlan has no concept of relating to Thelma other than sexually, and Thelma's husband Daryl shows only one dimension whether he is with his wife or with the authorities in his home. Waiting for phone calls, these men watch television, eat, drink, read. Although working side by side, they show no effort to bridge their isolation, or even a desire to do so.

Louise's lover Jimmy, a decent guy, is puzzled by Louise's wanting more than his kindness and his love. The more that she wants is understanding, and Jimmy is unable to offer it. It is for this reason that Louise does not trust him with her story or her life. At their farewell breakfast, after he has brought Louise her life savings, Jimmy speaks tenderly and movingly. Louise asks if he took a pill that helps him do that. I am choking on it, he replies. Jimmy may gag on stretching himself to be a proper lover, but he is suffocating from his aloneness as much as anything else.

This is a story of mutuality manqué. Thelma and Louise care for each other, but they will die because outlaws have to die in American films, and because mutuality is difficult to achieve in a culture confused and tormented about it. The adversary order is maintained by rape, inconsiderateness, and distancing, as well as by the deputies of law and order. The daily indignities and opportunism of truck drivers, detectives, and beer-hall dance partners are the norm. Two women try to flee their condition for a weekend, but it pursues them, as if to say there is no getting away from it, it surrounds you, it is your fate.

Louise is too smart, decent, and shrewd to kill; yet the accumulated pain of memory not only of the rape in Texas but of what must have been the indifference and callousness of men to whom she came for justice, enraged her. With Harlan, in the parking lot, she tries something beyond adversarialism. At first she says just, "Let her go." Harlan doesn't. Then she insults him. But shortly, she explains that what Harlan considers fun is not fun for women. She wants him to *comprehend*, she wants to touch him with her feelings, she wants him to get it and apologize. And she goes through the same routine with the oil truck driver.

Louise's efforts to move beyond adversarialism are powerful, but they fail. Neither man shows any recognition whatsoever, no fathoming of Louise's patient explanation, her anguished plea. *It is only after her humanity is rejected* that she becomes an outlaw. She and Thelma then turn their rage against the only possible objects remaining, themselves.

As they careen over the cliff, the two women are destroyed by adversarialism, but on their own terms. The hubcap that spins off the car as it goes over the edge is a teaser of their freedom to react as they have and to die as they will. But it is much more. In a dozen different ways, the car is one of this culture's leading emblems of adversarialism. It is a mechanical, environment-corroding, lifeless machine to which many men attach fantasies of power, sexuality, and freedom, all in adversary terms, and around which they have built largely adversarial forms of work, housing, entertainment, commerce, worship, and most other forms of behavior, including countless films with fast-driven cars. That very American symbol of freedom that the protagonists have adopted as signifying theirs is also a symbol of human separation, discord, and escape. For Thelma and Louise, the car was the agency of innocent vacation and then of desperate flight; the device itself, mark of male fancy and erotic displacement, will be destroyed with them, and even before they crash to bits at the bottom of the canyon, the car seems to begin to fall apart in mid-air.

If this is a story of revenge against two prototypical adversarial, raping men, it is also a story of women beseeching men to listen, to feel, to apologize, to grow, to learn to relate in mutualistic ways to other people. The men of their society will not meet their terms of humanity because they mistakenly think, adversarially, that that would mean submission and thus defeat. Refusing to accept the order they find degrading and inhuman, Thelma and Louise try to touch adversarial men and fail, but they succeed in coming to care fully for each other. By opting out of prostration before the law, which would be the adversary ending, and holding hands as they soar over the cliff, they come as close as they can to the mutuality for which they yearn. Contrast the decision of these two women to die united with the separation and violence directed toward their pursuers by Butch Cassidy and the Sundance Kid at the involuntary end of their lives on the run.

Mutuality

Peter Kropotkin observes that "mutual aid" has enabled people to work and live together for millennia.[1] Indeed, most human activity requires that people collaborate, and most people know how to do that. War, to Kropotkin, is an exceptional circumstance that draws certain people who are good at it.[2] While I think Kropotkin minimizes the fact that vast numbers of people passively accept whatever wars their government wages even though they may have mixed feelings about them, he usefully challenges theorists who assume cruelty to be more basic than cooperation.

Ashley Montagu criticizes the misuse of Darwin's work to support the "social Darwinist" view that competition is more fundamental than cooperation among humans. He points out that this popular misinterpretation of Darwin (who warned against applying the concept "survival of the fittest" to explain social behavior) fits a society trying to justify a competitive economic system,[3] and that it ignores the vast ranges of cooperative behavior in all species and the capacity of humans to value cooperation.

Given inclinations both to be adversaries and to work together, people can choose which direction to emphasize in their behavior. The choice begins with analysis, with understanding the paradigms as frameworks within which we behave, and with understanding that we are free to choose to shift our attention from winning to collaborating, from the pleasures of victory to those of shared accomplishment. It is not a question of sacrificing the familiar so much as gaining the joyous feelings of unity and community and in the accomplishments of mutuality.

Although adversarialism and mutuality probably do not exist in pure form and although each is to some extent an admixture of both, their predominant tendencies are clear. In the next passage, I intend the distinctions between the two to be understood as predominant tendencies: Where adversarialism is competition, mutuality is cooperation. Where the first wrenches people out of context, demonizes them, and makes them into enemies, the second seeks to understand people in individual, societal, cultural, and historical contexts. Where one attacks and humiliates, the other supports and nurtures. Where the adversary paradigm celebrates victory and submission, mutuality honors empathy and joint recognition of complex motives and aspirations. Where adversarialism negates emotional reality, mutuality esteems it. Where adversarialism exploits weaknesses, mutuality bolsters strengths. Where one is triumphant, the other is compassionate. Where one scorns faltering and failing, the other respects the meaning, universality, and humanness of frailties and struggles. Where one neither seeks nor grants forgiveness, the other knows both are essential to being fully human. Where one ignores vulnerability or mocks and hates it, the other accepts its inevitability and welcomes it.

More systematically, in mutuality:

1. The other is experienced as fully human. Central in the noblest aspirations of religion, humanism, democracy, and certain aspects of daily life, mutuality means retaining others' full personhood in one's consciousness,

emotions, and action. It also means realizing, directly or through sublimation, the full range of one's own feelings, fears, and inclinations.

—→   2. Compromise and harmony, openness and growth are prized, and contrasting realities are accommodated to each other. "Society (including structures of work) should be arranged to foster relationships of reciprocity and cooperation."[4] Rather than focusing on seeming losses resulting from compromise (of money, land, honor), attention is on *gains* of living harmoniously with others, self, and nature, and on the pleasures of working through emotional complexities while striving for varied goals.

3. Power is shared. Adversarialism assumes the necessity of power of some *over* others. Mutuality recognizes power as control over one's life in working *with* others.[5] "Social power," or power-over can be distinguished from "personal power," or "autonomy."[6] Personal power is associated with independence, self-reliance, self-actualization, and confidence. According to one piece of research, people feel better about themselves and they act more creatively and responsibly when they work with others toward a common end.[7] As an added outcome, increased opportunities for taking responsibility in the workplace (and elsewhere) affect people's sense of self-confidence and "political efficacy" *outside* the workplace.[8] It appears that the work site could be a modeling ground for mutualistic behavior that extends into family, community, and all other nonwork contexts.

4. Mutuality replaces subordination to hierarchy with interdependence of equals, the shared connectedness of human lives. There is a difference between "infantile dependence" based on primary identification with an adult, and the "mature interdependence" of accepting the self as separate from the other even while interconnected in relationship.[9] Both these concepts of dependence are relevant to mutuality. Mother and child, to name the obvious prototype of the infantile dependent relationship, can recognize each other, respond to each other, and meet each other's needs.[10] The same pattern applies to mature interdependence, except that here no one needs to identify with the other for survival; giving and taking are more nearly equal in the mature interdependent relationship than in infantile dependency, where the parent may be giving more than the child.[11]

5. Emotional responsiveness is essential. The mutuality paradigm embodies emotional understanding of people, situations, nature; the adversary paradigm derides it as unmanly. Where one paradigm bases relationship on distance, coldness, and domination, the other prizes closeness, warmth, and egalitarian acceptance.

6. Giving is a primal way of connecting. The adversary system assumes scarcity, such that taking more than giving, is essential for survival. In a complex practice in some preindustrial cultures, giving centers the act of connection itself, so that "things . . . are to some extent parts of persons, and per-

sons . . . behave in some measure as if they were things."[12] In such systems, gifts are put into endless circulation, so that the more they circulate, the greater their value. They represent connection, which is highly prized, in contrast with profit, another prize in our system of circulation. The "potlatch" of some Native American societies in the northwest United States was a massive giveaway and destruction of possessions as a way of joining with others. This sounds something like the detachment from things counseled by Buddhism as a way toward enlightenment and peace.

As gifts interconnect, they are inherently social. Profits isolate; they are inherently individual. Art is a gift when it "acts as an agent of transformation."[13] The artist models giving for the sake of affecting the other. The commodity negates emotional relationship, while the gift, like art, essentially *is* emotional relationship.[14] This perhaps explains how in U.S. culture, Christmas, which celebrates love, connection, and higher aspirations, is centered on gift giving. But when gifts are bought and given as commodities as well as, or sometimes in place of, expressions of love, they are peculiar. Built upon the adversarial assumption of scarcity, commodities as gifts may express love, but they are also the core of a consumer economy that favors "the bottom line" over emotional exchanges. The confusion of frantic monetary expressions of what is nonquantifiable is a painful example of a central contradiction of U.S. society. ↳ namely, love

7. Love and community are prime aspirations. The mutuality paradigm has never been absent in history. People do work and play and make love together as well as compete. Community, however romanticized by intellectuals, has always included the appeal of mutuality. Utopian communities, communes, and small religious "intentional communities" accurately reflect longings for connection beyond immediate relationships.

The mystique in Western cultures about love, about pure love, about falling in love and being in love also reflects, among other things, the universal longing for mutuality. The use of "love" in ads urging the viewer to "love" a car or food or whatever suggests a perversion of love; it is as if the desire to love and be loved is unreachable and one might as well settle for love with an inanimate object to be experienced as an extension of the self. The commercial exploitation of the word love thus mocks mutuality by turning love back onto the self, through its possessions.

Even if subordinated to the adversary paradigm, the mutuality countertheme exists in dialectical relationship with it. Visionary religions and political leaders recognize the appeal of mutuality. From the prophet Isaiah to Burmese democracy activist Aung San Suu Kyi, the ideal of mutuality is kept alive by extraordinary people who preach and practice it.

Mutuality movements include Quakers, Unitarian-Universalists, Mennonites, and numerous utopian experiments like the Amish and Bruderhof communities in the United States and kibbutzim in Israel. Whatever the intentions and accomplishments of mutuality figures, the institutions that follow them, such as religions and states, sometimes contradict the goal of mutuality by pursuing victory over the heathen or the irreligious or the political enemy or the unpatriotic of their own populations.

This is not to suggest, as is the fashion in some secular circles, that religion and state are simply hypocritical. Like other institutions, they embody the ambivalences and limitations of their founders and adherents. Enthusiasm for their claims distracts from recognizing the destructive effects of their inconsistencies, but just as strongly, condemning their misdeeds diverts attention from their merits and visionary potential. *A more helpful approach is to recognize the reality of ambivalence about and within both adversarialism and mutuality and to choose which valence to stress more than—rather than instead of—the other.*

States advance a rhetoric of mutuality in calling themselves a people or community, in proclaiming rights, goods, and services for all their citizens (whether actually provided or not) and in idealizing a concept of citizenship as in organic connection with the political community. Their failure to produce on these visions is not so much hypocrisy (the easy allegation) as it is a tormented inability, due in considerable part to blindness to the paradigm in which they operate, to recognize ambivalence and to strive to move past it. In the late 1980s, Mikhail Gorbachev was able to do just that. Stanley Hoffman observed in January 1988, that "the Soviet 'new thinking' attempts to contrast the obsolete approach to security, which is adversarial, with the need, in a nuclear world, to take into account the fears of the rival."[15]

Other institutions like schools and corporations hint at the appeal of mutuality in "family" metaphors created partly for social control and partly *to express authentic yearning.* The tenacity and possible sincerity of the rhetoric are as significant as its distance from actuality. The absence of true fulfillment implies perplexity and frustration, even helplessness and fear, more than evil intentions or a conscious denial of the historically fuller development of adversary inclinations.

If revolution is for the revolutionary an attempt to overcome domination, the defending order is determined not to yield either power or the adversary paradigm, which for both dominator and dominated remains unrecognized and unnamed. Conservatives and reactionaries see no possibility of mutuality. Although they may dislike the *idea* of domination inherent in the adversary paradigm, they suppress their own mutuality longings in their disbelief in the possibility of alternatives and thus are stuck, in their worldview, with the choice only of whether to dominate or be dominated. Liberals and radicals idealize overcoming conflict but also take adversarialism for granted. Hence their concepts of liberation ring hollow and, short of recognizing and

[margin handwriting: self-fulfilling prophecy, must have hope and optimistic will]

acting upon realities of internal conflict and the larger framework of paradigm conflict, are hollow. All four of these major political positions unwittingly share, then, an assumption that freezes them in place: that winning or losing is the only possible political goal and—at least as important—that the inner self plays no serious part in public action and need not be examined.

The Morality of Mutuality

If the externals of a relationship are the focus of the adversary paradigm, its complement works from awareness of inner states. In a psychoanalytic reformulation of the Golden Rule, Erik Erikson explores mutuality as a moral developmental issue:

> To recognize one of man's [sic] prime resources . . . we must trace back his individual development to his *pre-moral* days, his infancy. His earliest social experimentation at that time leads to a certain ratio of basic trust and basic mistrust—a ratio which, if favorable, establishes the fundamental human strength: hope. This over-all attitude emerges as the newborn organism reaches out to its caretakers and as they bring to it what we will now discuss as *mutuality*. The failure of basic trust and of mutuality has been recognized in psychiatry as the most far-reaching failure, undercutting all development. . . . It is my further proposition, then, that all moral, ideological, and ethical propensities depend on this early experience of mutuality.
>
> I would call mutuality a relationship in which partners depend on each other for the development of their respective strengths. . . . While the baby initially smiles at a mere configuration resembling the human face, the adult cannot help smiling back, filled with expectations of a "recognition" which he needs to secure from the new being as surely as it needs him. The fact is that the mutuality of adult and baby is the original source of hope, the basic ingredient of all effective as well as ethical human action. . . .
>
> Here we must add the observation that a parent dealing with a child will be strengthened in *his* [sic] vitality, in *his* sense of identity, and in *his* readiness for ethical action by the very ministrations by means of which he secures to the child vitality, future identity, and eventual readiness for ethical action.[16]

Mutuality throughout life echoes the earliest experiences of infants with adults. Note that it is not competition but a very subtle interdependent cooperation that marks that very complex early bond of child and others. From the start, cooperation is essential for the well-being of infant and those who care for it.

Most public concerns with matters like mutuality, partnership, and love are hortatory pleas of the form, "Humankind must/should/needs to/has to/ought to." They are of little value unless the psychology of interference with realizing them is explored fully.[17] The problem is not intentions or articulations of mutuality but structures that could realize it and strategies for struggling with feelings contradicting it. Calling for "intellectual humanism," Theodore Geiger implies that in the realm of change, insight is more useful than opinion or entreaty.[18] Alexander and Margarete Mitscherlich observe that

> If one thinks about morality, it is possible to conceive of something other than a catalogue of prohibitions; men [sic] might, for instance, be called on to contribute to a mutually satisfactory existence. This, however, presupposes that social conditions permit individuals to take an interest in each other and to enter understandingly into each other's feelings. But for this the individual needs practical guidance; ways of making contact must be available to him if he is not to lapse into emotional isolation or emotional autism, which are quite consistent with controlled conformism.[19]

Modern society advises people how to adapt to it; no new morality is defined, nor, of course, is any way of achieving it. The Mitscherlichs suggest a morality that is strikingly like that of Erik Erikson in his revised Golden Rule: "[D]o to another what will strengthen you even as it will strengthen him [/her]—that is, what will develop his[/her] best potentials even as it develops your own."[20] The Mitscherlichs' version of this attitude is:

> *In order to be moral, I must try to act in such a way that in my pursuit of pleasure and gain*—in both the concrete and the wider meaning of these words—*I do not harm anyone else.* I must adhere to this principle even if it brings me into conflict with my own urges and I must reconcile myself to renunciations. Even fear must not make me forget the other person.[21]

Adversary morality is a major part of the morality of capitalism, whose rhetoric also includes respect for the rights of individuals, freedom of expression, human rights, and also, ironically, for the rights of the Sixties' counterculture that criticized it. It is a morality that is a half-morality, for it recognizes that moral people must honor their own needs and inclinations. But by ignoring *relationship*, it becomes a morality of self-absorbed indulgence, lack of empathy for others, and denial of the self's possible pleasures in relating, in feeling with and for others, in loving and being loved. The morality of adversarialism is the logical outcome of relations based on besting other people.

Insight into others and oneself and cultivation of the capacity for critical understanding are crucial for human survival. Although they lack a full analysis of the structures that sustain adversarialism, the Mitscherlichs see these traits as part of an evolutionary process whereby moralities of reason will replace moralities of faith. The strengthened ego will create a morality honoring respect and affection for others and the self as part of mutual regulation that issues in support, understanding, and love. In this vein, Marcia Lugones and Elizabeth Spelman reason that desires to excel and to be seen as distinctive and significant need not be realized solely in competition. If recognition and appreciation are sought, there are other ways to come by them, as in communal projects[22] and, by extension, simply in people appreciating one another's endeavors.

One way to bring emotions more nearly into integration is to focus on understanding them, that is, to pay explicit attention to them and to allow them full recognition and where appropriate, expression. It is the denial of their centrality in organized social existence that gives virtually free rein to their destructive possibilities.

Pseudomorality can be distinguished from genuine morality; the difference is determined by examining motives underlying attitudes.[23] By understanding the nature of projection and the self's tendency toward it, people can allow themselves to see in themselves and others, systematic distortions based on otherwise unacknowledged parts of the self.[24] It is important to recognize that just as anger one cannot face in oneself can be attributed to an "enemy," so can decency and kindness one has difficulty acknowledging in oneself be attributed to a "saint."

This approach to morality moves beyond ethics and the rational analysis of decent behavior. By calling for insight into emotional understrata of expressed beliefs and behavior, it suggests that introspection that illuminates inner dynamics and ambivalence can connect with other forms of moral analysis and aspiration.

Lack of a habit of empathizing is a function either of absence of a superego, as in psychopathy, or of a superego too strong for the ego to handle. Rigidity and absence of empathy reflect a punitive conscience one feels unable to affect; this seems common in people whose fears and confusions lead them to be dogmatic.

> The permanent stunting of development by a too early, too stringent moral indoctrination, one which is devoid of empathy and allows no room for opposition or the taking-up of a dialectical, critical counterposition, can lead to an overly close tie between the super-ego and the

ego. [This can lead] to an inhibition of critical ego-functions, and moreover to a restriction of critical self-observation. The ego is able to see itself only through the eyes of "Big Brother," or of a less loving than inexorable and vengeful God-the-father. The very thought of an alternative to the rules that have been laid down is a punishable transgression.[25]

The seeming strength of absoluteness and rigidity is actually a form of weakness, an admission of "the inability to face despotic father figures."[26] If as Freud suggests, the deepest emotional issues involve sexuality and destructiveness, morality is meant to curb them. But so far in history, most societies permit far more destructiveness to be expressed than love and eroticism.[27]

As the Mitscherlichs suggest, there is an inverse relationship between freely expressed eroticism and the expression of destructiveness.[28] A morality of mutuality would acknowledge this relationship and instead of fearing eroticism, as conventional repressive morality does, would understand it as fulfilling in itself and also as crucial to reducing destructive behavior.

Empathy allows one to respect the reality of the other and to recognize its resonance in oneself. This is the groundwork for respecting the differentness of others and experiencing them as valuable complements to oneself.[29] Interdependence in mutuality is crucial for understanding one's own motives; for such knowledge does not issue only from looking inward. Fullest self-understanding demands a listening other who is different from oneself, for knowing that the self in its rich, contradictory, strange beauty is at its heart dialogic. Most forms of psychotherapy formalize a stylized version of a human process essential to clear and true understanding of the self as well as of the other: as open, honest, and full an examination of history and motives as both parties can engage in. The sympathy and empathy implied are part of a method of discovery, joy in which is shared by the partners in dialogue.[30]

A morality of mutuality, then, is based on liberating the self from the tyranny of an overly rigid conscience and overly rigid people who threaten to disapprove of or punish the self.

The counterpart to demoralization and unscrupulousness is moral over-adjustment, sanctimonious docility, over-conscientious compliance with moral dictates, over-scrupulosity. Both are signs of a pathological character development. . . . In the great majority of people, the ready-made, collective code will stifle the development of a personal conscience. In the past, the whole emphasis of moral education was on establishing a state of manipulable impotence. . . .

Over-adaptation, in which the individual merely acts as a puppet of the rules governing his social role, is usually rewarded from very early on.[31]

There is a retreat in recent history from the overly severe conscience but, as well, a corresponding pulling back from expressing ideals. Rather than viewing this situation with alarm, it can be seen as part of a healthy process of moving from rigid superego controls of behavior to flexible, ego-centered ones that take account of real changes in history, individuals' assessments of them, and the actors' own experiences.[32]

Such changes could also include abandoning extraordinarily powerful emotional ties to objects. The anality and oral aggression of property-owning, with their central focus on money and other possessions, is metaphoric for people from whom the self has had to separate but to whom they are still unconsciously attached.[33] It could give way to emotional ties to people. This could have as a crucial consequence, the renunciation of self-righteous moral posturing and punitive behavior.

Destructive energies—and this is crucial for positive social change—can be directed toward liberation rather than domination. Aggressive energy hitherto invested in cruelty could be freed for engaging in life-preserving, sublimated action. "Fighting" to end war, preserve the environment, and liberate people from domination is what I mean by adversary rituals of resistance or liberation, as contrasted with coercive ones. They need to proceed in full recognition and appreciation of the emotional reality and complexity of the other as well as objective ideologies and issues.

The morality implied by this analysis calls for learning a critical stance toward morality itself. A morality of competitive possession and self-display could give way to a morality of insight into and compassion for the self and others and their interrelationships. The inner deadness implied by what Veblen called "conspicuous consumption" would yield to the inner richness that would result from honest confrontation with others and honest confrontation with the self in its complexity. Unlike having and consuming, this project by its very nature would need to be social. As crucial insights gained with others can release people from inner fears and confusions, they can bind people together into larger entities of those self-consciously attempting to become liberated in this way. The issue is not sentimental declarations of unity or "idealism" or "utopianism" or clinging to early internalized authorities. Rather it is the empathetic act of putting oneself in the place of another person and reflecting critically on what one thereby learns about the other, the self, and the two in relationship.[34]

On the international scale, empathy is correspondingly important in allowing people collectively to replace fearing and opposing the other with joint understanding of historical context and current reality. It can mean transnational scopes of concern and critical intelligence replacing nationalism as a basic human identification.[35] As the transformative nature of the nuclear and environmental threats becomes more and more clearly understood, the method of grasping that the other's fears and dangers are similar to one's own deepens its effects on its users. The morality of "national self-interest" will then, for the sake of survival, give way to the morality of empathy and global identification. If not, some new catastrophe will intervene to derail humans from this mutually enhancing survival project.

TWELVE

The Emergence of Empathy

> [Empathy is] an "emotional knowing" of
> another human being rather than intellectual
> understanding. . . . Both empathy and intu-
> ition, to which it is related, are means of
> obtaining quick and deep *understanding*.
> —*Glossary* of the American
> Psychoanalytic Association

The Prisoner's Dilemma

There is fascination in certain quarters with the "prisoner's dilemma."[1] In this logical and political chestnut of a game, two people have to try to figure their chances of gaining light sentences if they behave in certain ways; each has to calculate the probable behavior of the other. Invented in 1950 at the RAND Corporation, the game focused on military strategy issues just as the U.S.-USSR arms race was seriously accelerating.[2]

Here is the prisoner's dilemma: Unable to communicate with each other and both presumably guilty of something, two prisoners are faced with choices that could reduce their period of incarceration. If one confesses and the other does not, the term of imprisonment for the former will be very low and for the latter, very high. If neither confesses, the stay in prison for each will be medium in length. If both confess, the term will be high for both but lower than that for the loser in the confess–no confess outcome and higher than that for the winner in that option. A graphic illustration may make this clearer (figure 12.1).

Since the shortest sentence is in the interest of both prisoners, each has to guess what the other will do. Logically, the risk of high incarceration is minimized by going for the medium resolution of neither one confessing. But if one therefore does not confess and the other does, the former gets stuck with the long sentence, and the latter benefits from the shortest possible one.

		Prisoner B	
		Not Confess	Confess
Prisoner A	Not Confess	2 years each	10 years for A and 1 year for B
	Confess	10 years for B and 1 year for A	5 years each

FIGURE 12.1

The voluminous literature on the prisoner's dilemma focuses on the game-theory aspect of the problem: How can one calculate which course of action maximizes the chances for a light sentence? Rationally, of course, neither prisoner should confess, and each should assume the other will make that choice. But of course if one assumes that that is what the other is doing, it makes sense to confess and benefit from the lightest sentence, unless, of course, the other prisoner has made exactly the same calculation.

It is a gorgeous logical game—enticing, titillating, a genuine paradox. Those who enjoy analyzing this matter appear to take for granted its paradigmatic boundaries. I think a significant part of its appeal lies precisely in its illumination of a crucial aspect of the adversary paradigm.

The prisoner's dilemma is not on the face of it adversarial in the pure sense, as each actor has the task of getting out rather than of doing in the other.[3] The adversary is not the other prisoner, but rather *the system that presents the options*. The prisoners can gain respite from defeat by "winning" against the system directly and against the other prisoner indirectly.

Because compliance with the adversary norm robs the actor of the pleasures of mutuality and the possibility of pursuing it, the norm itself dominates and subjugates the competitor. The exercise is premised on the desirability of the light sentence *regardless of what happens to the other prisoner*. It does not matter why the people are in prison, whether as thieves who may not trust each other or as political comrades who do. They are assumed to be generic rational actors. The calculations of each prisoner are thus instrumental; the second person is seen as an agent whom one may be able to work to one's advantage. Where are anger, fear, hope, identification with the duplicate plight of the fellow prisoner? Where are still other feelings that must infuse imprisonment and the complexities of the deal potentially to be struck? The terms of the game dehumanize whoever contemplates the game as well as the pair of prisoners. In typical adversary fashion, those who present the problem define objective conditions and hyperrationality as norms, excluding emotional reality.

The prisoner experiences antagonism at three levels. Overtly, there is a specific competitor. Covertly, the norms governing the encounter are adversarial. And on the third level, as the prisoners are considered void of emotions, each also experiences his or her self as adversary, for the logical reality of each is in effect pitted against his or her emotional reality.

The greater society diverts attention from the peculiarities and limits of the framework of competition to specific people within it. The norm is dictated by patriarchal and social class authority that prescribes how it is permissible to behave. The "successful" competitor must not empathize with the opponent, for conquest is not possible if feelings of connection intervene.

The no confession–no confession option in the prisoner's dilemma need not be seen as based only on self-interest, for it is the one choice that can fully consider the condition and feelings of the other. This has a certain intuitive logic of its own. Both share the condition of prisoner. Facing a difficult task, both are forced to make one of the two choices presented.

Suppose each actor considers empathy as key to the outcome. Suspecting that the other has similar feelings about being in jail, about being used in this decision-making exercise, and about being coerced to submit to adversary norms that dehumanize—each could feel into the feelings of the other rather than relying exclusively on cold calculations. On the basis of that empathic method, each could realize that not confessing is the one solution that honors the emotions of both parties.

But, the dispassionate observer must insert at this point, how can we assume that both actors are attuned to empathy as a methodological alternative in such calculations? The answer is, of course, we cannot make that assumption at all. In fact, we can suspect that neither actor, especially if male, is so oriented and that the chances of them both invoking empathy are small indeed.

Further, we can guess that anyone assuming empathy would run the risk of exploitation by the other prisoner. In one version of the game, subjects classified as predisposed to cooperate with others do cooperate with those they see as tending to be cooperative and compete with those they see as fundamentally competitive. By striking contrast, those classified as predisposed to compete *assumed all the other players to be likewise competitive.*[4] It would thus appear that tending to cooperate combines with empathy in ways that tending to compete does not. It would also appear that assuming cooperation or competition by others has all the hallmarks of a classic self-fulfilling prophecy.

Imagine, then, two prisoners inclined to cooperate and skilled in empathizing. Making the no-confession decision on the basis of empathy would establish a distinctive bond between them, a feeling that would contrast with the loneliness of the isolated prisoner trying to match wits with the other. The bond would also be reinforced by the decision each prisoner will have made to refuse to yield to the devilish terms of the dilemma, which demands the profoundly adversarial process of trying to outwit the other. Thus the outcome that works best for both prisoners is also the closest they can come to defying the dehumanizing terms of their situation. By not confessing and counting on the other prisoner to do likewise, each settles for the two-year sentence, considerably longer than the one year that would be their lot if they could successfully finesse the dilemma, but much shorter than the five years or ten years facing them if the finesse fails.

To make this decision, one has to identify with the other as a fellow prisoner caught in the same unwanted dilemma rather than as someone to be bested. One can imagine that freed of jail after the two-year term, the two might enjoy meeting and might feel gratitude for the empathic set of the other that made the "best" solution to the dilemma possible. Each would have the option to recognize and enjoy a unique connection with the other. Were that felt to be desirable as an end in itself, it would contrast with the logic of the formal dilemma, which assumes only a cognitive orientation to "self-interest." That feeling human connection, compassion, and caring is also "self-interest" is outside the range of what most political and economic thinkers mean by that term.

The empathic approach is in conventional terms "feminine," while the standard game-theory analysis is in conventional terms "masculine." In truth, of course, many men are empathic and many women are not. The conventional terms are useful, though, in recognizing how members of each gender have in general been socialized to think of themselves as innately one thing rather than another. If all human qualities belong to all people, then members of neither gender need feel either more entitled to one set of behaviors than another or less.

To pose empathy as an emergent political category necessary for the "best" resolution to the prisoner's dilemma and for species survival is to suggest an opening of both male behavior and political theory to qualities and processes that had by sleight of definition been denied them by being labeled feminine. Here is an example of how binary thinking deprives people of access to what is part of the human heritage. The people who so far determine normative thought are adversarially inclined men and women, and there is yet no widely recognized force calling for an alternative way of organizing political activity. Feminist political theory is emerging, to be sure, but little of it appears to challenge the adversary paradigm on its own terms.

The Return of the Repressed Freud

Although Marx acknowledged the centrality of the sensuous, free, and spontaneous in human existence, and although he denounced the degradation of women in class society, his analysis of domination and his prescription for ending it are masculinist to the core. His vocabulary is confrontative and triumphalist—conventionally male in its base in the adversary paradigm.

The feminine remains only a vision in Marx, never part of analysis or praxis. Although his concept of "species being"—recognition of the common condition of all humans—may imply empathy, Marx never develops his concept that far. His most fully anchored terms, like "objectivity," "relations of production," "use value," "exchange value," "commodification," "proletariat," "bourgeoisie," "lumpenproletariat," and "revolution" build from assumptions about hardness, toughness, the superiority of objectivity to subjectivity, and the inevitability of conflict.

Marxism is increasingly bankrupt as prescriptive theory because of a growing recognition, except among its most die-hard adherents, that something fundamental is missing in a system of explanation that lends itself to totalitarian manipulation, exclusion of the softer human qualities, and elevation of abstract principles over real human lives as they are lived day to day. This is true despite Marx's insistence that his work lay entirely in understanding the real world of real human beings and despite his still useful moral and structural critique of capitalism.

Because of these limits of Marx's analysis, feminism and psychoanalysis become crucial for survival. Although Freud is out of favor in much of feminism, one of its most crucial "discoveries" builds upon Freud. It is Freud who in modern social thought insisted on the centrality of feelings in human experience. This insight, radical in its implications, is complicated by—and thereby missed by many critics because of—some of the leading contradictions in Freud. Psychoanalysis, unhappily, assumes the adversary paradigm. The patient is riddled with "defenses" against feelings. The patient engages in "resistances" to the analyst. Problems are sought to be attacked and ended, rather than strengths sought from which growth and pleasure can ensue. Not that psychoanalysts do not help patients gain in their strengths but rather that the process is seen by some less as collaborative, mutualistic to the core, than adversarial, with the patient neurotically dependent on the analyst until the time comes when the patient becomes autonomous, needing the services of the analyst no more.[5]

This assumption replicates Freud's vision of the child becoming autonomous from the parent. In orthodox Freudian analysis (I realize there are numerous more humane deviations from this model by now), analysts oftener than necessary withhold their own feelings from patients, thus removing themselves in a crucial way from what could be a fully mutualistic, satisfying encounter. By now, thanks to "object relations" theorists and many feminist psychoanalytic thinkers, the concept of the child's becoming healthily interdependent with parents, and the patient's enjoying interdependence with the analyst, has for many people superseded Freud's more adversarial notions of autonomy and independence.[6]

For all its limits, psychoanalysis nonetheless celebrates the release of blocked feelings and sees that as crucial to human well-being. One piece of that release, that I believe is crucial for the development of mutuality, is empathy.

Warren Poland locates what could be the emergence of empathy as a fundamental political category in the contingencies of this historic era:

> [O]ur efforts to define and master the concept of empathy take place in a context of historical inevitability. The broad theme of reconciling individual identities and needs with group pressures and demands is in the air for all aspects of Western civilization. As if in an unconscious historical unfolding beyond any conscious-theoretical awareness, psychoanalysis has come to express its own manifestation of these historical forces.[7]

Psychoanalysis offers empathy as essential in humans' understanding not only of themselves privately but as selves in their relationship to, and in the functioning and changing of, institutions, leadership, ideas, and history itself. The salience of empathy and cooperation is historically contingent; it is an evolutionary issue.[8] Its time has come.

Psychoanalysis finds empathy crucial in the work of analyst with patient. Freud sees any human relationship as a drama to which are brought feelings from prior relationships, particularly those of dependence. Clients become increasingly aware of their tendency to "transfer" feelings and expectations from elsewhere to the analytic setting, and analysts monitor "countertransference," their propensity to bring their own unresolved needs and fears to the analytic encounter. The capacity of both participants to deal with transference and countertransference depends on empathy.

Empathy is the apprehending of another's feelings and the feelings of those feelings. In empathizing, people use their own feelings and experiences to guess at the feelings of others and to be willing to feel those feelings with them. Empathizing allows people to understand what might motivate their behavior.

Empathy is part of the process by which one recognizes others as also human. Despite his limitations, Marx's "nothing human is alien to me"[9] suggests Freudian wisdom: one knows others through knowing oneself. Empathy with others corresponds to introspection.[10] It includes imagining others' experiences.[11]

> Through empathy we aim at discerning, in one single act of recognition, complex psychological configurations which we could either define only through the laborious presentation of a host of details or which it may even be beyond our ability to define.[12]

The empathizing subject temporarily gives up her own ego for that of the object.[13] In empathizing, one feels with and for the other but preserves separateness.[14] In this respect, empathy differs from identification, which is taking on another's qualities that one finds attractive. Not everyone is worth identifying with, as some people may present qualities none of which one likes. It is possible to empathize with Hitler or Charles Manson without identifying with them at all. And the distinction is crucial, for some people assume that to understand others is to condone their behavior. On the contrary, whatever one's values and actions, it is crucial to everyone to know that others listen and understand. Indeed, it is possible that figures like Manson became destructive in response to early overpowering experiences of the absence of understanding and empathy.[15]

Empathy is both a capacity and a process, an active mode and a passive mode, a means of understanding and a means of communicating, a way of gathering data. A form of nonrational understanding,[16] it originates in the early nonverbal relationship of mother and child. Whatever traits are associated with each gender are originally learned in relationship with parents and other elders. Empathy permits establishing contact where no other mode seems to work and reestablishing contact in ways one may have known in very early years.[17]

In contrast to the distancing and dehumanization central to adversarialism, empathy connects. It "is anathema to killing, to torture, and to the waging of war. It stands in contrast and in contradiction to the demonization of the enemy, to scapegoating, to that polarization of good and bad which creates a world view . . . of heroes and villains, and little else."[18]

By its nature, empathy is inclusive rather than exclusive. Roy Schafer reasons that empathy involves substituting "and" for "but" in approaching the other. His discussion of the analysand's ambivalence about adversarialism applies to all encounters:

> Conflict theory is a theory of irrational antitheses, of the proliferation of the stated or implied use of "but" in mental functioning. For "but," analysis substitutes "and.". . . "And" points toward diversity and away from the simplistic "but," the alleged mutual exclusiveness of that which is wished for, feared, and deplored by the analysand.[19]

Louis Agosta suggests that empathy is a form of receptivity that is also a form of understanding and that it allows another to be seen as a whole rather than as disconnected parts.[20] He sees interhuman or intersubjective experience is possible only with empathy.[21] Heinz Kohut sees it as "vicarious introspection, . . . introspecting one's own vicarious experience of another's experience, and thus establishing a connection between self and other through this vicarious dimension of experience."[22] In empathy, "the subject becomes aware that the other's feeling is the source of his [/her] own." By interpreting the other's feeling through one's own experience of that feeling, one understands.[23] And one becomes capable, finally, of empathizing with oneself.

Charles Darwin is not remembered for his work on feelings, yet he distinguished between sympathy, "compassionate feeling for another's painful state" and empathy, "a sensitive sharing of a feeling-state so as to understand the other person."[24] The distinction remains crucial today in that compassion does not imply understanding so much as kind support; the understanding made possible by empathy allows for action with the other, whereas compassion often does not.

The Risks of Empathy

Through empathy, one enjoys attachment to others and enhances feelings of well-being, but it is also problematic. Feeling oneself into another assumes a strong enough sense of self that one does not fear being lost in the other or swallowed up. One's sense of boundaries must be firm and clear in order to make the empathic relation,[25] for the other may be so appealing or powerful that one could feel controlled, or the other may seem so repulsive that one could feel diminished through empathizing.

Empathy is hazardous for another reason: the pain of feeling another's pain. One can feel discomfort not only from the pain but from the introspection it may foster, and the problematic feelings that ensue. Enabling another to work through pain can help in healing both parties, but uneasiness is undeniable.[26]

From this perspective, it is possible to see the desire for power over others, and the implementation of the desire, as pathological. It is likely that people who exert power over others are unable to empathize because of a limited sense of self and fear of losing themselves in others. The self is aggrandized not so much to enact some craving for control, but rather to compensate for fear of being controlled and for feelings of inadequacy and incompleteness. The self unable to master itself in a satisfying way, unable to empathize freely, in desperation seeks to control other selves as if in compensation. This is also a way of gaining recognition; indeed Hegel claims this as one of the primary motives for domination. The self fully experienced in recognition, though, understands it to be a process of mutuality.[27]

The first reason, then, for insufficient empathy is inadequate sense of self. The second, related, is the problematic nature of pain. Feeling pleasure in another's victories may have meaning in itself but it often represents compensation for painful feelings about one's own limits and failures. It is, further, less than pleasant to identify with the loser's regret and disappointment and with the miser's greed, and it is disturbing to empathize with the bereaved person's grief, the pain of the batterer and the battered, the killer's obsession, the addict's internal torment, the psychopath's sick desires. The reason Freud insisted that psychoanalysts must be psychoanalyzed is so they will not yield to the temptation to bypass their clients' pain through fear of inability to handle their own pain. This is as true outside the clinic as in it. The reward of empathy is the experience of surmounting pain in a way that allows good feelings of deep human connection—some would call it spiritual—with another person.

Empathy and Victimization

In 1986, I was on a political study tour of Israel and the West Bank. For complex historical reasons, some Israelis had been moving to predominantly Palestinian areas in territories outside Israel but occupied by it. On one of our stops, a Jewish settler presented a slide show and talk promoting Jewish immigration to the West Bank. In the discussion that followed, one of our number asked the lecturer, a woman in her forties, how she supposed a Palestinian woman of her generation living nearby, with children the same ages as hers, would feel about the talk we had just heard.

Our speaker was startled. She darted back as if slapped in the face. She stammered, "I don't know, I have never been asked such a question, I don't know how to answer it. I will have to think about it." We remained quiet for a very long moment, and then she said, now with a tone of impatience, annoyance, and finality, "I cannot answer that question. I *cannot afford* to answer that question. Why do you ask it of me? You might as well ask me how I would feel if I were an Eskimo woman. I am not an Eskimo woman, I am not a Palestinian woman, I am an Israeli, and I am doing what I have to do."

Her reply moved me by its honesty and perceptiveness. Indeed, were she to take her Palestinian neighbor into account, how could our speaker have continued to act as if the West Bank was there for Jews to enjoy with no regard for Palestinians she was daily dominating by her very presence? I was struck by what appeared to be her capacity to seal off her ability to empathize. This habit may have been seared into her by traumatic adversary experiences, personal or collective or both, and could impel her to disregard a reality that would impinge more fully upon her life with the onset of the *intifada*, the Palestinian uprising, a year and a half later and peace negotiations five years after that.

John Mack writes, "Groups that have suffered repeated injuries in their own national experience rarely seem able to show much empathy for the suffering of other peoples." Mack calls this the "egoism of victimization." With respect to Jews, victimized for millennia, many of their number have in fact been able to empathize with other victims in many parts of the world. But some Jews, including many of those whose policies have often governed Israel, have tended to concentrate almost exclusively on their own victimization. Speaking generally, Mack continues, "By this dynamic one's own victimization is experienced as of overriding importance, and there is little empathy spared for the suffering of another people."[28] Mack refers to

> the apparent unwillingness of victimized peoples to surrender their victim status. . . . [G]roups who have internalized centuries, or even millennia, of historically confirming experience as victims and mourners . . . may unconsciously perpetuate the victim state to reap the benefits and justifications which accrue from being wronged and, in turn, from perceiving other peoples as responsible for these wrongs.[29]

Empathy means not only feeling into the feelings of another person, it also means accepting the feelings in oneself that correspond to them. There are at least two implications in the prospect of that settler allowing herself to acknowledge the humiliation, hatred, fear, and pain of her Palestinian counterpart: feeling her connection to those issues in her neighbor and facing those same issues in herself. In both cases, she would have to move beyond the obvious pleasures of adversary victory. She would need to deal with her own pain. How can she, how can Jews, effectively come to terms with the suffering, powerfully kept alive in memory and ritual, of millennia of insults and barbarities?

I cannot help but wonder, seeing some West Bank settlers with a fervent sense of mission, if the settlement policy of the Israeli government arose, among other meanings, as a collective defense against the pains of Jewish history familiar to so many Jews: the destruction of the Temples and the dispersion of Jews by the Babylonian and Roman conquerors in ancient times; the vast annihilations of the Crusades, the Inquisition, and the Holocaust; the pogroms, the expulsions, the accusations and persecutions of the past 2,000 years. Many Jews identify that pain with the role of passive victim. As if in counterpoint, settlement is very active. The enthusiastic settler, like many other people, forgoes introspection in favor of vengeance and action. The alternative, reflecting on pain, arouses the pain again, which may be experienced as too much to bear. Anger is a reaction to pain repressed, pain not adequately addressed and released.

A minority of Jewish settlers are in Gaza and the West Bank, which settlers prefer to call by its ancient name of Judea and Samaria, for religious ideological reasons (God, they believe, wants Jews to live there) or secular nationalist reasons (strength and appropriation are the way of the world; finally Jews are strong enough to do what other peoples have done for eons). Most settlers are there simply because of cheap real estate. For many years, government policy determined that less new housing would be built in Israel than in the occupied territories and that such housing would be heavily subsidized by the Israeli government so as to encourage resettlement on ancient Jewish lands or colonization of Palestinian lands, depending on one's point of view. Either way, settlement offers a two-step denial of the history of pain. First is the commitment to settlement without regard for the feelings and lives of Palestinians who already live there, some as refugees from Israel itself. Second is the decision to dwell upon fresh pain only when settlers are inconvenienced, wounded, and killed in clashes between them and resident Palestinians. Past pain is denied, then it is shifted from past to present and is dealt with as if insult or injustice in the present represents the entire range of issues that need to be managed, as if the self played no part in creating the pain it now suffers.

The process is not only one of disavowing earlier pain through getting even somehow with history and one's victimization, but also of disavowing empathy. Many settlers recognize that few people have empathized with Jews and conclude that Jews are under no obligation to empathize with anyone else. When Israelis point out that the great liberal Western democracies of the United States and England did nothing to end the Holocaust, did nothing to destroy the death camps, refused Jewish refugees during the war, and shunned the few tens of thousands of Jewish survivors, they are speaking truth. But that line of reasoning also leads them to defensiveness, denial, and continued suffering.

Empathy is not simply an ethical injunction, or a "nice" way of being human. Empathy is crucial in the process of moving beyond the debilitating effects of one's own suffering and in living in emotionally gratifying connection with other people. The refusal to empathize is a subtle, convoluted way of prolonging one's own hurt and one's own isolation from humanity, or what some call the "collective self," as if the person does not feel really entitled to advance beyond hurt and one's physical boundaries.

Pain's source can originate outside the self, as in the suffering caused countless Jews for millennia, but it can also be internal, as in guilt for mundane acts, desires, fantasies. To take a common example, a child feels guilty when, enraged, it wishes a parent's death. Not able to recognize the normality of the wish or to articulate it to more experienced others who could help absolve feelings of guilt, the child represses the wish and lets it fester in feelings of unspecific discomfort. The child's cultural context directs how the discomfort is translated into guilt for other deeds, including deeds not one's own, like the collective suffering of humankind.

If the normal guilt the child feels is prolonged indefinitely, it becomes neurotic guilt. In the treatment of neurosis, the therapist empathizes with the client and communicates through recognizing cognate experiences in his or her own life with which, presumably, the therapist has come to terms. Correspondingly, the client comes to health in part through empathizing with the therapist and trying on feelings perceived there. The client can feel the therapist's participation in the guilt. By empathizing with the other empathizer's empathy, the client can thus, by choice, recognize that guilt for an ancient, innocent thought is not unique after all (a misperception the inexperienced child is apt to take for granted) and that it does not warrant the relentless, continuing punishment of neurosis.

To put it another way, the client has the opportunity to identify with the therapist as someone who seems in good command of his or her life and emotions and who is like the client in basic, crucial ways. Part of that process of identification is empathically feeling into the therapist's feelings.

In therapy, ordinarily both parties are committed to the client's well-being. In this respect, therapy formalizes, though without full reciprocity, the routine experience of friendship; indeed, therapy seems useful when the mutuality, empathy, and support in friendship are not sufficient to help someone through crisis. The mutuality of therapy and friendship is, of course, the opposite of adversary encounters. Thus therapy, although an exceptional circumstance by design, offers an alternative model for how people can relate to each other. I believe the liberating potential of therapy includes applying the empathic model outside the clinic, intimacy, and friendship, to all relationships structured as adversarial. This calls of course for a vast change in orientation in nearly all institutional behavior.

Empathy and Projection

Empathy is the inverse of projection. In the latter process, people attempt to rid themselves of unwanted feelings by denying them in themselves and attributing them to other people. The aftermath of projection is distance, whereas the effect of empathy is feeling common humanness and therefore also closeness.

In projection, one attributes one's own feeling to someone else while denying it in oneself. In empathy, one allows oneself to feel and admit the feeling one identifies in someone else. The process is a loop. In order to feel the feeling one identifies in someone else, one has to be aware of one's own experience of that feeling. To empathize means to be able to accept that feeling in the other and, as well, in oneself.

Imagine an adult babysitting for a child who has a nightmare. Through empathy and his own memories of childhood terrors, he comforts the child and helps her come to terms with her fear. He explains that he knows how terrifying it is to have a nightmare, and can invite the child to talk about the nightmare's imagery and feelings, all of which will be acceptable to the empathizing adult. In helping the child cope with her fears, the adult can not only recall such feelings in his own history, he can opt to reexamine them, renegotiate the ways he handles them, perhaps even enjoying a new insight into resolution of the pain caused by the memories.

But suppose the adult angrily demands that the child return to bed, or ridicules her anguish. Her problem touches a raw nerve of unresolved pain in the grown-up and his corresponding inability to deal with the fears that empathy would allow to surface.

Lloyd deMause identifies three ways in which an adult can relate to children:

> (1) He [sic] can use the child as a vehicle for projection of the contents of his own unconscious (projective reaction); (2) he can use the child as a substitute for an adult figure important in his own childhood (reversal reaction); or (3) he can empathize with the child's needs and act to satisfy them (empathic reaction).[30]

DeMause claims that the empathic mode developed in Western culture in this century. The capacity of adults to empathize with children is a part of the process by which full humanization becomes possible. When parents make their children into their adversaries and vice versa—as some of them sometimes do—the parents unwittingly reveal their own failures to come to terms with qualities they long for—like spontaneity in joy and rage—that they were somehow forced to repress in their own childhood years.

When parents empathize with children, they can transcend temptations to act as if children are adversaries; they can recognize clear boundaries and accept the child as a separate being with separate needs. They can also end the temptation to confuse the child with the parent's own self (by projective identification) or to confuse the child with the parent's own parents (reversal reaction), with whom the parent may want to get even. Acting in the empathic mode means, then, not attributing anything to the child that is not really there.

For adults to empathize with children means to lay the groundwork for mutuality in the larger culture as well as in the family. When the adults are more familiar with adversarialism than mutuality, this is a problem. Yet it can be surmounted, even though the effort can be enormous to try to undo the habit of adversarialism. I am, for example, used to arguing, but since working on the ideas in this book, I have begun, when someone tries to pick a fight, not to feel like engaging in it. I can feel the other person's passion for arguing and remember how much I used to invest in trying to "win" such conflicts. Sometimes, I just say I don't feel like fighting, and that ends it. I rarely ask, "Why do you want to fight over this?" or "Can we talk about what you are feeling right now?" Such responses would bring me further along in the mutuality process I am trying to develop.

Empathy allows feelings to be shared, aired, relieved by being said. But cultural taboos against opening up such conversation, except in intimacy and friendship, remain strong. Sometimes I just go ahead with the argument and then later wonder what the point of it was and why I accepted the adversary terms of it.

For many people, keeping others away by fighting feels safer than inviting them to join in feeling emotions in their complexity, variety, and intensity. Fighting is protection against vulnerability, against unconsciously anticipated pain; it means ignoring the liberation of releasing pain and joining with another who can acknowledge and accept it.

In empathy, one recognizes distress, joy, any condition in another person and allows oneself to face the corresponding feelings in oneself. To do so means to enjoy access to the full range of one's feelings. If that is defined as a major criterion of adulthood, then the species as a whole, and societies as subunits of the species, have yet to achieve it in broad, useful ways.

Opposition of individuals and groups to each other preserves the isolation of the self on the assumption that the self really cannot handle all its feelings. This misconception of ego and reality is understandable in the child and tragic in the adult. As society has evolved so far, it has not only permitted children to perpetuate the misconception, but it has created institutions that embody that unfortunate decision and that even allow a tacit feeling of community with others who have made the same decision.

A small example comes to mind of everyday difficulties of empathizing. I usually try to understand my students' points of view and their struggles when discussing their difficulties with class materials; one of the joys of teaching is the occasional moments of true mutuality that happen in and out of the classroom, with students with whom I share interests in any number of topics. But occasionally I lose that perspective. One day I met individually with two students on papers I recommended be rewritten. The class was large, and I did not know the authors personally. Although I made a supportive comment or two on their papers, I mainly addressed unclear and inaccurate statements and did so a bit harshly. In talking with both students, I came to appreciate and have a better feeling for their struggles to understand the material.

When reading a student's paper, a teacher can easily lose sight of the person groping toward understanding. The grading system, ostensibly an objective measure of performance that informs people how they are doing, focuses attention on the paper and away from the striving student. Rather than empathize with their attempts, I sometimes project onto such students as these two, my own unclarity of writing and fuzziness of understanding and then take pleasure of some perverse sort in coming down hard on them. I believe the comments I made on the two students' papers were fair and accurate, but I realized that on one, I had been unnecessarily hurtful. I had decontextualized the paper and reacted to it without regard for the author's reality. Neglecting his feelings, I did not set a comfortable tone for our discussion; I was more punitive than useful and imagined that the student felt he had to endure the conversation rather than learning from it, in a kind and friendly way, how to think and write more clearly.

Compare this with Israelis decontextualizing Palestinians' anger, acts of violence, and national aspirations, and with anti-Semites' decontextualizing Jewish strivings for sovereignty and security and historic reasons for living in homogeneous communities. Compare it too with housed people decontextualizing the panhandling of the homeless and with well-off people decontextualizing the agonies and anger of the poor.

Refusal and reluctance to empathize do not imply ill will or inhumaneness; they suggest that for some people, empathy cannot be engaged in without fear of overdoing it, of feeling too much for another person in pain. The fear is of stepping over the line of empathy into identification that blurs what is in some ways a boundary between self and other. It is one thing to open oneself up to another's suffering and to allow oneself to work further on one's own. But one can fear not having the resources to master the pain in the other or in oneself and to be able to move on from it. One can also fear not having the strength to maintain separateness even while connecting with another, of falling into the other's pain and not being able to leave it behind when one decides to move on. Narcissists hold onto their sense of a separate self by a tenuous refusal to empathize with others; so fragile are the self boundaries of narcissists that they unconsciously fear merging with others.[31] It is beyond the scope of this book to examine how such fragility arises and persists. But a fuller study of the role of empathy in mutuality will need to address this issue.

Bad feelings can be most fully relieved when recognized and accepted by other people. This happens in love, good parenting, good therapy, and good friendship. Drugs, alcohol, nicotine, and other numbing devices like compulsive television viewing and compulsive consuming all provide ways of not revealing feelings to other or self, of trying to stifle rather than deal with them.

Problems in empathizing can themselves be empathized with, so that people who seem unable or unwilling to empathize need not feel rejected or vilified. I have found that sometimes women who have freed up empathic responses to other women are reluctant to acknowledge that men who are not very good at empathizing are not necessarily stupid, craven, or evil. It is the adversary assumption, I believe, that discourages such women from empathizing with the common male difficulty in empathizing. Refusal to empathize, like perpetuating the projection of denied parts of the self onto others, can be interrupted only by a fuller understanding of these processes and of ways to experiment with undoing them.

The delight and fullness of allowing oneself the broadest possible range of feelings have profound implications for fulfillment in relationships and in institutions. They are also crucial for coming to peace with oneself. Recognizing and respecting the humanity of the other is, finally, contingent on recognizing and respecting one's own humanity. The liberation of one, as has been said, is a precondition for the liberation of all. Empathy is crucial to this entire project.

Reappropriating the Self

A human being is part of the whole, called by us "universe." A part limited in time and space. He [sic] experiences himself, his thoughts and feelings as separated from the rest—a kind of optical delusion of his consciousness. This delusion is a kind of prison for us, restricting us to our personal desires and to affection for a few persons nearest us. Our task must be to free ourselves from this prison by widening our circle of compassion to embrace all living creatures and the whole nature in its beauty. Nobody is able to achieve this completely, but the striving for such an achievement is, in itself, a part of the liberation and a foundation for inner security.

—Albert Einstein,
New York Times, March 29, 1972

It is really a thought that built this portentous war establishment, and a thought shall also melt it away.

—Ralph Waldo Emerson,
"War"

this concerns me. if it takes our whole life to be know ourselves, and we must know ourselves to emphathize and must empathize to be mutualistic... how can one expect the world to achieve muctuality if we cannot individually?

The Child in the Self

In his films *Close Encounters of the Third Kind* and *E.T.*, writer and director Steven Spielberg suggests that kindness, rather than ferocity, may inhere in the "alien." As if he grasped the global dimension of our current crises, Spielberg chooses the planet as his focus of analysis rather than the state, the people, a movement, or an ideology. Rejecting a common science-

161

fiction formula of humans facing outer space enemies, he favors a vision of the other as potential friend.

In *Close Encounters*, Earth people greet an extraterrestrial ship with a musical pentad duplicating the ship's signal to earth. The space vessel responds with the original pentad and increasingly complex variations.

It is customary, in this genre, for aliens to be greeted by grim-looking, jaw-clenched, fully armed men fearful of losing family, honor, and planet. But in *Close Encounters*, Spielberg chooses another tack. In an especially compelling moment of the film, as the space object approaches there are no insignia or guns in sight, just ordinary-looking people in ordinary clothes and scientists in white coats. By recognizing what is likely a widespread wish to end isolation and discord, *Close Encounters* transmits to the audience a sense of anticipation and a longing to connect with something larger and transhuman. Playfulness and spirituality come together in this movie; that is, perhaps, part of its charm.

The news is not simply the aliens' presence, it is their character; something amicable out there is trying to talk with us openly, musically. Spielberg suggests that speech may not be the most effective way to make contact. At the beginning of life, children respond to the tone and timbre of adults' voices, not to the content of their words. Rhythm in voice as well as music echoes the prenatal cadence of the mother's heartbeat. Although music can also frighten, and although there is not yet a psychology of music that would explain why the pentad in *Close Encounters* is compelling, something about it clicks. One can think of the role of music in sustaining African Americans' hopes and dignity throughout slavery and beyond, in defining youths' objections to war and duplicity, and in regularly stirring audiences in religious and political ceremonies. By his spin on music in this film, Spielberg hints at the liberating possibilities of moving past some of the constraints of spoken language.

The delicacy of childlike space visitors and their graceful, soft movements contrast with the roughness of military personnel earlier removing residents from the area around the mountain on which the spaceship lands. The occasional use of army and police is strained, almost apologetic, half-heartedly mimicking the usual machismo marshalled to "greet" strangers from space. But the mimicry is faint. We see no artillery, no tanks, no helmet and shield-bearing agents of the state ready to fend off crazed, flesh-seeking killers from beyond. We do not even see a gun. The strange is benevolent rather than hostile, fragile instead of menacing, gentle not ferocious. Although Spielberg suggests no politics other than contempt for conventional authority, particularly that of parenthood, or perhaps because of that, the film presents the possibility of the other as accepting and acceptable, at a time (1977) when the customary demonizing of political enemies begins to be in trouble. If the United States needed time to relinquish the adversary assumption about the

Soviet Union, the film offers a way to imagine the other in a liberating light.

At a deeper level, outer space is a convenient metaphor for inner space; delight in the attractive mystery of the other is ultimately the discovery of hitherto hidden parts of the self.

Spielberg does essentially the same thing in *E.T.* There too, an alien is warm, nice, and in some ways superior, not menacing. Little E.T. is odd-looking and cute, perhaps reminding viewers of their discomfort with vulnerable and knowing childlike aspects of themselves. Although seemingly weak— E.T. is homesick, clumsy, and scared—he has hidden powers that enable him to heal with a touch and communicate extraplanetarily.

He also, where engaged appropriately, communicates brilliantly with an earthling. E.T. and Eliot, the ten-year-old fatherless boy who befriends him, are drawn to each other in their common condition of loneliness and neediness. "Through an exhaustive series of trial-and-error efforts, we see E.T. and Eliot striving to reach, engage, and understand one another, with the ultimate achievement of an interactive mutual empathy."[1] The relationship that builds between the two is a condensed model of empathy as it evolves between child and mother.[2]

Both stories suggest that the seemingly strange other is needed on earth. The smallness and innocence of the space creatures, their heads quite large in proportion to their bodies, could remind one of fetuses in their full potential, and perhaps wise children, as earthlings' possible saviors. The star child at the end of Kubrick's *2001: A Space Odyssey* comes to mind. Spielberg hints that release from oppressive adult authority may lie in something childlike. He seems to be saying, Look not to technology and domination but to the child unexpressed, to learn of liberation and how to gain it. Freud had the same idea. And we may recall the biblical notion that a child shall lead us.

Spielberg does less well with destructive parts of self: they appear as terrorizing sharks from the ocean or malevolent dinosaurs from the primeval past. The depth, water, and time metaphors suggest he is on the right track, of looking inward, but he continues to locate the self's destructiveness outside, and proposes mastering it in conventional macho ways. Even in *Schindler's List*, destructiveness is identified only with Nazis.

Deprojection

If people are ever to renounce the adversary compulsion, they must learn how to accept estranged parts of themselves—anger, contempt, jealousy, rage, and other such feelings people are taught to deplore and even to deny in themselves and instead to attribute to other people and censure in them. By dedemonizing other people, one can welcome them as partners rather than rivals in organizing the world. Adversarialism not only demands projection of the self's unsavory parts onto others; *it also encourages projection outward of inhibited altruism.* The macho strong repress their tenderness and compassion just as New Age gentle souls deny their tyrannical, intolerant tendencies. So much of the hippie and New Age cultures seems inauthentic to many people because by disavowing the self's cruel, angry leanings, hippies and New Agers *are* inauthentic. The reverse is true of mainstream macho culture. George Bush, Deng Xiao Ping, and Saddam Hussein are just as inauthentic as many flower children in that such world figures, at least in their public behavior, do not express their caring, tender inclinations. That this is normative reveals the larger culture's grounding in the adversary paradigm, which dictates that life-destroying impulses are more acceptable in politics than life-enhancing ones. It also bespeaks adversary insistence on binary, either-or formulations rather than inclusive, both-and ones.

"Reappropriating the self" means reacquiring what has been lost or denied in socialization as either too odious or too heroic to be acceptable to most people. Retaking all the self's characteristics helps liberate the self from the burden of its lies, the burden of attributing to others and impugning or overadmiring there what rightfully belongs to the self. Once one takes responsibility for the full self, one can choose how to engage each of its aspects. Rage can explode into racism and environmental abuse, or it can energize determination to replace damaging social forms with life-enhancing ones. Honestly felt idealism can fuse with that energy in successful public action. The task is to reappropriate all of one's humanness. This means not seeing the self as tainted—inferior in its badness that denies its goodness. This also means not seeing the self as sainted—superior in its goodness that denies its badness.

To shift primary emphasis from adversary relations to mutuality, the self can "deproject" what it attributes to the other that is actually in itself. Deprojection means recognizing in oneself qualities one finds objectionable in others. Instead, for example, of scorning individuals or groups as slothful, and distancing myself from them, I can use my perception of sloth in others as a way of identifying it in myself. Through empathy, I can feel for what sloth is in them and find ways to cope with it in myself. I will thus identity with others by admitting what we have in common instead of pretending myself superior to them.

Projection is separative, while identification is integrative. It enables me to feel akin to others through recognizing parts of myself in them, and vice versa. Deprojection opens the way to rehumanization. Recognizing what I share with those I see as slothful allows me to experience them and myself as fully human.

When, despite Reagan's sabre-rattling, U.S. media began showing daily life in the Soviet Union in the 1980s, it became possible for people here to appreciate their common humanness with people who for decades had been demonized. It was a revelation to see Soviet citizens going to school, waiting for buses, brushing their teeth. With developments in the Israeli-Palestinian peace process, however hesitant and ambiguous as of this writing, something analogous may be under way.

Reappropriating the Past

Much of the self is lost in the course of normal socialization or through idiosyncratic neurotic processes. Some psychotherapies help people examine personal histories to locate roots of current problems. It is, for example, recognized that many physically abused children later abuse their own children. It appears less widely accepted that many people emotionally abused as children later abuse their own children emotionally.

One gains nothing by accusing such people or their parents of evil or immoral behavior. One gains much in locating what lies behind decisions to do unto others that which one has hated having done unto oneself.

In both physical and emotional abuse, the central issue is hurt. The integrity of the body, the integrity of the psyche, the integrity of the soul are at stake.

Excuses for hurting others—that children have to be broken like wild animals in order to become social, or that obedience is the highest good in society—are rationalizations. They are exercised by people who compulsively recreate their own early abuse, this time as active rather than passive members of an abuse system, or by people thoughtlessly accepting the norms of some part of their society.

Think of violence that has until recently been taken for granted in our society: people who batter partners and children; soldiers and police who beat prisoners; politicians and military officers who revel in claims that the enemy is "beaten" or "only understands the language of force"; bureaucrats who punish the poor, the homeless, the derelict; teachers who humiliate children; professors who ridicule students and colleagues with whom they disagree; men who take out anger from many sources on women, homosexuals, children, foreigners, and others; women who undermine other women in pursuit of goals like career, marriage, and public office and who undermine men whom they see specifically or generally as having hurt them; parents who thwart their children's curiosity and their warm, caring impulses; religious leaders who instill guilt and doubt in their followers rather than nurturing joy and compassion.

It is one of the tragic functions of socialization to encourage people to forget (by suppressing—willfully forcing from consciousness, or repressing—unconsciously removing from consciousness) hurts felt to be unbearable. They return in disguised form as powerful but mysterious impulses that allow for brutalizing familiar and unfamiliar people alike, in contexts all the way from the nuclear family to international economics and politics. When I see politicians dedicating themselves to destroying other politicians, I think not only of the norms of their trade, but also of individuals who must either have known terrible hurt in early years or have accepted their culture's norms of adversarialism without any questions.

It is understandable, if sad, that people learn in our society to sentimentalize their childhoods. "Family values" has come to mean a romantic notion of health, solidity, and integrity in the nuclear family. Those who advocate "family values" do so as if nuclear families are pristine nurturers of goodness whose program had somehow come undone from recent outside pressures; in truth, nuclear families commonly, even if not universally, spawn jealousy, hatred, confusion, resentment, and wrath to the point of abuse that appears to cut across class, race, and ethnic lines. The nuclear family offers some children a loving beginning in the world; it offers others a cruel, tormented initiation. It brings to most people a complex mixture of those two modes.

A hallmark of fanciful rhetoric about the nuclear family is the avoidance of its destructiveness, both latent and expressed; but the avoidance is romantic, not malevolent. A hallmark of rhetoric critical of the nuclear family is denial of its virtues. This denial, like the romantic avoidance, is not pernicious but rather suggests the same problems of puzzlement, confusion, and fear of facing the realities of one's early years. If society has much at stake in avoiding such realities, there must be a reason: not the machinations of the powerful but rather a shared covert fear of re-encountering the misery of early years. The obstreperous child often responds to hurt in a sadly cruel (to self or others or both) but understandable way. And thus with the obstreperous adult as well.[3] Although the Gulf War cannot be reduced to a contest between two men early victimized by violence,[4] that background to their behavior is surely consequential.

Freud suggests that reappropriating the self includes a very difficult process of recovering events and feelings from childhood. Many methods of psychotherapy allow this kind of introspection, and people who have engaged in them know how slow and uncertain they can be. I know less about meditation but know that meditators often let themselves recognize feelings, whatever they are, and learn how to allow the feelings not to overwhelm or undo them.

Coming into the self's present includes linking it with the past, and that goes beyond family to groups and culture. In 1972, I first visited Masada, an Israeli site where 1,900 years earlier a thousand Jews retreated from mighty Roman armies in a last-ditch effort to avoid defeat after Jerusalem and the

Temple had been destroyed. This remaining handful of free people lived for three years on a hilltop provisioned with food and water. Eventually the Romans built an earthen ramp to the top of Masada and overcame the Jews' resistance. Rather than suffer enslavement and exile by the victors, the Jews made a suicide pact. Men killed their wives and children and then turned their swords upon each other. A few women and children hid and survived to tell the tale.

I was moved by the story and the site. I pondered how extraordinarily stubborn these Jews were. Then came an unexpected insight about my own stubbornness, which has both enabled me to persevere on projects until their completion and also has prevented me from being more spontaneous and flexible. After visiting Masada, I thought how the two most stubborn people I knew other than myself were my parents. In them too, stubbornness was both advantage and limit. And then I realized this was not just my own idiosyncratic problem or a peculiar family one; it was located in a tradition of a people who in the Bible are referred to as "stiff-necked," which I take to mean both rigid and stubborn. Whatever the survival value of those attributes—how else could Jewish identity maintain itself in two thousand years of diaspora?—they were also hell to cope with. My own fascination with Jewish history and culture has been in part an effort to learn enough about that problematic part of myself that I need not succumb to its frequently destructive wiles.

One way to reappropriate oneself is to retrieve one's story in its several dimensions, including social class. As a son of a lower-middle-class family, I realized that the confidence I envied in other children often—not always—reflected financially secure homes. That envy later turned into a critique of social class and its depriving many people of modest means of confidence and pleasure who are as entitled to them as anyone else.

Some African Americans reach back to their histories in this country and Africa to learn about themselves as fully as they can. Others, like many upwardly mobile people, disparage their past and identify with powerful individuals and groups whom they hope to join and with whom, intentionally or not, they are likely to abuse other people. Thus identifying with the aggressor, upwardly mobile people frequently do not let themselves face the humiliations and brutalities of their class, race, ethnic, and gender histories. I do not mean that people familiar with their past necessarily integrate it helpfully into their present. In fact, some people use it for the opposite purpose. I am made uncomfortable by fellow Jews who dwell on the Holocaust and Jewish victimization not to come to terms with its many-layered meanings but to justify self-pity, self-absorption, and the neglect of other people's suffering. Corresponding processes are likely common to all victim peoples.

A healthy society, one in which reappropriating the self would be a major project, would routinely provide contexts in which people examine their pasts. Discussions in classrooms, friendship and neighbor groups, associations at places of worship and places of work could evolve as either self-led or conducted by trained facilitators helping people connect their present lives with their personal and group histories. It is a struggle for many to come to terms with the U.S. concept of superindividualism, which tends to wrench people from feelings of real connections with others, in the long-time idealization of the solitary cowboy or adventurer—more recently that of the "successful" entrepreneur who is somehow self-sufficient rather than pathetically alone.

I interpret TV talk shows as revealing people's desires to know themselves, as well as, for many, pleasures in seeing people worse off than they. Many of the guests are marginal people who behave in melodramatic ways, rather than representative of people with ordinary problems. Sensationalistic though many stories and hosts' styles may be, there is likely a kernel there of wishes for self-knowledge and liberation from troubling behavior.

Good camera work often shows the complete absorption of talk show audience members in the stories of people who act out what most of us limit to fantasies or forbid to enter our consciousness at all. If as a society we are going to discover roots of our joys and sorrows in order better to cope with them, it makes sense to start at the edges, pay attention to extreme cases, such as bigamists, incest survivors, and people who have had sex-change operations. It is not just a matter of voyeurism; fascination with extreme behavior suggests that we see it as analogous our own troubled behavior, and that we desire, however unconsciously, to come to terms with the fullness of our varied inclinations. Most people are taught not to do or even want that, and many lack ways to proceed with support and friendly concern.

When talk shows, alternately, present people with nonspectacular problems, viewers gain the chance to explore familiar issues in ways that allow more than just gaping and tsk-tsking their way through a program. This effort has long been accomplished in popular advice columns like Dear Abby and Ann Landers. Perhaps letter writers and readers look to advice columnists for comfort and practical advice. When they get it, it is, interestingly, usually in the mutuality mode. This suggests a desire for advice about how to be mutualistic.

Reappropriating Body

It is natural to enjoy one's physical being; thinking ill of it and feeling bad about it is learned. Obsessions with looks reflect not only admiration of the aesthetically advantaged, as it were, but also subtle self-disparagement.

Involvement in spectator sports means, among other things, vicarious thrills through projective identification with well-trained, graceful, powerful athletes' bodies that seem to be superior to one's own.

Body dissatisfaction is so profitable that entire industries, such as diet, body-building and fitness, cosmetics, clothing, and commercialized sport make money from belittling the body. These business pursuits would be in peril were people to reappropriate their bodies and enjoy them without consumerist tinkering.

Losing pleasurable touch with one's body is a deleterious effect of the Cartesian notion that thinking defines the self. Sadly, much of education promotes this view. A healthy athletics program in schools and universities would emphasize finding forms of satisfying body expression in such varied traditions as dance and Asian body disciplines as well as athletics. Learning skills, grace, and confidence in movement would correspond in importance to learning skills of literacy, numeracy, and analysis.

In much of modern medicine, the body is treated "objectively" when not functioning normally. A deviant, alternative tradition sees the body as part of a complex system of emotions, ideas, spirit, and body feelings. It is these together than define the self and make possible an integrated sense of the self. In a healthy society, obsessive judgments and comparisons about bodies and faces would give way to natural pleasure in one's physical self as well as one's personality, character, and spirit. Were it used with an eye toward liberation rather than diversion and profits, television could discuss such matters in helpful ways. Educators could help teachers respect themselves so fully that they would encourage corresponding pleasure in their students.

People can consider how they feel about their bodies and their appearances. Where they feel lacking, they can ask others for help in determining whether the perceived lack is realistic. One whose body is flabby can turn to exercise. But one can also learn whether one is neurotically hard on oneself in obsessing over flaws and dismissing acceptance and praise as untrustworthy or misguided. One can experiment with diet. Some people avoid meat. Some feel better when they leave alcohol, caffeine, and sugar behind. Others do not. The point is that media could move beyond seductive advertising, stories about faddish diets, and endless cooking programs and cooking paraphernalia infomercials to discussing the role of food in self-perceptions and in health.

Given the place of sex in most people's experiences of their bodies, how wonderful it would be to move toward an ethic of frank discussion of its problems and its pleasures. Our society's preoccupation with sex indicates, among other things, yearning for free and open pleasure in thinking about bodies, talking about bodies, enjoying bodies, facing and dealing with problems with bodies. Complex matters of shame and guilt, confusion about lust, rage, and exuberance, children's natural delight in their physical being and parents' problems in accepting and encouraging that, all call for open discussion and shared struggle to surmount archaic, life-inhibiting taboos often passed on in media, religion, and families. Media fascination with the sexual behavior of celebrities suggests misplaced attention to substitutes for readers' and viewers' selves. Everyone's adequacies and inadequacies would better be addressed openly and directly in a society committed to reappropriation of the body.

Reappropriating Feelings

For years I have struggled, often reluctantly, sometimes angrily, frequently in confusion, with how to stop denying various parts of myself. Rather than dismissing someone with a feeling of contempt for his rigidity, for example, I try—sometimes successfully, sometimes not—to locate my own rigidity and work on reducing it. Correspondingly, when I feel admiration and envy for another person's confidence, generosity, or whatever, beyond a certain point I realize I am struggling to release locked-up feelings about those matters in myself. Real freedom means not only accepting the less pleasant parts of myself but the more attractive ones as well. Socialization tends to discourage comfort with emotions at the further reaches of both what is considered desirable and what is considered bad.

The dangers of mislocating one's struggles onto others appear in the classroom as well as elsewhere. Control is one of the leading unacknowledged issues in almost every context. Students are subject to enormous degrees of control by teachers who design the content of the class and its flow. It is up to them whether and how to mix lectures with discussion, whether to encourage students to work alone or in groups, how to assign grades, how to respond to students' insights, confusion, and delights. As part of the rarely recognized agenda of the classroom, teachers, from grade school through university, prepare students for being controlled by employers, political authorities, and mates. This enables the teachers, of course, also to sidestep struggling with their own discontents about being controlled.

By looking inward and trying to work with what is there, one approaches a new ethic in relating to the self as well as to others. Talk about feelings has been institutionalized into various systems of counseling and psychotherapy, a profession that tends to be politically conservative; most therapists avoid issues of broad social discontent and possible social reconstruction. This is a leaning not inherent in the therapeutic project itself. Freud caught on in the United States when the popular and professional cultures "Americanized" the unconscious, by draining it of its radical social under-thrust.[5] Most of the more socially perceptive, politically radical, and daring

European psychoanalysts dropped their counterestablishment, or socialist, political orientations in the course of becoming refugees in the United States.[6]

Psychoanalysts in the United States have devoted themselves mainly to adapting individuals to society rather than vice versa. Because most patients have money, many have little interest in social change. But analysts could work to reshape the environment to meet the needs of people unhappy in it. Were they to pursue this path, psychoanalysts could become in effect non-violent revolutionaries.[7]

Psychotherapy that satisfies clients teaches that expressing feelings allows comfort with them, which denial and repression make impossible. Understanding that feelings can be examined with other people, that they can be heard and accepted, legitimizes a candor that might be new in history, a candor that would allow even public figures to consider where their personal pain, rage, hope, talents, fears, humiliations, and insecurities fit into their ideas and behavior. Rather than Edmund Muskie being ridiculed for crying in public while running in the presidential primary, it would have been healthy for our society to celebrate his emotional freedom and inquire as to the issue at hand. It was sad also that as a candidate for president, Michael Dukakis had to defend entering therapy to deal with the pain of his brother's death in a bicycle accident. It would have been politically daring of him to question the maturity of anyone who did not struggle—whether or not with professional help—to come to terms with such a tragedy.

Such socialization would best begin in childhood. Benjamin Spock's recommendations for raising children are far more mutualistic than adversarial. He emphasizes the value of "growing up in a loving family—being loved and learning to love in return."[8] Children, he claims, learn in healthy circumstances to be cooperative and likable because they want to be liked. Around the age of three, feelings of enjoyment and affection for other children develop.[9] Daniel Stern writes in detail of the mutuality between mother and child, including the child's early responsiveness to the mother's feelings in healthy circumstances.[10]

Spock criticizes the child-centeredness of much child-rearing, with parents often devoting too much energy to making sure their children's needs are met. He suggests that it is vital that children learn what others, including the community, need from them as well as what the children themselves need.

> I think we've brought up our children not only less ready to do their part in solving the world's urgent problems but actually less happy in the sense of less fulfilled. For human beings, by and large, can only be really happy when they feel they are part of something bigger than themselves and when a lot is expected of them and when they are living up to those expectations.[11]

Spock implies that focusing on one's own feelings to the exclusion of those of other people is a major failing of middle-class socialization and ought to be corrected. Feelings of people with whom one interacts, from parents on outward, are as central to the child's reality as its own.

Philip Rieff sees psychoanalytic therapy as addressing that issue by creating new norms of relationship.[12] All cultures, Rieff reasons, develop means for people to release themselves periodically from the overly harsh constraints that culture imposes on them, for the purpose of conformity to norms and values.[13] Ritual orgies and confession are two examples of these.

In some circumstances, a culture may alter in such a way that more and more of what had been prohibited is now permitted. Bread and circuses substitute for right and duty and even for desire. Spectacle becomes a functional substitute for sacrament. Massive regressions can occur, leading to reckless and violent behavior. At times of impending transition to a new moral order, symbolic forms and their institutional objectifications change their relative weights. Competing symbolisms gather support in competing elites; they jostle each other for priority of place as the organizers of the next phase in the psychohistorical process.[14]

Rieff speculates that the coming normative order will require a new character type (to replace what I am calling the adversary) which he calls the "therapeutic." He sees that contemporary psychotherapies generate norms that contradict dominant ones. Respect for the reality of inner needs, for example, competes with respect for conventional community morality. Rieff points out that these two basic orientations conflict with each other and that neither is dominant.[15] (The condition is reflected in the current split on the abortion issue.) The fluidity of this peculiar situation suggests that "the therapeutic" is positioned to succeed the puritanical, the combative, the exploitative, as the dominant mode of relating in postmodern society.

Rieff suggests that self-fulfillment and the comforts and styles of consumerism are the major components of the emerging character type both East and West.[16] Such a commitment lacks in community orientation, though, and Rieff suggests that that, for the moment, is the way things appear to be.[17]

Building from Rieff, I suggest that the process of paradigm change proceeds dialectically in such a way that the therapeutic provides an antithesis to both the externally defined self of Western "individualism" and the underlying stifling norms of conformity to consumerism and the adversary paradigm. The therapeutic experience of self, others, and the relationship to others and society is a piece of the emerging mutuality paradigm. The modes of behavior that will be congruent with it will draw upon the liberating potential of inner awareness, and the joys of nurturing, caring, and loving within and beyond the nuclear family. Consider how one might go about reappropriating experiences of hurt and rage. Hurting is an unusual word; as a gerund, it means the experience both of being hurt and of causing hurt to others. There is no such ambiguity in revenge. It is a ritual that assumes that hurting can be met properly not by understanding, compassion, empathy, mediation, or anything but hurting in return. As understandable as the emotions of the hurt-and-revenge transaction are, the alternatives we seek might help to harness the seemingly boundless impulse to retaliate and use the energy of the impulse for constructive change rather than destructive action.

For hurt to be accepted by all parties involved, hurters will have to come to terms with what led to their anger and ensuing actions against others. Rituals of forgiveness might develop, and those, lest they become rote and inauthentic, would need to include accepting complex feelings in self and other. Through such rituals and through art, people might see honesty and cleansing portrayed in many appealing ways. Rituals of self-reflection, whether through therapy, art, meditation, or spiritual exercises, would help all parties to face inner and outer components of struggle.

Although anger can be expressed directly against whoever set it off in the present, it must be remembered that much anger that seems situational and present may hark back to early experiences with it. As well as being expressed directly, anger can be used to understand the angry other and oneself, and to conceive of anger as having positive implications. Writing of possibilities of women of different colors overriding their suspicions toward one another, fears, and guilt, Audre Lorde writes, "It is not the anger of other women that will destroy us but our refusals to stand still, to listen to its rhythms, to learn within it, to move beyond the manner of presentation to the substance, to tap that anger as an important source of empowerment."[18]

Lorde sees anger often entwined with guilt in unhelpful ways. She alludes to the common self-flagellation and paralysis of well-meaning, privileged people who are unclear how to act on the discrepancy between their condition and their humane values.

> If [guilt] leads to change then it can be useful since it is then no longer guilt but the beginning of knowledge. Yet all too often, guilt is just another name for impotence, for defensiveness destructive of communication; it becomes a device to protect ignorance and the continuation of things the way they are, the ultimate protection for changelessness.[19]

A culture of recognizing feelings, of accepting responsibility for behavior, of learning to ask for forgiveness, to give it, to receive it, would displace that of hurt/anger/vow-to-vengeance/revenge. The Catholic Church in the confession and Judaism on the Day of Atonement offer some sense of what this is about. Even though for some people such rituals are mechanical and mindless, for others they are genuine ways of coping with troublesome parts of the self.

one is better at empathizing when one is well-read because you have a read understanding of things you have not yet even experienced

The way to move beyond hurt, anger, and revenge is through emotional candor, flexibility, and practicing the honest expression of the self. I can think of two ways of reappropriating feelings of blaming, or mutuality alternatives: In the first, people in conflict can begin by looking at the system by which they usually play out their differences, noticing the presence of a theme of domination, victims, and victimizers. Joint struggle toward redesigning the processes can transform their adversarial feelings into mutual support, empathy, and respect. This mutuality alternative suggests that we find and work with *institutions* that promote mutuality, such as mediation.

The second alternative to blaming is coping with adversary feelings, recognizing the universality of offensive behavior and one's share in it. Talking about specifics of a situation is useful, as is working with literary prototypes. Presumably, as we participate in these alternatives, additional creative options will arise, helping us eventually to renounce blaming altogether.

People who address their own adversarialism learn self-knowledge that affects conversations with lovers, relatives, friends, teachers, students, clergy, therapists, and others who can, often in ritualized ways, invite reflection and inner honesty. They learn to ask: "Why did you say that? What did you mean by it?" "What were you feeling?" "What does that remind you of?"

A small example: For a while, I found a good friend pretentious, annoying, disruptive, contentious, and power-hungry. The irritation I felt became so strong that I considered ending the friendship. But as I contemplated that, I reminded myself that the problem must be in me, not him, as what suddenly seemed unbearable had been his style for years and had not previously bothered me much. Over a period of weeks I performed a painful self-examination. I asked myself, am I also disruptive and power-seeking in ways I do not want to face? For some time, I rejected that possibility. Then one day, with a sinking, somewhat anguished feeling, I remembered a recurring fantasy from my childhood in which I loudly and obnoxiously disrupted orderly proceedings. This pseudo-plan I imagined in Sunday School, at weddings, at family dinners. So powerful were these imaginings that I bore down with all my might to keep from yelling out at the top of my lungs, as I deeply longed to do. I had no specific cry in mind. I just wanted to scream.

I remembered another fantasy, a messianic scheme I was reluctant to abandon. Presumptuous as befits childhood and adolescent plans and visions, I entertained a megalomaniacal fantasy that compensated for some feelings of insignificance. I realized I had never given up the fantasy and that it was time for me to face and come to terms with it. As for control, wanting to control others and loathing others' controlling me is a common package of concerns. As I began examining these memories and issues, my antagonism to my friend dissolved. To my surprise and pleasure I started feeling more tolerant and compassionate toward certain problematic qualities in this friend, other people, and myself. Reflections associated with this work have helped me gain greater control over certain odious judgmental tendencies with which I have struggled for decades.

Reappropriating Altruism

Altruism is considered "unrealistic" in our society.[20] Finding pleasure in working for something beyond the self is not widely understood as gratifying unless, like patriotism, it is in the adversary mode. It is a credit to the power of the adversary paradigm that its justifying rhetoric devalues programs that recognize interests beyond opposition, comfort, and appearances. It is also true that many positive mutual feelings like thrill, exhilaration, and simple fun are reserved for family and friends, and only for "recreation," as if those feelings could not also suffuse school, work, and life in the community.

It takes a stretch to recognize in oneself both Gandhi and Hitler, both Florence Nightingale and Lucretia Borgia, but they are all there. The self is violated in equal measure by denying altruism and by denying destructive inclinations.[21]

Reappropriating the self includes reconnecting with the mutuality already there. It appears in art and social criticism that contrast adversary realities with possibilities of empathy and human connectedness. Some of journalism, social science, and philosophy also point in that direction. With appropriate expressions of mutuality, the task of how to deal with the destructive parts of self will no longer be solved in ersatz fashion through cheap projection and persecution but rather will allow recognition, without harming others, of the less pleasant parts of all selves.

To move toward mutuality, people will have to guard not only against inauthentic versions offered by social movements promoting growth as a commercial endeavor, they will need to realize it lurks in quieter places too. Some people, striving for mutuality because they find it attractive, embrace an inauthentic version in their closest relationships. Joyce Lindenbaum calls "pseudomutuality" (what I call compulsive mutuality) the condition created by couples who pretend they are alike.

> Pseudomutuality is an effort to solve the inevitable problems of separateness and envy. It is an avoidance of "felt difference," and an establishment of a unified front. A kind of exaggerated accommodation develops; one that goes beyond the sort of compromise that is essential in order for any two people to maintain a relationship.[22]

Pseudomutuality is a strained effort to become mutual without working with rage, hatred, and other real emotions that pseudomutualists apparently wish to avoid. The rejection of hippie and New Age harmony and cooperation by the majority of people may well be based on implicit recognition of the confusion between intention and emotional reality that appear so often to characterize and confuse people who try to deny the nastier parts of themselves.

Recognition of common humanity and true emotional complexity allows fulfillment, feeling, and exuberance possible in no other way. When drug experiences are attempts at finding such feelings, they caricature those possible without the aid of chemicals; they imply feelings of futility in the search for the real self in real connections in the real world of real human beings.

The so-called drug crisis in drug-infested societies will likely cease with the end of the predominance of the adversary compulsion that demands feelings of separation and opposition and discourages larger feelings and actions of mutuality. The way to end unhappy dependence on drugs is not through prison sentences for drug dealers, methadone programs, and antidrug advertising. The way to end unhappy dependence on drugs is to create a society where people's joys in daily life are full and reliable enough that drug dependence will no longer attract them.

None of this is to deny that drugs can be used for fun and for "consciousness expansion." Not all drug use is destructive or reckless. But to the extent that drugs are used to numb the hurt, despondent self, then reappropriating the self fully would make such drug use meaningless. Drugs, like alcohol in potential, could be reserved for ceremonial occasions and for times of relaxation and exploration, not, again, to deaden the felt pains of living.

The Restored Child Syndrome

Philip Pomper suggests that leader-follower relations in history are usually based on the model of the father's relationship with the child. Citing Erikson, Pomper considers the mother-child relationship, with its normative mutuality, a better model for containing and ritualizing violence in ways less destructive than those with which we are familiar.[23]

Erikson imagines a mutuality ritual "through which men [sic], equipped with both realism and spiritual strength, can face each other with a mutual confidence analogous to the instinctive safety built into the animals' pacific rituals."[24] If people project their antagonisms outward, then deprojecting is crucial. Parents, for example, frequently take out their frustrations, exasperations, and disappointments on their children. It is a way of expressing their own feelings of victimization and neglect in their lives.

An alternative way of "getting even" is for the parent *to give to the child what the parent needed but was denied.* The parent then "gets back" at her or his own insufficient parents by showing that what was essential but missing is now provided for someone else. In contrast to the battered child syndrome, this could be called the *restored child syndrome.* It corresponds to Erikson's concept of "generativity," by which adults give to younger people (they need not be biological offspring or family members) what they need in ways that fulfill both giver and recipient. Honoring the syndrome would include imagining what it would have been like to be given to properly and then moving from passive recipient of inadequate giving to active giver of adequate giving.

The restored child syndrome could be adapted as a way of moving beyond fear and opposition to connection and empathy with others. It would include renouncing one's own petulance and resentment about childhood disappointments and the failures of elders to behave adequately. It would entail forgiving the insufficiencies of those one has resented and hated. It would move the self to resolve to "get even" by learning the empathic, giving, caring, nurturing skills deficient in the people who have hurt one for whatever reasons in whatever period of one's life. It would become true that, unlike the advertisement that claims that "living well is the best revenge" (against what is left unsaid), living kindly and compassionately would be the best "revenge."

For this potential seed of mutuality to develop, counseling, art, and sensitive media programming could model and inspire understanding the restored child syndrome and ways of realizing it. In the media, this would call for a major shift in content from adversarialism to working seriously on real people struggling in their real lives with real problems. Feelings of hurt, fear, and anger would be explored in friendly settings, where people would be participating from their own experiences, failures, and hopes. People would recognize and respond to each other's feelings, experiences, and aspirations, and see themselves there.

FOURTEEN

ᘒᘓᘔᘍᘕᘖ

Seeds of Mutuality I:
Old Seeds in Old Institutions

Come writers and critics
Who prophesize with your pen
And keep your eyes wide
The chance won't come again
And don't speak too soon
For the wheel's still in spin
And there's no tellin' who
That it's namin.'
For the loser now
Will be later to win
For the times they are a -changin'.
                              —Bob Dylan,
          "The Times They Are A-Changin'"

I believe that mutuality can emerge from the adversary thickets of contemporary institutions—it need not be invented from scratch. Mutuality is already here, as seeds of cooperation, connection, love, and care in institutions familiar to us. Like some good mutant gene, these seeds bear the code of growth into mutuality. The turn of the century and millennium may be their time to flourish. In this and the next two chapters, I examine some places where it is possible to see mutuality already in play, although a fuller listing and view of these seeds of mutuality would be another book. The instances discussed are meant only as examples; readers can undoubtedly think of dozens more.

Mutuality in Everyday Life

Mutuality is of course familiar to everybody but so far lives out its lines in fewer places than does adversarialism. It thrives in pockets of institutions

whose adversary themes are more evident. For example, as cut-throat as relationships may be in many workplaces, there are also joys in colleagueship.
Whatever the color of the collar and whatever the highest degree held, people
sometimes enjoy each other, savor devising projects and learning together,
and create a culture of appreciating work, colleagues, and clients. As gossip is
part of the soul of any workplace, small talk allows that indulgence to shade
over into advice and exploration of personal troubles and triumphs. At its best,
work, even after hours, allows friendship, play, and mutual acceptance of
decency and vulnerabilities.

The family is the primary site of mutuality, even as it is the primary
training ground for adversarialism. "Dysfunctional" families seem unable to
move back and forth between the two modes, but in reasonably functioning
families, feelings of caring, respecting, responding, supporting, loving, and
other such behaviors abound. Early on, the delicate tunings of infants and parents develop mainly in the mutuality mode, or there is trouble ahead for
everyone. Love between consenting adults is, at its fullest, the essence of
mutuality, with its giving and taking, feeling the needs and hurts and hopes of
the other, and emotional and sexual fusion at moments of joy.

Part of the beauty of observing a young child entering into friendship is
seeing the child's ability to extend mutuality skills learned in the family. A
healthy society would be aware of the importance of this transition, for just as the
child learns mutuality first inside the family, then outside, so it eventually can
extend that attitude to groups, locales, society itself, and eventually the Earth.
Good child-rearing and good education would focus on these processes as essential not only for personal satisfaction but for survival of species and planet.

Among the pleasures of team sport is the mutuality of coordinating well
with other players. This is not only a technical feat, it is also a question of feeling respect and enjoyment with teammates. The same is true of groups of
musicians playing together. In music as diverse as jazz and the Indian raga,
performers work within forms that allow them to improvise, based on attune-
ment to other players. That state is emotional and personal, even while it is
embedded in technical competence in musical skills.

Even in nationalism, politics, business, and law, where adversarialism is
the norm, people on the same "side" appreciate the advantages of solidarity
with others. Unfortunately, there are times when potential adversary tensions
among people on the same side are defused by being projected outward onto
"enemies," such that enjoyable mutuality seems contingent on collective
opposition to others. Such scapegoating in the name of solidarity is not
inevitable but is at least in part a consequence of the self depriving itself of
access to its full emotional range. It is that deprivation, I believe, that underlies adversarialism in its compulsive form. It is a loss to those stuck in it. It
would be as if one denied oneself speaking the vowels of one's language and

compulsively limited oneself to consonants, all the while deriding seemingly hateful others as the vowel people.

Mutuality can suffuse everyday life in brief encounters with clerks in stores, receptionists, repair people, and neighbors in the elevator or on the street. In classrooms that work well, teachers and students bask in some degree of mutuality relations with each other. Although these encounters are fraught with possibilities of adversary nastiness, it is not prominent in all of them. Both adversarialism and mutuality suffuse electronic mail (e-mail) relationships; the visual anonymity there likely encourages in some people rather free play of either tendency in the expectation, often met, that the other is similarly inclined. Mutuality in everyday life offers a permanent echo-chamber, as it were, reminding us of its possibility and its potential. It is those echoes that remind us to notice the seeds of mutuality in all institutions, traditional and new.

Seeds of Mutuality in Organized Religion

In many ways, religion incarnates mutuality. Love of God, a Savior, the Pope, preachers, Chassidic rebbes, the Prophet and his successors, Nirvana, Enlightenment, all bespeak yearnings for mutuality relations. The binding together of worshippers depends to some extent on their mutuality feelings for each other and their shared attachment to religious figures and ideas they adore in common.[1]

Mutuality has no interest in hate. It is part of the complexity of much of organized religion, though, that it can celebrate mutuality in theology and enact it in ritual but can also undercut it. The world's religions have, from the beginning, spoken messages of mutuality, but except for deviant side movements, they have operated very much in the adversary mode.[2] To many people, religion means "human sacrifice and scapegoating, fanaticism and persecution, the Christian Crusades and the holy wars of Islam . . . witch hunts in Massachusetts, monkey trials in Tennessee."[3] In their dominant forms, Christianity and Islam envision universal peace based on their victory over other faiths. In its commanding shape in contemporary Israel, Judaism remains exclusivist and parochial. Despite cosmologies stressing interconnectedness, Hinduism and Buddhism also sometimes lend themselves to adversarialism. A Buddhist activist friend points out that Hinduism in India and Buddhism in Cambodia, to cite but two examples, have been used to justify war.[4]

Religion and the Need for Continuity of Vision

It is part of the conceit of revolutionaries to imagine that entirely new institutions can be created. It may be that when revolution fails, it is in part because people enjoy continuity of visions and symbols that revolutionaries dismiss. Resistance to change proceeds partly from fear but also from real attachment to what is familiar even if problematic.

In the modern era, secular movements and institutions, including the nation-state, have attempted to provide organizing, inspiring metaphors to replace those of religions. Visions of the free market as savior, of democracy as empowering, of socialism, of communism, of Aryan superiority run the gamut of pictures of the desirable presented forcefully to populations of nation-states. The failure of all of these visions to speak to yearnings for ethical direction and human respect is probably what accounts for massive returns to religion in the 1980s and 1990s. It is inadequate to see such behavior as reactionary. The yearning for meaning in this sense of comprehensive ethical visions is the theme of Michael Lerner's *The Politics of Meaning*[5] and conferences and movements stemming therefrom.

Although with the Enlightenment religion supposedly went into eclipse, and although secularism defines the political institutions of most industrial societies, religion continues to offer congenial frameworks for celebrating changes in nature and the human life cycle and for meaning in the broadest sense. Proponents of liberating change can better draw on the strengths of religious traditions than dismiss them for their failings.[6]

Religion, though, is often invoked in ineffective ways. Some religious leaders meet the suffering of their flocks from injustice with pleas to "return" to old practices. A past that never was is romanticized along with an assumption that will power, or possibly coercion, is adequate to accomplish the fantasied return. Rather than try to renew earlier *forms* of worship, family, or community, it makes more sense to me to link religious *values* that have inspired people with cooperative institutions rather than competitive ones.

Uneasy tension between the adversary and mutuality paradigms is evident in the three Western world religions. Christianity has promoted war, Inquisition, and superiority throughout much of its history, but in their original forms, Jesus's messages of healing and love were stronger. Jesus attempted to counter what had become rigid and adversarial in Judaism by urging a return to a mutuality message in the Jewish bidding to "Love thy neighbor." This appears to be the intention in his explanation, "Think not that I am come to destroy the law, or the prophets: I am not come to destroy, but to fulfill."[7]

In Western stereotypy, Islam is a religion of Holy War and intolerance. This image is part of the "orientalism" that has painted the Islamic Middle East in an unfavorable light even while romanticizing its sensuousness and exotic glamour.[8] Muhammed was born into a world described by Muslim scholars as barbaric: "Incessant war for supremacy, perpetual internecine strife, combined with the ceaseless wrangling of creeds and sects, had sucked

the lifeblood out of the hearts of nations and the people."[9] It was this fragmentation, this adversary setting, that Muhammed sought to change.

Like all world religions, Islam encompasses messages of both mutuality and adversarialism. Muhammad the adversary is an accessible image to
Westerners, and indeed adversarialism is an integral part of the Muslim tradition, as it is of Judaism and Christianity. Islam both accepts and rejects coercion with regard to religion. In Muhammed's words, "Wilt thou then force
men to believe when belief can come only from God?"[10]

Islam claims the highest stage of virtue as spreading goodness despite
the good or injury inflicted upon the Muslim.[11] Muhammed embodied the
virtue of forgiveness in unconditionally pardoning the murderers of his
daughters.

Judaism shares with Christianity and Islam a historical commitment to
mutuality. The commandments of Judaism are meant to contribute to an ethical, disciplined life. The tenet of *tikkun olam*, the repair and transformation
(literally the "fixing") of the world, is for some a metacommand to act for
peace and social justice in the world (*olam*), through mending and healing
(*tikkun*). Judaism's mutuality is illuminated in Talmudic commentary on such
behavior as responses to enmity, intent to inflict injury, and persecution.[12]

Jewish textual prescriptions for reconciliation, like Gandhi's, recommend control of the urge to hate and acting in a manner in which an enemy
can become a friend. The Torah says, "If you see the ass of one who hates you
lying under its burden, you shall refrain from leaving him with it, you shall
lift it up."[13] A midrash (a Talmudic commentary, often in the form of a story)
addresses the complex dynamic that results in such an encounter:

> When your enemy sees that you came and you helped him, he will say
> to himself, "I thought that he is my enemy. God forbid! If he was my
> enemy he would not have helped me, but if he is my friend, then I am
> his enemy in vain. I will go and pacify him."[14]

Talmudic discussion of intent to inflict injury further clarifies and
asserts Judaism's commitment to mutuality. When confronted by Esau and
four hundred soldiers, Jacob sat down with them to show that he considered
them friends, not enemies. The underlying assumption of Jacob's strategy is
that such an overt expression of faith and love for one intent upon inflicting
injury will appeal to that same sense of love in the opponent and nonviolence
will ensue.[15] The midrash reaffirms its commitment to mutuality in its instruction on persecution, wherein it is advised that as God is always on the side of
the oppressed, suffering must not be inflicted.[16]

All of this is to emphasize the presence of a mutuality alternative to the
adversarialism overwhelmingly apparent in the Pentateuch, the Five Books of

Moses. There, times almost without number, peoples are annihilated entirely, often at God's command. Treachery, hatred, enslavement, betrayal, and other adversary behaviors suffuse this complex sacred text. But not only that. Even in the midst of the adversary worldview, which is prominent in all three Western religions, mutuality remains a kind of beacon, even if the fog before it has not yet fully lifted. Now is the time to bring it into clear focus and elaborate it more fully than it has ever been elaborated before.

Just as the story of Muhammed reveals the intertwinings of adversary and mutuality themes, so does that of David in the Jewish tradition. The same David who "was benevolent to all, saying: 'Even to a murderer as well as to the slain, to a pursuer as well as to the pursued, I shall show kindness'"[17] also said, "How long shall my enemy be exalted over me?"[18]

Like all world religions, Hinduism sometimes contradicts its mutuality prescriptions in its practices. Thus did Nehru claim that India was "the least tolerant nation in social forms while the most tolerant in the realm of ideas."[19] Hinduism, though, like Buddhism, considers all religions as equal paths to the same God and denies that any religion can monopolize salvation.

Buddhism was as much a reaction to Hinduism's contradicting its mutuality tradition as Christianity was to Judaism's doing the same thing. The distortions of Hindu values at the time of Buddha sound like what Jesus objected to in the spiritual rigidity and corruption of the Pharisees. Buddha criticized the structure of authority in Hinduism. By the 5th century B.C., the authority of the Brahmin or priestly caste was being used to rationalize its members' extravagant lifestyles.[20]

By rejecting the adversary ritual of comparing, with which the caste system of Hinduism was rife, Buddha offered an alternative vision of human interconnectedness. He forswore speculation about the supernatural and found little attraction to Brahminic disputations on whether the world had been created, what the upper and lower worlds looked like, and the exact substance that transmigrated after death.[21] As he put it, "greed for views tends not to edification."[22]

As with other world religions, the spirit of Buddhism became partially lost in adversary organization. Pieces of what is essential for human and planetary survival live in all religions, waiting to be synthesized into a whole that is larger than all the institutional parts.

Charlene Spretnak suggests that the Buddhist traditions of introspection and release from unnecessary inner pain, the Native American legacy of comfort and oneness with the cosmos, and the earth- and body-centeredness of Goddess spirituality can combine with the emphases on social justice, social change, and community in Judaism, Christianity, and Islam.[23] She sees these ways as "fully subversive to the monstrous reduction of the fullness of *being* that the Earth community currently faces through the dynamics of an increasingly

manipulative, globalized, consumption-oriented political economy."²⁴ She also
sees them as bases for establishing a new reality proceeding from the "felt connections between the person and the family, the community, the bioregion, the
country, other peoples, other species, the Earthbody, and the cosmos."²⁵

Spretnak offers a vision of a metareligion, interconnecting but not
replacing religions as we have known them so far. A meta-religion, integrating the mutualistic tendencies of the world religions, would be an essential
piece of the emerging world culture I suggest in chapter 17 is under way.

Seeds of Mutuality in Organized Sport: The Slam Dunk

Organized sport combines adversarialism and play, which can be seen
as "any nonutilitarian physical or intellectual activity pursued for its own
sake."²⁶ The pleasure derived from play comes in doing rather than in what has
been done. It is the fun of the activity itself, apart from its outcome, that gives
pleasure to the player. Philip Slater contends that because of its nontotalitarian
structure, play is "democracy in action."²⁷

Johan Huizinga writes of play in his classic *Homo Ludens*: "Into an
imperfect world and into the confusion of life it brings a temporary, a limited
perfection. . . . The least deviation from it 'spoils the game,' robs it of its character and makes it worthless. . . . Play has a tendency to be beautiful."²⁸
Because play can have meaning apart from contest, it can be considered when
noncompetitive as a mutuality ritual.

It is easy to think of organized sport as only adversarial. Alfie Kohn
writes: "But we do not even need to point to the trophies and the money: The
very experience of having beaten someone else is extrinsic to the process
itself. The presence of this reward structure in competition disqualifies it as
play."²⁹ Not every action on the field or in the arena, though, is only adversarial. Deep within organized sport lie seeds that subvert the dominant paradigm. The slam dunk in basketball can be understood in this context as a
moment of play in an otherwise fiercely adversarial contest. Most people can
only dream of the exhilaration and rush of joy that must fill the player at the
moment in which the basketball is slammed down through the hoop. What
does it feel like in mid-air, to be suspended in time, to test the laws of physics?

A ritual that awakens the dormant spirit of mutuality, the dunk combines
play and celebration in athlete and onlooker. Yet as it operates within the
structure of competitive sport, the dunk can not entirely escape the constraints
of adversarialism. The dunker's frequent "In your face!," suggests the dominant paradigm, as does the annual slam dunk "contest" in which the most creative, athletic, and stylistic aerial artists compete for the "honor" of Slam
Dunk Champion.

The ritual of the dunk is nonutilitarian. According to one observer, "The dunk has assumed an importance that far exceeds its role in the game."[30] The act of scoring a basket may be undertaken for winning the game as well as for the individual to bolster his statistics, and the slam dunk is a surer two points than a shot that may bounce off the rim of the basket, but the dunk seems undertaken primarily as a pleasurable end in itself and an act of proud display.

The breakaway dunk, particularly striking, begins when a player intercepts a pass or picks up a loose ball and heads straight to the basket. With no opponent near enough to interfere, the player can be completely uninhibited in choosing how to appear in flight.

For the athlete and spectator the pleasure is primarily derived not from the two points tallied, but from the burst of self-expression and audience participation in the successful dunk. The response is adversarial: the home crowd is ignited, and the visiting one is silenced. The moment of take-off signals a glimmer of brief celebration, a respite from the intense adversary strivings of sport, a moment when athlete and spectator are reminded of a time in their lives when it was considered all right to play, to experience joy at no expense to another.

The dunk transcends team loyalties, geographic sympathies, and the adversary parameters of sport. It is not altogether unique, though. The appreciation in any sport for the move expertly executed—the successful long pass in football, the winning home run in the last half of the last inning in baseball, the brilliant scoring of a goal in hockey or soccer—all partake of admiration for play performed at its highest level as well as for adversary victory. Other traces of play in sport often evoke powerful responses. Willie Mays's basket catch, Mark Fydrich talking to the baseball, endzone dances, and coaches doused by buckets of Gatorade correspond in playfulness, for athletes and spectators, to playful aspects of the dunk. Thus one finds seeds of mutuality even in the intensely adversary setting of organized sport. The next step in the possible move toward greater mutuality is to reclaim and emphasize the lost spirit of play in all sports. And to renew and discover anew play in other institutions as well.

FIFTEEN

Seeds of Mutuality II:
New Seeds in Old Institutions

If I am not for myself, who is for me? And
being only for my own self, what am I? And if
not now, when?
                                   —Rabbi Hillel, Mishnah 14

Experiments in transcending traditional adversary relations are taking
place in many conventional institutions—politics, business, education, architecture, popular music, and others. Implicitly challenging norms of adversarial behavior, emerging mutuality attitudes reflect cooperation and sensitivity
to other people and to the planet.

International Politics

Nonviolence and civil disobedience are seeds of mutuality in international politics. Gandhi insisted that the enemy must be recognized and
respected as human. The challenge for nonviolent activists is to find points of
possible touch, vulnerabilities within self and other where human connection
can be made. There is an adversary element to this, as the nonviolent practi-
tioner directly challenges the paradigm of the party encountered. This is a liberatory, as distinct from a coercive, use of adversary inclinations. A dramatic
example of a major leader driven by mutuality rather than adversarialism
came from the Soviet Union. Whatever his misjudgments about the durability
of the Soviet Union, Mikhail Gorbachev's healing inclinations have been
remarkable. He played a crucial part in ending the Cold War and in challenging the cultures of militarism and terror it embodied.

Often overlooked, Nikita Khrushchev was brave enough to back off from the adolescent brinkmanship of the Cuban missile crisis. In the words of *Us and Them: The Psychology of Ethnonationalism*, a report by the Group for the Advancement of Psychiatry, Khrushchev "seemed to exemplify a leader who was able to absorb shame and respond maturely."[1] When President Kennedy refused to withdraw U.S. missiles from Turkey in exchange for Khrushchev removing his from Cuba, Khrushchev avoided the obvious temptation to confront. Speaking of advisors who urged him in what could have been a catastrophic direction, he said:

> They looked at me as though I was out of my mind or, what was worse, a traitor. . . . The biggest tragedy, as they saw it, was that the Chinese or Albanians would accuse us of weakness. I said to myself: To hell with these maniacs. . . . What good would it have done me in the last hour of my life to know that though our great nation and the United States were in complete ruin, the national honor of the Soviet Union was intact?[2]

The capacity to give up the practice of demonizing the other, which Khrushchev presents, requires an expansion of self in ways that would finally move beyond what Erikson calls *pseudospeciation*. This effort requires recognizing humans as a single species whose members share fundamental traits, fears, and hopes.

It is very hard to find seeds of mutuality in international relations. Because of the adversarial nature of the nation-state, its leaders put the interests of their populations ahead of those of other nation-states. The United Nations and the European Community stress interdependence over independence and on the surface appear to represent a transitional stage between the realpolitik of the nation-state and a world predominantly based on mutuality. Yet while it is true that both challenge the absolute sovereignty of the nation-state in favor of possible large-scale coordination and peacekeeping, this alone is not sufficient for mutuality to flourish. To paraphrase Gandhi, one must not only think of the ends but of the means. Empires stress interdependence, but they are not thereby mutuality associations.

The UN moves in mutuality directions when it creates the UN Declaration of Human Rights, sponsors the International Court of Justice, works for children's issues in UNICEF, and promotes general interests through WHO and UNESCO. These are its positive directions, in laying infrastructure for a world in which conflicts are resolved peacefully and peoples work together for the common good. All this, though, is very partial and very fragile so far, as the forces that contradict it often hold sway.

The UN continues, even after the Cold War, to be in some major ways an adversary organization, with all the pitfalls that implies. The UN-sanctioned Gulf War, which promised a "New World Order," gave us yet another victory and defeat in terms of the old paradigm, which both Saddam Hussein and George Bush reasserted.

The European Community works in two opposite directions. On one hand it suggests, on a regional level, what could be extended to relations of all states and nations to each other. National sovereignty is blurred as European states move from units pitted against each other to working together on common problems. Yet the adversary paradigm remains in force in a new way. The European market seems of greater benefit, in some countries, to merchants and politicians than to publics. And while its members struggle with impediments to cooperating with one another economically and politically, the end goal is to form a bloc that can more efficiently compete on the world market. It appears to be inevitable that a step toward mutuality is made hesitantly and with significant backpedaling, as if the old paradigm somehow must be honored even as mutuality develops.

In Israel, the West Bank, and the United States there have for some years been serious attempts at "dialogue" between Israelis and Palestinians in small, private settings. The ensuing process is laborious and difficult but edifying—the work of would-be enemies revealing hope, anger, stereotypes, and pain to each other. With patience, time, and sometimes the help of experienced facilitators, people slowly learn to honor the reality of those they have experienced as enemies and to connect with them rather than remain in frozen adversary stasis.

Thousands of teenage Palestinians and Jews in Israel have met in weekend workshops in organized settings like those of Neve Shalom/Wahat al-Salam ("Oasis of Peace" in Hebrew and Arabic—an Israeli Jewish-Arab village founded by a Jew who became a Catholic priest) and Givat Haviva, a kibbutz center for study, action, and arts. Other contexts in which Jews and Arabs collaborate are Shutafut ("Partnership," an Arab-Jewish friendship group that works in both communities for mutual recognition and respect), Interns for Peace (a Peace Corps–like program in which two-year volunteers work in adjoining Arab and Jewish villages in Israel), and joint business ventures by Jews and Arabs in Israel. For years, Prof. Herbert Kelman of Harvard University has brought Israelis and Palestinians together to work on their mutual recriminations, hopes, and the like; some of the people who attended his weekends have become principal negotiators between the two peoples.[3]

These discussion processes live at the edge of political reality; if known at all, they are scorned by most people in power. But they go on all the same, in a fashion like "Second Track Diplomacy," a term coined during the Cold War to refer to citizens of the two superpowers meeting with each other against the will of their respective governments. Such citizens recognized that their governments' adversary commitments made it impossible for them to leave the hardened, archaic forms of adversary politics. Often by conscious design, second track diplomats and dialoguers pioneer the mutuality alternative in their collective efforts to develop empathy as a crucial category of political analysis and response.

Reproductive Rights and Pro-Life Politics

The reproductive rights debate is as adversarial as any in recent years in the United States, but even here seeds of mutuality are evident. B. J. Isaacson-Jones, director of Reproductive Health Services in St. Louis, writes of an effort begun in 1990 to find common ground between the sides:

> It was shockingly easy to identify issues we agree on, like the need for aid to pregnant women who are addicted to drugs, the need for better prenatal care and the need to reduce unwanted pregnancy. Neither side wants women to need abortions because they don't have the money to raise a child.[4]

Loretto Wagner, past president of Missouri Citizens for Life says,

> No one is ever going to convince me that it's all right to kill unborn babies, and I'm going to go on working to make abortion illegal. But that doesn't mean we need to demonize each other. If this is not to become the Vietnam of the 1990's we have to sit down and talk to each other.[5]

According to Charlotte Taft, director of a Dallas Clinic that performs 4,000 abortions a year,

> It has become very clear to me that the polarization I have engaged in for years has not served the women in my community, has not helped to resolve anything, and was a self-indulgence. I'm trying to figure out who in the other side I can talk to, but it's scary, since I don't trust them any more than they trust me.[6]

A pregnant ten-year-old came to the St. Louis abortion clinic but decided to have the baby. Her pregnancy was medically complicated, and there was no one to take care of her during the hours when her mother was at work. The head of the clinic called Ms. Wagner, who raised money in antiabortion circles to help the young girl. The baby was born and put up for adoption.

Both St. Louis groups joined efforts in 1991 to promote state legislation to fund treatment of pregnant drug addicts. A reporter observes that people who run abortion clinics and those who run homes for pregnant women are more willing to seek accommodation than are the advocacy groups that support them.[7] As so often, people's real involvement with real people, as distinct from ideological commitment at far remove from people, suggests recognition of the other, respect, however grudging, and the capacity, based at least partly on empathy, to work with the other not as abstract foe but as specific human other.

Three years later, and three weeks following the shooting of two people in Boston-area abortion clinics, opponents in the debate identified shared concerns: "making adoption easier, curbing teen-age pregnancy and providing support for poor, single mothers who keep their babies."[8] This approach, however mutualistic, is not without risks and limits. The compromise that permits working together allows reproductive rights activists to acknowledge—without reciprocity, according to some—passions felt by pro-life people. The sticking point for the former is that the latter does not recognize the former's values and politics as legitimate at all. Whether and how to accommodate in contrast with overcoming the other remains a live issue for both sides to the conflict.[9]

One observer notes that

> the simplistic rhetoric of both sides of the abortion debate in America is a symptom of, and for that matter, a cause of the impoverished moral thinking that has led to the runaway plague of abortion. Thus those who claim absolute primacy for "a woman's right to choose" trivialize the other values that often outweigh that right. Likewise, those who, in the name of preventing abortion, insist on discussing it in the context of the Holocaust, murder or infanticide are themselves impeding the kind of mature moral reasoning—a movement through complexity instead of away from it—that would properly make abortion the rarest of outcomes instead of an increasingly frequent one.
>
> The so-called "right to life" movement denounces the careful drawing of distinctions, the defense of nuance and the effort to appreciate the often tragic web of complications as complicity in murder—when in fact the ability to do such things is the essence of responsible moral reasoning.[10]

In the summer of 1996, a conference was held in Washington, D.C., on the topic "Reach for Common Ground." The program booklet states,

> We believe that there is a space—it could be for dialogue, it could be for work on issues—where pro-choice and pro-life people can come

together in a non-adversarial way. We also believe that such coming together is a good thing. It produces positive outcomes for the individuals and groups involved, as well as for society.[11]

The reproductive rights debate reveals a limit to the paradigm shift analysis of this book. As always, one party—if absolutist—can insist on an adversary construction of the encounter. Unless the other party can "open the frame of adversarialism" (see chapter 16), it must slug it out. James Carroll suggests that *both* sides maintain absolutist commitments. The problem is that although the parties can admit that preventing unwanted pregnancies is desirable, they are unable to agree either that women ought to be free to make their own choices, or that they ought not to be. Where this kind of disagreement can go is beyond the scope of this book but needs eventually to be addressed in order more fully to work out the possibilities of transcending adversary relations.

Education

Mathematician Uri Treisman was puzzled about why college students of Black and Hispanic backgrounds in the California State University system rarely received high grades in calculus courses, while students of Chinese and Jewish backgrounds did very well.[12] Each year, 600,000 first-year students in that system take calculus and 250,000 fail.[13]

Treisman and his colleagues compared a group of Black students with a group of Chinese students. In an imaginative methodological move, Treisman asked students' permission to videotape them as they studied calculus in their dormitory rooms. By doing so, he solved the mystery. It turned out that Black students spent the recommended eight hours a week studying calculus, alone. Chinese students worked within a similar range of hours each week, but also worked in groups for an additional four to six hours. They pooled their strengths and helped each other. When Black and Hispanic students studied in cooperative learning groups, their grades were at the same high level or higher than those of their Chinese and Jewish peers.[14]

In our society, students are ordinarily taught to struggle on their own since they are led to believe one or another version of the cliché, "It's a dog eat dog world."[15] They are socialized to compete for the apparently scarce goods of high grades and honors.[16] But it is now clear that learning is often faster, surer, easier, and more rewarding when students share what they understand. What is defined under the adversary paradigm as cheating turns out in a mutuality mode to enhance learning. While fairly new and daring, methods of cooperative learning have been used at all levels of education with excellent results.[17] Practices such as placing students near enough each other that they can share materials and creating an atmosphere wherein all feel responsible for the learning of everyone in the group, contribute to the cooperative education goal of "positive interdependence." That, together with face-to-face interaction in which students promote each other's success, forms the conceptual foundation for cooperative learning, a major seed of mutuality.

The cooperative learning instructor creates a supportive classroom in which students feel comfortable taking risks. By conveying warmth, openness, and a focus on students' ways of learning, the instructor encourages rapport of everyone with everyone. Classroom mutuality depends on behaviors like encouraging students to ask questions, welcoming their personal viewpoints, acknowledging their feelings about assignments and classroom policy, and revealing interest in them as individuals. Even the teacher quickly learning students' names contributes to mutuality by partly decentralizing traditional authority.

The mutuality vision "Education 2000" emphasizes crucial tenets of cooperative education including (1) students rather than curriculum driving the system, (2) teachers acting as facilitators of learning rather than imparters of information, (3) students learning the democratic process by participating in it, (4) students being encouraged to participate in service projects for their communities, (5) students developing feelings of connectedness, love, and compassion for the needs of people.[18]

Business

Some people are working for significant changes in attitudes and behavior in business. Although they are minor in influence so far and do not address the overall structure of the economic order, they offer hints of what real metamorphosis might be like. The authors of "Re-inventing the Corporate Self: The Inner Agenda for Business Transformation" describe the potential for such a shift:

It concerns most basic assumptions about companies' mission, accountability, and internal and external power relationships. . . . Consider the range of social and environmental controversies affecting, and affected by, corporate policies: pollution control, community rights to information, consumer safety, affirmative action and parental leave, sensitive arms and technology exports. All these involve a profound challenge to conventional notions of responsibility in a corporate setting. . . . Some companies are defining this shift as a win/win situation.[19]

Opened in 1984, the Women's Economic Development Corporation (WEDCO) helps low-income women enter business. In its first two years it assisted more than a thousand women, two-thirds of them with family incomes under $12,000 and one-fifth currently or formerly on welfare or social security. Helping to start 98 businesses and to expand 144 in those first two years, WEDCO persuaded banks to lend money at the market rate on their own discretion while relaxing the equity and collateral requirements that normally lock women out. Here is an example of WEDCO in action: a woman who wanted to be a florist was not a traditional credit candidate. WEDCO started her with a $500 loan to buy roses to sell on Valentine's Day. She made six times that amount that day, paid back the loan, and successfully expanded her new business.[20]

Another example of a business organization trying to transcend adversarialism is the Industrial Cooperative Association, which provides technical assistance to employee-owned businesses. This includes business advice, education, and legal work for cooperative groups around the country.[21] By establishing a loan fund directly for those who want to start a cooperative business or buy a firm to run as a cooperative, the ICA moves past the adversarial and hierarchical chains of command of the traditional corporation and helps empower those who have been systematically alienated from policy making. The ICA helped start a health care cooperative in the Bronx and a camping goods manufacturing cooperative in the San Francisco Bay area. A Latina worker/owner of the latter spoke of the empowerment she experienced as a result of ICA's efforts: "In our culture, a woman doesn't make many decisions. But being in the co-op, I'm part of the decision-making, and I like it."[22]

Cooperation among people takes form in relation to the natural environment through respect for its limits and vulnerabilities. Renewable energy technologies that do not deplete resources or pollute are in development, significant even if small in scope so far. In short, the seeds for a discernible shift in business philosophy and practice from adversarialism to mutuality are being planted. "Socially responsible investing" is growing, characterized by decisions on the part of firms concerned with these issues not to invest in companies connected with alcohol, animal testing, tobacco, gambling, and arms manufacture but rather in companies good for the environment and human well-being.

Although capitalism remains intact, deviations from its classical mode are growing: companies that develop positive relations with their community and employees, fair treatment of women and minorities, product quality, and a caring attitude towards consumers have found a rapidly increasing number of investors.[23]

Social investing has grown into a vibrant broad-based movement. . . . Financial professionals realized that by putting their money where their hearts were, they would make money and advance their causes. They spread the word and investors began to come to them. U.S. social investing is only a little more than twenty years old and still growing.[24]

Among socially responsible businesses, Ben and Jerry's ice cream is especially famous. Stoneyfield Yogurt, which says it was inspired by Ben and Jerry's, gives 15% of its profits to employees and another 10% to organizations like Oxfam America, National Public Radio's "Living on Earth," and the Earth Day Everyday Network.[25]

People who use the Working Assets VISA card and the affiliated Working Assets Long Distance phone company decide each year which of several dozen social change organizations will get how much of the hundreds of thousands of dollars of profits these two businesses give away, according to how much business they have done during the year.

The seeds of mutuality have recently been planted, even if barely, in the weapons business. Selling arms is still highly profitable, but more and more firms are seeking ways to keep their own economies going through research, development, and production to meet peacetime needs. For what Eisenhower called "the military industrial complex," the threat from the Soviet Union was never that it might use nuclear devices to destroy or cripple the United States, the threat was always that it would cease its nuclear threat. Mikhail Gorbachev was able to see through this charade to the vision of mutuality:

> The spiraling arms race, coupled with the military and political realities of the world and the persistent traditions of pre-nuclear political thinking, impedes cooperation between countries and peoples, which—East and West agree—is indispensable if the world's nations want to preserve nature intact, to ensure the rational use and reproduction of her resources and, consequently, to survive as befits human beings.[26]

Gorbachev issued a direct challenge to the political economy of the United States, a plea that resources no longer be used for the wasteful purpose of war production but for meeting real human needs:

> The arms race, just like nuclear war, is unwinnable. . . . All of us face the need to learn and live at peace in this world, to work out a new mode of thinking, for conditions today are quite different from what they were even three or four decades ago. The time is ripe for abandoning views on foreign policy which are influenced by an imperial standpoint. . . . From the viewpoint of long-term, big-time politics, no one will be able to subordinate others. . . . Along with the above-said

realities of nuclear weapons, ecology, the scientific and technological revolution, and informatics, this also obliges us to respect one another and everybody.[27]

When Gorbachev removed an entire superpower from nuclear competition, the U.S. war economy began to yearn for its lost enemy. The bombing of Libya, the invasions of Grenada and Panama, the Gulf War, and subsequent military involvement in Iraq all represent attempts to reinvigorate the adversary paradigm. Presidential candidate Bob Dole campaigned in 1996 partly on stepping up defense spending. Whether the United States will continue conflict with Iraq or escalate enemy rhetoric against Cuba, North Korea, or international terrorism remains to be seen. It is clear as of this writing that President Clinton remains committed to policies promoting transnational corporate interests in the world rather than embracing a grander vision, in the style of Gorbachev's, to replace familiar life-threatening policies.

A demand for reducing arms spending was initiated in June 1996 by a group of thirty-six Boston based business leaders in banking, food retailing, ice cream, law, and other areas. The action took the form of an ad in the *New York Times* on Sunday June 16 and a press conference later in the week.[28]

Architecture

Art can stimulate and challenge, but it can also deaden and divert attention from real human concerns. Like muckraking journalism and social criticism, art can provide lively outlets for critical insights and deep-felt emotions. It can also renew and arouse the human spirit and motivate its spectators to act on those feelings. The arts are

> a form of organization of social energy, and the flood which they set in motion may at any moment, in favorable conditions, reverse its direction. The artist leads his [sic] fellow men [sic] into a world of fantasy where they find release, thus asserting the refusal of the human consciousness to acquiesce in its environment, and by this means there is collected a store of energy which flows back into the real world and transforms the fantasy into fact. Thus, then, is the connection between such masterpieces of human culture as Greek tragedy and the mimetic dance, in which the savage huntsmen express both their weakness in the face of nature and their will to master it.[29]

Until very recently, following the lead of Le Corbusier's vision of the home as a "machine for living in," architecture has sought to declare its separation from the realm of nature. Today, however, architects are tending to merge their art with the needs of the planet in ways that were inconceivable a short time ago.

A quarter of a century ago, Buckminster Fuller, a quirky, visionary architect, designed the "World Game," intended to spread as broadly as possible information about the state of world resources. The purpose of the game was to put aside ideological biases. Efforts to dominate would disqualify anyone from playing the game, whose emphasis was on peaceful means, intelligent use of resources, and cooperative exploration toward a sustainable, pollution-free use of resources.[30]

A later shift in this direction in architectural philosophy appeared in 1989 with the introduction of the "Critical Planet Rescue" resolution to the American Institute of Architects. It emphasized a building material's life cycle and covered natural resource depletion, ecosystem effects, energy consumption, waste generation, and indoor air pollution.[31] Attention to such developments questions what Gary Coates calls "the narcissistic phase of architectural education that predominated in the 1980s."[32] According to AIA member Bob Berkebile,

> The overall goal is to create a cultural change for our society. Joseph Campbell pointed out that the focus of the tallest building has changed as society has changed—from church steeple to capital dome and currently, the corporate high-rise. Now we need a new paradigm and appropriate symbol.[33]

In "A Manifesto for Building Professionals," James Wines calls for what amounts to mutuality:

> The next stage is to create architecture where both function and image celebrate the environmental message. . . . In the post-industrial world, any architecture whose work continues to draw inspiration from the machine age is hopelessly out of touch with reality. . . . Architecture is now about rediscovering humanity's debt to the earth and connecting this awareness into a new iconography."[34]

One author suggests that architecture is the collective unconscious made visible and that architecture can move to celebrating cooperation with ecosystems rather than celebrating power over materials like aluminum and glass.[35] Whether architecture makes this transformation remains to be seen. The issues are at least before it now.

The theme of the summer 1993 convention of the American Institute of Architects (AIA) was "Architecture at the Crossroads: Designing for a Sustainable Future."[36] The conference designed a new set of architectural guidelines called a "Declaration of Interdependence for a Sustainable Future." Implicitly speaking to the need to move beyond the adversary relationship humans have had with our environment and with each other in our environment, the declaration declares:

> Buildings and the built environment play a major role in the human impact on the natural environment and on the quality of life; sustainable design integrates consideration of resource and energy efficiency, healthy buildings and materials, ecologically and socially sensitive land use, and an aesthetic sensitivity that inspires, affirms, and ennobles; sustainable design can significantly reduce adverse human impacts on the natural environment while simultaneously improving quality of life and economic well being.[37]

Declaring "that they fully support the development of the already evolving planetary culture of interdependence,"[38] the architects declare that "in a context of limited information there should be an avoidance of decisions and actions that may result in irreversible damage to environmental assets of air, water, soil, flora and fauna, and the ecosystems of which these are part."[39] Further decision is made to

> emphasize that innovation and design be directed to the creation of products, services, and technologies, and buildings and structures, that operate and function in ways that are environmentally beneficial or neutral, rather than in ways that result in irreversible harm to the environment.[40]

The mutualistic orientation of the architects' statement includes the entire planet in its scope:

> A planetary culture of interdependence requires that design professionals operate with professional practices and ethics. . . . Environmental auditing, monitoring, and forecasting are used to ensure that the wellbeing of both present and future generations and of other species is adequately protected and nurtured . . . [and that s]imilar environmental standards are applied in all countries and locations, irrespective of their socio-economic status.[41]

The architects and design professionals also call for working from an integration of understanding and insights from the arts and humanities and the social and natural sciences as well as from architectural and design traditions themselves.[42] They call upon themselves to emphasize approaches based on indigenous cultures and on alternatives to traditional Western science.[43]

This is mutuality in the fullest, to be sure in an orienting document. Like so many other seeds of mutuality, the idea is evolving in a specific professional context; whether and how it takes hold depends on the insights, vision, and determination of the people who become inspired by it.

Popular Music

Like movies, popular music expresses a culture's conscious and unconscious values and beliefs. The adversary and mutuality themes are not hard to find there. However obvious adversarialism is in rock, rap, and reggae, calls for cooperation and mutuality are also present, as so often elsewhere, in minor but recognizable form.

Although their rap celebrates a tradition of African American male strength dating back to boxers Jack Johnson and Muhammad Ali, there is nothing paradigm-shaking in NWA's "Fuck the Police," Public Enemy's "Fight the Power," or KRS-One's repeated urgings "you can't trust a big butt and a smile."

By contrast, in the early seventies, John Lennon sang, in "Imagine," a fundamental piece of the paradigm shift from adversarialism to mutuality: imagining something different, something that abjures aggression, something that works to unite people "in perfect harmony."[44]

The theme of mutuality is prominent in the music of the rap group Arrested Development. Its top-ten 1992 album *3 Years, 5 Months, and 2 Days in the Life of* . . . diverges from the traditional divisive, misogynistic, adversarially drenched music of gangsta' rap and much popular music in general.[45] It begins with the anthem "Space ain't man's final frontier, man's final frontier is the soul." The tone of the album is one of inward journey, a search for connection and meaning in an adversary world. The songs focus on love, empathy, and inner strength.

In "Mama's Always on Stage," the lead rapper Speech tells a woman friend who is a teenage mother, "Anytime you need help sister, / We'll be there just give us a ring. / We will help you to raise that king" and then urges, "Can't be a revolution without women." In "Mr. Wendal" the group tells of the wisdom of a homeless man. The meeting between the rapper and Mr. Wendal becomes the occasion for self-reflection: "Uncivilized we call him. / But I just saw him eat off the food we waste. / Civilization, are we really civilized, yes or no who are we to judge?" In a moment of fear and insecurity in "Fishin' 4 Religion," Speech observes, "Staring at the sea that's full of violence. / Scared to put my line in that water."

Arrested Development is not wishy-washy feel-good music. Seeing the state of affairs in the world as calling for a kind of revolution, it calls for people to "get political," yet its visions transcend the "Fuck the Police" mentality. The words of Speech echo Freud's concept of sublimation: "Direct your anger-love. / Nothing's ever built on hate. Instead love!" Arrested Development urges, "Dig your hands in the dirt / Children play with dirt." The hit single "Tennessee" presents the pain and anguish of watching "brothers on the corner playing ghetto games." The group counsels progress not by avenging, hurting, comparing, blaming, or insulting, but by turning inward.

Sixties and seventies reggae Jamaican musician Bob Marley drew on his experiences of Third World oppression and the uniting power of the Rastafari religion to sing a message of peace, love, and unity. Perhaps in the service of his critique of imperialism and domination, Marley's larger message embraces all of humanity. In "One Love / People Get Ready," he proclaims: "One love / One heart / Let's get together and feel all right."[46] Marley sang of a place where the sinners, who are equally ourselves and the "man" who dominates others, are all accepted in unity and love. Looking back to an earlier song, "Get Up, Stand Up," Marley makes it clear that this place is not some heaven above, "But if you really know what life is worth / You will look for yours here on Earth."[47] Marley accepted the struggle that engulfed his people and land, but his larger musical message was of a greater love and a greater unity where all could come together as brothers and sisters.

Many years later, the reggae band Spearhead voiced another dimension of this message. In "People in the Middle," Spearhead recognizes the humanity in the "other," in our supposed enemies. Michael Franti sings: "so many is out there—that's livin' undercover / your motha, your fatha, your sista, your brotha, your friends and their enemies all have their lovers. Yeah!"[48] This message of recognition, of realizing that even so-called enemies have their lovers, mothers, fathers, and so on is a proclamation of recognizing the humanity in everyone. Mutuality builds on exactly this realization that all humans are trying to live their lives and in most essential ways are alike. The next step might be to question whether enemies are a necessary part of life or are constructed out of unfaced inner issues.

Even such adversarially oriented groups like the Beastie Boys have moved in some of their work toward mutuality. In "Bodhisattva Vow," the Beastie Boys voice what they have found in Buddhism. They proclaim: "The Bodhisattva vow is one of power and strength / . . . Seeing others are as important as myself / I strive for a happiness of mental wealth / With the interconnectedness that we share as one."[49] By putting these ideas to music, they have spread their own learning from Buddhism to a popular music audience. The widening of circles and teaching the message of mutuality suggest the potential power of music.

It remains to be seen how much of art as we know it is adaptable to mutuality. Much of art is based on conflict, and it is not clear to me if among the countless meanings of art, the repeated representation of it is part of an effort to come to terms with the conflicts portrayed or a ritual reinforcement of the adversary paradigm or perhaps both. Art in a predominantly mutuality society might take quite other forms than art as we know it now. The kind of society I am suggesting would unfold in ways we cannot clearly foresee. That is the way of new institutions, new societies, new paradigm emphases.

☙〰❧

SIXTEEN

Seeds of Mutuality III:
New Seeds in New Institutions

> What has been long neglected cannot be
> restored immediately. Fruit falls from the tree
> when it is ripe. The way cannot be forced.
> —The Buddha

The rudiments of fuller mutuality are apparent in some budding new institutions. Media make little of them except as curiosities. When universities teach about them they are likely to tuck them into marginal and esoteric courses not commonly taken very seriously. Even people working in relatively new mutuality settings may fail to notice their larger contexts and resort unnecessarily to adversarialism from time to time.

It is true of nonviolence, self-help, new games, mediation, and other examples of empathy and cooperation that appropriate skills for pursuing them can be learned. It is not easy to talk about hurt and bewilderment if one is used to striking out to express rage, it is not easy to cooperate if one is accustomed to competition as the heart of daily activity, it is not easy to consider others' feelings if one has been trained to act only on one's own emotional reality. At the same time, it was also not easy to learn to cut off empathy in the first place, to curtail desires to be understood, and to assume only the worst of other people.

Socialization in the family, school, and elsewhere will, if mutuality is to come into its own, include teaching mutuality habits so far not very familiar to most people. The challenge to media is enormous to make love and decency as appealing as violence and hate. Surely people clever enough to celebrate the negative could be marvelously inventive were they motivated to see mutuality as desirable and as essential for human and planetary survival. Parents and others in authority can learn and then teach mutuality. Agents for such *every child has parental figures. If each taught every child to be inherently mutualistic...new world could emerge with this generation?*

teaching are out there, in certain world figures, in some parts of world religions, in psychotherapy and teaching at their best, in crevices and pockets of many institutions, and in classes and organizations that consult on such matters. Musicians, painters, architects, sculptors, and other artists could find ways to make mutuality appealing and intriguing to vast numbers of people. The same is true in medicine, law enforcement, education, and all other institutions.

World Exponents of Nonviolence: The Politics and Teaching of Mutuality

As best he can, Rambo enacts the adversarialism his culture and military training instill in him, but it comes, finally, to naught. The Godfather's fate, substituting Mafia for military, is about the same. Nuclear competition does not make sense, since no one can "win" an all-out nuclear face-off. Environmental exploitation either shifts from the full adversary stance to mutuality-preservation or we will all have had it. "Free market" competition maintains such an uneven distribution of goods and services that billions of people are apparently doomed to marginal existences, feeling no hope of change in their individual fates or in the institutions that consolidate and perpetuate the limits suffered.

Adversary advocates run all the way from Saddam Hussein and international terrorists and their version of adversarialism to Milton Friedman, Bob Dole, Bill Clinton, and their varied versions of it. Unlike the others, though, Clinton shows, however unevenly, intimations that working toward the common good is preferable to the pursuit of adversary interests. I have the impression of Clinton as less driven by the adversary compulsion than by his version of normative adversarialism. If I am right, then he might see his way, more easily than most of his counterparts, to taking part in working toward the shift in paradigms that I am claiming is necessary for human survival. Clinton's penchant for compromise, whatever its many political implications, suggests a willingness to take more than one interest into account in settling conflicts. He has passed up several opportunities, although not all, for military engagement. It is that inclination toward mutuality, I believe, that accounts in part for the determination of some political forces in the United States to reinforce the weakening adversary paradigm, by reinvigorating the defense budget, ending compassionate programs for needy citizens, and turning back mutuality gains for women, minorities, homosexuals, and others.

The moral content and political contexts of adversarialism differ, but the framework assumptions—that winning and losing are central to meaning in life and that "losers" must shut up and accept their fate or be marginalized to political ineffectiveness—remain fixed. It is that condition that this book challenges.

If those who speak for the old paradigm are abundant—and they are—what of those who promote mutuality instead? Jesus, Gandhi, and Martin Luther King Jr. come to mind. Each had, it appears, a pretty good idea that he was ahead of his time and was asking people to behave in ways they would find strange. All of them surely understood that many people they hoped to reach would resist their recommendations for how to live kinder, fuller lives that accept the realities of other people as well as their own. The mutuality messages of these figures is honored oftener than not, in the breach. It is not evil or viciousness, I suspect, so much as unfaced, unresolved ambivalence and compulsions that account for this. Piety commonly accompanies the memories and teachings of these mutuality visionaries, but institutions for the most part, even some of those claiming to promote the messages, behave more adversarially than mutualistically. Although this would not seem to be essential to the task, each of these visionaries was killed in the course of carrying out what he defined as his mission.

The adversary has the inherent strategic advantage over the mutualistic person (note that there is no single word in the mutuality realm that corresponds to "adversary"). Adversaries can insist on adversary relations and can force them on others, by, among other techniques, murdering or inspiring the murders of those who challenge what adversaries represent. The assassination of Martin Luther King Jr. had what was likely the intended effect: it removed charismatic leadership from the civil rights movement and thereby slowed its pace of accomplishment. The assassination of Yitzhak Rabin in Israel had a corresponding effect on the elements of a peace process that had been in place between Israelis and Palestinians for about two years.

As of this writing, there are three world figures who seem especially effective in keeping alive the imagination and spirit of mutuality: Nelson Mandela, Aung San Suu Kyi, and the Dalai Lama. Each not only offers a vision of mutuality; each pursues it actively.

Nelson Mandela

As President of South Africa, Nelson Mandela is the only one of the three to head a state. I had grown up to believe, as a truism, that in order to end *apartheid*—state-sponsored racism—in South Africa, Blacks would massacre great numbers of Whites. It appears that among the reasons that did not happen is that the last president under the old regime, F. W. de Klerk, for years secretly arranged for Nelson Mandela to be taken out of prison for short periods of time and toured throughout South Africa, to familiarize himself with the situation over which de Klerk understood Mandela would eventually preside.[1]

When apartheid dissolved and he became the first Black president of South Africa, Mandela did not follow what could have been impulses to avenge his twenty-seven years in prison and the decades of Black suffering at the hands of White South Africans. Instead, he included his opponents in his government and worked immediately toward rapprochement of all contending parties. Not too long after his inauguration, Mandela established the Truth and Reconciliation Commission, headed by major anti-apartheid activist Bishop Desmond Tutu, "to investigate apartheid-era abuses, apportion reparations and amnesties, and to compile an official history of the road from repression to democracy."[2] That a hated social order would be examined dispassionately, by a body headed by an activist cleric, to determine responsibility and measure out pardons carefully, according to complex, compassionate criteria, rather than jailing and executing the former victimizers, suggests a major movement toward mutuality in extremely difficult political circumstances. Although the African National Congress, of which Mandela was long a major figure, did have an armed operation, the thrust of Mandela's learning in his twenty-seven years in prison, and his behavior since his release, has been generous, open, empathic—mutualistic far more than one might have imagined, given the trying circumstances of the system whose political (but not, note, economic) dimensions he helped bring to an end.

Whatever the internal and external constraints on him, Mandela has come closer to true mutuality in governing than have most national political leaders. His task is very hard; competing factions, most of them adversarial, try his patience and his inventiveness, but the commitment appears firm. The day of his election as president, Mandela said, "We place our vision of a new constitutional order for South Africa on the table, not as conquerors, prescribing to the conquered."[3]

Mandela's inclusion of former enemies in his government, his establishing a truth and reconciliation commission, and his efforts to create a government for all people in South Africa suggest mutuality intentions and procedures, however limited circumstances beyond Mandela's control may make them.

Aung San Suu Kyi

Burmese liberation leader Aung San Suu Kyi has insisted on nonviolence as the spirit and strategy of her movement, the National League for Democracy. Under house arrest from July 1989 through July 1995, Suu Kyi is the daughter of Aung San, a man who was expected to lead Burma once the British granted it independence in 1948. Aung San was assassinated in 1947 and has since remained an inspiration to democratic forces in his country.

After her house arrest ended, Suu Kyi was urged by the military government of Burma (which the current leaders call Myanmar) to leave the country. Knowing that would diminish her effectiveness as freedom leader, she stays, under a sort of voluntary house arrest. Several times a week, with periodic interruptions by the government, Suu Kyi addresses crowds of thousands of people in question-and-answer sessions outside her house. Although there are pressures on her to endorse violence against the military government, she says that the use of arms would support the principle that those with superior arms are to rule the country. In what can be read as a complex mutuality statement, she says, "But we have always said that we will never, never disown those who have decided to take up arms, because we understand how they feel."[4] Suu Kyi accepts feelings and motives of arms-bearers all the while rejecting their strategy. She and they thus need not be totally at odds with each other. While Suu Kyi has been urged to organize a massive campaign of civil disobedience, she has so far not done so. Whatever the complexities of her situation and her plans, she remains committed to nonviolence in opposing the military government of her country.

Two scenes in the movie *Beyond Rangoon* portray the nonviolent commitment of the liberation movement Suu Kyi heads. In the first, Suu Kyi is leading a group of several hundred followers down a Rangoon street in a peaceful evening pro-democracy demonstration. They arrive at a phalanx of armed soldiers whose rifles point at the demonstrators. Radiating a charismatic presence and in full harmony with her followers, Suu Kyi approaches the line of armed men, moving toward one in particular. As she looks him in the eye, we see no trace of anger, contempt, or impatience in hers. Suu Kyi's gaze is strong, kind, and warm. His bayonet directed at her, the soldier begins to sweat. He watches her nervously. Clearly under orders, the soldier holds firm, his bayonet pointing toward the liberation leader. Suu Kyi slows down as she approaches him, never losing eye contact or the warm smile. As she gets closer to the young military man, he begins to tremble. She does not. She slows down, advancing ever so gently and steadily toward him. He could shoot or lunge his bayonet forward but appears to be frozen. Suu Kyi proceeds, steadily and slowly. About 3–4 feet from him, she gently, carefully, raises her right arm, and, although the camera does not show us her complete gesture, appears to bring her arm past the man and his rifle. As if performing an intricate ballet movement, the soldier along with his gun moves sideways, and Suu Kyi leads her people past him and through the soldiers on duty. A clearer, more exquisite example of nonviolent confrontation with power can hardly be imagined.

Another striking scene appears near the end of the film. The professor who turned tour guide after losing his university position for political reasons is attempting to lead students and other rebels out of the growing dangers they face in Burma by fleeing to neighboring Thailand. Nearly there, they are suddenly faced by another armed young soldier whose assignment is to prevent such desertions from Burma. The old man, risking death just as Suu Kyi does in the earlier scene, hesitantly walks up to the soldier. He does so cautiously, with no sense of threat or incipient trick. Quietly, he and the soldier talk. We do not hear the words, but we see the soldier listening intently. We expect the professor will persuade the young man to let him and his group pass, but we are unprepared for the drama of the soldier laying down his rifle and joining the refugees in their flight into Thailand.

Both these incidents offer dramatic illustrations of the concept and power of opening the frame of adversarialism (see below) and of nonviolence as a political strategy and philosophy. In the Burmese context and outside it, they are to be sure fragile buds of what Gandhi and King attempted to practice; as such they offer a tantalizing prospect in terms of two successful limited actions, not a massive paradigm shift but a provocative hint of one.

It is, I have been claiming, partly the accumulation of such strivings that will at some point create a critical mass of mutuality changes that will shift into a leading mutuality mode. We are not there yet but are approaching it through such phenomena as Mandela's and Suu Kyi's deliberate, careful movements toward political and social change without violence.

The Dalai Lama

Mandela and Suu Kyi are political actors whose remarks about their beliefs and their behavior help clarify it. Nonviolence as a philosophic concept and a religious discipline is developed differently and fully in the person I see as the third in the current series of major nonviolence world figures: the Fourteenth Dalai Lama.

Chosen in traditional ways by a council of religious elders, a two-year-old boy from a farming family was determined in 1937 to be the reincarnation of the Thirteenth Dalai Lama. As such, he was educated, as are all monks studying for the doctorate in Buddhist studies, in religious and secular subjects. The Dalai Lama became the spiritual leader of seven million Tibetan Buddhists.[5]

In 1949–50, when the Dalai Lama was fifteen, China invaded and occupied Tibet and began a course of action that appears to be designed to eliminate Tibetan culture, religion, and language, and to outnumber Tibetans in their own land with Chinese forcefully brought there for resettlement. The Chinese project to destroy an entire culture was resisted by the young Dalai Lama, who tried in meetings with Chinese leaders to work out an accommodation that would allow Tibetans at least cultural and religious autonomy. The Chinese have rejected all such proposals and have continued their culture-cide campaign. In 1959, the Dalai Lama fled with thousands of his followers to India, where in Dharamsala a government-in-exile has been in place ever since.

Against his will and preferences, the Dalai Lama's role has shifted from that of solely spiritual leader to political leader as well. Somewhat like Jews in exile,[6] Tibetans have been moving from a local identity to a world one, with their religion and cause being noted in ever widening circles by political and laypeople who otherwise would likely be oblivious to both. It is possible that part of the appeal of the Dalai Lama and his cause is connected with growing interest in the United States in Buddhism, of which in this country, Tibetan Buddhism is one of the leading forms.[7]

In the course of making the case for his people's integrity and independence, the Dalai Lama has had to become a world figure. As a Buddhist monk, he has chosen to bring his message of nonviolence to the case for Tibetan independence, both as a philosophy of living and as a strategy for resisting the Chinese. Although some of his followers would prefer violence against the Chinese, the Dalai Lama rejects that option, not only because it would surely be futile but because he teaches compassion for all, even for enemies.[8] A documentary on the Chinese persecution of Tibetan nuns makes this idea vivid in the nuns' sustained compassion for their persecutors, torturers, and rapists.[9]

The Dalai Lama is so apart from the framework of the power and ruthlessness that passes as political leadership in the world that it takes an effort to consider that his message not only has political relevance but that it is a design for a politics that could ensure survival of our species and planet. The Dalai Lama counsels, in effect, a politics of mutuality.

If a single word is adequate to represent the Dalai Lama's message, it is "compassion," which combines what I have been calling empathy with what I have been calling mutuality. The Dalai Lama's mutuality offering to China is so far massively rejected. China retains a full adversary commitment in its relationship with Tibet.

Like Aung San Suu Kyi, the Dalai Lama observes that violence begets violence. He also believes that human beings are fulfilled only when they practice compassion "for all sentient beings" and realize their potential by giving to others. Adversaries by definition take—resources, honor, fealty; they give rancor and contempt. The Dalai Lama offers that only caring, compassionate relating can meet the needs of all parties to any encounter. "Ultimately," he writes, "the reason why love and compassion bring the greatest happiness is simply that our nature cherishes them above all else."[10]

The Dalai Lama began a speech, "Compassion in Global Politics," to the Los Angeles World Affairs Council[11] with his basic proposition that all human beings want happiness and want to avoid suffering. On the basis of this universal truth, he says, all people are brothers and sisters and can talk with each other.

Based on such genuine human relation—real feeling for each other, understanding each other—we can develop mutual trust and respect. From that, we can share other peoples' suffering and build harmony in human society. We can create a friendly human family.[12]

Recognizing differences in ideologies and cultures, the Dalai Lama reasons that on the basis of "the basic sameness of humanity," joint efforts can be made

to solve the problems of the whole of humankind. The problems human society is facing in terms of economic development, the crisis of energy, the tension between the poor and rich nations, and many geopolitical problems can be solved if we understand each others' fundamental humanity, respect each others' rights, share each others' problems and sufferings, and then make joint effort.[13]

He then goes on to relate the possibility of that joint effort succeeding, to something individual and also transindividual:

Everybody loves to talk about calm and peace whether in a family, national, or international context, but without *inner* peace how can we make real peace? World peace through hatred and force is impossible. Even in the case of individuals, there is no possibility to feel happiness through anger. If in a difficult situation one becomes disturbed internally, overwhelmed by mental discomfort, then external things will not help at all. However, if despite external difficulties or problems, internally one's attitude is of love, warmth, and kindheartedness, then problems can be faced and accepted easily.[14]

This is the Dalai Lama's version, I believe, of a crucial aspect of what I have been calling reappropriating the self. The normative adversary is capable of doing this, were his/her culture to offer appropriate opportunity and encouragement for it. It is the person who seems unable to transcend the adversary compulsion whom all who work for peace in the world need to understand. The understanding is a prerequisite for figuring out how to suggest to the person so inclined that greater fulfillment might lie in learning to release oneself from the bonds of the compulsion.

It is, then, the intricate and infinitely challenging project of seeking peace inside oneself and outside oneself, and working on both issues in interactions with others, that defines the Dalai Lama's convictions about possibilities of peace in the world. Although this seems idealistic and naive to some, it is worth pondering that "hard-headed" and "realpolitik" approaches that have dominated world politics for millennia have brought us to vast and grow-ing disparities in life chances and happiness between a minority of the world's population and the majority, the continuing possibility of nuclear annihilation, and proliferating environmental crises that could, singly or in combination, wreak havoc on species not yet wiped out by industrialization. It is increas-ingly difficult to make the case for continuing in the hard-headed, realpolitik directions that have defined most of world, national, and local politics for thousands of years. The question is not how to figure out how to make the old ways work better. The question is how to conceptualize new ways of relating, new ways of organizing institutions, new ways of pursuing peace and happi-ness in the world. And how to implement them in raising children, in politics, and in everyday life.

The Dalai Lama is a world force for rethinking assumptions about polit-ical behavior and individual behavior along what he sees as realizable ethical lines. He does not, as they say, just talk the talk; he walks the walk. And he does not do so as naively as it may seem. As if responding to the Rambo ele-ment in human behavior, he is fully aware that selfishness, anger, and hatred, us well us love, gentleness, and compassion, are in us all. Through examining these inclinations carefully, both conceptually and emotionally, people can find ways in which the destructive tendencies can be deliberately diminished in their power over us. It is worth remembering that Rambo's understandable rage got him nothing, nothing at all, that he wanted. That he yearned for respect, recognition, and love were apparent, but he knew no means by which to find them.

An advantage the Dalai Lama offers over Rambo and the Godfather is the vision of peace and happiness realizable through sustained, difficult, and gratifying disciplines of examining the inner self and outer reality in ways that allow for changes from destructive, adversarial behavior to that of compas-sion, mutuality, love. As little as Westerners know of Buddhism, even less is known about the activist implications and traditions in it.[15] It is these feelings and the relationships that make them possible, not revenge and brutal vindi-cation, that humans seek. Not finding them is a function of not having ade-quate concepts to define the problems and ways of pursuing happiness and peace. World figures like Nelson Mandela, Aung San Suu Kyi, and the Dalai Lama, through words and actions, model what is possible by way of paradigm transformation. It is my hope that my analysis of the adversary compulsion and the possible imminence of paradigm shift offer conceptual tools, visions, and actions that further the project of real liberation from the ill consequences and bad feelings of adversary behavior.

What I offer in this book is not a complete analysis and not a complete program of action. I hope, all the same, that it is a stimulating beginning that will lead to much more inquiry and investigation, to much more analysis and prescription, to experiments with taking useful part in individual and social change efforts. If survival is our project, the old ways no longer work. It is time to understand why and to create ways that do work, toward freeing us from unnecessary suffering and enabling us to bring all of us—not simply some at the expense of others—but all of us, closer to the happiness and fulfillment we all desire.

Organizations Promoting Nonviolence

For many years, nonviolence was a rather esoteric philosophy and practice. The War Resisters' League, the American Friends Service Committee, and the Fellowship of Reconciliation are among organizations known for promoting it in this century in the United States. In the 1930s and 1940s, Gandhi offered himself and millions of followers as exemplars of nonviolence by conducting campaigns of civil disobedience against the British occupation of what became India, Pakistan, and Bangladesh. Two decades later, Martin Luther King Jr. further developed these ideas in the United States through his many successful campaigns for African Americans' rights.

By the 1990s, the Albert Einstein Institution in Cambridge, Massachusetts, the Resource Center for Non-Violence in Santa Cruz, California, and Non-Violence International in Washington, D.C., emerged as organizations promoting nonviolence in this country and throughout the world. The founder of the Albert Einstein Institution, Gene Sharp, is probably the foremost Gandhi scholar and advocate in the world.[16]

Since 1993, Non-Violence International has published a journal called *International Journal of Non-Violence*. The Albert Einstein Institution and Garland Publishing produced *An Encyclopedia of Non-Violent Action* in 1997.

Although "hard-headed" military and political people have long ridiculed or ignored nonviolence, major accomplishments in the 1980s and 1990s can be attributed to people practicing this approach to conflict. Peaceful changeovers of government have taken place in the Philippines and Nicaragua, for example, and fundamental changes of political systems in South Africa, much of the former Soviet Union, and most of its former East European satellites have taken the nonviolence road. The seemingly intractable conflict between Israel and the Palestinians has not been without sporadic, limited violence, and the "peace process," which has included changes proceeding nonviolently, has been interrupted by rogue terrorist acts on one side and a government hesitant to proceed toward full peace on the other. It is too early to know how effective the forces in both communities that oppose a mutualistic settlement of the conflict will be.

A new campaign to stop U.S. arms sales to dictators suggests another phase of the possibility of nonviolence growing as a viable way of resolving conflicts within and among nations. War is still more popular and more often invoked to solve conflicts, but it is likely that in the modern period, nonviolence has made more gains than ever before in history.

It is conceivable that peoples of our planet will tire enough of war and its waste of lives and resources to demand peaceful ways of resolving all conflicts. I imagine one day the Pentagon being turned into a gigantic museum of the history of war, complete with exhibits of all its technologies, the political and economic systems that promoted it, the social psychology of support for it, and the nature of people who promoted it. The purpose of this vast museum would be to educate, so that people would understand how war arose, how it declined, and how to prevent its ever arising again.

Therapies and Self-Help Groups

Numerous psychotherapies have as their goal the restoration of the self's powers to act on behalf of its desires. Therapeutic efforts of necessity include working effectively with desires that threaten the social order and one's own well-being. Most psychotherapies help people speak what they mean, listen carefully to others, understand complexity in the self and in relations with others, act thoughtfully on the understanding, and be responsive in an enlightened way to one's own feelings and those of others.

The alliance of therapist and client becomes a model for care and joint endeavor. Therapy takes many forms. The classic model is client and therapist. Group therapy, wherein a number of clients and one or two therapists work together on clients' issues, is a variation. Workshops and retreats are other contexts in which people work together on inner issues.

Among the numerous variations on therapy is the self-help movement. Self-help is "a process, group or organization comprising people coming together or sharing an experience or problem, with a view to individual and/or mutual benefit."[17] It assumes that power over one's life is desirable and possible. While the former claim is news to no one, the latter is often greeted with disbelief. The normative image of self-help in the United States is the individual striving for what he or she wants: success in play, work, wealth, prestige, power. The idea that one can emotionally empower oneself not by comparing and competing but through inner exploration in the company of amiable others lies at the heart of the mutuality practice of self-help. In a Sunday edition, one midwestern newspaper lists Cocaine Anonymous, Codependents Anonymous, Gamblers Anonymous, Grief Support Group, Prostitutes Anonymous, Family Members of Youth Involved in Gangs, Words that Hurt:

Dealing with Verbal Abuse, Parents of Lesbians and Gays, Nicotine Anonymous, and ninety more support groups.[18]

Our Bodies, Ourselves, first published in 1970, was designed to help women understand and decode the mysteries of their physical beings. It was typical of physicians to sustain an adversary relation with women patients by mystifying their bodies and withholding information and decision-making rights from them. The authors of this self-help compendium not only explain technical issues of anatomy, physiology, and health but also instruct how to conduct breast and vaginal examinations on oneself. The sensibilities, language, and approach of the book contribute to the reader's empowerment.[19]

In the 60s and 70s, "consciousness-raising" groups encouraged women to overcome tendencies to think of their unsatisfying circumstances as unique and as their own individual problems. Women tended to assume that they could do nothing about, and maybe ought not even to question, what we can now characterize as adversary relations with men. With no formal or paid leadership, women learned in these groups to think together about women in history and society, to find ways to live their lives more fully, and to work for others' liberation as well.

Alcoholics Anonymous is the original twelve-step program, upon which subsequent efforts are based. Built on ultra-democratic structure with no paid staff, no professionals, and rotating roles of facilitator, recovery, when it happens, appears to be based on telling one's story to people with similar addiction problems who listen in supportive and empathic ways. There are twelve-step groups for families of alcoholics, drug-dependent people and their associates, people with eating disorders, bereaved people, disabled people, sufferers of the same disease, and more. There is, for a further example, a program called Stepping Stones, which runs weekend workshops for children 6–18 years of age and their families who are grieving for deceased relatives.[20]

Adversary rituals such as hurting, mistrusting, comparing, competing, and inducing fear may not be fully foreign to self-help groups, but their members make great efforts to minimize them by being self-conscious about their emergence and struggling to move past them. Self-help groups have at least this much in common: (1) members are equal in status, (2) all make decisions for themselves, (3) the group is responsible for its behavior, (4) members join because of their own problems, (5) proceedings are confidential, and (6) participation is free.[21] The emphasis on mutuality distinguishes self-help from normative competition and selfish individualism. (It is at the same time true— liberatory developments do have downsides—that some claims for success in such groups are exaggerated, some people "hustle" mutuality, such as professional facilitators who exploit clients for money and self-importance, and courts may coerce people to undergo group experiences that work only when entered voluntarily.)

Among the conditions that self-help groups address are these two: addictions and victimization. The first refers to food, drug, alcohol, or any other addictive behavior (imagine groups to help break addictions to adversarialism). The second refers to victims of painful circumstances over which they have no control, like being an abused person, the partner or child of an addict, the victim of a disease or crime, or the survivor of the death of someone close. Members of both kinds of groups support and comfort one another through identification, understanding, and empathy.

An anonymous author characterizes the distinctiveness of groups such as these:

> The self-help group is an American invention, and, in improvisational, pragmatic, egalitarian, and anti-hierarchical character, it bears an American stamp. . . . The language of self-help literature, which is the form in which self-help is most accessible to anyone who wishes to form an opinion about it . . . is entirely practical. . . . Everybody in a self-help group is . . . very obviously an equal.[22]

Self-help is an alternative to paid services for people whose income and subculture may not allow for professional help. In an organization free from the constraints of adversarialism, there is no room for malpractice lawsuits, emotional abuse, or financial exploitation. Moreover, self-help cuts across social classes, races, and ethnic groups. Participants learn they are not isolated and that their problems are common to a broad range of people. Self-help builds from models of grassroots democracy, empowerment, and mutuality. It is possible that self-help is not even the most precise term for this ritual. As it stresses the *sharing of experience,* it might more aptly be termed "mutual help."[23]

Self-help can be a diversion from trying to make changes in society rather than just in the self. At the same time, it offers a method whereby honesty with the self is cultivated. This, from a mutualistic point of view, is crucial for becoming sensitive and responsive to the needs and projects of other people. Empathy, to put it another way, is fundamental to the kinds of successful relating to others that is part of liberating social change. Self-knowledge thus is essential for gaining the strength to move effectively into social action.

New Games

The New Games Foundation is a nonprofit organization that promotes cooperation in play. Since 1974, New Games celebrations have been held at training programs, urban recreation departments, physical education proceedings, and conservation and community centers in the United States and other countries.[24]

New Games retrieve the somewhat abandoned spirit of play which is an essential part of mutuality. Invoking adversary imagery (and unwittingly suggesting difficulty in leaving it), *The New York Times* wrote in 1973, during the infancy of this mutuality ritual, "the occasion may be to a change in sports what the storming of the Bastille was to the French Revolution."[25]

New Games separate play from competition. In conventional musical chairs, a chair is removed after each round of the game until every player has lost but one, who had to be very aggressive to win. In the New Games variation, when the music stops, all people sit on the chairs that are left. At the end of the game, everyone is piled up on the last chair. The fun is in fitting together on remaining chairs rather than in defeating others.

In New Games, rules are flexible and can be adjusted to meet players' needs; gender, age, and size do not determine capacity for having fun. New Games rely less on forms and rules than on an attitude that encourages skilled exertion, playing, cooperating, and trusting rather than ranked comparison of abilities.[26] They invite spontaneity and participation.

"Infinity Ball" is a cooperative variation of volleyball. Beyond the fact that any number of people can play, the standard rules of volleyball generally apply, including that only three hits per side are allowed before the ball must be sent over the net. The main twist is that the score, kept track of by both teams in unison, is the number of times the ball is hit over the net without hitting the ground. Thus both sides "win,"[27] or more accurately, joint accomplishment and fun replace concern with victory of one side over the other.

The New Games "tug of war" also builds toward mutuality. While teams pull at opposite ends of a long rope as in the usual form of the game, as a side begins to lose ground, others join in.[28] What is traditionally referred to as "cheating" is "helping."

"Planet Pass" is played with a six-foot inflatable ball depicting the earth's continents and oceans. Players lie on their backs in a line. The object of the game is to keep the Earthball in the air, so that after passing the ball, one runs to the end of the line to receive it again. While the game could go on forever, a goal is set, such as keeping the planet "alive" for 2000 taps.[29] Other games such as waterslide, people pyramids, caterpillar, hug tag, and blob also represent seeds of new play.[30]

Emphasizing preparation for lifetime health rather than varsity competition, New Games are gaining momentum in children's physical education classes.[31] Gym teachers offer their students a choice of climbing the rope, swinging on it, or simply holding on. Rather than shooting a basket once or twice during the class period, students can handle a ball of size and weight right for them, hundreds of times a day, with a movable target that can be adjusted as their shooting improves. The aim of this new philosophy in physical education is not to learn to score a basket, but to develop body awareness and the confidence to try other activities. Many gym teachers have de-emphasized the whistle and stop-watch, to encourage students to play at their own pace. Benefits of alternatives to competition are being discovered in many places. In Jemison, Alabama, for example, a high school teacher has brought nature exploring, hiking, and nutrition into the gym curriculum.[32]

Cooperation appears in board games as well as in the gym and on the playing field. The publisher of "Eagle Eye Agency—The Cooperative Detective Game" explains,

> Any detective game we have tried has ultimately disappointed us because in the end the mystery itself was not so important as who won. Eagle Eye provides the opportunity for the players to work as a team of detectives much as a real team works in a police force or as a team works in a detective agency.[33]

Participants can freely test their ingenuity and deductive skills. Because they need not focus their energy on defeating one another, the game more closely resembles play than contest.

The recently evolved sports of frisbee and hackeysack began as purely playful pastimes. It is by now possible to play frisbee competitively, and perhaps hackeysack will move in the same direction, but so far, each offers itself at least part of the time as a context for fun with no winning-losing encumbrances.

Mediation

In mediation, a third party intervenes to help people resolve their conflicts. Mediator and clients work together to develop options, consider alternatives, and reach a consensual settlement that will accommodate their needs. As mediation recognizes participants' potential for directing their lives, it is a form of mutual empowerment. Disputants have increasingly turned to mediation as a means of addressing conflicts regarding housing, police, the workplace, minority relations, environmental issues, criminal justice, family and divorce proceedings, and education.

People who act on feelings of anger and rage in socially destructive ways threaten everyone's struggles to cope with personal violent inclinations. Separating and vilifying people who act against society is a way of avoiding the noncriminal's own tendencies to do the same thing. Although it is obvious that the majority wish to protect themselves against antisocial behavior by a criminal minority, it is not at all obvious that retribution contributes effectively to that goal. Retribution must be about venting feelings of rage, not about preventing anything.

Family and divorce mediation offers couples a less combative and more emotionally reassuring way of making important decisions about restructuring their family than is usually provided in litigation-based proceedings. Within the adversary framework a recalcitrant spouse often displaces his or her anger and resentment onto the divorce action itself, onto matters of child custody, visitation, or financial arrangements. The spouse's resistance to cordial settlement is expressed in such adversarial slogans as "Fine, divorce me. But I'm not going to lose the car/house/children with the marriage."[34] In litigation-based divorce, personal bitterness, for whatever reasons, is joined to the adversary compulsion so that the litigant sees the spouse as an opponent who must be defeated lest one lose to him or her. Mediation allows escape from this all-or-nothing thinking. Mediators clarify what disputants stand to gain and lose from continuing their conflict. They teach that noncooperation in the divorce will result in lowered esteem in the former spouse or children and that unilateral decision-making will not provide a mutual and lasting agreement. And they help the couple to visualize the long-term social and psychological ramifications of the struggle. Mediation fosters a sense of individual empowerment as well as the ability to respond cooperatively to changed circumstances. The consensual nature of mediation can, for example, lessen the probability of child-support violations.[35]

The mutuality ritual of mediation is also crystallizing in education. Mediation is increasingly seen as an effective way of resolving conflict among students and between teachers and parents. Urban Community Mediators, a volunteer organization founded in Massachusetts in 1975, trains high school students in techniques to mediate fights and other conflicts among school peers. The goal in such situations is a win-win outcome. At a conference on peer mediation and violence prevention held at the University of Massachusetts–Boston, then state Attorney General James Shannon "asked the audience to imagine how different Boston would be 'if our young people were armed with the weapons of communication and mediation instead of guns and knives.'"[36] Robin Brooke, a peer education coordinator at a neighborhood health center in Boston, observes, "It has been proven with my program and other studies that teens are very influential with other teens. When they see it work, it gives them a lot of self-esteem and pride."[37]

Games are used to teach mediation and the idea of compromise in resolving conflict. David Felder has designed games that simulate the Arab-Israeli conflict and parent-child conflict, as well as one entitled "Saddam vs. Uncle Sam." The games have fact sheets instructing each side on its real interest and on how to be an effective mediator. Such developments in the field of education strengthen mutuality by way of mediation. Felder claims, "Sometimes people turn to violence because they don't know alternative ways to handle conflict. The games can show an alternative to people going to court all the time."[38]

Mediation is increasingly common in disputes between parents and teachers over ways to meet a child's special needs. It helps to resolve such issues by providing a neutral third party to help along mutually agreeable decisions. In one case, a mother demanded three hours of instruction in reading, language, mathematics, and spelling for her mentally retarded twelve-year-old daughter. The school district argued that it was not its policy to cater to such demands. After successful mediation, the girl was provided one hour of academic instruction per day.[39]

Mediation is not only practiced in isolated cases. Twelve states and the Washington D.C. school district currently have special education mediation programs. The Neighborhood Justice Center of Atlanta has developed training models that address conflicts between parents and teachers. The program emphasizes learning about the "adversary" by playing each of the three basic roles of mediator, parent, and school representative.[40] The mediator acts as facilitator and agent of reality who asks participants to doubt the certainty of their perceptions about the other and to try to find convergent hopes and expectations.

The historical and cultural roots of mediation go as far back as ancient China. It is embedded in laws and customs of Japan, the Judeo-Christian tradition, and parts of Africa.[41] Its elements of openness, nonviolence, and cooperation, and capacities to listen, connect, and compromise are the mutuality bases of this seed of great potential change. Yet mediation is still a relatively unknown approach to conflict resolution in U.S. society.

Although negotiation differs from mediation in relying on the authority of the negotiator to a greater extent than happens with the mediator, nonetheless it shares with mediation the commitment to nonviolence as the preferred method for resolving conflicts. FBI agent Clint van Zandt was overruled in his claim that Ruby Ridge, Idaho (antigovernment militants) and Waco, Texas (Branch Dravidians) confrontations between citizens and federal authorities could be resolved by persuasion. After the Oklahoma City bombing in April 1995, that appeared to be vengeance for the Ruby Ridge and Waco violence, van Zandt was allowed to head the crisis team handling the 1996 standoff in Montana between the Freemen and the FBI. The resolution took time; it involved no violence. Lucinda Franks writes of this as a "victory of patience over force," which has vindicated van Zandt's approach.[42]

Van Zandt speaks of this transformation within the FBI in terms implicitly recognizing the scope of what amounts to a crucial piece of the paradigm shift I claim may be under way:

During my years with the F.B.I., we agents who believed that outsmarting the bad guys was better than trying to outshoot them were fighting an uphill battle against the Bureau's traditional mind-set, which held that you didn't try to figure out who the enemy really was, you just said, "Come out with your hands up or I'll blow you away . . ." As far as I'm concerned, the Freemen operation was a demonstration of *real* strength.[43]

In 1994, the Boston school system offered a nine-week pilot course introducing students to the Program for Young Negotiators, offered to a number of sixth through eighth graders in several middle schools. Created by the Consensus Building Institute in Cambridge, the program is meant to promote nonviolence in handling any kinds of conflicts.[44]

Restorative Justice

The Spring 1992 issue of *Odyssey*, a magazine subtitled Creative Alternatives to Criminal Justice, is built upon the theme of restorative justice contrasted with retributive justice. The latter, pure adversarialism, is captured by Howie Carr, a columnist for the *Boston Herald*:

We're human beings. We're carnivores. We're by nature a warlike species. I think we are always going to have certain violent people especially among the males due to testosterone or hormones or whatever you want to say. We're always going to have crime and the people who commit those crimes, male or female, need to be locked away from the rest of us so they can't hurt us.[45]

Favoring incarceration and incapacitation over rehabilitation, Harvard political scientist James Q. Wilson writes that

It is a measure of our confusion that such a statement will strike many enlightened readers today as cruel, even barbaric. It is not. It is merely a recognition that society at a minimum must be able to protect itself from dangerous offenders and to impose some costs . . . on criminal acts; it is also a frank admission that society doesn't know how to do much else."[46]

Leonard Zehr contrasts two forms of justice:

Retributive justice is a contest between state and offender, using systematic rules to determine blame. Restorative justice sees crime as a violation of people and relationships and seeks repair, reconciliation, and reassurance.[47]

Ruth Morris adds, "Respect, integration, democracy, advocacy, and honesty are among the core principles of restorative justice. Unfortunately, retributive justice, as we know it, violates all these principles."[48] As a model of restorative justice, she cites the Canadian Victim Offender Reconciliation Program started by Mennonites in Kitchner, Waterloo, in 1974. A judge was persuaded to allow two young offenders who had vandalized twenty-two properties to visit each of the homes and their owners. Two studies, one in British Columbia and one in the United States, "show that more than 90% of victims and offenders are satisfied with [this kind of] process and would like to do it again."[49]

Morris compares restorative justice with the revenge of retributive justice. The former attends to victims' needs by recognizing that they have been wronged and that their anger is legitimate, that they need to feel protected from further harm, that compensation of some kind is forthcoming, and that their experience can be used by society to help understand and better treat victimizers and their victims. Restorative justice emphasizes the larger context of victimizers' and victims' life histories, the institutions in which they are embedded, and the goal of harmonious relations rather than opposition and revenge.

Victim offender mediation services bring victimizers and victims to question each other, explain effects of the crime on them, work out a restorative plan, and provide counseling for the offender. In addition to print works cited, much of the conceptual framework and process of restorative justice appears in a video called "Restoring Justice," which shows pain, fear, hope, and other emotions on the faces and in the behavior of offenders, victims, and people who facilitate productive contact between the two.[50] In a study at the Center for Victim Offender Mediation in Minneapolis, very high rates of satisfaction are reported from both offenders and victims.[51]

Restorative justice embraces mediation, restitution, arbitration, and reconciliation as means to mend quarrels. As its social vision transcends an inefficient adversary trial system that increases division and alienation, it is a form of mutuality. The idea of reciprocal recognition and response could be the start of a process that would transfer weight on the scales of justice from retributive justice to restorative justice. By granting full recognition of the feelings and needs of all parties involved, this shift in conceptions of how to work with law-breakers contributes to an ethic of responsiveness that could transform the conditions that foster crime in the first place.

The issue is not whether alternative ways to deal with criminal justice are possible, for they already exist, in, for example, neighborhood justice experiments. The City Attorney's Office in Columbus, Ohio, operates a project in which conflicts ranging from assault to telephone harassment are mediated by a Capital University law student in order to encourage informal settlement between the parties involved.[52] In a program of the Justice Resource Institute in Boston, interpersonal matters involving relatives, neighbors, friends, and other relationships such as that between landlord and tenant are mediated by a panel of two or three local volunteers prepared in an intensive three-week training course.[53]

At the New York Dispute Resolution Center, disputants over harassment, assault, and theft seek agreements that subsequently are legally recognized and therefore binding under an enactment by the state of New York.[54] In Japan, West Germany, France, and Great Britain there is growing sentiment for reconciliatory forms of justice in preference to traditional retributive ones.[55]

Opening the Frame of Adversarialism

Adversarialism confronts everyone in everyday life, but most people are probably pulled into its destructive snares by those who are truly compulsive about it. It takes two or more to create and sustain a mutuality relationship but just one to insist on adversarialism. "Power can be stopped only by power."[56] Most people reluctantly go along with it because they feel they have no choice. There are, all the same, ways of cultivating alternatives to adversarialism, even with driven adversaries. The term "opening the frame" is useful for this process.

In 1987–88, during my sabbatical in Israel, I took part sometimes in a vigil against the Israeli occupation of the West Bank and Gaza. It was common for people who agreed with us to flash a V sign or call out words of encouragement. Often, opponents to our position shouted that we were finishing the Nazis' work, Arab-lovers, and the like.

One day, another vigiler and I engaged an antagonist in an exchange that opened the frame of adversarialism. The Israeli norm in confrontations with demonstrators is either for the demonstrator to yell back at the vilifier in equally passionate response, or to remain silent. We chose a third tack. The conversation went something like this:

HE (with strong emotion): You are feeding into Hitler's plans; you are going to destroy the Jewish people.

WE (also with strong emotion): You sound really angry.

HE (seeming a bit startled, probably because we did not give back the expected hostile reply): Yes, I am very angry.

WE: What are you angry about?

HE: I am afraid of the Arabs, they want to destroy us.

WE: We're afraid too. We're really afraid. The history of the thing is not good. What do you suppose we ought to do about our fear?

HE: Transfer [deport] the Arabs out of Israel and the territories. (At this point, it would be usual for the vigiler to accuse the other of being a racist, obstructing peace.)

WE: Transfer them out! What an interesting idea. How do you imagine going about it? (We had the impression that people who use deportation as a slogan have not thought out the actual details of what it would mean.)

HE (startled again): I'm not sure.

WE: Well, it would have to be buses or trucks, right? Israeli buses hold 44 passengers. Figure 2 or so million Palestinians, divided by 44. (Now the fellow seemed confused.) It would take a lot of busloads and truckloads. How would you get them on? They would not go willingly. Guns to their heads? (He did not like this idea.) What if they resisted? Would you shoot them, or what? And anyway, where would you take them? (Again, he may not have thought this out.) It would pretty much have to be Jordan, right? Now if you actually could get a couple million Palestinians to the border with Jordan and drop them off, do you suppose they would say Goodbye, you win, we quit. Or would they vow to work to get even and to come back to the land from which you had expelled them, just as you surely would were the situation reversed?

Now the other fellow said he had to leave, and did. I was moved by the conversation past my clichés about people who favor deporting Arabs from Israel. Although I did not accept his way of handling that fear, I felt for the first time I was starting to de-dehumanize someone whose politics I rejected. At the time, there seemed nothing more to do than have the conversation as we had it. In retrospect, I regret my partner and I did not ask for the chance to have an extended discussion whereby rather than simply showing the limits of the deportation argument, we might have explained our own reasoning (we did not), our own fears, and our hopes that people of clashing opinions learn how to examine the emotions underlying the positions and to work toward resolutions that address feelings as well as security concerns. This was, then, a partial opening of the frame of adversarialism, with an adversary component (we were in effect showing him limits to his position without real compassion for why he held it and what it meant to him) by stepping outside the shouting right-and-wrong format but not achieving real mutuality either.[57]

The point of opening the frame of adversarialism is to refuse the invitation to play by its terms. Doing so means the would-be adversary has the chance to respond to an invitation to find another way to talk, one that can lead to some place other than winning and losing. Gandhi drives at this in his suggestion of trying to touch the heart of the other and the Dalai Lama in his call for compassion toward *everyone*.

Another example of opening the frame: In an Alternatives to Violence program, a New York woman tells the story of her walking home across Central Park at dusk. She was carrying books she had just checked out at the New York Public Library. A menacing man approaches her, and she smiles at him. Explaining that the books are heavy, she asks him to help her home with them. The man does so and when he gives the books back to her at her apartment door admits that he had intended to mug her.[58] In class, when I have used this example, some students complain that one could not count on the non-mugging. True, but it seems a safer risk than running.

Etiquette columnist Judith Martin writes of telling a New York taxi driver her destination. His reply: "Lady, do you have any idea how far that is and how hard it is to get there?" Martin, were she committed to the adversary response the driver invites, might have said something like, "I'm the paying customer and you're the driver; now take me where I want to go." Or "Let me have your license number; I'm going to report this." Instead, she sat back, smiled, and said, "Well, then, where would *you* like to go?" The driver laughed, and apparently complied with her request.[59]

Derik Abelson, a seventeen-year-old high school student with cognitive and learning disabilities, was mocked and mimicked at his school in Ayer, Massachusetts. He complained to the school principal, who suggested Abelson tell the students of his hurt feelings. Two other students helped him organize his talks to several classrooms. One student reported that when Abelson told students how he felt, "he made us all talk and act differently in a positive way." Former tormentors have become admirers of Abelson, who was given an award by the Anti-Defamation League's A World of Difference Institute for his stand against prejudice.[60]

Another example of the power of opening the frame appears in the story of a Nazi and a Jew. In June 1991, Cantor Michael Weisser, newly moved to Lincoln, Nebraska, was told by a telephone caller, "You will be sorry you ever moved into 5810 Randolph St., Jew boy." Two days later, a packet of caricatures demeaning Blacks and Jews was tossed onto the Weisser's porch, with a note reading, "The KKK is watching you, Scum."

The police, whom the Weissers called, warned that the harasser was likely Larry Trapp, a local KKK activist and Nazi sympathizer. Although diabetic and in a wheelchair, Trapp was believed to be responsible for firebombings of African Americans' homes in the Lincoln area and an Indochina Refugee Assistance Center in nearby Omaha.

The Weissers began to wonder what made Trapp so hateful. The cantor left messages on Trapp's answering machine telling him that the Nazis killed disabled people like him and suggesting that Trapp let go of his hatred. He told Trapp that justice is for everyone and asked what would happen when one day Trapp meets God.

The two men finally connected on the phone, and Trapp demanded that Weisser stop harassing him. Following his wife's advice should actual phone contact come about, Weisser abjured the adversary frame and instead opened up a mutuality possibility. He said he knew Trapp was in a wheelchair and asked if he could take him to a grocery store or help in some other way. Trapp said no.

Some time later, Trapp in his wheelchair was helped onto an elevator by a Vietnamese woman. Trapp wept when he remembered the Omaha bombing. Later, he called Weisser to tell him he was rethinking some things. He apologized for his cruelties.

That evening, the cantor led his congregation in prayers for Trapp. Later, Trapp called the Weissers and said he wanted to "get out" but did not know how. The Weissers visited him. Julie gave Trapp a braided silver friendship ring. Trapp was moved to tears by the Weissers' visit and took off his two silver swastika rings, saying he could not wear them anymore.

Later, Trapp quit the Klan and all other racist organizations and wrote apologies to people he had offended. Eventually he learned he had just a year to live and accepted an invitation from the Weissers to spend it in their home. Julie, a nurse, left her job in order to take care of him. During that year, Trapp decided to convert to Judaism and did. He died a few months later.[61] Not surprisingly, Trapp's racism and sadism appear to have grown from a traumatic childhood. He was beaten and humiliated by a racist father. The story is told in greater detail in a *Not by the Sword* by Kathryn Watterson.[62]

Peace Movements

In places as diverse as Ireland, South Africa, and the Middle East, people have begun to cross adversary lines in working toward nonviolent solutions to continuing major political conflicts. During the Cold War, "track two diplomacy" developed in which United States and Soviet citizens made informal contacts with each other to establish interpersonal familiarity, common ground, and common aspirations. These actions served as statements of exasperation with conventional political processes and also prods to political authorities to move beyond the adversary fixations that seemed an essential part of the glue that kept adversary Cold War structures in place.

In more recent times, numerous groups have evolved to promote peace across national lines. Seeds of Peace is a summer program that brings together adolescents from eight Middle Eastern countries—seven Arab ones and Israel—to meet each other as members of a new generation who will be in a position in another decade or two to try to make peace in ways that may not have been available to their elders. The youths spend three weeks in a summer camp in Maine, building trust, friendship, and skills in learning about each other and getting along together.[63]

In Boston, the "Book of Peace" grew from the Louis D. Brown Peace Curriculum, created by the parents of Brown, a fifteen-year-old high school student who was shot to death while on his way to an antigang-violence meeting. In the book, teenagers' essays express their understandings and hopes for peace. One reads,

> There are people . . . who believe that violence is a normal part of life because they grew up watching their parents fight each other or their neighbors. These people have lost touch with basic humanism. They don't realize that life is more important than everything, more important than a pair of sneakers, more important than a million dollars, that nothing can ever be comparable to life.[64]

And Much More

Even to list new institutions adequately would require another book. Among them can be found the American Green movement, with its Ten Key Values of "ecological wisdom, grassroots democracy, personal and social responsibility, non-violence, decentralization, community-based economics, postpatriarchal values, respect for diversity, global responsibility, and future focus."[65] There are hundreds more. Readers are invited to consider other mutuality innovations and bring them to other people's attention.

Part V

☙⚓❧

Conclusion

I conclude this discussion with observations and speculations that push further the possibility that the foundation of a mutuality society is already under way. It is time for global visions, not to negate local visions so much as to bind them together into a project that recognizes the organic relation of the human species to all others and to the planet and the cosmos. The challenge of learning to live in harmony can replace that of learning to oppose and conquer. It is the fitting project for our era, the survival project itself.

The idea of global visions is not new; part of our challenge is to renew them and reshape them according to the imperatives laid out by our material circumstances of nuclear threat, environmental devastation, and rapidly expanding population. It is on that material base that we can rethink and rework our relations with the planet, with other people, and with ourselves. It will help develop what I call the "mutuality of growth," suggesting how best to work with others in developing our own strengths and theirs.

One can appreciate the self as active agent in history and the complexity of the circumstances in which the self acts by keeping one's eyes on both levels of analysis and their intersection. By so doing, the self can extend beyond adversarialism, can base actions on empathy far more than has been the norm so far in history, and can enjoy the extraordinary feelings—some call them spiritual—of connections with other people, other species, the planet, and the universe.

SEVENTEEN

ↄ◠◇◠ↄ

Three Stretches
toward Globalism

War is no longer legitimate, but peace is not
yet legitimate.

—Kenneth Boulding,
Stable Peace

What is happening in this world-order revolution in the shift from civilization to planctiza-
tion is the return of the seasonal round, a
return to connectedness with the biosphere, a
shift from masculine, linear, binary modes of
thought to feminine, cyclical, and analogical
modes of being. . . . From the restructuring of
civilization comes the unimaginable creation
of planetization.

—William Irwin Thompson,
Darkness and Scattered Light

The Defeatist Temptation and the Hope Beyond It

We are like flies crawling across the ceiling of the Sistine Chapel: we
cannot see what angels and gods lie underneath the threshold of our perceptions. We do not live in reality; we live in our paradigms, our habit-
uated perceptions, our illusions; the illusions we share through culture
we call reality, but the true historical reality of our condition is invisible
to us. How can you fix up history if you cannot see it? And what if history cannot be fixed from inside history? What if the attempt to fix
human history is an effort to seek out the dark with a searchlight?[1]

I include this warning simply to acknowledge that attempting to discover the boundaries of our consciousness and how to move beyond them is

fraught with difficulties. But if we are to surmount the potentially deadly consequences of our moment, it is essential to make the effort. If we advance in the project to sustain life and to integrate ourselves with each other and our planet, we will eventually do so in transnational conversations which will extend indefinitely our abilities to act on what we learn.

Yes, I know many readers are dubious about the usefulness of understanding and the potentialities of human action. Thus, what I see as the dialectical counterpoint to the quotation above:

> Let no one be discouraged by the belief there is nothing one man or one woman can do against the enormous array of the world's ills—against misery and ignorance, injustice and violence. . . . Few will have the greatness to bend history itself; but each of us can work to change a small portion of events, and in the total of all those acts will be written the history of this generation.
>
> It is from numberless diverse acts of courage and belief that human history is shaped. Each time a man [or woman] stands up for an ideal, or strikes out against injustice, or acts to improve the lot of others, he [she] sends a tiny ripple of hope, and crossing each other from a million different centers of energy and daring, those ripples build a current which can sweep down the mightiest walls of oppression and resistance.[2]

Some News That's Fit to Print

News media, one is told, have to report on violence and sensationalism because that is what readers want (and that, supposedly, is what sells the media). Yet occasionally the adversary frame is opened. Here are mutuality stories in the first section of the *Boston Globe* of August 21, 1993.

One (p. 1): Both sides cheer settlement that shares Vt. boy
    The adoptive mother openly wept in joy. The biological father walked out of the courtroom proudly. Family and friends on both sides applauded. And nothing turned out as anyone expected yesterday, when all parties to the complicated adoption tussle over Baby Pete arrived at a surprise solution.
    Under a creative settlement that even Addison County Probate Judge Chester Ketcham called "unique," Donna McDurfee—who, with her husband Richard, has been fighting to adopt the nine-month-old child—becomes his legal mother. She will have "primary custodial responsibility" for the boy who is to be known henceforth as Peter Elliott Harriman McDurfee.

But Daniel Harriman—the biological father, who had been fighting for custody of his only son—is officially recognized as the baby's
father, with full legal and visitation rights.

. . . "Nobody lost, and the baby won," said [Richard McDurfee].
"It's the best day of my life."

In a season when a boy of twelve divorced his biological parents in
order to relate exclusively to his adoptive parents, when a girl of two was
forced to leave her adoptive parents and live with her biological parents, and
when a teenage girl sued to prevent her biological parents from visiting her at
all—a season of adversarial proceedings and outcomes in family matters—the
Vermont decision is striking for its mutuality character.

Two (p. 2): Israelis bury their dead and hold their fire
Despite a surge of anger among Israelis over the loss of nine soldiers in southern Lebanon, Prime Minister Yitzhak Rabin held fast yesterday to an agreement reached with Syria and did not send forces to
flush Iranian-backed guerrillas from Lebanese villages. . . .

"The way to avert such tragedies in the future is a peace agreement," a senior Rabin adviser said.

The commitment to forgo retaliation is a far cry from the usual Israeli
response to such provocations. This action anticipated the peace accord
signed by Israel and the Palestinians in September 1993.

Three (p. 3): Hunger strikers on bus in Texas allowed to ship supplies
to Cuba
Ministers on a three-week hunger strike in a school bus along the
U.S.-Mexico border won permission yesterday to deliver supplies to
Cuba. They were protesting the U.S. trade embargo against that com-
munist nation. . . .

The standoff ended after the government declared the bus to be
humanitarian aid instead of an illegal export. . . .

[The bus was on a convoy] carrying computers, medicine, wheel-
chairs, school supplies and other materials for Cuba.

Although it is likely that the government backed off from its original
position because of embarrassment caused by the fast of determined clergy
in very hot weather, the resolution of the issue is not the usual adversary
one.

In our last example from the same issue of the *Boston Globe*, excerpts
from Salman Rushdie's *The Satanic Verses* were published without Rushdie's

permission by Turkish newspaper editor Aziz Nesin. Riots ensued, and a hotel where Nesin was staying in Turkey was set on fire. He escaped, but thirty-seven people died.

> Four (p. 4): Rushdie in Germany for Rapprochement
> The real turning point comes around midnight. . . . When the company rises from the dinner table to retire, the two central figures embrace . . . the friendliness that manifests itself is spontaneous and mutual.
> Rushdie and Nesin agree on an important point—that the fate of Islamic fundamentalism will be decided by how it is confronted on its own turf.
> While postponing plans to publish *The Satanic Verses* in Turkish, the two agreed to Turkish translations of some of Rushdie's other works. They also discussed plans for a petition in support of Rushdie to be circulated among the 1.8 million Turks in Germany.

The same day's paper, needless to elaborate, is also filled with stories of murders, kidnappings, the arrest of a con man, and other adversary proceedings.

Strangers in Good Company: A Mutuality Tale

Strangers in Good Company is a film in its own genre. I have so far been able to find none other I would call fully mutuality films. With its nonprofessional cast, the acting in *Strangers* is so direct that it feels like a documentary.

The storyline of *Strangers* is minimal. Seven women in their seventies through nineties, six of them White and one Mohawk, and their young Black woman driver, are stranded in the Canadian countryside after their excursion bus breaks down. They find shelter in an abandoned house. As the little food they happen to have with them gives out, they pick berries and catch frogs and fish. Gradually, they reveal their vulnerabilities to each other.

There is nothing adversarial in the story, even though each of the women is miffed by the inconvenience of being stranded. One complains after their first night in the house that she could not sleep. It was, she says, the worst night of her life; she lets it go at that. Another could not sleep because someone snored. She does not complain to that woman, and nothing more is said.

What holds the audience, I think, is the gentle sharing of adversity that the women take for granted. If there is an adversary, it is their plight; it is not each other. There are no prima donnas among the women, no whiners, no clowns, no scapegoats. Constance, because of whose search for a childhood home the bus broke down in deserted territory, says early on that she feels guilty for what happened, but she is talked out of that rather easily. No one is blaming anyone for anything. No one hurts anyone.

As the women tell their stories, there are no unfavorable comparisons. Cissy, super-straight but open, kind, and fully alive, is fascinated by Mary's lesbianism and does not judge it. Everyone's vulnerabilities are accepted and respected. There are no contrasts of achievements or hard-luck stories. Nobody contradicts another. Even a card game is played just for fun.

The women accept each other as they are. They are curious about their companions, and although no complex histories are revealed, each tells enough about herself that she risks being ridiculed or misunderstood. That does not happen.

Every woman in the story speaks quietly and moves softly. Even big, tough Alice is gentle and graceful in her voice and her walk. Bus driver Michelle, young, vibrant, wise, and a bit large, does not complain about her sprained ankle; she manages her misfortune with dignity. She does not seek sympathy; from this group, she can take it for granted.

This is the stuff of mutuality. While picking berries, Alice tells Cissy how she loves it when her almost two-year-old great-grandson runs to her. She regrets that she will not live to see him to manhood. Cissy reveals she has two grandchildren but fears that something could happen to her only child, their father, and where would that leave her? She is sorry she had no more children. Alice, also a mother of one, does not express a corresponding fear; she comments she feels better now that they have told these things. The women talk about family and their lives. The film shows stills of each one (except Michelle, the driver) as a girl and as a young woman. They talk of work, which most of them did not like. The exception is Catherine, who loves being a nun and who cannot fully explain her joy in serving others, although we see it in her effort to repair the bus engine and in her determination, despite arthritic feet, to go for help when her attempt fails. Mary enjoys drawing. Alice once worked on an assembly line she hated and quit. Winnie disliked her job on a cigarette factory assembly line during World War II, but she stuck it out.

There are no lawyers or doctors among them, nor, except for the incapacitated Michelle, are there younger women either. Four are of a certain conventional woman's experience, but we are reminded that even in their era, there were lesbians and of course nuns.

So powerful are all seven of the older women, in who and what they are, that Michelle falls in easily with them. (She, though, tells nothing of herself; nor is she asked.) Sometimes she is amused; she asks Beth to take off her wig and wear a scarf over her natural hair. Beth does, and Michelle tries to convince her how attractive she is that way. Beth looks wistful for a moment, as if she would like to lighten up but just does not seem to have that in her. Kindly, Michelle does not press the point.

Strangers in Good Company leaves viewers with no story to savor, no plot to examine, no tensions that need resolving. The director has coaxed from the women who and what they are, albeit in a contrived setting. Were mutuality a more common focus for movies, wider audiences might appreciate such real people as these.

How to Make an American Quilt shares with *Strangers in Good Company* the device of women relating to each other mutualistically through telling their stories. In *Quilt*, a young woman, Finn (Wynona Ryder), retreats to her grandmother's house to write her master's thesis and figure out whether she wants to marry the man who wants to marry her. Her grandmother and several friends, a group long experienced in collective quilt-making, are making a quilt for what they believe is the impending wedding.

The film is largely a series of stories about marriage and its problems, gently and compassionately told to Finn by women two generations older than her. Each embodies what she tells of her story in her contributions to the quilt. That lives are interrelated is a major theme of the movie and its central material trope, as is the claim that people connect sympathically through revealing their vulnerabilities to each other.

This same insight, according to one author, underlay the NBC network's strategy in programming the 1996 Olympic games in Atlanta. NBC discovered that more women than men watch the Olympics and that "Before they can get interested in an event, [women] need to know the characters and sympathize with them. For women, winning and losing are secondary; *story* is the main thing."[3] Olympic reportage (in between commercials, many of them also presenting ministories) thus built upon the same insight used by the directors of *Strangers* and *Quilt*: that women tend more than men to relate through recognizing and accepting vulnerabilities and to sympathize with the people in the stories behind those vulnerabilities. It appears that the unprecedentedly fully scripted Republican and Democratic National Conventions in 1996 were also addressed to a majority female audience by dwelling on personal stories more than on issues or conflicts.[4] The presidential and vice-presidential "debates" in 1996 were unusually civil in tone and featured many illustrative anecdotes. All this further suggests responding to the "gender gap" appeals, that is, to what is perceived as women's inclination to prefer civility and the humanization of real stories to heavily adversarial political confrontations.

Two 1996 films add to this analysis of women's relations as central to their life experiences. In *The Spitfire Grill*, a young woman ends five years in prison and seeks a small town to begin anew. A kindly sheriff persuades Hannah (Ellen Burstyn), the old widowed proprietor of the Grill, to take on Percy (Allison Elliott) as an employee. Conscientiously and diligently, Percy learns the ropes and has to take over when Hannah is temporarily immobilized by an accident. Shelby (Marcia Gay Harden), wife of Hannah's nephew who looks with disfavor on an ex-convict living among them and working for his aunt, joins Percy in keeping the restaurant going. The three women develop warm, close relations. They are kind and mutually supportive and delight in each other's company. Appearing to respect what is pretty clearly her sorrow, neither Hannah nor Shelby probes into Percy's past, although Hannah's nephew becomes obsessed with it. He introduces the conventionally male, competitive, dominative element into the story, and his doing so brings tragedy for Percy and redemption for another male, Hannah's Vietnam-war damaged son, and finally for the nephew too, who at the funeral service for Percy admits his error in judgment about her.

Whatever the plot problems of *Spitfire*, it continues in what appears to be the genre in growing numbers of films about women in mutualistic relations with each other. Unlike the women in *Strangers* and *Quilt*, though, those in *Spitfire* bond through work before they tell much of their stories. They seem to intuit and appreciate pain, loneliness, and exasperation and let their recognition of those and of each other's emotions suffice for connection. Near the denouement of the film, when Percy reveals her story to Shelby, Shelby's compassion and affection for her, already fully developed, are now solid enough that she can be sure, correctly, that Percy is not guilty of a crime newly attributed to her in the film.

A fourth such movie is *Manny and Lo*. Two orphaned sisters, about sixteen and eleven years of age, leave foster homes for the road. The older one, Laurel, called Lo (Aleksa Palladino), drives the car that is, as in *Thelma and Louse* as well as countless male films, the emblem of freedom, but also, inevitably, of trouble. In perhaps all such stories, it is as if the machine of freedom does not produce. Sometimes outer realities, and often inner ones ignored in the frantic quest for no binds and no bonds beyond one buddy, haunt the outlaws and eventually destroy them. But not so in *Manny and Lo*. Lo becomes pregnant by a casual boyfriend. Once she seeks medical advice, she is too far along to abort and so has to figure out how to get help to have the baby. She and Amanda, called Manny (Scarlett Johansson), kidnap a sad-looking, slightly daffy baby store employee Elaine (Mary Kay Place), whom they think, from hearing her conversations with customers, knows much about babies and could help them at the crucial time.

Lo seems to play a traditional male role, in charge of her and Manny's meanderings, contemptuous of her sex partner's gift of a flowery blouse, and determined not to inform Elaine why they have kidnapped her until Elaine accepts that Lo is in control. Because Lo refuses Manny's suggestion that she level with Elaine, Elaine keeps emotional distance between her and her kidnappers, goes on a prolonged hunger strike, and tries one combination after another to open the padlock on her ankle chain. But after a while, Elaine begins taking care of the girls. Even though she is slowed by the chain, she begins to make proper meals for the three of them and to offer the right advice to the pregnant Lo, such as to stop smoking.

Gradually, Manny, Lo, and Elaine become a family. Elaine, who was "too cluttered" in earlier years to have a family, becomes mother-sister-aunt-friend to Manny and Lo. She helps Lo give birth, and not only is a new life born, a new family is too.

In this film, to the extent that stories are told, it is through indirection and occasional references. As in *Spitfire*, connection is based less on disclosure of personal narratives than on respect for complex feelings and absence of judgment about them.

These films, then, largely mutualistic in character, emphasize vulnerabilities explained in stories or intuited through emotional recognition or both. And they reveal respect for emotions, whether ordinary or not, without judgment. As judgment is a prime adversarial technique, its absence is a core piece of mutuality.

I have found it a challenge to locate more mutuality films. What Philip Slater calls "reconciliation plots" are partial fits.[5] *The Mission* tells of an idealistic, compassionate Catholic priest (Jeremy Irons) who establishes a mission in southern South America in the seventeenth century. A tough, angry former slave trader (Robert DeNiro) murders his brother in a fit of jealousy over the woman they both love and atones for his sin by a drawn-out process of self-mortification, at the end of which he and the cleric who has chastised him come to respect and enjoy each other fully; DeNiro becomes a priest.

This reconciliation takes place in the context of Irons setting up a cooperative, joyful, mutualistic agricultural and living community among the Indians for whom he built his mission. The Spanish and Portuguese authorities, alarmed at resistance to enslavement in the name of empire, destroy the mission, killing DeNiro and vast numbers of the Indians, who, against Irons's wishes and commitment, take up arms against the imperialists.

Slater mentions as other reconciliation films, several from the fifties and sixties (*Me and the Colonel, The Defiant Ones*, and *In the Heat of the Night*) and more from the late eighties (*Midnight Run, Outrageous Fortune, 48 Hours, Kiss of the Spider Woman, Alien Nation, Baghdad Cafe, Ruthless People, Orphans, Russkies, Mona Lisa, Enemy Mine, Throw Mama from the Train, Running Scared*, and *Driving Miss Daisy*, as well as *The Mission*. In all cases, hostilities between unlike people, usually antagonists, are transformed, through compassion and accepting the other, into respect and mutuality.[6]

Slater adds a category of films that seem to express "a hunger to understand the experience of others, an empathic questing that anticipates the democratic [in my terms, mutualistic—GF] future.'"[7] In this genre he includes *Trading Places, All of Me, Vice Versa, Big*, and *Like Father Like Son*. He also includes transvestite films like *Tootsie, La Cage aux Folles*, and *Victor, Victoria*,[8] to which I will add the more recent *Priscilla, Queen of the Desert*, and *Birdcage* (a remake of *La Cage aux Folles*). In all these cases, ordinary adversary relations are questioned, tested, challenged, and in some critical ways, discarded.

These films tell stories that potentially liberate the tellers, their complementary figures in the films, and the audience. It is useful to remember that psychoanalysis and numerous forms of psychotherapy center on clients telling their stories to professional listeners, who help clients interpret and come to terms with them. The dehumanization that is essential to adversarialism is discarded in personal storytelling that thereby lays a basis for mutuality.

Freud teaches us that people have very complex, painful stories and that those stories can confuse and inhibit them. People in our society are discouraged from admitting their vulnerabilities and working on them; they are guarded about where, if at all, to tell their stories, although women tend to tell them more easily to one another than do men. At present, many social norms and decades of neurotic repressions have eradicated, for vast numbers of people, the ordinary but sublime processes of unburdening, recognition, and acceptance in close relationships. By talking and by learning to listen and respond, some competence can be gained in coming to terms with lingering hurts, rages, confusions, and longings by both tellers and listeners. *Strangers in Good Company* is a mutuality poem, a dance revealing how people learn to move in harmony with each other, to enjoy and respect their strengths and tender places, to empathize, share, and care in easy, natural ways.

Whither Adversarialism?

If humans are on the cusp of major paradigm shift, as I claim, then we can focus not on how to end adversarialism, but rather on how best, from the point of view of survival, to express the elements of each paradigm in this era. Both paradigms are forever in tension with each other; we have choices to make when we feel impelled to act on them. If to survive we need to move toward greater mutuality, we will also need to sustain adversary contexts in which to continue to play out our adversary tendencies—the results of accumulated anger and rage—unless and until we perfect ways through conversation and art that make adversary encounters no longer necessary or desirable.

When Freud talked about sublimation, he meant that since we cannot express all sexual urges directly, it is useful for civilization and for our own individual survival, to sublimate such energies into socially useful behavior. Work and art, as well as affection and play, embody many aspects of Eros, Freud's term for the energy at the foundation of all life-preserving and life-enhancing inclinations. In his writings on sublimation, it is possible to include destructiveness in the discussion. Although Freud does not do so, it is plausible to apply a corresponding analysis to destructiveness, which seems to come from experiences of the self not being affirmed rather than from biology itself. Nature provides us with the potential to destroy, but the potential is engaged only in experiences that often could have been more gratifying had those disconfirming the self been more in tune with themselves, their own histories, and the realities of the people they affect. To sublimate destructiveness means to use it creatively for the benefit of others. Earlier, I suggested that some athletic activity is a way of siphoning off destructiveness toward others while benefiting the body and soul.

The use of adversary inclinations in politics could, for another example, mean opposing domination in place of furthering it. Thus the same internal juices could be called upon to oppose racism as to be a racist. And thus with promoting or helping move beyond sexism, anti-Semitism, homophobia, the maldistribution of resources in a society, and all other forms of domination.

Adversary vigor can engage the self in self-examination, the point of which is not self-deprecation but coming to terms with universal tendencies toward defeat, sloth, indifference, and resignation to seemingly insuperable forces in the self and outside it. Argument can be debilitating, but friendly analysis can be rousing and productive. The point of argument is to overcome the other, and nothing good comes of it; but friendly analysis has as a goal elucidation, the challenge to make things clear, to improve skills, and to sharpen insight and understanding, putting adversarialism to very good use.

Conflict can, then, be adversarial when the goal is overcoming the other, or mutualistic when the goal is learning and growing from understanding through opening oneself to the other and exploring differing views and experiences. Hearing the other in order to overcome or submit is adversarial. Listening to the other in order to absorb viewpoints and feelings, allowing the vulnerability of reassessment, of considering real change, is mutualistic. Readers can undoubtedly think of other useful ways to engage adversary tendencies at no harm to self, others, and environment.

In order to sustain adversarialism, society has produced, in abundant numbers, what we might call the adversary character type. A transition to mutuality as the salient mode of expression will bring the mutuality character type, already with us in nooks and crannies of most institutions, to the fore. Mutuality types at present are often suppressed and repressed, even, likely, unto the ranks of the mentally disturbed. I do not foresee pathologizing adversarialism in a corresponding way but rather working to bring out the mutuality tendencies in everyone, so as, in the more adversarial types, to suggest choices and balance where once mutuality might have been subordinated and even dismissed.

Toward Globalism

Two unforeseen developments preoccupy the post–Cold War world: the expansion of fundamentalist religion and nationalism. Although the bulk of attention to the former has been given to Islamic fundamentalism, Jewish, Christian, and Hindu fundamentalism, dogmatic and intolerant, also appear to be holding their own. This is a time of renewed ultranationalism and violent ethnic assertiveness in what were Yugoslavia and the Soviet Union and in Sri Lanka, the Sudan, India, Rwanda, Burundi, and other countries.

At the end of the Middle Ages, the Renaissance and the Reformation opened the way to capitalism and democracy. The promise of the former was unfettered entrepreneurship that would bring comfort and abundance to all. The promise of democracy was opening politics to universal participation. These two meaning systems, capitalism and democracy, appeared to be succeeding the narrowness and rigidities of the feudal economic system, fundamentalist religion, and ethnic identification in the form of virulent nationalism.

While the ideas and enthusiasms behind capitalism and democracy were impressive, the actual systems evolved with very mixed results. Capitalism created massive forced movements of peasants from the countryside to cities where vast numbers of men, women, and children became desperately poor laborers, working in unsafe, unhealthy working conditions and living in crowded, filthy slums. Social order broke down. Disease, prostitution, crime, alcoholism, and despair were rampant, and remain so in many cities of industrial and industrializing societies.

Various socialist thinkers, culminating in Marx, came along, as did sociology, to inquire into the reasons for this turn of events in which the bourgeoisie prospered and vast numbers of other people suffered. "Utopian socialists" imagined humane alternative communities that would bypass the dehumanizing effects of capitalism. Seeing that these would serve very few people at best, Marx envisioned another way. He believed that capitalism was necessary to develop full industrialization, which in its eventual automated form would free people from boring work and create the material preconditions for universal comfort and freedom for the fulfillment of skills and potentials in everyone. Get through capitalism as rapidly as possible, Marx advised, then create socialism, which will distribute abundance equitably (its disinterest in fair distribution is one of many limits of capitalism) and will free people to realize themselves in ways previously available only to bohemians and elites.

Democracy, Marx explained, became manipulated by the very wealthy in order to promote profit-making. In the name of manipulated democracy, business and political elites, in addition to providing abundance for some and order for many, also hoodwinked, stole, lied, and killed. They initiated wars to control markets, bought or were bought as politicians, and directed media and education so as to limit how much real truth about society was going to reach the public. The elites, crucially aided by some journalists and some academics, eventually deceived most people with bizarre if seductive notions that human fulfillment and consumerism are one and the same, and that watching TV for hours day and night is happiness itself. These deceptions, whether or not intentionally cruel, have served for two centuries to confuse people and to distract them from facing and resolving the real problems, external and internal, that beset them.

As Russia was entering capitalism at the turn of the century now nearly ended, Lenin imagined that socialism could be created without first going through capitalism, even though Marx warned against such a foolish effort and especially advised that if the Russians tried to do so, they would fail. They did.

But meanwhile, "socialism/communism," as the world movement sponsored by the Soviet Union promoted it, offered hope to millions of people who wanted out of the horrors of capitalism and the mockery of democracy that often accompanied it. In the Third World especially, after shaking off the colonial order, there was widespread yearning for justice and equality rather than the rapacious opportunism of capitalism, with greedy local elites running societies for their own benefits and those of their partners, transnational owners in the industrially developed world.

Socialism/communism did not create the millennium; although it brought universal education and medical care for all, and concepts of justice and decency, it also brought new versions of elitism and injustice. With its collapse, one entire world meaning system is about over. It lingers in China, Cuba, North Korea, Vietnam, and a few other places, but most have long since given up on creating new economic systems; they have already joined, or will soon, the capitalist world market system.

The other gigantic meaning system is in trouble too. Social decay permeates the United States, and Europe and Japan are not far behind. The social inequities that capitalism seems to demand are coming now to haunt it. Elites seem insatiable as, particularly in the United States, they succeed in influencing the government to redistribute income upward. Crime, homelessness, addictive drug use, family collapse, decay of urban services, disease, hopelessness, despair—all these pervasive phenomena suggest that the one remaining superpower did not "win" anything with the collapse of the Soviet system but rather has a little more time to decline in its own way.

The crisis is that faith in the capacity of our system to produce comfort, opportunity, dignity, and self-respect for everyone is dwindling rapidly, because the system seems unable to provide that. The response to bitter disappointment in both major postmedieval systems seems to be massive regression to earlier meaning systems. The recent wave of "return" to fundamentalist religion vividly demonstrates that some people handle confusion and fear by embracing absolutist, dogmatic systems of meaning. Turn yourself over to the clergyperson (rabbi/imam/preacher/priest), and he (in these contexts, rarely she) will tell you what to do, when to do it, and with whom. It is not hard to understand the appeal of a return to early childhood certainties, before moral judgments and critical thought became familiar and seemingly problematic.

Rabid nationalism is also massively regressive. With the breakdown of economy, polity, and meaning in Eastern Europe and the former Soviet Union, unscrupulous leaders promote the politics of nationalism and opposition. It is not just that Serbs and Croats have sustained long-standing hatreds of each other, and Serbs and Bosnians, Armenians and Azeris, Chechnyans and Russians, and so on, it is also that the kinds of people whose compulsions lead them to seek power sometimes take the relatively easy way by fueling latent hatreds into full-blown conflagrations. Love and respect among people are sacrificed to the gods of cynicism and opportunism, and before you know it, everything is out of hand. With the collapse of postmedieval meaning systems, there is a grotesque if understandable tendency to accept leaders who point the way, in truly regressive and reactionary ways, to prior meaning systems, none of which can possibly deliver on their promises.

As if that were not bad enough, the end of the stable if sick Cold War oppositions between two gigantic systems has redounded into intensifications of intranational adversary relations particularly among races, ethnic groups, classes, genders, and sex orientations. All of these also represent regression from possibilities of mutuality to archaic systems of adversarialism.

If the current movement is backward, there is another option, a crucial choice that can be made: movement forward. There are local and national strivings toward cooperation and transnational problem-solving, in place of retreating to worn-out, warmed-over meaning systems that will produce at least as much damage now as they did centuries ago. These strivings are crucial parts of the alternative, *globalism*, which takes the entire planet as a reference point, and preservation of all its human and ecological systems as a goal with which people can identify for the first time (save for rare, far-seeing people of times past) with the planet Earth. Building from the fragility of our globe, long understood by many preindustrial peoples but only recently and barely recognized in the larger societies, the goal is to use Earth's resources for everyone's benefit and to consider all people as equally entitled to all political liberties.

Some bases for globalism are already apparent. Global ecological crises make a mockery of national borders and thus hasten the development of global awareness, a survival necessity. Overfished seas, depleted rain forests, thinned ozone, and fallout from Chernobyl have planetary, not only national, consequences. Global awareness begins, perhaps then, with the objective material realities of environmental crises.

The UN Declaration of Human Rights and evidence from nearly every part of the planet make it clear that democracy and human rights are emerging as global political values. Chinese students demonstrating for democracy, the increasing successes of Amnesty International in freeing prisoners who have spoken their minds in repressive societies, and yearnings for real democratic participation just about everywhere underscore the observation.

A global culture must have a language, and English is indeed emerging as just that. It is the language increasingly of business, intellectual interchange, and much of entertainment. Global English will most likely supplement, not replace, national languages. And as it develops globally, English will almost certainly be infused with words from Hindi, Chinese, Russian, French, Swahili, Arabic, Hebrew, German, Japanese, and many other languages. A world English will gradually evolve that will differ from any of the national English languages now spoken, and it will be taught and used as the language of globalism.

A global culture needs music. There are already two world music forms: jazz and rock. Both originate in the U.S. slave experience and hence are African in origin. Both appear to contain in sometimes subtle, sometimes obvious ways, expressions of scorn for domination and exploitation and yearnings for real freedom.

A global religion may well, as Charlene Spretnak anticipates, blend the action-orientation of Judaism, Christianity, and Islam, and their attention to working in community, with the disciplined inner awareness of Buddhism, the reverence for nature and for humans' integration with it common to Native American religions, and celebration of the human body common to many feminist spiritual endeavors. Buddhism can also be included among the religions teaching and practicing environmental awareness, social activism, and community.[9]

World clothing styles are well developed. They include T-shirts, with texts of art, politics, and almost anything else on them; jeans; sneakers and sandals; and ethnic jewelry that is sold in bazaars and flea markets throughout the planet.

These so far are integrating features of a budding globalism. At the same time, so far they tend to disparage local cultures and encourage their dissolution and to promote private profit rather than human engagement, compassion, and understanding. Global TV informs, and in that way is liberating, but it also conveys images of reckless violence and rabid consumerism, which not only cannot be available to everyone but which distract attention from issues that desperately need collective human attention. Among their complexities, transnationals' accomplishments include a world cuisine of junk food, much of it made from animals whose feeding requires taking vast amounts of land out of production of grains that are far more efficiently grown and healthy to eat than meat. Fast food also uses too many ingredients like fat and preservatives that are not good for the body. World consumer culture includes cigarettes, pushed upon poor populations more relentlessly than any other drug, and advertised as if smoking and health were compatible.

The world, as Marx predicted, is becoming united in a single economic system. He could not foresee that it would also come together into a single, integrated information system. Both these global systems bear the seeds of greater degradation and also seeds of real liberation, through development of "sustainable" agriculture and technologies and through the ease of conveying information about politics, technology, and just about everything else.

Just barely but noticeably, the lineaments of a global culture have begun to emerge, like the first traces of a photograph in the pan of developing fluid. The potentials for real freedom and for exploitation are all there. Identifying them and learning how to promote the ones we favor and discourage the others are crucial to what will be the emerging global politics.

The Self and Its Strengths: The Mutuality of Growth

If Freud was an archaeologist, as he claimed in one of his favorite metaphors, he dug into the foundations of the adversary paradigm but did not recognize it as such. Ego defense, Freud's term for a way the self manages its conflicts, is a mechanism that can also sustain the adversary paradigm. Freud's awareness of love and the problems in achieving it[10] let him see defenses as issues to be worked through in order that one can love. He also makes much of defending the self against the onslaughts of nature, the body, and other people.[11]

In psychoanalysis, Freud provides tools for gaining competence and experience in mutuality. The concept of "transference" suggests that the client brings to therapy, as to other relationships, earlier expectations, suspicions, and fears. Looking at this tendency carefully allows both client and analyst to examine fundamental problems in feeling and relating. Philip Rieff sees that the clinical encounter is a model for learning to identify and express feelings honestly, for openly and fully listening to another person, and for learning that the self is fulfilled in crucial ways only in relationship with others.

To contrast this with Freud's theory of ego defenses, which dig into the foundations of the adversary paradigm by describing our unconscious tendencies to rigidify and reject various forms of input—from nature, other people and even our own bodies—I would like to propose a theory of *ego advances*, to indicate ways by which the self unites with others, society, culture, nature, and the planet in ways that enhance them all. Loving is the classic strategy for this, but there are many other ego advances as well.

Freud formulated his theory of ego defenses with nouns: projection, repression, denial, displacement, undoing, intellectualization, and the like. The nouns suggest something fixed, a mechanism that is there, to be engaged when necessary.

The word *defense* is adversarial; it is from war vocabulary. Freud fails in his work to use words that suggest the ego at peace and preparing for more and better peace.

Although ego defenses imply action, they do so primarily by *protecting the self from others, not enhancing the self with others*. Ego advances are efforts to relate, described by gerunds to imply *ongoing work*. Empathizing, for example, moves one beyond isolation and responds to pain as well as pleasure in others.

My notion of ego advances is a slight variation on terms developed by Erik Erikson for understanding how the self evolves.[12] Erikson refers to "virtues," or strengths of the self that guide it through the complex encounters of development. By renaming this "ego advances," I mean to emphasize movement forward, and by using gerunds rather than nouns, I call attention to process.

Erikson identifies the first issue between a new person and its caretaking adult as "trust." A baby has to learn to trust the adult to meet its needs. But since no one can meet all the child's needs all the time, it also has to learn mistrust. Both kinds of learning are crucial in preparation for encounters with other people. In my system, the first ego advance is called *trusting*—and is, as Erikson explains, essential as the basis for any relationship. Mistrust, by contrast, belongs in the defense system as an often necessary barrier against being hurt, abandoned, betrayed. It enables one to recognize and respond appropriately to people who are untrustworthy.

Erikson's second stage of development is autonomy, which he contrasts with shame and doubt. Autonomy does not mean simply freedom from restrictions by or ties with others. It suggests *mutual* recognition of rights to independence. It means a self confident in its strengths and purposes confronting other selves confident in their strengths and purposes. The negatives of autonomy, in Erikson's phenomenology, are shame and doubt, defensive responses to punishment and humiliation that follow from certain kinds of control by others. I suggest *venturing* as the second ego advance, the gerund for what Erikson calls autonomy. Venturing with pleasure beyond the familiar and secure includes overcoming what could be crippling shame and doubt. The capacity for spontaneity, growth, and delight is part of venturing.

The ego learnings of the Oedipal period Erikson calls initiative and guilt. To initiate is to relate to others through the pleasures of competence, imagination, and risk. The child is filled with fantasies of heroism, conquest, and derring-do, and as the healthy child of this age moves into society, it acts out, often in inventive play, whatever projects occur to it. The child unable to achieve full functioning at this stage may expect defeat to be the inevitable outcome of imagined initiatives. When neurotic guilt, which debilitates unnecessarily, is overcome, initiative, unfettered by neurotic inhibition, is an exciting way of acting that may include combining with others through joint projects. In my system, I will call this ego advance *initiating*.

Erikson names the fourth stage of development "industry," effective interaction with the material and social environment at a time when a child begins to acquire its culture's work, play, and interpersonal skills. The unhealthy child suffers from "inferiority," crippling inhibitions that make effective learning and behavior frightening and thus taboo. I propose to call the ego advance of industriousness and gaining competence, *learning*.

At the core of Erikson's work is "identity," the consolidation of developing fragments of the self. Although the self is reconsolidated continually, it is ordinarily in adolescence that one creates a recognizable, more or less predictable self that feels right to oneself and that others can recognize as having meaning and purpose. Identity includes family, group, societal, and cultural dimensions that enable feeling part of larger structures that welcome and embrace one as belonging there. The self that fails to achieve a viable identity is beset by "identity confusion," a defense against bewilderments and pains that prevent pleasurable and meaningful self-integration. I will call this ego advance *integrating*, bringing disparate pieces into a personal, societal, and cultural whole, even while moving and changing.

With a firm identity, the self can move toward other selves and form deep emotional, intellectual, spiritual, and physical ties, including those of sexuality. What Erikson calls "intimacy" is that capacity and that goal, but where the self is incapable of establishing intimacy, it suffers "isolation," a defense against the anticipated pain of close involvement with another. The gerund for intimacy, the ego advance of the period of mature connections with others, is *loving*.

At some point in the delicate interweaving of lives that intimacy means, people may pass themselves on to others in their species. The cultural continuity this indicates need not be biologically based; it can be managed through parenting nonbiological offspring and by caring for others in teaching, nursing, library work, social work, and medicine. Erikson calls this relationship to coming generations "generativity" and contrasts it with "stagnation," a later stage of isolation in which one feels stifled, worn out, used up. In the broadest sense, I think it is right to call the ego advance that engages generativity, *parenting*. It means growing as one gives and giving as one grows.

The last stage of life Erikson formulates as "ego integrity" in contrast to "despair." Ego integrity includes forswearing regret and bitterness. If not an enthusiastic acceptance of all one's life has been, it is at least a realistic integration into the self of reasons for sadness as well as for joy, renunciation of wistful or angry wishes that the past can now be made otherwise and that there is any point in remorse.

Ego integrity is a later stage of identity. Whereas identity is prospective, bringing the experiences of the first decade or two into a workable and satisfying whole from which the adult self can develop, ego integrity is an analogous retrospective process. It is an ego advance that allows the aging person to present a model to younger people of closure, of completion that feels right and looks right both to the aging person and to the community. I recommend calling this ego advance *completing*.

Erikson's ego strengths focus on the ego's development of the capacity to enjoy challenge and growth, all the while learning how to maneuver among numerous temptations and hazards that would keep it from healthy assertion and gratification. If ego defenses ward off attacks on self-esteem, then ego advances actively seek experiences that enhance pleasure in activity and self-esteem. Identifying with the strengths of the other, empathizing with the other in such a way as to extend the range of one's own feelings, initiating activities that challenge and extend one's repertoire of competencies—are ego advances.

A society that is more adversarial than mutualistic supports traits like mistrust, shame, guilt, inferiority, and the like, for they are parts of processes of opposition. The institutions of a society committed to building mutuality would devote themselves, in education, religion, government, the family, medicine, law—every institution—to learning how to overcome processes that inhibit the exercise of ego advances. Neither domination nor profit would define the purpose of people in such a society. Purposes would be growth, sharing, and vibrant interdependence.

The Self and Globalism: Three Stretches

Whether the world moves toward globalism and mutual reinforcement of strengths rather than exploitation of weaknesses depends on willful decisions by large numbers of people to act in ways that will do just that. *The self as active agent in history has never had greater opportunity.* Anyone who wants to contribute to the paradigm shift toward mutuality that, if we will it, lies ahead, is challenged in at least three ways to participate. Each calls for stretching beyond familiar, comfortable parameters.

1. *Extending beyond adversarialism.* Most people are so accustomed to adversarialism and so inexperienced with mutuality that moving from predominance of one to the other requires a real stretch of imagination and emotions. It can be done; that is part of what "free will" is about. But leaving the customary, however destructive it is, is like a neurotic leaving neurosis. One is nervous about losing "old friend" feelings toward whatever is familiar in destructive parts of the self and in destructive relationships and institutions. The stretch requires sustained support of like-minded others.

Exploring mutuality can, for some people, draw on pleasurable adult experiences and, as well, on faint memories of experiences and feelings vaguely remembered from early years. As it calls for honest responses to others about feelings and goals, it will involve honest self-criticism and will proceed in the company and colleagueship of other people with the same commitments and determination.

This stretch includes parents learning not to browbeat children into competing for the sake of competing, and it includes struggling to identify unnecessary adversary practices in one's life and finding ways to move beyond them.

This stretch means *(a)* finding institutions with seeds of mutuality, working with them, helping strengthen and extend them; *(b)* teasing out seeds, however tiny, already in institutions and working with others to enhance and enlarge them; *(c)* planting seeds of mutuality in institutions that appear devoid of them.

This stretch also includes focussing on ego advances in responding to others so as to respect and support their strengths and positive strivings, as well as one's own. This means attuning oneself to one's own growth separate from *and* in connection with that of others.

At a very broad level, this stretch challenges political, economic, and other elites and all who work for them to see through the deadly and deadening adversarialism of contemporary institutions. It strongly suggests working, for example, toward economic activity that requires minimal use of nonrenewable resources and that takes human well-being and that of the planet fully into account in deep senses rather than superficial ones.

2. *Feeling and accepting connections of empathy and equality with the rest of the human species and with nature too.* Most people are conditioned to think of their ethnicity, race, gender, class, religion, and other demographic categories, as well as their species, as superior or inferior to others. To feel the

oneness of the human species means to overcome what Erikson calls pseudospeciation and achieve what Marx called species being, consciousness of the common condition and nature of all humans. Feeling an integral part of nature and the cosmos draws heavily on wisdom sustained in Buddhism, Native American traditions, and more recent New Age efforts to address contemporary crises.

Accomplishing this stretch will probably require dialogue groups of many kinds, some of them perhaps televised as models of such explorations of self and others, of stereotypes, hatreds, fears, cliches, and common misinformation. The deprojecting called for in chapter 13 will be a crucial part of this particular stretch, for feeling at one with the species means overcoming tendencies to attribute to others what really is part of the self.

3. *Accepting and feeling organic connections with other species and the whole planet.* It takes stretching to move past the assumption that animals are on earth for humans to hunt and eat or to stare at in zoos. It is difficult to abandon what is familiar and tasty. Yet when I read about the inefficient use of grain in producing meat and the appalling conditions in which animals are grown for human use,[13] and realize the problems of overfishing the seas, I continue to shift toward vegetarianism.

One morning a few years ago, I started thinking about what I was doing in throwing away a cheap disposable razor. I envisioned a city dump with my razor added to it. Ah, don't be silly, I told myself, it's just a very small piece of plastic, what can one more discarded razor mean for the environment? Then I multiplied by millions of other men and women disposing of the same item and saw mountains of nonbiodegradable plastic. To pass beyond my sense of me as adding just a tiny bit to the problem to me as exemplar of the very large problem required a mighty stretch. I no longer use disposable razors, but it really takes effort to turn my eye to that larger context. The issue comes up too in using products that once came in aerosol cans and in investing in IRAs with a company that does not put money into tobacco, alcohol, environmentally polluting companies, and arms production.

By stretch, I mean stretch. I mean stretch as in limbering up a too tight body before jogging or Tai Ch'i or any other athletic effort. I mean stretch as in uncomfortable effort with the promise of eventually increasing comfort and pleasure, albeit with a bit of uncertainty as to what will come of this endeavor. I also mean identifying with other people also trying to stretch.

Stretching also means reshaping one's concept of oneself. To commit oneself to these stretches may draw ridicule—from fear and confusion more than from malice—from people denying the numerous crises facing us. It might mean being marginalized by some friends and family. It could include wrenching oneself away from the concept one has had of oneself as ineffective in public matters.

The three stretches, the reader will note, deal with individual consciousness and individual behavior. As of this writing, I am unable to conceptualize the structural actions that might be taken to hasten the move toward mutuality. The global pervasiveness of capitalism, consumerism, and maldistribution of wealth and resources—complex manifestations of adversarialism on the broadest world level—is staggering, and the complicity of most politicians in perpetuating these problems in the world is overwhelming. The theory of armed revolution, whatever its merits and failings earlier in this century nearly ended, seems unworkable and inapplicable in the current situation. We who imagine massive nonviolent social change have, as of this moment, no coherent or comprehensive theory of how to bring about structural changes that would free people from the hard and soft tyrannies they currently endure. With such a view, one can retreat into despair or renew determination to work effectively as an individual and join with others of similar dispositions in continuing the search for ways to effect massive liberatory changes.

This book suggests that reappropriating the self, working with mutualistic people in institutions already inclined in that direction, and working within adversarial institutions with likeminded people, to persuade them to move in mutualistic directions, are modest steps that can be taken now to further the work of mutuality. This is a piece of a larger theory of change that has yet to be worked out by me or anyone else. At least this might contribute to its invention: It is possible that once a critical mass is reached of people willing, able, and eager to work in the direction of mutuality, their effects will move beyond the stages on which they carry out their dramas of reducing human suffering and enhancing human fulfillment by making that a means as well as an end of their daily interactions, their work, their lives in communities, and their relationship with their species, locations, and our planet itself.

As far as I can take them right now, the three stretches call for reconceptualizing who one is and how one takes responsibility, not only for one's actions on the planet but toward institutions of waste and injustice. The stretches imply working with other people in political contexts for fundamental institutional change. If globalism is to create a pan-cultural religion, I suspect that effective liberatory political action will be experienced as a kind of communion. I hope I live long enough to see this.

Notes

Acknowledgments

1. Gordon Fellman, "Peace in the World or the World in Pieces," Policy Studies, No. 34, The Leonard Davis Institute, Hebrew University, Jerusalem, 1989.

Chapter 1

1. I am one of six authors (William Schwartz, Charles Derber, Gordon Fellman, William Gamson, Morris Schwartz, and Patrick Withen) of *The Nuclear Seduction: Why the Arms Race Doesn't Matter and What Does* (Berkeley: University of California Press, 1990).

Chapter 2

1. William Raspberry, "A search for common ground on abortion," *Boston Globe*, September 16, 1995.

2. See two books by Riane Eisler for the fullest explication of this history that I know: *The Chalice and the Blade* (San Francisco: Harper & Row, 1988) and *Sacred Pleasure* (San Francisco: Harper & Row, 1995).

3. For a nuanced, complex discussion of the relation of motherhood to life in general as well as babies' lives, see Roberta Pfeufer Kahn, *Bearing Meaning: The Language of Birth* (Urbana: University of Illinois Press, 1995).

4. Patrick E. Tyler, "U.N. Forum Hears Speech by Burmese," *New York Times*, September 1, 1995.

5. Marilyn Ferguson, *The Aquarian Conspiracy: Personal and Social Transformation in the 1980s* (Los Angeles: Tarcher, 1980); Fritjof Capra, *The Turning Point: Science, Society, and the Rising Culture* (New York: Bantam, 1982); and Capra, *Uncommon Wisdom* (New York: Simon & Shuster, 1988). Ferguson and Capra discuss figures in public life, literature, and science who are convinced that this era is ripe for major, fundamental change: Pierre Teilhard de Chardin, Nikos Kazantzakis, Pierre Trudeau, Ilya Prigogine, Gardner Murphy, C. S. Lewis, Marshall McLuhan, Abraham Maslow, Michael Lerner, Michael Rossman, John Middleton Murray, Martin Buber, Henry Miller, Arthur Clarke, Gregory Bateson, Stanislav Grof, Margaret Lock, Hazel Henderson, E. F. Schumacher, and Carl Simonton, among others.

6. Alvin Toffler defines agriculture as the first "wave" of civilization, industrialization as the second, and a third, in formation now, one based on a synthesis of information, decentralization of production, renewable energy, appropriate-scale technology, de-urbanization, return of work to the home, a reconnection of production and consumption in the household, decentralized political decision-making, and more. Alvin Toffler, *The Third Wave* (New York: William Morrow, 1980).

Riane Eisler, Pierre Teilhard de Chardin, Marshall McLuhan, Paolo Soleri, Lewis Thomas, Charlene Spretnak, Gregory Bateson, William Irwin Thompson, Philip Rieff, Philip Slater, Ursula LeGuin, Andrew Bard Schmookler, Adrienne Rich, Lee Halprin, Thomas Berry, Wendell Berry, Judith Jordan, and Marge Piercy are among scores of others who envision serious and basic change.

Chapter 3

1. Louis Lamour, as reported to me by Thomas Doherty in a personal communication.

2. I am grateful to Tom Doherty for this insight.

Chapter 4

1. Philip Slater, *The Glory of Hera* (Boston: Beacon Press, 1968), 36. Slater draws on Johan Huizinga's *Homo Ludens* in this discussion.

2. Ibid., 40.

3. I am grateful to Mathew Johnson for this insight.

4. Alfie Kohn, *No Contest* (Boston: Houghton Mifflin, 1986).

5. Ibid., chapters 2–5.

6. I thank Lee Halprin for pointing this out, in personal communication. The position is developed by Daniel Quinn, in *Ishmael* (New York: Bantam/Turner, 1993)

that species eat other species to survive. They can do this with full respect for the other species, and with a feeling of integral relationship with it; they can also do it at a remove that suggests no respect for or feeling of relationship to the species in question or nature and humans' place in it.

7. Charles E. Nathanson, "Sacred Principles: A Reinterpretation of Human and Cultural Origins," Ph.D. dissertation, Brandeis University, 1979, 217–20 and passim.

8. Ibid. See also William Irwin Thompson, *The Time Falling Bodies Take to Light* (New York: St. Martin's, 1981), 76.

9. For surveys of the ideas of major object relations theorists, see Howard A. Bacal and Kenneth M. Newman, *Theories of Object Relations: Bridges to Self Psychology* (New York: Columbia University Press, 1990), and Gregory Kohor, ed., *The British School of Psychoanalysis* (New Haven: Yale University Press, 1986). See also works by theorists Michael Balint, John Bowlby, Nancy Chodorow, W. R. D. Fairbairn, Melanie Klein, Margaret Mahler, and D. W. Winnicott.

10. Erik H. Erikson, *Insight and Responsibility* (New York: Norton, 1964). See especially chapter 4, "Human Strength and the Cycle of Generations," 109–57.

11. George Herbert Mead, *Mind, Self, and Society* (Chicago: University of Chicago Press, 1934), especially part III.

12. Sam Keen, *Faces of the Enemy* (San Francisco: Harper & Row, 1986), 31. Nixon himself is an outstanding, if sad, example of a man driven by the adversary compulsion.

13. For provocative speculations on this matter, see Eisler, *The Chalice and the Blade,* and *Sacred Pleasure* and Quinn, *Ishmael.*

14. Eisler, *The Chalice and the Blade.*

15. Quinn, *Ishmael.*

16. See Dorothy Dinnerstein. *The Mermaid the Minotaur* (New York: Harper Colophon, 1976). See also Nancy Chodorow, *The Reproduction of Mothering* (Berkeley: University of California Press, 1978).

17. David Bakan, *And They Took Themselves Wives* (San Francisco: Harper & Row, 1979).

18. Bruno Bettelheim, *Symbolic Wounds* (New York: Collier, 1962); Karen Horney, "The Flight from Womanhood: The Masculinity Complex in Women, as Viewed by Men and by Women," *International Journal of Psychoanalysis* 7 (1926): 324–39; Karen Horney, "The Dread of Women: Observations on a Specific Difference in the Dread Felt by Men and by Women Respectively for the Opposite Sex," *International Journal of Psychoanalysis* 13 (1932): 348–60.

19. Maurice N. Walsh and Barbara G. Scandalis, "Institutionalized Forms of Intergenerational Male Aggression," in Martin A. Nettleship, R. Dale Givens, and Anderson Nettleship, *War: Its Causes and Correlates* (The Hague: Mouton, 1975), 138–39.

20. Bettelheim, *Symbolic Wounds.*

21. Barbara Katz Rothman, *Recreating Motherhood* (New York: Norton, 1989), part I.

22. I thank Lee Halprin for this observation.

23. Thomas Kuhn, *The Structure of Scientific Revolutions* (Chicago: University of Chicago Press, 1970).

24. Herman E. Daly, *Toward a Steady State Economy* (San Francisco: W. H. Freeman, 1973), 149ff.

25. Ibid., 2.

26. Ibid., 5.

27. John Stuart Mill, *Principles of Political Economy*, vol. II (London: John W. Parker and Son, 1857), 320–26, with omissions; in Daly, ibid., 12–13.

Chapter 5

1. Sanders was a football coach at Vanderbilt University in 1948, around when he made the statement. Lombardi, to whom it is usually attributed, actually said, "Winning isn't everything—but making the effort to win is." Both quotations are in Jay M. Shafritz, *Words on War* (New York: Prentice Hall, 1990), 484, where the original sources are cited.

2. J. William Gibson, *Warrior Dreams: Violence and Manhood in Post-Vietnam America* (New York: Hill and Wang), 1994.

3. Ibid., 183.

4. Ibid., 187.

5. Ibid., 188.

6. Ibid., 189.

7. Ibid.

8. Arthur Koestler, *Janus* (New York: Random House, 1978), 91.

9. William Peters, *A Class Divided* (New Haven: Yale University Press, 1971).

10. Georg Simmel, *Conflict* (Glencoe, IL: Free Press. 1955), 29.

11. Ibid.

12. Ibid., 30.

13. Ibid., 31.

14. Charles Derber, *The Wilding of America* (New York: St. Martin's), 1996, passim.

15. The works of Sigmund Freud, Erik Erikson, Anna Freud, Abraham Maslow, Heinz Kohut, Robert White, Gregory Rochlin, and many others speak to this.

16. Kohn, *No Contest*, 6, 89.

17. William Schwartz et al., *The Nuclear Seduction* (Berkeley: University of California Press, 1990), chapter 8.

18. For a most vivid portrayal of this in the historical and cultural context of American Blacks in the 1930s through the 1950s, see Ralph Ellison, *Invisible Man* (New York: Vintage, 1989).

19. For an extended and by now classic discussion of the nature of competence, see Robert W. White, *Ego and Reality in Psychoanalytic Theory* (New York: International Universities Press, 1963).

20. See Sam Fussell, *Muscle: Confessions of an Unlikely Bodybuilder* (New York: Poseidon Press, 1991).

21. Howard F. Stein, "Adversary Symbiosis and Complementary Group Dissociation: An Analysis of the U.S./USSR Conflict," in Howard F. Stein and Maurice Apprey, eds., *From Metaphor to Meaning: Papers in Psychoanalytic Anthropology* (Charlottesville: University Press of Virginia, 1987), 273.

22. Melanie Klein, "On Identification," in Klein, *Our Adult World and Other Essays*, quoted in ibid., 273.

23. For a helpful, fuller discussion of the dynamics of projective identification, see Michael J. Scavio, Andrew Cooper, and Pamela Scavio Clift. "Freud's Devaluation of Nietzsche," *The Psychohistory Review* 21.3 (Spring 1993): 311–12.

24. Erik H. Erikson, "Ontogeny of Ritualization," in R. M. Loewenstein, A. Solnit, and M. Schur, eds., *Psychoanalysis: A General Psychology* (New York: International Universities Press, 1966), 606.

25. Joel Kovel, *White Racism* (New York: Vintage, 1971).

26. Charles A. Pinderhughes, "Differential Bonding from Infancy to International Conflict," in John E. Mack, issue editor, "Aggression and Its Alternatives in the Conduct of International Relations," *Psychoanalytic Inquiry* 6.2 (1986): 2.

27. See Eric Saida, "On Love and Violence," Senior Honors Thesis, Sociology Department, Brandeis University, May 1996.

28. I thank Mathew Johnson for pointing this out.

29. See, e.g., Jean Briggs, *Never in Anger* (Cambridge, MA: Harvard University Press, 1970) for a fascinating discussion of Eskimos' ways of restraint.

30. Stein, "Adversary Symbiosis," 298.

Chapter 6

1. Franco Fornari, *The Psychoanalysis of War* (Garden City, NY: Anchor, 1974). This chapter owes much to Fornari's analysis not only of the possibility of nuclear holocaust but of war in general.

2. Fornari, citing Bouthoul, ibid., 27.

3. The notion of surplus something that goes awry begins in Marx's concept of "surplus value," the worth that workers put into products that comes to owners in the form of profit rather than coming back to workers in the form of wages. See, e.g., Karl Marx, "Wages, Price and Profit," in Karl Marx and Frederick Engels, *Selected Works* (New York: International Publishers, 1972), 215–17. Herbert Marcuse uses this trope in creating the concept of "surplus repression," in his Marxo-Freudian classic *Eros and Civilization* (Boston: Beacon Press, 1955). Michael Lerner continues the tradition in coining "surplus powerlessness" in his book by that name (Oakland, CA: Institute for Labor and Mental Health, 1986).

4. I am grateful to Steve Berger for this clever adaptation of D. W. Winnicott's notion of "good-enough mothering."

5. "Why War?" Chapter 25 in Sigmund Freud, *Collected Papers*, vol. 5 (New York: Basic Books, 1959).

6. "Thoughts for the Time on War and Death," Chapter 17, Sigmund Freud, *Collected Papers*, vol. 4 (New York: Basic Books, 1959).

7. Fornari, *Psychoanalysis of War*, xv.

8. Binkley's closet of nightmares, in "Outland," successor to the now-defunct comic strip "Bloom County," offers an especially vivid illustration of this.

9. For a full development of this analysis, see Gordon Fellman, "The Truths of *Frankenstein*: Technologism and Images of Destruction," *Psychohistory Review* 19.2 (Winter 1991).

10. Edward Glover, *War, Sadism and Pacifism* (London: Allen and Unwin, 1946), 19.

11. Sigmund Freud, *Civilization and Its Discontents* (New York: Norton, 1961), 57n. Freud is quoting Heine's *Gedanke und Einfalle*, section I.

12. See David Shipler, *Arab and Jew* (New York: Penguin Books, 1986), especially chapters 5–10, on reciprocal stereotyping of Palestinians and Israeli Jews.

13. Fornari, xv. Emphasis in original.

14. Glover, *War, Sadism and Pacifism*, 44.

15. Fornari, *Psychoanalysis of War*, xvii.

16. Ibid., xviii.

17. Ibid., xxvi.

18. H. H. Gerth and C. Wright Mills, eds., *From Max Weber* (New York: Oxford University Press, 1946), 48, 77–78, 334; Max Weber, *The Theory of Social and Economic Organization* (New York: Oxford University Press, 1947), 156.

19. Fornari, *Psychoanalysis if War*, xxvii-ix.

20. Ibid., xxix.

21. Ibid., 17.

22. The psychoanalytic literature is voluminous on this. The Buddhist tradition of facing destructiveness and handling it nondestructively is less well known in the West. See, for example, the Vietnamese Buddhist Thich Nhat Hanh, in *Miracle of Mindfulness* (Boston: Beacon Press, 1976); *Being Peace* (Berkeley: Parallax Press, 1987); and *Peace Is Every Step* (New York: Bantam Books, 1992). See also Tenzin Gyatso, The Fourteenth Dalai Lama, "Compassion and the Individual" (Boston: Wisdom Publications, 1991), and the Dalai Lama, *Kindness, Clarity, and Insight*, trans. and ed. by Jeffrey Hopkins (Ithaca, NY: Snow Lion Publications, 1984).

Part III Introduction

1. Erik H. Erikson, "Ontogeny of Ritualization," in R. M. Lowenstein, A. Solnit, and M. Schur, eds., *Psychoanalysis: A General Psychology* (New York, International Universities Press, 1966), 601–21.

Chapter 7

1. Dr. Seuss, *The Butter Battle Book* (New York: Random House, 1984).

2. Elliott Jaques calls these sources of anger "bad objects." Elliott Jaques, "Social Systems as Defence against Persecutory and Depressive Anxiety," in Melanie Klein et al., eds., *New Directions in Psycho-Analysis* (London: Tavistock, 1955), 478–98.

3. Ibid., 483–84.

4. Freud's discussion of this phenomenon remains classic. See his *Future of an Illusion* (New York: Norton, 1961), and his *Group Psychology and the Analysis of the Ego* (New York: Norton, 1959). For a much fuller examination of the same idea, put differently, see Kovel, *White Racism*.

5. See Alix Strachey, *The Unconscious Motives of War* (London, George Allen and Unwin, 1967), 181.

6. Jaques, "Social Systems," 486.

7. Keen, *Faces of the Enemy.*

8. Paul Fussell, *Wartime* (New York: Oxford University Press, 1989), 137–38.

9. Ibid., chapter 10, "The Ideological Vacuum."

10. Keen, *Faces*, passim.

11. Ibid., passim.

12. Maurice N. Walsh and Barbara G. Scandalis, "Institutionalized Forms of Intergenerational Male Aggression," in Martin A. Nettleship, R. Dale Givens, and Anderson Nettleship, eds., *War: Its Causes and Correlates* (The Hague: Mouton, 1975), 135.

13. Ibid., 138.

14. Ibid., 138–39, 147.

15. I thank Colquitt Meacham, who grew up in the South, for this observation.

16. See, for example, Heinz Kohut, *Self-Psychology and the Humanities* (New York, Norton, 1985), 63–65, 84–93.

17. The issue is not simple, and it appears that the United States learned to condition soldiers to be more efficient on the battlefield in wars since 1945. The basic source on soldiers not automatically wanting to shoot is S. L. A. Marshall, *Men against Fire: The Problem of Battle Command in Future War* (Washington, DC: Combat Forces Press; New York: William Morrow, 1947), chapter 5. For discussions of this and later developments and some of the intricate arguments about aggression, killing, and resistances to killing, see Dave Grossman, *On Killing: The Psychological Cost of Learning to Kill in War and Society* (Boston: Little Brown, 1995), chapters 2 and 3. Also see Richard Holmes, *Acts of War: The Behavior of Men in Battle* (New York: Free Press, 1985), chapter 8.

18. Hans Gerth and C. Wright Mills, *From Max Weber: Essays in Sociology* (New York: Galaxy, 1958), passim. Weber observes that once charismatic leaders pass, their accomplishments are made routine and bureaucratized. They become "rationalized" according to some principles of value and efficiency.

19. For a further elaboration of the matching of humans and high technology in the form of cyborgs and military thinking about new technological war, see Chris Hables Gray, *Postmodern War: The New Politics of Conflict* (New York: Guildford Press, 1997).

20. Howard Zinn, *A People's History of the United States* (New York: Harper Perennial, 1980), 86.

21. Schwartz et al., *The Nuclear Seduction*; Joseph Gerson, *The Deadly Connection: Nuclear War and U.S. Intervention* (Philadelphia: New Society Publishers, 1986).

22. For a provocative discussion of the ambiguity of the Russian situation as of 1992, see Ken Gluck, "The New Russian Imperialists," *The Nation* 255.7 (September 14, 1992): 243–46.

23. Schwartz et al., *The Nuclear Seduction*.

24. Mikhail Gorbachev, *Perestroika* (London: Collins, 1987), 141.

25. Erikson, "The Golden Rule," 242.

26. Ibid., 243.

27. See Wilhelm Reich. *The Mass Psychology of Fascism* (New York: Farrar, Straus and Giroux, 1970), esp. chapter 2, "The Authoritarian Ideology of the Family in the Mass Psychology of Fascism," 34–74. And see also Otto Gross, "Zur Uberwindung," quoted in Russell Jacoby, *The Repression of Psychoanalysis* (New York: Basic Books, 1983).

28. Gross, ibid., 43.

29. Otto Fenichel, "Gedanken," 310–11, in Russell Jacoby, *Repression of Psychoanalysis*, 61.

30. Michael Lerner, *Surplus Powerlessness* (Oakland, CA: Institute for Labor and Mental Health, 1986), 237.

31. Gregory Rochlin, *Man's Aggression* (New York: Delta, 1973), 120.

32. Heinz Kohut, quoted on p. 55 of Rafael Moses, "The Group Self and the Arab-Israeli Conflict," *International Review of Psychoanalysis* 9 (1982): 54–65.

33. Samuel I, 15:2, *The Jerusalem Bible* (Jerusalem: Koren Publishers, 1977).

34. Samuel I, 15:3, in ibid.

35. Exodus, 17:14, in ibid.

36. Exodus 21:24, in ibid.

37. Brandeis sociology graduate student Dave Shafer discusses this vividly in "Dissolution of Rage" (unpublished paper, July 1994), about weight-lifting as a way to cope with anger.

38. Steven Wangh, personal communication, July 2, 1992. Wangh's suggestions and insights about the relationship of pain, anger, and revenge have been crucial in my thinking throughout this chapter.

39. *Boston Globe*, August 16, 1993, 6: "The new prime minister, Morihiro Hosokawa, who already had labeled Japan the aggressor in World War II, broke

another precedent yesterday by offering condolences to other nations' war victims on the 48th anniversary of Japan's surrender.

"Hosokawa's statement and lower house speaker Takako Doi's blunt admission that Japan caused 'horrible sacrifices' for Asians contrasted with the vague language of previous leaders about Japan's war role."

40. Harold F. Searles, "The Psychodynamics of Vengefulness," *Psychiatry* 19.1 (1956): 31.

Chapter 8

1. Philip Slater, *The Pursuit of Loneliness* (Boston: Beacon Press, 1990), 99.

2. See the intricate argument of Lloyd deMause, *History of Childhood* (New York: Psychohistory Press, 1974).

3. *Silence of the Lambs*, Jonathan Demme, dir. Orion Pictures Corporation, 1990 (motion picture).

4. See Freud's *Totem and Taboo* (New York, Norton, 1982), 82, and Eli Sagan, *Cannibalism: Human Aggression and Cultural Form* (New York, Harper & Row, 1974), chapters 1 and 2.

Chapter 9

1. An example of moving beyond right-left splits is that of long-time left activist Dave Dellinger, who at the August 1996 Chicago reunion of the 1968 antiwar protesters "the Chicago 8," called for grassroots organizing rather than expecting much from the government. Bobby Seale, another of the Chicago 8, spoke at the same venue of raising money for local environmental rehabilitation projects. At the same time such formerly outspoken leftists accept some of the right-wing critique of big government, so are right-wingers softening their opposition to feminism. These are movements, however hesitant and complicated, away from adversarialism, in the direction of mutuality. See Jon Keller, "Going back to the grass roots." *Boston Globe*, 9/2/96.

2. J. Wade Gilley, "Faust Goes to College," *Academe* 78.3 (May-June 1992): 9–11. Gilley sees no virtue in such rankings. For a reply to Gilley, see David S. Webster, "Academic Rankings: First on a List of One," *Academe* 78.5 (September-October 1992): 19–22.

3. Gary Warner, *Competition* (Elgin, Illinois: David C. Cook, 1979): 171.

4. Letter, *Boston Globe*, July 5, 1996, p. 14.

5. This "quotation" is the author's invention. It is based on impressions gleaned from experiences with a number of highly competitive people and does not exclude his own reflections on certain parts of himself.

6. John Berger, *Ways of Seeing* (London: BBC and Penguin Books, 1982), 148–54.

7. Herman Kahn. *On Thermonuclear War* (Westport, CT: Greenwood Press, 1969). See especially chapter 2, "Will the Survivors Envy the Dead?" Kahn's answer: Not necessarily.

8. Gorbachev, *Perestroika.*

9. Ibid., 137.

10. Ibid., 142.

11. For two poignant dramas on the issue of ending life voluntarily, see Brian Clark, *Whose Life Is It Anyway?* (Ashover, Derbyshire: Amber House Press, 1978), in which a sculptor whose loss of function in an accident is so severe, he has no further desire to live. In another play (Marsha Norman, *Night, Mother* [New York: Hill and Wang, 1983]), a young woman's emotional state leads her to decide to end her life. See also the motion picture *Antonia's Line* (Marlene Gorns, dir. *First Look*, 1996), in which a woman in good health, a good love relationship, and a fulfilling family context, decides that after a rich, full life, she has lived enough and chooses now to die.

Chapter 10

1. Charles Derber, *The Wilding of America* (New York: St. Martin's, 1996), 46.

2. Erikson, *Childhood and Society*, chapter 8.

3. Howard F. Stein, "Adversary Symbiosis . . ."

4. William Ryan, *Blaming the Victim* (New York: Vintage Books, 1971).

5. For a clear statement of this relatively new concept, see Jessica Tuchman Mathews, "Redefining National Security," *Foreign Affairs* 68.2 (1989): 162–77.

6. Max Weber, *The Protestant Ethic and the Spirit of Capitalism* (New York: Scribner's, 1956), esp. chapter 5; Hans Gerth and C. Wright Mills, eds., *From Max Weber*, chapter 8.

7. For appalling details, see Raul Hilberg, *The Destruction of the European Jews* (Chicago: Quadrangle Books, 1961).

8. Philip Slater, personal communication.

Chapter 11

1. Peter Kropotkin, *Mutual Aid* (Boston: Extending Horizons Books, 1955).

2. Selections from *Mutual Aid*, in Emile Capouya and Keitha Tompkins, eds., *The Essential Kropotkin* (London: Macmillan, 1975), 170–207.

3. Ashley Montagu, *Darwin, Competition and Cooperation* (New York: Henry Schuman, 1952), 47.

4. Martha Ackelsberg and Kathryn Pyne Addelson, "Anarchist Alternatives to Competition," in Valerie Miner and Helen E. Longino, eds., *Competition: A Feminist Taboo?* (New York: The Feminist Press, 1987), 224.

5. Starhawk, *Truth or Dare* (San Francisco: Harper & Row, 1987), 8–10 and passim. Her "power over" corresponds to my "adversarialism" and her "power with," to my "mutuality."

6. Nancy Klieber and Linda Light, *Caring for Ourselves: An Alternative Structure for Health Care* (Vancouver, BC: School of Nursing, University of British Columbia, 1978), 226.

7. Ibid., 226.

8. Carole Pateman, *Participation and Democratic Theory* (Cambridge: Cambridge University Press, 1970), chapters 4 and 5, cited in Ackelsberg and Addelson, "Anarchist Alternatives," 226.

9. W. Ronald Fairbairn, *Psychoanalytic Studies of the Personality* (London: Routledge and Kegan Paul, 1952), 36, 39, 145, 163.

10. Erikson, *Childhood and Society*, especially chapter 2, "The Theory of Infantile Sexuality," and chapter 7, "The Eight States of Man," part 1, "Trust vs. Basic Mistrust."

11. Fairbairn, *Psychoanalytic Studies*, 36.

12. Marcel Mauss, quoted by Lewis Hyde in *The Gift: Imagination and the Erotic Life of Property* (New York: Vintage Books, 1983), 33n.

13. Hyde, *The Gift*, 47.

14. Ibid.

15. Stanley Hoffman, "Coming Down from the Summit," *New York Review of Books*, January 21, 1988, p. 24.

16. Erik H. Erikson, "The Golden Rule in the Light of New Insight," in Erikson, *Insight and Responsibility* (New York: Norton, 1964), 231–32.

17. See Sigmund Freud, "Thoughts for the Times on War and Death," in Freud, *Collected Papers* (New York: Basic Books, 1959), vol. 4, chapter 17.

18. Alexander and Margarete Mitscherlich, *The Inability To Mourn* (New York: Grove, 1975), 89.

19. Ibid., 135.

20. Erikson, "The Golden Rule," 233.

21. Ibid., 154.

22. Marcia C. Lugones and Elizabeth Spelman, "Competition, Compassion, and Community: Models for a Feminist Ethos," in Valerie Miner and Helen E. Longino, eds., *Competition*, 236ff.

23. Mitscherlichs, *Inability to Mourn*, 155–56.

24. Ibid.

25. Ibid., 157–58.

26. Ibid., 163.

27. Ibid., 165.

28. Ibid.

29. Ibid., 166; see also Philip Rieff, *The Triumph of the Therapeutic* (New York: Harper & Row, 1968).

30. Ibid., 166–67.

31. Ibid., 167.

32. Ibid., 174.

33. Ibid., 183.

34. Ibid., 187.

35. Ibid., 187–88.

Chapter 12

1. The literature on this topic is vast. Some of the standard references are Robert Axelrod, *The Evolution of Cooperation* (New York: Basic Books, 1984); R. Duncan Luce and Howard Raiffa, *Games and Decisions* (New York: Dover, 1985), 94–102; William Poundstone, *Prisoners Dilemma* (New York: Doubleday, 1992); Anatol Rapaport and Albert M. Chammah, *Prisoners Dilemma: A Study in Conflict and Cooperation* (Ann Arbor: University of Michigan Press, 1965); Anatol Rapaport, Melvin J. Guyer, and David G. Gordon, *The 2 x 2 Game* (Ann Arbor: University of Michigan Press, 1976); Eric Rasmussen, *Games and Information* (Cambridge: Basic Blackwell, 1989).

2. Poundstone, *Prisoners Dilemma*, 8–9.

3. I am grateful to Maya Bar-Hillel for this observation.

4. Jeffrey Z. Rubin and Bert R. Brown, *The Social Psychology of Bargaining and Negotiation* (New York: Academic Press, 1975), 183–85.

5. The insights of Philip Slater have been crucial in developing this section.

6. Benjamin, *Bonds of Love*; Chodorow, *The Reproduction of Mothering*; Eisler, *The Chalice and the Blade*; Kahn, *Bearing Meaning*; Winnicott, *The Family and Individual Development.*

7. Warren Poland, "On Empathy in and beyond Analysis," chapter 14 in Lichtenberg et al., 331.

8. Esther Menaker and William Menaker, *Ego in Evolution*(New York: Grove Press, 1965); see chapter 12, "Ethics in Evolution," 186–211, esp. 194.

9. The line appeared originally in Terence's *Heauton Timoroumenos* (The Self-Tormentor), line 77, and was later quoted by Cicero. John Bartlett, *Familiar Quotations* (Boston: Little, Brown, 1980), 96.

10. Robert Waelder, quoted in Gail S. Reed, "The Antithetical Meaning of the Term 'Empathy' in Psychoanalytic Discourse," in Lichtenberg, Bornstein, and Silver, eds., *Empathy* (Hillsdale, NJ: Analytic Press, 1984), 16.

11. Heinz Kohut, ibid., 13.

12. Kohut, ibid.

13. Reed, "Antithetical Meaning," 12.

14. David Beres and Jacob A. Arlow, "Fantasy and Identification in Empathy," *Psychoanalytic Quarterly* 43 (1974): 33.

15. See the film *Helter Skelter* (Tom Gries, dir. Lorimar, 1976), a dramatization of the Tate-LaBianca murders and the trial of Manson and his "family."

16. Reed, "Antithetical Meaning."

17. Ralph R. Greenson, "Empathy and Its Vicissitudes," *International Journal of Psychoanalysis* 41 (1960): 423.

18. Rafael Moses, "Empathy and Dis-Empathy in Political Conflict," *Political Psychology* 6.1 (1985): 136.

19. Roy Schafer, "Discussion," in Lichtenberg et al., *Empathy*, 31.

20. Louis Agosta, "Empathy and Intersubjectivity," in Lichtenberg et al., *Empathy*, 46, 45.

21. Ibid., 47.

22. Ibid., 51.

23. Ibid., 55.

24. Quoted in Stanley Olinick, "A Critique of Empathy and Sympathy," in Lichtenberg et al., *Empathy*, 155–56.

25. Buie, ref. in Pinchas Noy, "The Three Components of Empathy: Normal and Pathological Development," in Lichtenberg et al., *Empathy*, 178.

26. Moses, "Empathy," 137–38.

27. For a full discussion of recognition and domination and also the tension between needs for recognition and needs for assertiveness, see Jessica Benjamin, *The Bonds of Love* (New York: Pantheon, 1988).

28. John Mack, "Nationalism and the Self," *Psychohistory Review* 2.2–3 (Spring 1985): 60.

29. Ibid., 64. Mack cites Willem van Leer here.

30. Lloyd deMause, "The Evolution of Childhood," in Lloyd deMause, ed., *The History of Childhood* (New York: Psychohistory Press, 1974), 36.

31. Beres and Arlow, "Fantasy," 34.

Chapter 13

1. Donald Silver, "Introductory Remarks," in Lichtenstein et al., *Empathy*, 3.

2. Ibid., 3–4.

3. Alice Miller, *For Your Own Good: Hidden Cruelty in Child-Rearing and the Roots of Violence* (New York: Farrar, Straus, & Giroux, 1990).

4. See chapter 8, note 3.

5. John R. Seeley, "The Americanization of the Unconscious," in *The Americanization of the Unconscious* (New York: Science House, 1967), 3–17.

6. Russell Jacoby, *The Repression of Psychoanalysis* (New York: Basic Books, 1983).

7. George Thomson, *Aeschylus and Athens* (London: Laurence and Wishart, 1946), 383.

8. Benjamin Spock, *Baby and Child Care* (New York: Pocket Books, 1970), 336. See also Daniel Stern, *The Interpersonal World of the Infant* (New York: Basic Books, 1988).

9. Spock, *Baby and Child Care*, 336–37.

10. Stern, *Interpersonal World*.

11. Spock, *Baby and Child Care*, xvi.

12. Philip Rieff, *The Triumph of the Therapeutic* (New York: Harper & Row, 1966).

13. Ibid., 233.

14. Ibid., 234.

15. Ibid., 238.

16. Ibid., 238, 253.

17. Ibid., 261.

18. Audre Lorde, *Sister Outsider* (Freedom, CA: Crossing Press, 1984), 130.

19. Ibid., 130.

20. For a full analysis of our culture's defamation of altruism and ambivalence about it, see Alfie Kohn, *The Brighter Side of Human Nature* (New York: Basic Books, 1990).

21. Ibid.

22. Joyce P. Lindenbaum, "The Shattering of an Illusion: The Problem of Competition in Lesbian Relationships," in Valerie Miner and Helen E. Longino, eds., *Competition: A Feminist Taboo?* (New York: Feminist Press, 1987), 201.

23. Philip Pomper, *The Structure of the Mind in History* (New York: Columbia University Press, 1985), 107–8.

24. Erik H. Erikson, *Gandhi's Truth* (New York Norton, 1969), 433; cited in Pomper, *Structure of the Mind*, 108.

Chapter 14

1. Cf Sigmund Freud, *Group Psychology and the Analysis of the Ego* (New York: Norton, 1959).

2. See Elise Boulding, *Building a Global Civic Culture* (New York: Teachers College Press, 1988), 60–61.

3. Huston Smith, *The Religions of Man* (New York: Harper & Row, 1958), 5.

4. Paula Green, personal communication.

5. Michael Lerner, *The Politics of Meaning* (Reading, MA: Addison-Wesley, 1996).

6. For an extended discussion of the strengths of Buddhism, Native American spirituality, Goddess spirituality, Judaism, Christianity, and Islam, in the context of a critique of structuralism, postmodernism, and deconstructionism, see Charlene Spretnak, *States of Grace* (San Francisco: HarperCollins, 1991).

7. Matthew 17.

8. On the former, see Edward Said, *Orientalism* (New York: Pantheon, 1978). On the latter, see William Leach, *Land of Desire* (New York: Pantheon, 1993), 104–5.

9. Sayyid Amir Ali, in *The Spirit of Islam,* quoted by Maqsood Ahmad in "A Critical Study of the Spirit of Islam," *Hamdard Islamicus* 9 (Winter 1988): 24.

10. Smith, *Religions of Man*, 222.

11. Muhammed Khan, "Moral Principles as the Basis Of Islamic Culture," in Ruth Nanda Anshen, ed., *Moral Principle of Action*, volume 6 (New York: Harper and Brothers, 1952), 22.

12. Reuven Kimelman, "Nonviolence in the Talmud," in Robert Holmes, ed., *Non-Violence in Theory and Practice* (Belmont, CA: Wadsworth Publishing, 1990), 20.

13. Exodus 23:5.

14. Proverbs 3:17.

15. Kimelman, "Nonviolence," 23.

16. Ibid., 25.

17. Psalms 13:6.

18. Psalms 13:3.

19. Smith, *Religions of Man*, 61.

20. Ibid., 92.

21. Ibid.

22. Ibid., 94.

23. Spretnak, *States of Grace*, chapters 2–5.

24. Ibid., 9.

25. Ibid.

26. Allen Guttmann, *From Ritual to Record* (New York: Columbia University Press, 1978), 3.

27. Philip Slater, *A Dream Deferred: America's Discontent and the Search for a New Democratic Ideal* (Boston: Beacon Press, 1991), 76.

28. Andrew Fluegelman, ed., *The New Games Book: Play Hard, Play Fair, Nobody Hurt* (New York: Headlands Press, 1976), 140.

29. Kohn, *No Contest* (Boston: Houghton Mifflin, 1992), 83.

30. Anthony Cotton, "This Was Some Kind of Jam Session," *Sports Illustrated*, February 6, 1984, p. 26.

Chapter 15

1. Group for the Advancement of Psychiatry, *Us and Them: The Psychology of Ethnonationalism* (New York: Brunner/Mazel, 1987), 119.

2. Ibid., 121.

3. The work of the Center for Jewish-Arab Economic Development, founded and co-directed by Sarah Kreimer, is reported in "The delicate business of coexistence," *Jerusalem Post International Edition*, week ending July 18, 1992. For a directory of Israeli groups composed of Jews and Arabs who work together on peace and other common interests, see Anita Weiner, Arnon Bar-On, and Eugene Weiner, eds., *The Abraham Fund Directory of Institutions and Organizations Fostering Co-Existence between Jews and Arabs in Israel.* New York: Abraham Fund, 1992.

4. Tamar Lewin. "In Bitter Abortion Debate, Opponents Learn to Reach for Common Ground," *New York Times*, February 17, 1992.

5. Ibid.

6. Ibid.

7. Ibid.

8. Anthony Flint. "Narrow areas of agreement may be key to abortion talks," *Boston Globe*, January 23, 1995.

9. See "'Common Ground' or Losing Ground? Choosing our Alliances," *Reproductive Rights Newsletter*, Spring 1992, PO Box 686, Boston, MA 02130. See also an organization called Common Ground Network for Life and Choice, 1601 Connecticut Avenue, NW, Suite 200, Washington, DC 10009; the letterhead for this organization lists over a dozen associated organizations.

10. James Carroll, "Abortion complexity," *Boston Globe*, April 23, 1996.

11. Reach for Common Ground, First National Conference, May 30–June 2, 1996, Madison, Wisconsin. Sponsored by Health and Human Issues, Division of Continuing Studies, University of Wisconsin–Madison and the Common Ground Network for Life and Choice, a project of Search for Common Ground, Washington, DC (see previous footnote for address).

12. Philip Uri Treisman, "Academic Perestroika: Teaching, Learning, and the Faculty's Role in Turbulent Times," FIPSE Lecture, California State University, San Bernardino, March 8, 1990.

13. Ibid., 26.

14. Ibid., 24.

15. For a discussion of the downsides of competition as a major theme in U.S. society, see Alfie Kohn, *No Contest.*

16. For a discussion of the limits of external rewards, all the way from grades and gold stars to prizes and incomes, see Alfie Kohn, *Punished by Rewards* (Boston: Houghton Mifflin, 1993).

17. See, e.g., "Cooperative Learning and College Teaching," newsletter, New Forums Press, P.O. Box 876, Stillwater, Oklahoma 74076; David Johnson and Roger T. Johnson, *Cooperation and Competition* (Edina, Minnesota: Interaction Book Company, 1989); David Johnson, Roger T. Johnson, and Karl A. Smith, *Active Learning: Cooperation in the College Classroom* (Edina, Minnesota: Interaction Book Company, 1991); David Johnson, Roger T. Johnson, and Karl A. Smith, *Cooperative Learning: Increasing Faculty Instructional Productivity* (Washington, DC: School of Education and Human Development, George Washington University, 1991); Chet Meyers and Thomas B. Jones, *Promoting Active Learning Strategies for the College Classroom* (San Francisco: Jossey-Bass, 1993); Neal A. Whitman, *Peer Teaching: To Teach Is to Learn Twice* (Washington, DC: ASHE-ERIC Higher Education Report No. 4, Association for the Study of Higher Education, 1988). Cooperative learning is not a new invention; students in orthodox Jewish learning centers (yeshivas), for example, have studied in pairs for centuries.

18. Taken from *Gateway: A Publication of the Global Alliance for Transforming Education*, Winter/Spring 1993, p. 3.

19. Melissa Everett, John E. Mack, and Robert Oresick, "Re-inventing the Corporate Self: The Inner Agenda for Business Transformation," Center for Psychology and Social Change, 1993, p. 1.

20. Jemadari Kamara, ed., *Socially Responsible Investment and Economic Development*, National Conference on Socially Sensitive Investing for Economic Growth. Flint: University of Michigan, 1986, p. 7.

21. Ibid., 12.

22. Ibid., 19.

23. Ibid., xvii.

24. Ibid., 20.

25. Mark Dagostino, "More than a matter of good taste," *Boston Globe*, January 4, 1995.

26. Gorbachev, *Perestroika*, 11–12.

27. Ibid., 138.

28. Peter S. Canellos, "Ben and Jerry's, other firms attack both parties on arms spending," *Boston Globe*, June 27, 1996.

29. George Thomson, *Aeschylus and Athens* (London: Laurence and Wishart, 1946), 384.

30. *Whole Earth Catalog* (Sausalito, CA: Whole Earth Catalog), May 1971, pp. 30–32.

31. Dick Russell, "A Garden of Earthly Designs," *The Amicus Journal* 15.2 (Summer 1993): 15.

32. Ibid., 19.

33. Ibid., 20.

34. James Wines, "Architecture in the Age of Ecology," *The Amicus Journal* 15.2 (Summer 1993): 23.

35. William Irwin Thompson, *Darkness and Scattered Light* (Garden City, NY: Anchor, 1978), 99.

36. Russell, "Garden," 14.

37. International Union of Architects/American Institute of Architects World Congress of Architects, Preamble, "Declaration of Interdependence for a Sustainable Future," Chicago, June 18–23, 1993.

38. Ibid., opening paragraph.

39. Ibid., Article 1.

40. Ibid., Article 1.

41. Ibid., Article 5.

42. Ibid., Article 10.

43. Ibid., Article 13.

44. John Lennon, "Imagine," in Lennon, *Imagine*, Apple, 1971.

45. Arrested Development, *3 YEARS, 5 MONTHS AND 2 DAYS IN THE LIFE OF* . . . , EMI Records Group, 1992.

46. Bob Marley and the Wailers, "One Love / People Get Ready," in *Exodus*, Island Records, 1977.

47. "Get Up, Stand Up," in ibid.

48. Spearhead, "People in the Middle," in *Home*, Capitol Records, 1994.

49. Beastie Boys, *Ill Communication*, Capitol Records, 1994.

Chapter 16

1. Allister Sparks, "Letter from South Africa: The Secret Revolution," *The New Yorker* (April 11, 1994).

2. "Apartheid's last head gives in explanation." *Boston Globe*, August 22, 1996, p. A2.

3. "A Unanimous, Dramatic Win for Mandela," News Tribune News Service, May 10, 1994.

4. Amitav Ghosh, "A Reporter at Large: Burma," *The New Yorker*, August 12, 1996, p. 50.

5. The Dalai Lama, *Freedom in Exile* (New York: HarperCollins, 1990), chapter 1; Michael Harris Goodman, *The Last Dalai Lama* (Boston: Shambhala, 1986), chapter 1. Both these books, the former an autobiography, are excellent introductions to Tibetan Buddhism and the history of the Chinese invasion and occupation of Tibet, as well as the Dalai Lama's life in Tibet and in exile.

6. See Rodger Kamenetz, *The Jew in the Lotus* (San Francisco: HarperCollins, 1994), for an account of the Dalai Lama's meetings with Israeli and U.S. Jewish leaders to discuss how a people, religion, and culture have remained alive in exile for 2,000 years.

7. "Spiritual Happening," *Boston Globe*, September 1, 1996. See also Diana L. Eck, "Neighboring Faiths," *Harvard Magazine* 99.1 (September/October 1996).

8. See the excellent documentary *Compassion in Exile* by Mickey Lemle (Lemle Pictures, 1992).

9. See Ellen Bruno's documentary *Satya: A Prayer for the Enemy* (Ellen Bruno, 1993).

10. The Dalai Lama, *Compassion and the Individual* (Boston: Wisdom Publications, 1994); see also the Dalai Lama, *Dimensions of Spirituality* (Boston: Wisdom Publications, 1995).

11. "Compassion in Global Politics," in The Fourteenth Dalai Lama. *Kindness, Clarity, and Insight* (Ithaca, NY: Snow Lion, 1984).

12. Ibid., 59.

13. Ibid., 60.

14. Ibid.

15. For a complex discussion of this topic, see Marin Goldstein, "Mahayana Buddhism: Precepts for Environmental Consciousness and Social Activism," Senior honors thesis, Brandeis University, May 1996.

16. See, e.g., Sharp's *Exploring Nonviolent Alternatives, Gandhi as a Political Strategist, The Politics of Nonviolent Action*, and *Social Power and Political Freedom*.

17. Robert Adams, *Self-Help, Social Work, and Empowerment* (London: Macmillan, 1990), 1.

18. "Support Group Calendar," *Omaha World-Herald*, October 6, 1996, 7E.

19. See the Boston Women's Health Book Collective, *Our Bodies, Ourselves* (New York: Simon & Schuster, 1976) and *The New Our Bodies, Ourselves* (New York: Simon & Schuster, 1984), and subsequent editions.

20. Stepping Stones is a program of Hospice Care, Inc., 647 Summer Street, Boston, MA 02210. 617-279-4100.

21. Adams, *Self-Help*, 11.

22. "Notes and Comment," *New Yorker*, April 23, 1990, 31–32.

23. Phyllis Silverman, *Mutual Help Groups: Organization and Development* (Beverly Hills, CA: Sage, 1980), 10.

24. Andrew Fluegelman, ed., *The New Games Book* (New York: Dolphin/Doubleday, 1976), 19. See also Susan Butler, *Non-Competitive Games* (Minneapolis: Bethany House Publishers, 1986).

25. Flugelman, *New Games Book*, 10.

26. Ibid., 20.

27. Ibid., 113.

28. Ibid., 153.

29. Ibid., 167.

30. Ibid., 55, 57, 107, 115, 117.

31. Melinda Henneberger, "New Gym Class: No More Choosing Up Sides," *The New York Times*, May 16, 1993, p. 1.

32. Ibid., 37.

33. Family Pastime (producer of the game), "Eagle Eye Agency—The Cooperative Detective Game."

34. Jay Folberg and Alison Taylor, *Mediation: A Comprehensive Guide to Resolving Conflicts Without Litigation* (San Francisco: Jossey-Bass, 1984), 163.

35. Ibid., 172.

36. Jocelyn R. Coleman, "Students Named Peer Mediators," *Boston Globe*, June 14, 1990.

37. Ibid.

38. Felder Books & Games, 9601–30 Miccosukee Road, Tallahassee, FL 32308, pamphlet entitled "Mediation Games: Games for All Types of Conflicts."

39. Folberg and Taylor, *Mediation*, 197.

40. Ibid., 200.

41. Ibid., 1.

42. Lucinda Franks, "Don't Shoot: In the New F.B.I., Patience Comes First," *The New Yorker*, July 22, 1996, 27.

43. Ibid., 27.

44. Jordana Hart, "The Classes Cut Violence: Boston Middle-Schoolers Learn Art of Negotiation, Compromise," *Boston Globe*, October 10, 1994.

45. Luke Janusz, "The Smiling Terminator: An Interview with Howie Carr," *Odyssey*, Spring 1992, 36.

46. James Q. Wilson, *Thinking about Crime* (New York: Vintage Books, 1975), 172–73, quoted in Luke Janusz, "The Politics of Punishment," *Odyssey*, Spring 1992, 10.

47. Quoted in Ruth Morris, "Restorative Justice: Path to the Future," *Odyssey*, Spring 1992, 91. Morris misnames Leonard Zehr as Howard Zehr.

48. Ibid.

49. Ibid., 92, citing Leonard Zehr, *Changing Lenses* (Scottsdale, AZ: Herald Press, 1990), 164–66.

50. *Restoring Justice*. Video produced for the National Council of Churches, by the Presbyterian Church (U.S.A.), 100 Witherspoon Street, Louisville, KY 40202–1396.

51. Mark Umbreit, "The Impact of Victim Offender Mediation: A Case Study," in *Odyssey*, Spring 1992, 118–21.

52. Tony Marshall, *Alternatives to Criminal Courts: the Potential for Non-Judicial Dispute Settlement* (Brookfield, VT: Gower Publishing, 1985), 67.

53. Ibid., 73.

54. Ibid., 74.

55. Ibid., 79–88.

56. Andrew Bard Schmookler, *The Parable of the Tribes* (Berkeley: University of California Press, 1983), 21 and passim.

57. I am grateful to Phyllis Greenwood for pointing out the adversary component in this exchange and the limits there in reaching toward mutuality.

58. This anecdote is from an e-mail posting on the Peace Studies Association Network, of October 30, 1995. I have lost the name and address of the individual sender.

59. Julie Hatfield, "Miss Manners' polite efforts to 'Rescue Civilization,'" *Boston Globe*, June 26, 1996.

60. Gloria Negri, "10 students who find a better way are honored," *Boston Globe*, May 15, 1996.

61. David O'Reilly, "Beyond Hate: The Klansman Who Became Jewish," *Detroit Free Press*, April 20, 1995.

62. Kathryn Watterson, *Not by the Sword* (New York: Simon and Schuster, 1995). The book is subtitled: How the Love of a Cantor and His Family Transformed a Klansman.

63. "Youths meet to promote Mideast peace," *Boston Globe*, August 19, 1996.

64. Patricia Smith, "How I refilled my hope tank," *Boston Globe*, May 3, 1996.

65. Spretnak, *States of Grace*, 262n2.

Chapter 17

1. Thompson, *Evil and World Order*, 81.

2. Robert Kennedy. South Africa, June 1966. (I do not have a source for this quotation. I found it years ago and have no idea where.)

3. David Remnick, "Inside-Out Olympics," *The New Yorker*, August 5, 1996, p. 27.

4. Michael Kelly, "Glasshouse Conventions: How the Parties Built Their Pretty Facades—And Why They're So Fragile," *New Yorker*, September 9, 1996.

5. Philip Slater, *A Dream Deferred* (Boston: Beacon Press, 1991), 114.

6. Ibid.

7. Ibid.

8. Ibid.

9. Goldstein, "Mahayana Buddhism."

10. For an analysis of Freud's claims about the force of love in human existence, see Jonathan Lear, *Love and Its Place in Nature: A Philosophical Interpretation of Freudian Psychoanalysis* (New York: Farrar, Straus, & Giroux, 1990).

11. Freud, *Civilization and Its Discontents*, 24, and throughout much of Freud altogether.

12. Erik H. Erikson, *Childhood and Society*, chapter 7, and *Insight and Responsibility*, chapter 4. See also Erikson, *The LifeCycle Completed* (New York: Norton, 1982).

13. Peter Singer, *Animal Liberation*.

Bibliography

Ackelsberg, Martha and Kathryn Pyne Addelson. "Anarchist Alternatives to Competition." In Valerie Miner and Helen E. Longino, eds., *Competition: A Feminist Taboo?* New York: The Feminist Press, 1987, 221–33.

Adams, Robert. *Self Help, Social Work, and Empowerment*. London: Macmillan, 1990.

Adorno, Theodor W. and Max Horkheimer. *Dialectic of Enlightenment*. New York: Seabury, 1972.

Agosta, Louis. "Empathy and Intersubjectivity." In Joseph Lichtenberg, Melvin Bornstein, and Donald Silver, eds., *Empathy 1*. Hillsdale, NJ: Analytic Press, 43–61.

Ali, Sayyid Amir. *The Spirit of Islam*. Quoted by Maqsood Ahmad in "A Critical Study of the Spirit of Islam," *Hamdard Islamicus* 11 (Winter 1988).

All Quiet on the Western Front. Lewis Milestone, dir. Universal-International, 1930, motion picture.

Antonia's Line. Marlene Gorris, dir. First Look, 1996, motion picture.

"Apartheid's last head gives an explanation." *Boston Globe*, August 22, 1996, p. A2.

Arlow, Jacob A. and David Beres. "Fantasy and Identification in Empathy." *Psychoanalytic Quarterly* 43 (1974): 26–50.

Arrested Development. *3 YEARS, 5 MONTHS AND 2 DAYS IN THE LIFE OF* . . . New York: EMI Records Group, 1992, sound recording.

Axelrod, Robert. *The Evolution of Cooperation*. New York: Basic Books, 1984.

"A Unanimous, Dramatic Win for Mandela." *News Tribune* News Service, May 10, 1994.

Babe. Chris Noonan, dir. Universal, 1995, motion picture.

Bacal, Howard A. and Kenneth M. Newman. *Theories of Object Relations: Bridges to Self Psychology.* New York: Columbia University Press, 1990.

Bakan, David. *The Duality of Human Existence.* Boston: Beacon Press, 1966.

————. *And They Took Themselves Wives.* San Francisco: Harper & Row, 1979.

Bar Hillel, Maya. Personal communication.

Bartlett, John. *Familiar Quotations.* Boston: Little, Brown, 1980.

Beastie Boys. *Ill Communication.* Capitol Records, 1994, sound recording.

Benjamin, Jessica. *The Bonds of Love.* New York: Pantheon, 1988.

Beres, David and Jacob A. Arlow. "Fantasy and Identification in Empathy." *Psychoanalytic Quarterly* 43 (1974).

Berger, John. *Ways of Seeing.* London: BBC and Penguin Books, 1982.

Berger, Steven. Personal communication.

Bettelheim, Bruno. *Symbolic Wounds.* New York: Collier, 1962.

Beyond Rangoon. John Boorman, dir. Castle Rock, 1995, motion picture.

Bonnie and Clyde. Arthur Penn, dir. Warner Brothers, 1967, motion picture.

Boyz N the Hood. John Singleton, dir. Columbia Pictures, 1991, motion picture.

Boston Women's Health Book Collective. *Our Bodies Ourselves.* New York: Simon & Schuster, 1976. (See also *The New Our Bodies, Ourselves.* New York: Simon & Schuster, 1984 and subsequent editions.)

Boulding, Elise. *Building a Global Civic Culture.* New York: Teachers College Press, 1988.

Boulding, Kenneth. *Stable Peace.* Quoted in Michael N. Nagler, "Peace as Paradigm Shift," *Bulletin of the Atomic Scientists* 37 (December 1981): 49–52.

Breathed, Berke. *Outlander*, comic strip.

Briggs, Jean. *Never in Anger.* Cambridge, MA: Harvard University Press, 1970.

Brown, Norman O. *Life against Death.* Middletown, CT: Wesleyan University Press, 1970.

Bruner, Jerome. "Foreword." in *Infants and Mothers.* New York: Dell, 1983.

Butler, Susan, ed. *Non-Competitive Games*. Minneapolis: Bethany House Publishers, 1986.

Canellos, Peter S. "Ben and Jerry's, Other Firms Attack Both Parties on Arms Spending." *Boston Globe*, June 27, 1996.

Capouya, Emile and Keitha Tompkins, eds. *The Essential Kropotkin*. London: Macmillan Press, 1975.

Capra, Fritjof. *The Turning Point: Science, Society, and the Rising Culture*. New York: Bantam, 1982.

———. *Uncommon Wisdom*. New York: Simon & Schuster, 1988.

Carroll, James. "Abortion complexity." *Boston Globe*, April 23, 1996.

Chammah, Albert M. and Anatol Rapaport. *Prisoners Dilemma: A Study in Conflict and Cooperation*. Ann Arbor: University of Michigan Press, 1965.

Chodorow, Nancy. *The Reproduction of Mothering: Psychoanalysis and the Sociology of Gender* (Berkeley: University of California Press, 1978).

Clark, Brian. *Whose Life Is It Anyway?* Ashover, Derbyshire: Amber House Press, 1978, play.

von Clausewitz, Carl. *On War*. Princcton: Princeton University Press, 1976.

Close Encounters of the Third Kind. Steven Spielberg, dir. Columbia Pictures, 1977, motion picture.

Coleman, Jocelyn R. "Students Named Peer Mediators." *Boston Globe*, June 14, 1990.

"'Common Ground' or Losing Ground? Choosing our Alliances." *Reproductive Rights Newsletter*. PO Box 686, Boston, MA 02130, Spring 1992.

Compassion in Exile. Mickey Lemle, dir. New York: Lemle Pictures, 1992, documentary film.

Cooley, Charles Horton. *Human Nature and the Social Order*. New York: Scribner, 1922

"Cooperative Learning and College Teaching." Newsletter, New Forums Press, Inc., P.O. Box 876, Stillwater, Oklahoma 74076.

Coser, Lewis. *The Functions of Social Conflict*. New York: Free Press, 1956.

Cotton, Anthony. "This Was Some Kind of Jam Session." *Sports Illustrated*, February 6, 1984.

Dagostino, Mark. "More than a matter of good taste." *Boston Globe*, January 4, 1995.

Dalai Lama. "Compassion and the Individual." Boston: Wisdom Publications, 1994.

————. "Dimensions of Spirituality." Boston: Wisdom Publications, 1995.

————. *Freedom in Exile*. New York: HarperCollins, 1990.

————. *Kindness, Clarity, and Insight*. Ithaca, NY: Snow Lion, 1984.

Daly, Herman E. *Toward a Steady State Economy*. San Francisco: W. H. Freeman, 1973.

Davis, Kingsley and Wilbert E. Moore. "Some Principles of Stratification." *American Sociological Review* 10 (April 1945).

"The delicate business of coexistence." *Jerusalem Post* (International Edition), week ending July 18, 1992.

DeMause, Lloyd. "The Evolution of Childhood." In Lloyd deMause, ed., *The History of Childhood*. New York: Psychohistory Press, 1974.

————. "The Gulf War as a Mental Disorder." *Journal of Psychohistory* 19.1 (Summer 1991): 1–22.

Derber, Charles. *The Wilding of America*. New York: St. Martin's Press, 1996.

Dinnerstein, Dorothy. *The Mermaid and the Minotaur: Sexual Arrangements and Human Malaise*. New York: Harper & Row, 1976.

Doherty, Thomas. Personal communication.

Dolman, Fred, "Republican revolution was a sham." Letter to the *Boston Globe*, July 5, 1996.

Durkheim, Emile. *The Division of Labor in Society*. New York: Free Press, 1964.

Dylan, Bob. *Lyrics, 1962–1985*. New York: Knopf, 1985.

Eck, Diana L. "Neighboring Faiths." *Harvard Magazine* 99.1 (September/October 1966): 38–44.

Einstein, Albert. *New York Times*, March 29, 1972, 20.

Eisler, Riane. *The Chalice and the Blade*. San Francisco: Harper & Row, 1987.

————. *Sacred Pleasure: Sex, Myth, and the Politics of the Body*. San Francisco: HarperCollins, 1995.

Ellison, Ralph. *Invisible Man*. New York: Vintage Books, 1989.

Emerson, Ralph Waldo. "War," in *The Complete Works of Ralph Waldo Emerson, XI*. New York: AMS Press, 1979.

Erikson, Erik H. *Childhood and Society*. New York: Norton, 1950.

————. *Young Man Luther*. New York: Norton, 1958.

——. *Insight and Responsibility*. New York: Norton, 1964.

——. *The Life Cycle Completed*. New York: Norton, 1982.

——. "Ontogeny of Ritualization." In R. M. Loewenstein, A. Solnit, and M. Schur, eds., *Psychoanalysis: A General Psychology*. New York: International Universities Press, 1966.

——. *Gandhi's Truth*. New York: Norton, 1969.

E. T. Steven Spielberg, dir. Universal City Studios, 1982, motion picture.

Everett, Melissa, John E. Mack, and Robert Oresick. "Re-inventing the Corporate Self: The Inner Agenda for Business Transformation." Cambridge, MA: Center for Psychology and Social Change, 1993.

Fairbairn, W. Ronald. *Psychoanalytic Studies of the Personality*. London: Routledge and Kegan Paul, 1952.

Family Pastime. "Eagle Eye Agency—the Cooperative Detective Game," board game.

Felder Books & Games. "Mediation Games: Games for All Types of Conflicts," pamphlet. Address: 9601 30 Miccosukee Road, Tallahassee, FL 32308.

Fellman, Gordon. "Peace in the World or the World in Pieces." *Policy Studies* (The Leonard Davis Institute, Hebrew University, Jerusalem) 34 (1989).

——. "The Truths of Frankenstein: Technologism and Images of Destruction." *Psychohistory Review* 19.2 (Winter 1991).

Fenichel, Otto. "Gedanken." Quoted in Russell Jacoby, *The Repression of Psychoanalysis*. New York: Basic Books, 1983.

Ferguson, Marilyn. *The Aquarian Conspiracy: Personal and Social Transformation in the 1980s*. Los Angeles: Tarcher, 1980.

Fine, Reuben. *Narcissism, the Self, and Society*. New York: Columbia University Press, 1986.

First Blood. Ted Kotcheff, dir. Carolco Pictures, 1982, motion picture.

Flint, Anthony. "Narrow areas of agreement may be key to abortion talks." *Boston Globe*, January 23, 1995.

Fluegelman, Andrew, ed. *The New Games Book: Play Hard, Play Fair, Nobody Hurt*. New York: Headlands Press/Dolphin/Doubleday, 1976.

Folberg, Jay and Alison Taylor. *Mediation: A Comprehensive Guide to Resolving Conflicts without Litigation*. San Francisco: Jossey-Bass, 1984.

Fornari, Franco. *The Psychoanalysis of War*. Garden City, NY: Anchor, 1974.

Franks, Lucinda. "Don't Shoot: In the New F.B.I., patience comes first." *The New Yorker*, July 22, 1996.

Freud, Anna. *The Ego and the Mechanisms of Defense*. New York, International Universities Press, 1946.

Freud, Sigmund. "Thoughts for the Time on War and Death." In *Collected Papers*, vol. 4. New York: Basic Books, 1959.

———. "Why War?" In *Collected Papers*, vol. 5. New York: Basic Books, 1959.

———. *Group Psychology and the Analysis of the Ego*. New York: Norton, 1959.

———. *Future of an Illusion*. New York: Norton, 1961.

———. *Civilization and Its Discontents*. New York: Norton, 1961.

Fromm, Erich. *Zen Buddhism and Psychoanalysis*. New York: Grove Press, 1960.

Fussell, Paul. *Wartime*. New York: Oxford University Press, 1989.

Fussell, Samuel. *Muscle: Confessions of an Unlikely Bodybuilder*. New York: Poseidon Press, 1991.

Gandhi, M. K. *Gandhi's Autobiography: The Story of My Experiments with Truth*. Washington, DC: Public Affairs Press, 1948.

Gateway: A Publication of the Global Alliance for Transforming Education (Winter/Spring 1993).

Gerson, Joseph. *The Deadly Connection: Nuclear War and U.S. Intervention*. Philadelphia: New Society Publishers, 1986.

Gerth, Hans and C. Wright Mills. *From Max Weber: Essays in Sociology*. New York: Galaxy, 1958.

Ghosh, Amitav. "A Reporter at Large: Burma." *The New Yorker*, August 12, 1996.

Gibson, J. William. "The Making of a Gunfighter," unpublished manuscript.

———. *Warrior Dreams: Violence and Manhood in Post-Vietnam America*. New York: Hill and Wang, 1994.

Gilley, J. Wade. "Faust Goes to College." *Academe* 78.3 (May-June 1992): 9–11.

Glover, Edward. *War, Sadism, and Pacifism: Further Essays on Group Psychology and War*. London: George Allen and Unwin, 1946.

Gluck, Ken. "The New Russian Imperialists." *The Nation* 255.7 (September 14, 1992): 243–46.

The Godfather. Francis Ford Coppola, dir. Paramount Pictures, 1972, motion picture.

Goldin, Hyman. *Ethics of the Fathers*. New York: Hebrew Publishing, 1962.

Goldstein, Marin. "Mahayana Buddhism: Precepts for Environmental Consciousness and Social Activism." Senior honors thesis, Sociology Department, Brandeis University, May 1996.

Gonen, Jay. *A Psychohistory of Zionism*. New York: Mason/Charter, 1975.

Goodman, Michael Harris. *The Last Dalai Lama*. Boston: Shambhala, 1986.

Gorbachev, Mikhail. *Perestroika*. London: Collins, 1987.

Gordon, David G., Melvin J. Guyer, and Anatol Rapaport. *The 2x2 Game*. Ann Arbor: University of Michigan Press, 1976.

Gouldner, Alvin. *The Coming Crisis of Western Sociology*. New York: Basic Books, 1970.

Grand Illusion. Jean Renoir, dir. Tamarelle's French Film House, 1938, motion picture.

Gray, Chris Hables. *Postmodern War: The New Politics of Conflict*. New York: Guilford Press, 1997.

Green, Paula. Personal communication.

Greenson, Ralph R. "Empathy and Its Vicissitudes." *International Journal of Psychoanalysis* 41 (1960): 418–24.

Gross, Otto. "Zur Uberwindung." Quoted in Russell Jacoby, *The Repression of Psychoanalysis*. New York: Basic Books, 1983.

Grossman, Dave. *On Killing: The Psychological Cost of Learning to Kill in War and Society*. Boston: Little, Brown, 1995.

Group for the Advancement of Psychiatry, *Self-Involvement in the Middle East Conflict*. New York: Mental Health Materials Center, 1978.

———. *Us and Them, the Psychology of Ethnonationalism*. New York: Brunner/Mazel, 1987.

Guttmann, Allen. *From Ritual to Record*. New York: Columbia University Press, 1978.

Halprin, Lee. "On Anticommunism in the United States." *The Boston Exchange* 5.1 (May 1989).

Hart, Jordana. "The classes cut violence: Boston middle-schoolers learn art of negotiation, compromise." *Boston Globe*, October 10, 1994.

Hatfield, Julie. "'Miss Manners' Polite Efforts to 'Rescue Civilization.'" *Boston Globe*, June 26, 1996.

Hawthorne, Nathaniel. *The Scarlet Letter*. New York: Knopf, 1992.

Hegel, Georg Frederick. *Phenomenology of Mind*. New York: Harper, 1967.

Helter Skelter. Tom Gries, dir. Lorimar, 1976, motion picture.

Henderson, Hazel. *Building a Win-Win World*. San Francisco: Barrett-Koehler, 1966.

————. *Paradigms in Progress*. Indianapolis: Knowledge Systems, 1991.

Henneberger, Melinda. "New Gym Class: No More Choosing Up Sides," *The New York Times*, May 16, 1993, p. 1.

High Noon. Fred Zinnemann, dir. Republic Pictures, 1952, motion picture.

Hilberg, Raul. *The Destruction of the European Jews*. Chicago: Quadrangle Books, 1961.

Hobbes, Thomas. *Leviathan*. New York: Collier Books, 1962.

Hoffman, Stanley. "Coming Down from the Summit," *New York Review of Books*, January 21, 1988.

Hollingshead, August. *Elmtown's Youth*. New York: Wiley, 1949.

————. *Social Class and Mental Illness*. New York: Wiley, 1958.

Holmes, Richard. *Acts of War: The Behavior of Men in Battle*. New York: Free Press, 1985.

Horney, Karen. "The Flight from Womanhood: The Masculinity Complex in Women, as Viewed by Men and by Women." *International Journal of Psychoanalysis* 7 (1926): 324–39.

————. "The Dread of Women: Observations on a Specific Difference in the Dread Felt by Men and by Women Respectively for the Opposite Sex." *International Journal of Psychoanalysis* 13 (1932): 348–60.

Hospice Care, Inc. 647 Summer Street, Boston, MA 02210, 617-279-4100.

How to Make an American Quilt. Jocelyn Moorhouse, dir. Universal, 1995, motion picture.

Huizinga, Johan. *Homo Ludens*. London: Routledge and Kegan Paul, 1949.

Hyde, Lewis. *The Gift: Imagination and the Erotic Life of Property*. New York: Vintage Books, 1983.

International Journal of Nonviolence. Washington, DC: Nonviolence International, 1993–.

International Union of Architects/American Institute of Architects. "Declaration of Interdependence for a Sustainable Future." World Congress of Architects. Chicago, June 18–21, 1993.

Jacoby, Mario. *Individuation and Narcissism*. London: Routledge, 1990.

Jacoby, Russell. *The Repression of Psychoanalysis*. New York: Basic Books, 1983.

Janusz, Luke. "The Politics of Punishment." *Odyssey*, Spring 1992.

————. "The Smiling Terminator: An Interview with Howie Carr." *Odyssey*, Spring 1992.

Jaques, Elliott. "Social Systems as Defence against Persecutory and Depressive Anxiety." In Melanie Klein et al., eds., *New Directions in Psycho-Analysis*. London: Tavistock, 1955.

The Jerusalem Bible. Jerusalem: Koren Publishers, 1977.

Johnson, David and Roger T. Johnson. *Cooperation and Competition*. Edina, MN: Interaction Book Company, 1989.

Johnson, David, Roger T. Johnson, and Karl A. Smith. *Active Learning: Cooperation in the College Classroom*. Edina, MN: Interaction Book Company, 1991

————. *Cooperative Learning, Increasing Faculty Instructional Productivity*. Washington, DC: School of Education and Human Development, George Washington University, 1991.

Johnson, Mathew. Personal communication.

Jones, Thomas B. and Chet Meyers. *Promoting Active Learning Strategies for the College Classroom*. San Francisco: Jossey-Bass, 1993.

Jordan, Judith V. "Clarity in Connection: Empathic Knowing, Desire and Sexuality," Work in Progress, a series published by the Stone Center for Developmental Services and Studies, Wellesley College.

Kahn, Herman. *On Thermonuclear War*. Westport, CT: Greenwood Press, 1969.

Kahn, Roberta Pfeufer. *Bearing Meaning: The Language of Birth*. Urbana: University of Illinois Press, 1995.

Kamara, Jemadari, ed. *Socially Responsible Investment and Economic Development*. National Conference on Socially Sensitive Investing for Economic Growth. Flint: University of Michigan, 1986.

Kamenetz, Rodger. *The Jew in the Lotus*. San Francisco: HarperCollins, 1994.

Keen, Sam. *Faces of the Enemy*. San Francisco: Harper & Row, 1986.

Keller, John. "Going back to the grass roots." *Boston Globe*, September 2, 1996.

Kelly, Michael. "Glasshouse Conventions: How the parties built their pretty facades— and why they're so fragile." *New Yorker*, September 9, 96.

Kennedy, Robert. Speech in South Africa. Source of quotation unknown.

Khan, Muhammed. "Moral Principles as the Basis of Islamic Culture." In Ruth Nanda Anshen, ed., *Moral Principle of Action*, vol. 6. New York: Harper and Brothers, 1952.

Kimelman, Reuven. "Nonviolence in the Talmud." In Robert Holmes, ed., *Non-Violence in Theory and Practice*. Belmont, CA: Wadsworth Publishing, 1990.

Klein, Melanie. "On Identification." In Howard F. Stein and Maurice Apprey, eds., *From Metaphor to Meaning, Papers in Psychoanalytic Anthropology*. Charlottesville: University Press of Virginia, 1987.

Klieber, Nancy and Linda Light, *Caring for Ourselves: An Alternative Structure for Health Care*. Vancouver, BC: School of Nursing, University of British Columbia, 1978.

Koestler, Arthur. *Janus*. New York: Random House, 1978.

Kohn, Alfie. *The Brighter Side of Human Nature*. New York: Basic Books, 1990.

———. *No Contest*. Boston: Houghton Mifflin Company, 1992.

———. *Punished by Rewards*. Boston: Houghton Mifflin, 1993.

Kohor, Gregory, ed. *The British School of Psychoanalysis*. New Haven, CT: Yale University Press, 1986.

Kohut, Heinz. *The Restoration of the Self*. New York: International Universities Press, 1977.

———. *The Search for the Self, Selected Writings of Heinz Kohut: 1950–1978*, vol. 2. Ed. by Paul H. Ornstein. New York: International Universities Press, 1978.

———. *Self-Psychology and the Humanities*. New York: Norton, 1985.

Kornfield, Jack. *Buddha's Little Instruction Book*. New York: Bantam, 1994.

Kovel, Joel. *White Racism, a Psychohistory*. New York: Vintage, 1971.

———. *Against the State of Nuclear Terror*. Boston: South End Press, 1984.

Kropotkin, Peter. *Mutual Aid*. Boston: Extending Horizons Books, 1955.

Kuhn, Thomas. *The Structure of Scientific Revolutions*. Chicago: University of Chicago Press, 1970.

Lacan, Jacques. *Écrits*. New York: Norton, 1977.

Lasch, Christopher. *The Culture of Narcissism*. New York: Warner Books, 1980

Leach, William. *Land of Desire*. New York: Pantheon, 1993.

Lear, Jonathan. *Love and Its Place in Nature: A Philosophical Interpretation of Freudian Psychoanalysis*. New York: Farrar, Straus, and Giroux, 1990.

Lennon, John. "Imagine." In Lennon, *Imagine*, Apple, 1971, sound recording.

Lerner, Gerda. *The Creation of Patriarchy*. New York: Oxford University Press, 1986.

Lerner, Michael. *The Politics of Meaning*. Reading, MA: Addison-Wesley, 1996.

————. *Surplus Powerlessness*. Oakland, CA: Institute for Labor and Mental Health, 1986.

Letter, *Boston Globe*, July 5, 1996, 14.

Lewin, Tamar. "In Bitter Abortion Debate, Opponents Learn to Reach for Common Ground." *New York Times*, February 17, 1992.

Lichtenberg, Joseph, Melvin Bornstein, and Donald Silver, eds. *Empathy*. 2 vols. New York: Analytic Press, 1984

Lindenbaum, Joyce P. "The Shattering of an Illusion: The Problem of Competition in Lesbian Relationships." In Valerie Miner and Helen E. Longino, eds., *Competition: A Feminist Taboo?* New York: The Feminist Press, 1987.

Loomis, Charles P. and John C. McKinney. "Introduction." In *Community and Society*. New York: Harper Torchbooks, 1963.

Lorde, Audre. *Sister Outsider*. Freedom, CA: Crossing Press, 1984.

Luce, R. Duncan and Howard Raiffa. *Games and Decisions*. New York: Dover, 1985.

Lugones, Marcia C. and Elizabeth Spelman. "Competition, Compassion, and Community: Models for a Feminist Ethos." In Valerie Miner and Helen E. Longino, eds., *Competition: A Feminist Taboo?* New York: The Feminist Press, 1987.

Lynd, Robert S. *Knowledge for What?* Princeton, NJ: Princeton University Press, 1948.

Lynd, Robert S. and Helen Merrell Lynd. *Middletown*. New York: Harcourt, Brace, 1929.

————. *Middletown in Transition*. New York: Harcourt, Brace, 1937.

Mack, John. "Nationalism and the Self." *Psychohistory Review* 2.2–3 (Spring 1985): 47–69.

————. "Some Thoughts on the Nuclear Age and the Psychological Roots of Anti-Sovietism." In John E. Mack, issue editor, "Aggression and Its Alternatives in the Conduct of International Relations." *Psychoanalytic Inquiry* 6.2 (1986): 267–85.

Manny and Lo. Lisa Krueger, dir. Sony Pictures, 1996, motion picture.

Marcuse, Herbert. *One-Dimensional Man*. Boston: Beacon Press, 1966.

————. *Eros and Civilization*. Boston: Beacon Press, 1974.

Marley, Bob and the Wailers. *Catch a Fire*. Island Records, 1973, sound recording.

――――. *Exodus*. Island Records, 1977, sound recording.

Marshall, S. L. A. *Men against Fire: The Problem of Battle Command in Future War.* Washington, DC: Combat Forces Press, and New York: William Morrow, 1947.

Marshall, Tony. *Alternatives to Criminal Courts: the Potential for Non-Judicial Dispute Settlement.* Brookfield, VT: Gower Publishing, 1985.

Marx, Karl. *The German Ideology.* New York: International Publishers, 1947.

――――. *Capital.* New York: Modern Library, n.d.

――――. "Estranged Labour." In Robert Tucker, ed., *The Marx-Engels Reader.* New York: Norton, 1978.

――――. "The German Ideology." In Robert Tucker, ed., *The Marx-Engels Reader.* New York: Norton, 1978.

――――. "Wages, Price and Profit." In Karl Marx and Frederick Engels, *Selected Works.* New York: International Publishers, 1972, 186–229.

Mathews, Jessica Tuchman. "Redefining National Security." *Foreign Affairs* 68.2 (1989): 162–77.

Meacham, Colquitt. Personal communication.

Mead, George Herbert. *Mind, Self, and Society.* Chicago: University of Chicago Press, 1934.

Menace II Society. Allen and Albert Hughes, dir. New Home Line Video, 1993, motion picture.

Menaker, Esther and William Menaker. *Ego in Evolution.* New York: Grove Press, 1965.

Merton, Robert. *Social Theory and Social Structure.* Glencoe, IL: Free Press, 1957.

Midnight Cowboy. John Schlesinger, dir. Jerome Hellman Productions, 1969, motion picture.

Mill, John Stuart. *Principles of Political Economy*, vol. 2. London: John W. Parker and Son, 1857.

Miller, Alice. *The Drama of the Gifted Child.* New York: Basic Books, 1981.

――――. *For Your Own Good.* New York: Farrar, Straus, and Giroux, 1990.

The Mission. Roland Joffe, dir. Kingsmere, 1986, motion picture.

Mitscherlich, Alexander and Margarete Mitscherlich. *The Inability to Mourn.* New York: Grove Press, 1975.

Money-Kyrle, R. E. *Psychoanalysis and Politics.* New York: Norton, 1952. Quoted in Ashley Montagu, *Darwin, Competition and Cooperation.* New York: Henry Schuman, 1952.

Montagu, Ashley. *Darwin, Competition and Cooperation.* New York: Henry Schuman, 1952.

Moore, Barrington Jr. *Social Origins of Dictatorship and Democracy.* Boston: Beacon Press, 1966.

Morris, Ruth. "Restorative Justice: Path to the Future." *Odyssey,* Spring 1992.

Moses, Rafael. "The Group Self and the Arab-Israeli Conflict." *International Review of Psychoanalysis* 9 (1982): 54–65.

———. "Empathy and Dis-Empathy in Political Conflict." *Political Psychology* 6.1 (1985): 135–39.

Nathanson, Charles E. "Sacred Principles: A Reinterpretation of Human and Cultural Origins." Ph.D. dissertation, Brandeis University, 1979.

Negri, Gloria. "10 students who find a better way are honored." *Boston Globe,* May 15, 1996.

Nhat Hanh, Thich. *Being Peace.* Berkeley, CA: Parallax Press, 1987.

———. *The Miracle of Mindfulness.* Boston: Beacon Press, 1976.

———. *Peace Is Every Step.* New York: Bantam, 1992.

Nietzsche, Friedrich. *Twilight of the Idols.* In Walter Kaufman, ed., *The Portable Nietzsche.* New York: Viking Press, 1954.

Norman, Marsha. *Night, Mother.* New York: Hill and Wang, 1983, play.

"Notes and Comments." *The New Yorker,* April 23, 1990, pp. 31–32.

Noy, Pinchas. "The Three Components of Empathy: Normal and Pathological Development." In Joseph Lichtenberg, Melvin Bornstein, and Donald Silver, eds., *Empathy,* vol. 1. Hillsdale, NJ: Analytic Press, 1984.

Olinick, Stanley. "A Critique of Empathy and Sympathy." In Joseph Lichtenberg, Melvin Bornstein, and Donald Silver, eds., *Empathy,* vol. 1. Hillsdale, NJ: Analytic Press, 1984.

Onorato, Richard. Personal communication.

O'Reilly, David. "Beyond Hate: The Klansman Who Became Jewish." *Detroit Free Press,* April 20, 1995.

Osgood, Charles E. "An Analysis of the Cold War Mentality," *Journal of Social Issues* 17.3 (1961): 12–19.

Parkin, Frank. *Class, Inequality and Political Order.* New York: Praeger, 1972.

Pateman, Carole. *Participation and Democratic Theory.* Cambridge: Cambridge University Press, 1970.

Peters, William. *A Class Divided*. New Haven, CT: Yale University Press, 1971.

Pinderhughes, Charles A. "Differential Bonding from Infancy to International Conflict." In John E. Mack, issue editor, "Aggression and Its Alternatives in the Conduct of International Relation." *Psychoanalytic Inquiry* 6.2 (1986): 155–73.

Poland, Warren. "On Empathy in and beyond Analysis." In Joseph Lichtenberg, Melvin Bornstein, and Donald Silver, eds., *Empathy*, vol. 1. Hillsdale, NJ: Analytic Press, 1984.

Pomper, Philip. *The Structure of the Mind in History*. New York: Columbia University Press, 1985.

Poundstone, William, *Prisoners Dilemma*. New York: Doubleday, 1992.

Powers, Roger and William Vogele, eds. *Protest, Power, and Change: An Encyclopedia of Nonviolent Action from ACT-UP to Women's Suffrage*. New York: Garland, 1997.

Quinn, Daniel. *Ishmael*. New York: Bantam/Turner, 1993.

Rasmussen, Eric. *Games and Information*. Cambridge: Basil Blackwell, 1989.

Raspberry, William. "A search for common ground on abortion." *Boston Globe*, September 16, 1995.

Reardon, Betty. *Sexism and the War System*. New York: Teachers College Press, 1985.

Reed, Gail S. "The Antithetical Meaning of the Term 'Empathy' in Psychoanalytic Discourse." In Joseph Lichtenberg, Melvin Bornstein, and Donald Silver, eds., *Empathy*, vol. 1. Hillsdale, NJ: Analytic Press, 1984.

Reich, Wilhelm. *The Mass Psychology of Fascism*. New York: Farrar, Straus and Giroux, 1970.

Remnick, David. "Inside-Out Olympics." *The New Yorker*, August 5, 1996, pp. 26–28.

Restoring Justice. Produced for the National Council of Churches, by the Presbyterian Church (USA), 100 Witherspoon Street, Louisville, KY 40202–1396, video.

Rieff, Philip. *The Triumph of the Therapeutic*. New York: Harper & Row, 1968.

Rochlin, Gregory. *Man's Aggression*. New York: Delta, 1973.

The Rocky Horror Picture Show. Jim Sharman, dir. Twentieth Century Fox, 1975, motion picture.

Roheim, Geza. *Animism, Magic, and the Divine King*. New York: Knopf, 1930.

———. *Psychoanalysis and Anthropology*. New York: International Universities Press, 1950.

———. *Origin and Function of Culture*. New York: Johnson Reprint, 1968.

Rothman, Barbara Katz. *Recreating Motherhood*. New York: Norton, 1989.

Rothstein, Arnold. *The Narcissistic Pursuit of Perfection*. New York: International Universities Press, 1980.

Rubin, Jeffrey Z. and Bert R. Brown. *The Social Psychology of Bargaining and Negotiation*. New York: Academic Press, 1975.

Rushdie, Salman. *The Satanic Verses*. London: Viking, 1988.

Russell, Dick. "A Garden of Earthly Designs." *The Amicus Journal* 15.2 (Summer 1993): 14–20.

Ryan, William. *Blaming the Victim*. New York: Vintage Books, 1971.

Said, Edward. *Orientalism*. New York: Pantheon, 1978.

Saida, Eric. "On Love and Violence." Senior honors thesis, Sociology Department, Brandeis University, May 1996.

Satya, a Prayer for the Enemy. Ellen Bruno, dir. Prod. by Ellen Bruno, 1993, documentary film.

Scandalis, Barbara G. and Maurice N. Walsh. "Institutionalized Forms of Intergenerational Male Aggression." In Martin A. Nettleship, R. Dale Givens, and Anderson Nettleship, eds., *War: Its Causes and Correlates*. The Hague: Mouton Publishers, 1975.

Scavio Michael J., Andrew Cooper, and Pamela Scavio Clift. "Freud's Devaluation of Nietzsche." *Psychohistory Review* 21.3 (Spring 1993).

Schafer, Roy. "Discussion." In Joseph Lichtenberg, Melvin Bornstein, and Donald Silver, eds., *Empathy*, vol. 1. Hillsdale, NJ: Analytic Press, 1984.

Schindlers List. Steven Spielberg, dir. MCA Universal Home Video, 1994, motion picture.

Schmookler, Andrew Bard. *The Parable of the Tribes*. Berkeley: University of California Press, 1983.

Schwartz, William and Charles Derber, with Gordon Fellman, William Gamson, Morris Schwartz, and Patrick Withen. *The Nuclear Seduction: Why the Arms Race Doesn't Matter and What Does*. Berkeley: University of California Press, 1990.

Searles, Harold F. "The Psychodynamics of Vengefulness." *Psychiatry* 19.1 (1956): 31–39.

Seeley, John R. *The Americanization of the Unconscious*. New York: Science House, 1967.

Dr. Seuss. *The Butter Battle Book*. New York: Random House, 1984.

Shafer, Dave. "Dissolution of Rage." Unpublished paper, Sociology Department, Brandeis University, July 1994.

Shafritz, Jay M. *Words on War*. New York: Prentice Hall, 1990.

Sharp, Gene. *Exploring Nonviolent Alternatives*. Boston: Porter Sargent, 1970.

———. *Gandhi as a Political Strategist*. Boston: Porter Sargent, 1979.

———. *The Politics of Nonviolent Action*. Boston: Porter Sargent, 1973.

———. *Social Power and Political Freedom*. Boston: Porter Sargent, 1980.

Shipler, David. *Arab and Jew*. New York: Penguin Books, 1986.

Silence of the Lambs. Jonathan Demme, dir. Orion Pictures, 1990, motion picture.

Silverman, Phyllis. *Mutual Help Groups: Organization and Development*. Beverly Hills, CA: Sage, 1980.

Simmel, Georg. *Conflict*. Glencoe, IL: Free Press, 1955.

Skocpol, Theda. *States and Social Revolutions*. Cambridge: Cambridge University Press, 1979.

———. *States, Social Knowledge, and the Origins of Modern Social Policies*. Princeton, NJ: Princeton University Press, 1996.

Slater, Philip. *The Glory of Hera*. Boston: Beacon Press, 1968.

———. Personal communication.

———. *The Pursuit of Loneliness*. Boston: Beacon Press, 1990.

———. *A Dream Deferred: America's Discontent and the Search for a New Democratic Ideal*. Boston: Beacon Press, 1991.

Smith, Huston. *The Religions of Man*. New York: Harper & Row, 1958.

Smith, Patricia. "How I Refilled My Hope Tank." *Boston Globe*, May 3, 1996.

Social Science Research Council. *The American Soldier*. Princeton, NJ: Princeton University Press, 1949–50.

Sorokin, Pitirim A. "Foreword." In *Community and Society*. New York: Harper Torchbooks, 1963.

Southern Poverty Law Center. Mailing, May 1, 1996.

Sparks, Allister. "Letter from South Africa: The Secret Revolution." *The New Yorker*, April 11, 1994.

Spearhead. *Home*. Capitol Records, 1994, sound recording.

"Spiritual Happening." *Boston Globe*, September 1, 1996.

The Spitfire Grill. Lee David Zlotoff, dir. Castle Rock (via Columbia), 1996, motion picture.

Spock, Benjamin. *Baby and Child Care.* New York: Pocket Books, 1970.

Spretnak, Charlene. *States of Grace.* San Francisco: HarperCollins, 1991.

Starhawk. *Truth or Dare.* San Francisco: Harper and Row, 1987.

Stein, Howard F. "Adversary Symbiosis and Complementary Group Dissociation: An Analysis of the U.S./USSR Conflict." In Howard F. Stein and Maurice Apprey, eds., *From Metaphor to Meaning: Papers in Psychoanalytic Anthropology.* Charlottesville: University Press of Virginia, 1987.

Stern, Daniel. *The Interpersonal World of the Infant.* New York: Basic Books, 1985.

Strachey, Alix. *The Unconscious Motives of War.* London: George Allen and Unwin, 1967.

Strangers in Good Company. Cynthia Scott, dir. National Film Board of Canada, 1991, motion picture.

"Support Group Calendar." *Omaha World-Herald*, October 6, 1996, p. 7–E.

"Talk of the Town." *New Yorker*, April 23, 1990, pp. 31–32.

Thelma and Louise. Ridley Scott, dir. Metro Goldwyn Mayer, 1991, motion picture.

Thompson, William Irwin. *Evil and World Order.* New York: Harper & Row, 1976.

———. *Darkness and Scattered Light.* Garden City, NY: Anchor, 1978.

———. *The Time Falling Bodies Take to Light.* New York: St. Martin's, 1981.

Thomson, George. *Aeschylus and Athens.* London: Laurence and Wishart, 1946.

To Wong Foo, Thanks for Everything, Julie Newmar. Beeban Kidron, dir. Universal, 1995, motion picture.

Toffler, Alvin. *The Third Wave.* New York: William Morrow, 1980.

Treisman, Philip Uri. "Academic Perestroika: Teaching, Learning, and the Faculty's Role in Turbulent Times." FIPSE Lecture, California State University, San Bernardino, March 8, 1990.

Tucker, Robert. *Philosophy and Myth in Karl Marx.* Cambridge: Cambridge University Press, 1961.

2001: A Space Odyssey. Stanley Kubrick, dir. MGM, 1968, motion picture.

Tyler, Patrick E. "U.N. Forum Hears Speech By Burmese." *New York Times*, September 1, 1995.

Umbriet, Mark. "The Impact of Victim Offender Mediation: A Case Study." *Odyssey*, Spring 1992.

"A Unanimous Dramatic Win for Mandela." News Tribune News Service, May 10, 1994.

Volkan, Vamik D. *Cyprus—War and Adaptation: A Psychoanalytic History of Two Ethnic Groups in Conflict*. Charlottesville, VA: University of Virginia, 1979.

———. *The Need to Have Enemies and Allies: From Clinical Practice to International Relationships*. Northvale, NJ: Jason Aronson, 1988.

——— and Norman Itzkowitz. *Turks and Greeks: Neighbours in Conflict*. Cambridgeshire, England: Eothen Press, 1994.

Wallerstein, Immanuel. *The Capitalist World Economy: Essays*. Cambridge: Cambridge University Press, 1979.

———. *World Inequality: Origins and Perspectives on the World System*. Montreal: Black Rose Books, 1975.

Walsh, Maurice N. and Barbara G. Scandalis. "Institutionalized Forms of Intergenerational Male Aggression." In Martin A. Nettleship, R. Dale Givens, and Anderson Nettleship, eds., *War: Its Causes and Correlates*. The Hague: Mouton Publishers, 1975, 135.

Wangh, Stephen. personal communication.

Warner, Gary. *Competition*. Elgin, IL: David C. Cook, 1979. Cited in Alfie Kohn, *No Contest*. Boston: Houghton Mifflin, 1992.

Watterson, Kathryn. *Not By the Sword*. New York: Simon & Schuster, 1995.

Weber, Max. *The Theory of Social and Economic Organization*. New York: Oxford University Press, 1947.

———. "Class, Status, Party." In Reinhard Bendix and S. M. Lipset, eds., *Class, Status, and Power*. Glencoe, IL: The Free Press, 1953.

———. *The Protestant Ethic and the Spirit of Capitalism*. New York: Scribner's, 1956.

Webster, David S. "Academic Rankings: First on a List of One." *Academe* 78.5 (September-October 1992): 19–22.

Weiner, Anita, Arnon Bar-On, and Eugene Weiner, eds. *The Abraham Fund Directory of Institutions and Organizations Fostering Co-Existence between Jews and Arabs in Israel*. New York: Abraham Fund, 1992.

White, Robert W. *Ego and Reality in Psychoanalytic Theory*. New York: International Universities Press, 1963.

Whitman, Neal A. *Peer Teaching: To Teach Is to Learn Twice*. ASHE-ERIC Higher Education Report No. 4. Washington, DC: Association for the Study of Higher Education, 1988.

Whole Earth Catalog. Sausalito, CA: Whole Earth Catalog, May 1971.

Will, George F. "The morose liberals." *Boston Globe*. December 8, 1989.

Wilson, James Q. *Thinking about Crime*. New York: Vintage Books, 1975, 172–73. Quoted in Luke Janusz, "The Politics of Punishment." *Odyssey*, Spring 1992.

Wines, James. "Architecture in the Age of Ecology." *Amicus Journal* 15.2 (Summer 1993): 22–23.

Winnicott, Donald. *The Family and Individual Development* (New York: Basic Books, 1965).

Wright, Erik Olin. *Class, Crisis and the State*. London: Verso, 1979.

———. *Classes*. London: Verso, 1985.

"Youths meet to promote Midcast peace." *Boston Globe*, August 19, 1996.

Zehr, Leonard. *Changing Lenses*. Scottsdale, AZ: Herald Press, 1990.

Zinn, Howard. *A People's History of the United States*. New York: Harper Perennial, 1980.

Index

a child who can restrain themselves is considered more mature, but not an entire nation?

It'd be safer if we all came to class with guns?

psychologist
researcher
published author
journalist
teacher   write own curriculum
professor

take completely out of defense and put into education, environmental policies, working on overpopulation, settling internal problems first. why would anyone have reason to attack a nation like that. As a nation, we need inner peace before can have outer peace.